NORTHERN FRONTIER

NORTHERN HOMELAND

THE REPORT OF THE MACKENZIE VALLEY PIPELINE INQUIRY : VOLUME ONE

Design and Photocomposition:
Alphatext Ltd.

Available by mail from
Printing and Publishing
Supply and Services Canada
Ottawa, Canada K1A 0S9
or through your bookseller

Catalogue number:
English edition CP32-25/1977-1
French edition CP32-25/1977-1F

ISBN:
English edition 0-660-00775-4
French edition 0-660-00776-2

Price: Canada $5.00; other countries $6.00
Price subject to change without notice

Table of Contents

This is Volume One of a two-volume report. It deals with the broad social, economic and environmental impacts that a gas pipeline and an energy corridor would have in the Mackenzie Valley and the Western Arctic. In it certain basic recommendations are made. Volume Two will set out the terms and conditions that should be imposed if a pipeline is built.

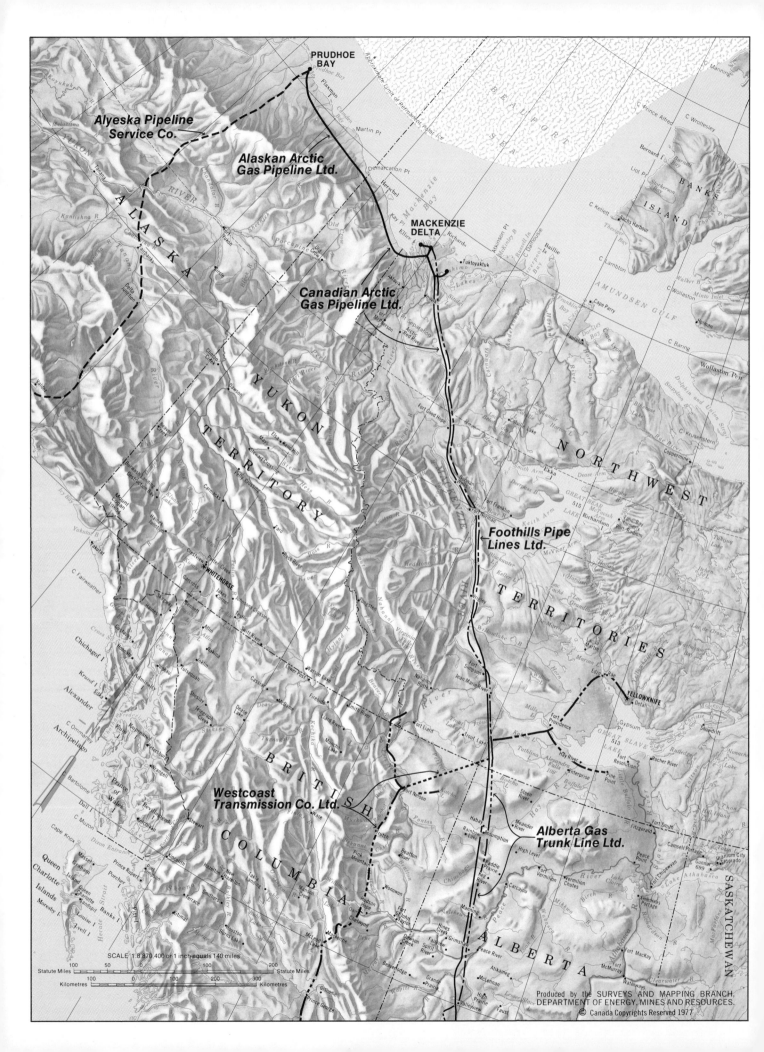

MACKENZIE VALLEY PIPELINE INQUIRY

COMMISSIONER
Mr. Justice Thomas R. Berger

10th Floor
One Nicholas Street
Ottawa, Ontario K1N 7B7

April 15, 1977

The Honourable Warren Allmand
Minister of Indian Affairs and Northern Development
House of Commons
Ottawa, Ontario

Dear Mr. Allmand:

We are now at our last frontier. It is a frontier that all of us have read about, but few of us have seen. Profound issues, touching our deepest concerns as a nation, await us there.

The North is a frontier, but it is a homeland too, the homeland of the Dene, Inuit and Metis, as it is also the home of the white people who live there. And it is a heritage, a unique environment that we are called upon to preserve for all Canadians.

The decisions we have to make are not, therefore, simply about northern pipelines. They are decisions about the protection of the northern environment and the future of northern peoples.

At the formal hearings of the Inquiry in Yellowknife, I heard the evidence of 300 experts on northern conditions, northern environment and northern peoples. But, sitting in a hearing room in Yellowknife, it is easy to forget the real extent of the North. The Mackenzie Valley and the Western Arctic is a vast land where people of four races live, speaking seven different languages. To hear what they had to say, I took the Inquiry to 35 communities — from Sachs Harbour to Fort Smith, from Old Crow to Fort Franklin — to every city and town, village and settlement in the Mackenzie Valley and the Western Arctic. I listened to the evidence of almost one thousand northerners.

I discovered that people in the North have strong feelings about the pipeline and large-scale frontier development. I listened to a brief by northern businessmen in Yellowknife who favour a pipeline through the North. Later, in a native village far away, I heard virtually the whole community express vehement opposition to such a pipeline. Both were talking about the same pipeline; both were talking about the same region — but for one group it is a frontier, for the other a homeland.

All those who had something to say — white or native — were given an opportunity to speak. The native organizations claim to speak for the native people. They oppose the pipeline without a settlement of native claims. The Territorial Council claims to speak for all northerners. It supports the pipeline. Wally Firth, Member of Parliament for the Northwest Territories, opposes the pipeline. I decided that I should give northerners an opportunity to speak for themselves. That is why I held hearings in all northern communities, where the people could speak directly to the Inquiry. I held hearings in the white centres of population, and in the native villages. I heard from municipal councillors, from band chiefs and band councils and from the people themselves. This report reflects what they told me.

The North is a region of conflicting goals, preferences and aspirations. The conflict focuses on the pipeline. The pipeline represents the advance of the industrial system to the Arctic. The impact of the industrial system upon the native people has been the special concern of the Inquiry, for one thing is certain: the impact of a pipeline will bear especially upon the native people. That is why I have been concerned that the native people should have an opportunity to speak to the Inquiry in their own villages, in their own languages, and in their own way.

I have proceeded on the assumption that, in due course, the industrial system will require the gas and oil of the Western Arctic, and that they will have to be transported along the Mackenzie Valley to markets in the South. I have also proceeded on the assumption that we intend to protect and preserve Canada's northern environment, and that, above all else, we intend to honour the legitimate claims and aspirations of the native people. All of these assumptions are embedded in the federal government's expressed northern policy for the 1970s.

The Corridor Concept and Cumulative Impact

The proposed natural gas pipeline is not to be considered in isolation. The Expanded Guidelines for Northern Pipelines, tabled in the House of Commons on June 28, 1972, assume that, if a gas pipeline is built, an oil pipeline will follow, and they call for examination of the proposed gas pipeline from the point of view of cumulative impact. We must

Spring on the Yukon Coastal Plain. (ISL—G. Calef)

Pingos near Tuktoyaktuk. (GNWT)

Old Crow River. (ISL—G. Calef)

Autumn on Mackenzie River. (R. Fumoleau)

consider, then, the impact of a transportation corridor for two energy systems, a corridor that may eventually include roads and other transportation systems.

The construction of a gas pipeline and the establishment of an energy corridor will intensify oil and gas exploration activity all along the corridor. The cumulative impact of all these developments will bring immense and irreversible changes to the Mackenzie Valley and the Western Arctic. And we must bear in mind that we have two corridors under consideration: a corridor from Alaska across the Northern Yukon to the Mackenzie Delta, and a corridor along the Mackenzie Valley from the Delta to the Alberta border.

The Project: Its Scope and Scale

A gas pipeline will entail much more than a right-of-way. It will be a major construction project across our northern territories, across a land that is cold and dark in winter, a land largely inaccessible by rail or road, where it will be necessary to construct wharves, warehouses, storage sites, airstrips — a huge infrastructure — just to build the pipeline. There will be a network of hundreds of miles of roads built over the snow and ice. Take the Arctic Gas project: the capacity of the fleet of tugs and barges on the Mackenzie River will have to be doubled. There will be 6,000 construction workers required North of 60 to build the pipeline, and 1,200 more to build gas plants and gathering systems in the Mackenzie Delta. There will be about 130 gravel mining operations. There will be 600 river and stream crossings. There will be innumerable aircraft, tractors, earth-movers, trucks and trailers. Indeed, the Arctic Gas project has been described as the greatest construction project, in terms of capital expenditure, ever contemplated by private enterprise.

Engineering and Construction

The gas pipeline across the North from Prudhoe Bay and from the Mackenzie Delta will confront designers and builders with major challenges of engineering and logistics. These relate not only to the

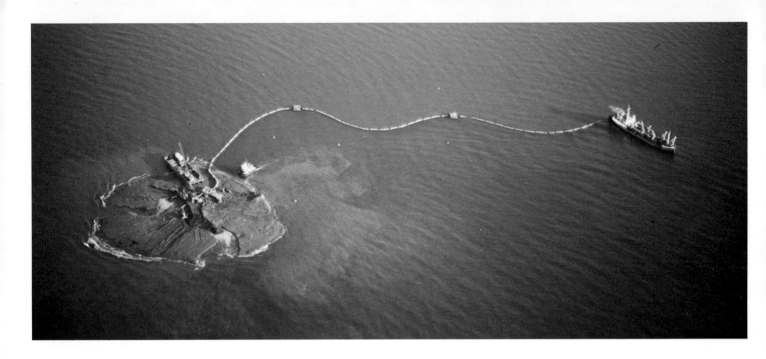

size and complexity of the project but also to its remote setting, the arctic climate and terrain, and those components of the project and its design that are innovative or lack precedent.

The question of frost heave is basic to the engineering design of the gas pipeline. Both Arctic Gas and Foothills propose to bury their pipe throughout its length, and to refrigerate the gas to avoid the engineering and environmental problems resulting from thawing permafrost. But where unfrozen ground is encountered, in the zone of discontinuous permafrost or at river crossings, the chilled gas will freeze the ground around the pipe, and may produce frost heave and potential damage to the pipe.

The pipeline companies are obviously having trouble in designing their proposal to deal with frost heave. They are making fundamental changes in the methods proposed for heave control; the methods seem to be getting more complex, and the conditions for success more restrictive. It is likely that the companies will make yet further changes in their proposals, changes that are likely to increase costs and to alter substantially the environmental impact of the project.

Another issue is construction scheduling. The pipeline companies propose to construct the pipeline in winter. But we have limited experience of pipelining in far northern latitudes and in permafrost. There are uncertainties about scheduling, so far as logistics, the construction of snow roads, and productivity are concerned. In this respect, the greatest challenges will be encountered in the Northern Yukon, which is also the most environmentally sensitive area along the route. I am not persuaded that Arctic Gas can meet its construction schedule across the Northern Yukon. Should this occur, there is a likelihood of cost overruns, of construction being extended into the summer, or even of a permanent road being built to permit summer construction. The environmental impact of a change to summer construction would be very severe. The project would then have to be completely reassessed.

Construction of artificial island in the Beaufort Sea.
(J. Inglis)

Compressor unit, Sans Sault Test Site. (Arctic Gas)

Drill site on the Eagle Plain, southeast of Old Crow.
(ISL—G. Calef)

Permafrost test at Sans Sault Test Site. (Arctic Gas)

I recognize, of course, that the proposals of the pipeline companies are in a preliminary, conceptual stage, not in their final design stage. I recognize, too, that improvements will appear in the final design. But my responsibility is to assess the project proposals as they now stand.

Given the uncertainties relating to design and construction, illustrated by the foregoing comments on frost heave and scheduling, and given the bearing they have on environmental impact and the enforcement of environmental standards, it seems to me unreasonable that the Government of Canada should give unqualified approval to a right-of-way or provide financial guarantees to the project without a convincing resolution of these concerns.

The Northern Environment

There is a myth that terms and conditions that will protect the environment can be imposed, no matter how large a project is proposed. There is a feeling that, with enough studies and reports, and once enough evidence is accumulated, somehow all will be well. It is an assumption that implies the choice we intend to make. It is an assumption that does not hold in the North.

It is often thought that, because of the immense geographic area of the North, construction of a gas pipeline or establishment of a corridor could not cause major damage to the land, the water or the wildlife. But within this vast area are tracts of land and water of limited size that are vital to the survival of whole populations of certain species of mammals, birds and fish at certain times of the year. Disturbance of such areas by industrial activities can have adverse biological effects that go far beyond the areas of impact. This concern with critical habitat and with critical life stages lies at the heart of my consideration of environmental issues.

We should recognize that in the North, land use regulations, based on the concept of multiple use, will not always protect environmental values, and they will never fully protect wilderness values. Withdrawal of land from any industrial use will be necessary in some instances to preserve wilderness, wildlife species and critical habitat.

The Northern Yukon

The Northern Yukon is an arctic and sub-arctic wilderness of incredible beauty, a rich and varied ecosystem inhabited by thriving populations of wildlife. The Porcupine caribou herd, comprising 110,000 animals or more, ranges throughout the Northern Yukon and into Alaska. It is one of the last great caribou herds in North America. The Yukon Coastal Plain and the Old Crow Flats provide essential habitat for hundreds of thousands of migratory waterfowl each summer and fall. This unique ecosystem — the caribou, the birds, other wildlife, and the wilderness itself — has survived until now because of the inaccessibility of the area. But it is vulnerable to the kind of disturbance that industrial development would bring.

The Arctic Gas pipeline, to carry gas from Prudhoe Bay, Alaska, to markets in the Lower 48, would cross this region, either along the Coastal Route or, as a second choice, along the Interior Route. Once a gas pipeline is approved along either route, exploration and development in the promising oil and gas areas of Northern Alaska will accelerate, and it is inevitable that the gas pipeline will be looped and that an oil pipeline, a road and other developments will follow.

Gas pipeline and corridor development along the Coastal Route, passing through the restricted calving range of the Porcupine caribou herd, would have highly adverse effects on the animals during the critical calving and post-calving phases of their life cycle. The preservation of the herd is incompatible with the building of a gas pipeline and the establishment of an energy corridor through its calving grounds. If a pipeline is built along the Coastal Plain, there will be serious losses to the herd. With the establishment of the corridor I foresee that, within our lifetime, this herd will be reduced to a remnant. Similarly, some of the large populations of migratory

Polar bear skins, Sachs Harbour. (M. Jackson)

Inuit women cutting up whale, Tuktoyaktuk. (D. Campbell)

Scraping a caribou hide. (A. Steen)

Arctic fox pelts, Sachs Harbour. (M. Jackson)

waterfowl and sea birds along the Coastal Route, particularly the fall staging snow geese, would likely decline in the face of pipeline and corridor development.

Gas pipeline and corridor development along the Interior Route would open up the winter range of the caribou herd. The impact of this development combined with that of the Dempster Highway could substantially reduce the herd's numbers and undermine the caribou-based economy of the Old Crow people.

Thus, I have concluded that there are sound environmental reasons for not building a pipeline or establishing an energy corridor along the Coastal Route. There are also sound environmental reasons for not building a pipeline or establishing an energy corridor along the Interior Route, although they are not as compelling as for the Coastal Route. A pipeline and corridor along the Interior Route would have a devastating impact on Old Crow, the only community in the Northern Yukon. All the people in the village told me they are opposed to the pipeline. They fear it will destroy their village, their way of life, and their land.

I recommend that no pipeline be built and no energy corridor be established across the Northern Yukon, along either route. Moreover, if we are to protect the wilderness, the caribou, birds and other wildlife, we must designate the Northern Yukon, north of the Porcupine River, as a National Wilderness Park. Oil and gas exploration, pipeline construction and industrial activity must be prohibited within the Park. The native people must continue to have the right to hunt, fish and trap within the Park. The Park must indeed be the means for protecting their renewable resource base.

You and your colleagues will have to consider whether Canada ought to provide a corridor across the Yukon for the delivery of Alaskan gas and oil to the Lower 48. I recommend that no such route be approved across the Northern Yukon. An alternate route has been proposed across the Southern Yukon, along the Alaska Highway.

Some of the concerns about wildlife, wilderness, and engineering and construction that led me to reject the corridor across the Northern Yukon do not appear to apply in the case of the Alaska Highway Route. It is a route with an established infrastructure. In my view, the construction of a pipeline along this route would not threaten any substantial populations of any species in the Yukon or in Alaska. But I am in no position to endorse such a route: an assessment of social and economic impact must still be made, and native claims have not been settled.

The Mackenzie Delta and the Beaufort Sea

The Mackenzie Delta and Beaufort Sea region supports a unique and vulnerable arctic ecosystem. Its wildlife has been a mainstay of the native people of the region for a long time, and still is today.

In my opinion, unlike the Northern Yukon, oil and gas development in the Mackenzie Delta-Beaufort Sea region is inevitable. Notwithstanding the disappointing level of discoveries so far, the Delta-Beaufort region has been rated by the Department of Energy, Mines and Resources as one of three frontier areas in Canada that potentially contain major undeveloped reserves of oil and gas.

A decision to build the pipeline now would act as a spur to oil and gas exploration and development in the Mackenzie Delta and the Beaufort Sea. Future discoveries will probably lead to offshore production. It is the impact of this whole range of oil and gas exploration and development activity that must concern us.

In order to protect the Delta ecosystem, the birds and the whales, I recommend that no corridor should cross the outer Delta. This means that the Arctic Gas Cross-Delta Route must not be permitted. Also, strict limitations will have to be placed on other oil and gas facilities on the Delta, particularly the outer Delta. Special measures will be needed to avoid disturbance to fish populations within the Delta. I also propose that a bird sanctuary should extend across the outer part of the Delta to protect migratory waterfowl, giving the Canadian

Caribou fording Porcupine River. (ISL—G. Calef)

Caribou with newborn calves migrating. (ISL—G. Calef)

Foraging caribou in the Northern Yukon. (ISL—G. Calef)

Bull caribou. (C. Dauphiné Jr.)

Wildlife Service jurisdiction to regulate industrial activity in the sanctuary.

The white whales of the Beaufort Sea — 5,000 in number — come to the warm waters bordering the Mackenzie Delta each summer to have their young. To preserve this population from declining in the face of pipeline construction and the cumulative stresses imposed by ongoing oil and gas exploration, production and transportation, I recommend that a whale sanctuary be established in west Mackenzie Bay covering the principal calving area. If the herd is driven from its calving area, it will die out. Unlike the bird sanctuary, the whale sanctuary will be an area in which oil and gas exploration and development would be forbidden at any time of the year.

Much of the oil and gas potential of the region is believed to lie offshore beneath the Beaufort Sea. You and your colleagues have decided that the risk entailed in the Dome exploratory drilling program in the Beaufort Sea is acceptable, on the ground that it is in the national interest to begin delineating the extent of these reserves. I am not offering any opinion on that decision. I am, however, urging that, once the Dome program is completed, careful consideration be given to the timing and extent of the drilling and development that may take place thereafter. A proliferation of oil and gas exploration and development wells in the Beaufort Sea will pose an environmental risk of a different order of magnitude than the risk entailed in drilling 16 exploration wells to see if oil and gas are to be found there.

The matter is not, however, simply one of Canadian drilling activity in arctic waters. We have preceded all of the other circumpolar countries — the United States, the Soviet Union, Denmark and Norway — across this geographic and technological frontier. We are pioneering on this frontier and establishing the standards that may well guide other circumpolar countries in future arctic drilling and production programs.

The greatest concern in the Beaufort Sea is the threat of oil spills. In my opinion, the techniques presently available will not be successful in controlling or cleaning up a major spill in this remote area, particularly under conditions involving floating ice or rough water. Therefore, I urge the Government of Canada to ensure that improvements in technology for prevention of spills and development of effective technology for containment and clean-up of spills precede further advance of industry in the Beaufort Sea. I further urge that advances in knowledge of the environmental consequences of oil spills should likewise keep ahead of offshore development. Here I am referring not only to impacts on mammals, birds and fish in the Beaufort Sea area but also to the possibility that accumulation of oil in the Arctic Ocean could affect climate. In this I am referring to the possibility that oil spills from offshore petroleum development by all the circumpolar powers could diminish the albedo (the reflective capacity of ice), causing a decrease in the sea ice cover and hence changes in climate. Canada should propose that research be undertaken jointly by the circumpolar powers into the risks and consequences of oil and gas exploration, development and transportation activities around the Arctic Ocean.

The Mackenzie Valley

The Mackenzie Valley is a natural transportation route that has already seen several decades of industrial development. It is the longest river system in Canada, one of the ten longest rivers in the world, and one of the last great rivers that is not polluted.

I have concluded that it is feasible, from an environmental point of view, to build a pipeline and to establish an energy corridor along the Mackenzie Valley, running south from the Mackenzie Delta to the Alberta border. Unlike the Northern Yukon, no major wildlife populations would be threatened and no wilderness areas would be violated. I believe that we can devise terms and conditions that will allow a pipeline to be built and an energy corridor established along the Mackenzie Valley without significant losses to the populations of

Snow geese feeding. (Arctic Gas)

Willow ptarmigan. (A. Steen)

Peregrine falcon. (R. Fyfe)

Gyrfalcon. (R. Fyfe)

birds, furbearers, large mammals and fish. A pipeline along the Mackenzie Valley would impinge on the outer limits of the winter ranges of the Bluenose and the Bathurst caribou herds, but would not cross their calving grounds or disturb their main migration routes. These herds are not threatened.

However, to keep the environmental impacts of a pipeline to an acceptable level, its construction and operation should proceed only under careful planning and strict regulation. The corridor should be based on a comprehensive plan that takes into account the many land use conflicts apparent in the region even today.

Comprehensive land use planning in the Mackenzie Valley can emerge only from a settlement of native claims, but, on purely environmental grounds, there are several areas of land that warrant immediate protection. I recommend sanctuaries to protect migratory waterfowl and the already endangered falcons. These sites have been identified under the International Biological Programme, namely: the Campbell Hills-Dolomite Lake site, which is important to nesting falcons, and the Willow Lake and Mills Lake sites, which are of importance to migratory waterfowl.

Northern Science and Research

Throughout the Inquiry, we found that there are critical gaps in the information available about the northern environment, about environmental impact, and about engineering design and construction on permafrost terrain and under arctic conditions. I have already referred to the inadequate state of knowledge about frost heave. This is a very practical question. Others, such as the albedo question, that seem to be less definite or to lie far in the future also demand our attention now. There is a whole range of issues that fall between, many of which are discussed in this report.

We are entering an era in the North when the government, its departments and agencies, will have to be in a position to assess — and to judge — the feasibility, desirability and impact of a whole series of proposals for northern oil and gas exploration and development. Industry proposes: government disposes. But for government to make an intelligent disposition of industry's proposals — whether they be for pipelining in permafrost, for drilling in the Beaufort Sea, for under the sea transporation systems, or for tankering in arctic waters — it must have an independent body of knowledge. A continuing and comprehensive program of northern science and research is called for.

Cultural Impact

It is, however, the people who live in the North that we ought to be most concerned about, especially the native people. Euro-Canadian society has refused to take native culture seriously. European institutions, values and use of land were seen as the basis of culture. Native institutions, values and language were rejected, ignored or misunderstood and — given the native people's use of land — the Europeans had no difficulty in supposing that native people possessed no real culture at all. Education was perceived as the most effective instrument of cultural change: so, educational systems were introduced that were intended to provide the native people with a useful and meaningful cultural inheritance, since their own ancestors had left them none.

The culture, values and traditions of the native people amount to a great deal more than crafts and carvings. Their respect for the wisdom of the elders, their concept of family responsibilities, their willingness to share, their special relationship with the land — all of these values persist today, although native people have been under almost unremitting pressure to abandon them.

Native society is not static. The things the native people have said to this Inquiry should not be regarded as a lament for a lost way of life, but as a plea for an opportunity to shape their own future, out of their own past. They are not seeking to entrench the past, but to build on it.

Today white and native populations in the Mackenzie Valley and Western Arctic are about equal in number. But it is the native people

Barge on Mackenzie River. (Arctic Gas)

Snowmobiles and sleigh, Tuktoyaktuk. (H. Lloyd)

Northern bush aircraft. (DIAND Yellowknife)

Boats used to hunt whale, Kugmallit Bay. (W. Hoek)

who constitute the permanent population of the North. There they were born, and there they will die. A large part of the white population consists of public servants, employees of the mining industry and of the oil and gas industry and their families. Most of them do not regard the North as their permanent home, and usually return to the South. There are, of course, white people in the North who have lived there all their lives, and some others who intend to make the North their permanent home, but their numbers are small in comparison to the native population.

So the future of the North ought not to be determined only by our own southern ideas of frontier development. It should also reflect the ideas of the people who call it their homeland.

Economic Impact

The pipeline companies see the pipeline as an unqualified gain to the North; northern businessmen perceive it as the impetus for growth and expansion. But all along, the construction of the pipeline has been justified mainly on the ground that it would provide jobs for thousands of native people.

We have been committed to the view that the economic future of the North lay in large-scale industrial development. We have generated, especially in northern business, an atmosphere of expectancy about industrial development. Although there has always been a native economy in the North, based on the bush and the barrens, we have for a decade or more followed policies by which it could only be weakened and depreciated. We have assumed that the native economy is moribund and that the native people should therefore be induced to enter industrial wage employment. But I have found that income in kind from hunting, fishing and trapping is a far more important element in the northern economy than we had thought.

The fact is that large-scale projects based on non-renewable resources have rarely provided permanent employment for any significant number of native people. There is abundant reason to

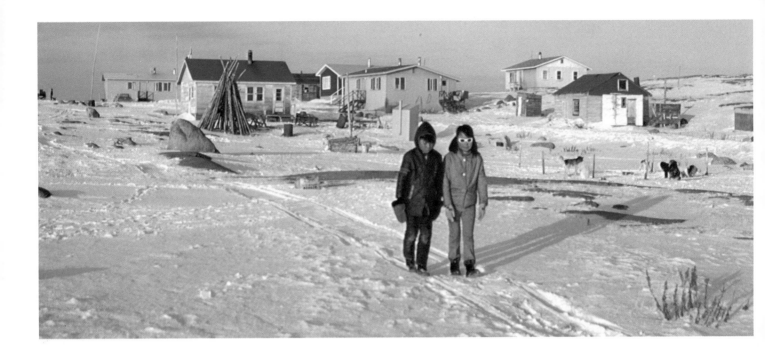

doubt that a pipeline would provide meaningful and ongoing employment to many native people. The pipeline contractors and unions have made it plain that native northerners are not qualified to hold down skilled positions in pipeline construction, and that they will be employed largely in unskilled and semi-skilled jobs. Once the pipeline is built, only about 250 people will be needed to operate it. Most of these jobs are of a technical nature and will have to be filled by qualified personnel from the South.

I have no doubt that terms and conditions could be imposed that would enable northern businesses to expand during the construction of the pipeline. But there are hazards for northern businessmen. Construction of the Mackenzie Valley pipeline could produce a serious distortion of the small business sector of the Northwest Territories. This would raise problems for the orderly development of regional economic and commercial activity in the long run.

If communities in the Mackenzie Valley and Western Arctic are made to depend exclusively on industrial wage employment and if the production of country food for local consumption ceases to be an important component in the economy, then the self-employed will certainly become the unemployed. The point is simple enough: the extension of the industrial system creates unemployment as well as employment. In an industrial economy there is virtually no alternative to a livelihood based on wage employment. Those who are unable or unprepared to work for wages become unemployed and then dependent on welfare. To the extent that the development of the northern frontier undermines the possibilities of self-employment provided by hunting, fishing and trapping, employment and unemployment will go hand-in-hand.

I do not mean to suggest that native people will not want to participate in the opportunities for employment that industrial development will create. Some native people already work alongside workers from the South. Many native people have taken advantage of

Detah Indian village. (R. Fumoleau)

Inuit housing. (GNWT)

Yellowknife. (A. Steen)

Fort Franklin. (R. Fumoleau)

opportunities for wage employment — particularly in the Delta — on a seasonal basis to obtain the cash they need to equip or re-equip themselves for traditional pursuits. But when the native people are made to feel they have no choice other than the industrial system, when they have no control over entering it or leaving it, when wage labour becomes the strongest, the most compelling and finally the only option, then the disruptive effects of large-scale, rapid development can only proliferate.

It is an illusion to believe that the pipeline will solve the economic problems of the North. Its whole purpose is to deliver northern gas to homes and industries in the South. Indeed, rather than solving the North's economic problems, it may accentuate them.

The native people, both young and old, see clearly the short-term character of pipeline construction. They see the need to build an economic future for themselves on a surer foundation. The real economic problems in the North will be solved only when we accept the view the native people themselves expressed so often to the Inquiry: that is, the strengthening of the native economy. We must look at forms of economic development that really do accord with native values and preferences. If the kinds of things that native people now want are taken seriously, we must cease to regard large-scale industrial development as a panacea for the economic ills of the North.

Social Impact

I am convinced that the native people of the North told the Inquiry of their innermost concerns and their deepest fears. Although they had been told — and some indeed had agreed — that the proposed pipeline would offer them unprecedented opportunities for wage employment, the great majority of them expressed their fears of what a pipeline would bring: an influx of construction workers, more alcoholism, tearing of the social fabric, injury to the land, and the loss of their identity as a people. They said that wage employment on the pipeline would count for little or nothing when set against the social costs. I am persuaded that these fears are well-founded.

The alarming rise in the incidence of alcoholism, crime, violence and welfare dependence in the North in the last decade is closely bound up with the rapid expansion of the industrial system and with its intrusion into every part of the native people's lives. The process affects the close link between native people and their past, their own economy, their values and self-respect. The evidence is clear: the more the industrial frontier displaces the homeland in the North, the greater the incidence of social pathology will be. Superimposed on problems that already exist in the Mackenzie Valley and the Western Arctic, the social consequences of the pipeline will not only be serious — they will be devastating.

The social costs of building a pipeline now will be enormous, and no remedial programs are likely to ameliorate them. The expenditure of money, the hiring of social workers, doctors, nurses, even police — these things will not begin to solve the problem. This will mean an advance of the industrial system to the frontier that will not be orderly and beneficial, but sudden, massive and overwhelming.

Native Claims

Native people desire a settlement of native claims before a pipeline is built. They do not want a settlement — in the tradition of the treaties — that will extinguish their rights to the land. They want a settlement that will entrench their rights to the land and that will lay the foundations of native self-determination under the Constitution of Canada.

The native people of the North now insist that the settlement of native claims must be seen as a fundamental re-ordering of their relationship with the rest of us. Their claims must be seen as the means to establishing a social contract based on a clear understanding that they are distinct peoples in history. They insist upon the right to

Inuit at Northern Games, Coppermine, 1976.
(GNWT–R. Wilson)

Reindeer round-up, Atkinson Point. (J. Inglis)

Holman youngster. (P. Scott)

Children playing in Holman, 1959. (J. Fyles)

determine their own future, to ensure their place, but not their assimilation, in Canadian life.

The federal government is now prepared to negotiate with the native people on a comprehensive basis, and the native people of the North are prepared to articulate their interests over a broad range of concerns. These concerns begin with the land, but are not limited to it: they include land and land use, renewable and non-renewable resources, schools, health and social services, public order and, overarching all of these, the future shape and composition of political institutions in the North.

The concept of native self-determination must be understood in the context of native claims. When the Dene refer to themselves as a nation, as many of them have, they are not renouncing Canada or Confederation. Rather, they are proclaiming that they are a distinct people, who share a common historical experience, a common set of values, and a common world view. They want their children and their children's children to be secure in that same knowledge of who they are and where they came from. They want their own experience, traditions and values to occupy an honourable place in the contemporary life of our country. Seen in this light, they say their claims will lead to the enhancement of Confederation — not to its renunciation.

It will be for you and your colleagues, in negotiations with the native people, to determine the extent to which native claims can be acceded to, and to work out the way in which self-determination might be effected in the North, whether by the establishment of native institutions on a geographical basis or by the transfer of certain functions of the Government of Canada and the Government of the Northwest Territories to native institutions.

The idea of new institutions that give meaning to native self-determination should not frighten us. Special status for native people is an element of our constitutional tradition, one that is recognized by the British North America Act, by the treaties, by the Indian Act, and by the statement of policy approved by Cabinet in July 1976. It is an ethnic thread in our constitutional fabric. In the past, special status has meant Indian reserves. Now the native people wish to substitute self-determination for enforced dependency.

The attainment of native goals implies one thing: the native people must be allowed a choice about their own future. If the pipeline is approved before a settlement of claims takes place, the future of the North — and the place of the native people in the North — will, in effect, have been decided for them.

The construction of the pipeline now will entail a commitment by the Government of Canada and the Government of the Northwest Territories to a program of large-scale frontier development, which, once begun, cannot be diverted from its course. Once construction begins, the concentration on the non-renewable resource sector and the movement away from the renewable resource sector will become inexorable. The goal of strengthening the native economy will be frustrated.

An increase in the white population in the wake of pipeline construction will entrench southern patterns of political, social and industrial development, will reduce the native people to a minority position, and will undermine their claim to self-determination.

The settlement of native claims is not a mere transaction. Intrinsic to settlement is the establishment of new institutions and programs that will form the basis for native self-determination. It would be wrong, therefore, to think that signing a piece of paper would put the whole question behind us, as if all that were involved was the removal of a legal impediment to industrial development. The native people insist that the settlement of native claims should be a beginning rather than an end of the recognition of native rights and native aspirations. In my opinion, a period of ten years will be required in the Mackenzie Valley and Western Arctic to settle native claims, and to establish the

Snowdrift children. (R. Fumoleau)

Johnny Crapeau of Detah. (R. Fumoleau)

Maggie Fisher of Fort Good Hope. (R. Fumoleau)

François Paulette of Fort Smith. (M. Jackson)

new institutions and new programs that a settlement will entail. No pipeline should be built until these things have been achieved.

It would therefore be dishonest to try to impose an immediate settlement that we know now — and that the native people will know before the ink is dry — will not achieve their goals. They will soon realize — just as the native people on the prairies realized a century ago as the settlers poured in — that the actual course of events on the ground will deny the promises that appear on paper. The advance of the industrial system would determine the course of events, no matter what Parliament, the courts, this Inquiry or anyone else may say.

In recent years in the North we have witnessed a growing sense of native awareness and native identity. The same phenomenon can be observed throughout the country. It is not going to go away. To establish political institutions in the North that ignore this fact of life would be unwise and unjust. Special status can be — and ought to be — a constructive and creative means by which native people, through the development of institutions of their own, can thrive in a new partnership of interests.

If There is no Pipeline Now

If the native people are to achieve their goals, no pipeline can be built now. Some will say this decision must mean that there will be no economic development in the North. If a pipeline is not built now, so the argument goes, the northern economy will come to a halt. But this view misconstrues the nature of the northern economy and northern development.

If there is no pipeline, the native economy based on hunting, fishing and trapping will scarcely be affected. The mining industry, which is the largest component of the private sector of the economy of both the Yukon Territory and the Northwest Territories, will not be greatly affected. Government, the largest employer and the main source of income for white northerners, and the federal and territorial bureaucracies are not likely to decrease in size simply because a pipeline is not built now.

A decision not to build a pipeline now would not necessarily bring an end to oil and gas exploration. There will be a setback to Inuvik and, to a lesser extent, to other Delta communities. If exploratory drilling in the Delta and the Beaufort Sea ought to continue in the national interest, the Government of Canada has the means to see that it does.

I am convinced that non-renewable resources need not necessarily be the sole basis of the northern economy in the future. We should not place absolute faith in any model of development requiring large-scale technology. The development of the whole renewable resource sector — including the strengthening of the native economy — would enable native people to enter the industrial system without becoming completely dependent on it.

An economy based on modernization of hunting, fishing and trapping, on efficient game and fisheries management, on small-scale enterprise, and on the orderly development of gas and oil resources over a period of years — this is no retreat into the past; rather, it is a rational program for northern development based on the ideals and aspirations of northern native peoples.

To develop a diversified economy will take time. It will be tedious, not glamorous, work. No quick and easy fortunes will be made. There will be failures. The economy will not necessarily attract the interest of the multinational corporations. It will be regarded by many as a step backward. But the evidence I have heard has led me to the conclusion that such a program is the only one that makes sense.

Implications

There should be no pipeline across the Northern Yukon. It would entail irreparable environmental losses of national and international importance. And a Mackenzie Valley pipeline should be postponed for ten years. If it were built now, it would bring limited economic

Northern Yukon. (E. Peterson)

Dogteams trek across sea ice. (GNWT)

Little Bell River. (ISL—G. Calef)

Winter — Yukon North Slope. (Arctic Gas)

benefits, its social impact would be devastating, and it would frustrate the goals of native claims. Postponement will allow sufficient time for native claims to be settled, and for new programs and new institutions to be established. This does not mean that we must renounce our northern gas and oil. But it does mean that we must allow sufficient time for an orderly, not hasty, program of exploration to determine the full extent of our oil and gas reserves in the Mackenzie Delta and the Beaufort Sea. Postponement will offer time for you and your colleagues to make a rational determination regarding the priorities to be adopted in relation to the exploitation of all our frontier oil and gas resources, at a time when the full extent of our frontier reserves has been ascertained.

I believe that, if you and your colleagues accept the recommendations I am making, we can build a Mackenzie Valley pipeline at a time of our own choosing, along a route of our own choice. With time, it may, after all, be possible to reconcile the urgent claims of northern native people with the future requirements of all Canadians for gas and oil.

Yours truly,

Thos. R. Berger

The North

Northern Frontier, Northern Homeland

This Inquiry was appointed to consider the social, environmental and economic impact of a gas pipeline and an energy corridor across our northern territories, across a land where four races of people — Indian, Inuit, Metis and white — live, and where seven languages are spoken. The Inquiry was also empowered to recommend terms and conditions that ought to be imposed to protect the people of the North, their environment, and their economy, if the pipeline were to be built.

Today, we realize more fully what was always implicit in the Inquiry's mandate: this is not simply a debate about a gas pipeline and an energy corridor, it is a debate about the future of the North and its peoples.

There are two distinct views of the North: one as frontier, the other as homeland.

We look upon the North as our last frontier. It is natural for us to think of developing it, of subduing the land and extracting its resources to fuel Canada's industry and heat our homes. Our whole inclination is to think of expanding our industrial machine to the limit of our country's frontiers. In this view, the construction of a gas pipeline is seen as the next advance in a series of frontier advances that have been intimately bound up with Canadian history. But the native people say the North is their homeland. They have lived there for thousands of years. They claim it is their land, and they believe they have a right to say what its future ought to be.

The question whether a pipeline shall be built has become the occasion for the joining of these issues.

In the past, Canada has been defined by its frontiers. In the words of Kenneth McNaught:

From the time of the earliest records Canada has been part of a frontier, just as in her own growth she has fostered frontiers. The struggle of men and of metropolitan centres to extend and control those frontiers, as well as to improve life behind them, lies at the heart of Canadian history — and geography determined many of the conditions of that struggle. [*The Pelican History of Canada*, p. 7]

H.A. Innis insisted that it was Canadian geography and Canadian frontiers that made possible and defined the existence of the country. The nation's lines of transportation and communications were based on the St. Lawrence River, the Great Lakes and western waterways. French and British dependence on fish, fur, timber and wheat influenced the course of Canadian history, one staple after another drawing the nation from one frontier to the next. Innis refuted the notion that Canada's economy is simply a series of projections northward from the economic heartland of North America.

The French, the fur trade, British institutions — these have all played a part from the earliest times in the development of a separate community in the northern half of the continent. But it is a northern tradition that in large measure makes Canada distinct from the United States today. We share a mass culture with the United States, but it is Canada that has — and always has had — a distinct northern geography and a special concern with the North.

What happens in the North, moreover, will be of great importance to the future of our country; it will tell us what kind of a country Canada is; it will tell us what kind of a people we are. In the past, we have thought of the history of our country as a progression from one frontier to the next.

Such, in the main, has been the story of white occupation and settlement of North America. But as the retreating frontier has been occupied and settled, the native people living there have become subservient, their lives moulded to the patterns of another culture.

We think of ourselves as a northern people. We may at last have begun to realize that we have something to learn from the people who for centuries have lived in the North, the people who never sought to alter their environment, but rather to live in harmony with it. This Inquiry has given all Canadians an opportunity to listen to the voices on the frontier.

In the past at each frontier we have encountered the native people. The St. Lawrence Valley was the homeland of the Huron and the Iroquois — they were overwhelmed; the West was the homeland of the Cree — they were displaced; the Pacific Coast was the homeland of the Salish — they were dispossessed. Now, we are told that the North is the homeland of the Dene, the Inuit and the Metis. Today in the North we confront the questions that have confronted Canadians before — questions from which we must not now turn away.

Should the future of the North be determined by the South? The question can, of course, be answered by saying that since 1867 the Government of Canada has had responsibility for the welfare of the native people, and that since 1870 it has had jurisdiction over the Northwest. This is to say that Ottawa is sovereign, and has the power to dispose of the North as it wills. But the Government of Canada has not been satisfied to make such an answer, and has established this Inquiry to make it plain that the goals, aspirations and preferences of the northern peoples should be fully explored before any decision is taken.

The choice we make will decide whether the North is to be primarily a frontier for industry or a homeland for its peoples. We shall have the choice only once. Any attempt to beg the question that now faces us, to suggest that a choice has already been made or need never be made will be an inexcusable evasion of responsibility.

The issues we face are profound ones, going beyond the ideological conflicts that have occupied the world for so long, conflicts over who should run the industrial machine, and who should reap the benefits. Now we are being asked: How much energy does it take to run the industrial machine? Where must the energy come from? Where is the machine going? And what happens to the people who live in the path of the machine?

It may be that, in the national interest, the gas pipeline and the energy corridor should be built. It may be that they should not. But we owe to the peoples of the North, and to future generations, a careful consideration of the consequences before we go ahead with such projects. This report is an attempt to set out what those consequences will be.

The Northern Biome

To most Canadians, "the North" is the immense hinterland of Canada that lies beyond the narrow southern strip of our country in which we live and work. Throughout this report, my view of the North is confined largely to Canada's northern territories — the Yukon Territory and the Northwest Territories — and my attention is addressed principally to that part of Canada, including the adjoining sea and islands, that

lies to the north of the provinces of British Columbia and Alberta.

In the course of this Inquiry, I have travelled throughout this region. I have learned how remarkably different the land is in winter and in summer. I have seen the great differences between the forest and the tundra. I have admired the vastness of the land, its variety, its beauty, and the abundance of its wildlife.

I have travelled throughout the Mackenzie Valley, and I have seen the great river in its varied moods. I have crossed the swampy and forested plains and the "great" lakes that extend eastward from the Valley to the edge of the Canadian Shield. I have seen the myriad lakes and ponds and the complex of river channels that form the Mackenzie Delta. I have flown over the Beaufort Sea — in winter covered by ice and snow, in summer by fields of ice floating in the blue water. I have seen the beaches, bars and islands of the Arctic coast, the pingos and lakes around Tuktoyaktuk, the rocky hills at Holman, and the clear rivers of the Yukon Coastal Plain.

On the Old Crow Flats, in the Mackenzie Delta, and along the Beaufort Sea coast I have seen the immense flocks of birds that migrate in their thousands to this arctic area each summer. I have seen the white whales swimming in the shallow coastal waters of the Beaufort Sea around the Mackenzie Delta. I have seen the Porcupine caribou herd in early summer at its calving grounds in the Northern Yukon, and the Bathurst herd at its wintering grounds north of Great Slave Lake. And in every native village I have seen the meat and fish, the fur and hides that the people have harvested from the land and water.

The Boreal Forest and the Tundra

Biologists divide the North into two great regions called "biomes": the boreal forest and the tundra. The boreal forest is characterized in the minds of most people by spruce trees and muskeg. It is the broad band of coniferous forest that extends right across Canada from Newfoundland to Alaska. The tundra, extending from the boreal forest northward to the Arctic Ocean, comprises one-fifth of the land mass of Canada, but most of us who have never seen it, and know of it simply as a land without trees, sometimes call it "the barrens." Yet the tundra biome includes landscapes as varied and as beautiful as any in Canada — plains and mountains, hills and valleys, rivers, lakes and sea coasts. In winter, land and water merge into a white and grey desert, but the summer brings running water, explosively rapid plant growth, and a remarkable influx of migratory birds.

The two northern biomes — the tundra and the boreal forest — meet along the tree line. The tree line is not really a line, but a transitional zone that is commonly many miles in width. This biologically important boundary, which separates forest and tundra, also separates the traditional lands of the Indians and the Inuit. The tree line may also be viewed as the southern limit of the Arctic, the boundary between the Arctic and the sub-Arctic; this is the distinction I shall adopt in this report. Thus, the entire Mackenzie Valley and most of the Mackenzie Delta lie south of the tree line and are described as sub-arctic. In contrast, the land along the coast of the Beaufort Sea and the islands to the north lie beyond the tree line and are described as arctic.

I have learned from experience that, arctic or sub-arctic, this region is one of great

Well head, Pointed Mountain pipeline, NWT. (GNWT)

Permafrost patterns on the Yukon tundra. (M. Church)

Landscape of the boreal forest. (C. & M. Hampson)

Hoar frost. (R. Fumoleau)

climatic contrasts. In mid-summer, it is never dark, but in mid-winter the only daylight is a combined sunset and sunrise. Summer weather can be pleasantly warm, and in the Mackenzie Valley temperatures in excess of 80°F are not uncommon. But summer weather can also be raw and damp, particularly near the coast where a switch from an offshore to an onshore wind will cause temperatures to drop rapidly almost to freezing, accompanied by fog and drizzle.

Both rainfall and snowfall are light. In the Mackenzie Valley, the amount of precipitation is similar to that at Saskatoon or Regina, but in the true Arctic, including the lands bordering the Beaufort Sea, precipitation is as low as that in the driest parts of the Canadian prairies. For this reason, the Arctic may be described as desert and semi-desert, and it is remarkable, therefore, that the land surface in summer is predominantly wet and swampy, and dotted with innumerable shallow ponds. This apparent anomaly is caused, in large part, by permafrost, perennially frozen ground, which prevents water from draining downward into the ground. The seasonally thawed active layer of the soil holds the water from rain and melting snow like a sponge.

Permafrost

In much of Southern Canada, the ground freezes downward from the surface every winter and thaws completely again in the spring. But in the northern half of our country, in the sub-arctic and arctic regions, frost has penetrated below the maximum depth of summer thaw, and a layer of frozen ground persists beneath the surface from year to year. This perennially frozen ground, called permafrost, modifies the character of the landscape in the North and profoundly

affects the works of man on and beneath the surface of the land.

In the southern part of the permafrost region, the perennially frozen layer beneath the seasonally thawed "active" layer is only a few feet thick and occurs as patches or islands surrounded by unfrozen ground. Northward, permafrost is more extensive, the layer of frozen ground becomes thicker, and areas of unfrozen ground are smaller and fewer. Farther north still, the permafrost is relatively continuous and may be several hundred to more than a thousand feet thick; but there are areas without permafrost beneath rivers and lakes. To describe the main differences in its distribution, we speak of the continuous and the discontinuous permafrost zones. The proposed pipeline route north of Fort Good Hope lies within the continuous permafrost zone, whereas the route south of Fort Good Hope to around the Alberta border lies in the discontinuous permafrost zone.

Permafrost also occurs offshore beneath the Beaufort Sea, but little is yet known about it there. We believe most of the undersea permafrost was formed on land and has since been inundated by a rising sea level and shoreline erosion.

All of this, of course, is not obvious, but has been learned through a great deal of study. But what is obvious in travelling in the North is the presence of surface features that accompany permafrost. In the discontinuous permafrost zone, there are peat mounds or palsas, speckled and string bogs, and drunken forests with trees tilted in various directions. Farther north, there are pingos, frost-crack patterns, exposed masses of ice, thermokarst depressions caused by the melting of underground ice, as well as characteristic slump features and other signs of thawing soil along the sea coast and river

banks, and around lakes and ponds. In summer, there is the all-pervading wetness of the ground surface. In a region that, under warmer conditions, would be desert or semi-desert, ponds, swamps, fens and water-filled frost cracks all bear witness to the inability of water to drain downward through the frozen ground. Permafrost keeps the ground in the North moist, and it profoundly affects the vegetation, insects, birds and other forms of life.

Tundra has been described as land floating on ice. This conception aptly emphasizes the fact that frozen water within the ground gives the terrain unique qualities and creates problems for engineers. Thus, in the permafrost region, rock (which contains little water) is normally no different from rock in temperate regions, but the unconsolidated earth material — the soil — changes radically when the water in it freezes to form ice. The frozen soil will not absorb more water nor can water pass through it: water must therefore remain on the ground surface. Soil cemented together by ice is not easy to dig or to use in construction projects, because it has taken on rock-like properties. True, so long as it is frozen, it provides a solid foundation. But, not uncommonly, when frozen soil thaws, particularly if it is a fine-grained soil, it loses its strength: the soil may flow under its own weight, and the ground surface may subside as water escapes. In ice-rich soils, the effect may be compared with the melting of ice cream. This drastic change in properties occurs whenever the melting of ice in the soil releases more water than the soil can absorb. Such soil is described as containing excess ice.

Thawing of permafrost is only one cause of frost-induced engineering problems in the Arctic and sub-Arctic. Seasonal frost action in the active layer above the perennially frozen ground also causes problems. In winter, moisture in the active layer freezes, producing an upward displacement of the ground, called frost heave; in summer, there is a loss of bearing strength as the active layer thaws and the excess water is released. In some situations, engineering projects can lead to perennial freezing of areas where the ground is unfrozen or to the thickening of (existing) permafrost. When such changes take place in fine soil with abundant water, ice can build up and may cause frost heave. As we shall see later in this report, frost heave represents a serious problem for the proposed buried, chilled pipeline.

When roads, buildings or pipelines must be built where permafrost occurs, the engineers usually try to avoid disturbing the natural temperature regime in the ground. Disturbance of the ground surface is, therefore, kept to a minimum, particularly where peat or other organic material serves as a natural insulating blanket over the frozen ground. Frequently, where the thawing of permafrost would cause engineering or environmental difficulties, the structures are built above the ground on piles to permit air to circulate under them. The trans-Alaska oil pipeline is built on piles for this purpose. A common alternative is to place the structure on a pad of gravel, or of gravel plus insulation, thick enough to prevent heat from reaching the frozen ground. Compressor stations for the proposed Mackenzie Valley gas pipeline would be built on such pads. On the other hand, if a structure must disturb the ground or must be placed underground, then more complex techniques are required to avoid frost problems. The proposal to refrigerate the buried Mackenzie Valley gas pipeline is an example of such techniques.

The Northern Ecosystem

I have heard hundreds of hours of evidence from experts and laymen alike on the nature of the northern environment. Soil scientists and geotechnical engineers have explained the environmental problems associated with permafrost. Experts on vegetation have described the flora and the measures that can be taken to reestablish plant cover on disturbed areas. Biologists, hunters, trappers and fishermen have told me about the northern animals and fishes — their life cycles, habitat requirements and susceptibilities to disturbance. Throughout all this evidence, I have heard detailed expressions of concern for the northern ecosystem and of the measures that might be used to preserve it in the face of industrial development.

To understand the impact of industrial development on the northern ecosystem and the appropriateness of mitigative measures, it is essential first to understand its general nature and the features that set it apart from more familiar ecosystems in the South. Merely to characterize the North as sensitive, vulnerable or even fragile will not help. Granted, certain species are sensitive: falcons, for example, cannot tolerate disturbances near their nesting sites. The massing of some species such as caribou, white whales and snow geese in certain areas at certain times will make whole populations of them vulnerable. And the response of permafrost to disturbance suggests that its very existence is fragile. But anyone who has visited the North during the long winters and the short mosquito-infested summers will know that northern species must be hardy to survive.

Every ecosystem is built on both living and non-living elements. The two are inextricably linked, and the characteristics of the one are reflected in those of the other. It is not surprising that the combinations of climate and topography in the northern biomes have produced plant and animal populations unique to the North. The relations within the northern ecosystems are not well understood, but at least three characteristics appear to distinguish them: the simplicity of the food chains, the wide oscillations in populations, and the slow growth rates. Dr. Max Dunbar, a marine biologist of international repute, provides an overview of these features in his book *Environment and Good Sense*:

Arctic ecosystems are simple compared with those in temperate and tropical regions; that is to say, they consist of a comparatively small number of species. There are about 8,600 species of birds in the world; of these only some 56 breed in Greenland, and perhaps a little over 80 in Labrador-Ungava. Colombia, on the other hand, has 1,395, Venezuela 1,150. Of the 3,200 species of mammals known in the world, only 9 are found in the high Arctic, on land, and only 23 in the Cape Thompson area of Alaska. The world is full of fish; well over 23,000 are known. But only about 25 live in arctic waters. The same proportions, approximately, are shown in other groups of animals and plants.

As an example of such simple systems: the lemmings (there are two species in the North, but with fairly separate distributions, so that they are seldom found together) form the herbivore link between the mosses and grasses (the primary producers) and the foxes, snowy owls, and weasels. Here we have only one dominant herbivore, three common predators, and a few species of plants: so far only four species of mammals and birds in any one region. In certain areas, add two more predators: the rough-legged hawk and the gyrfalcon; elsewhere, add caribou and ground squirrels, two other herbivores; here and there, a wolf. In more southerly regions of the North another fox, the red fox, is also found; and a few herbivorous and insectivorous birds,

The Mackenzie Delta. (CAGPL)

Caribou on the move. (G. Calef)

Arctic ground squirrel. (C. & M. Hampson)

Arctic grayling. (R. Read)

perhaps five species. This gives only 15 species of homotherms or warm-blooded animals, and it is rare to find all of them in one "system" or restricted region. To these must be added the invertebrates and the plants, but this is enough to show how simple the pattern is when compared with the variety of birds and mammals found together in temperate parklands, or, even more so, in the tropical rain forest. In arctic lakes the number of species is very small indeed, and in the sea the same general proportion of species numbers is maintained in comparison with lower latitudes. Other similar examples could be given for coastal communities and for islands.

The cause of this simplicity is not the low temperatures themselves, contrary to common belief. Living organisms can adapt very easily to low temperature as such; this is true not only of the warm-blooded forms but of the poikilotherms ("cold-blooded" species) as well. The limiting factor is the ability of the system to produce life in abundance. In the sea, at least, and in lakes, this means that the limiting factor is the supply of inorganic nutrients.... On land the limiting factors may be both this lack of nutrients and the long frozen winter when the food supply is very greatly, though not entirely, reduced. In either instance it is food supply rather than low temperature....

One important result of the simplicity of arctic systems is that the component species oscillate in abundance over periods of time. In the example given above, the period of oscillation is controlled by the length of life and reproductive capacity of the lemming, and is maintained at from three to five years with quite remarkable regularity. These oscillations are severe in amplitude, so that they give rise frequently to what amounts to local extinction of species; the populations then have to be built up again by immigration from adjacent areas. The upsetting of this already rather shaky equilibrium by man's activity is probably very easy to do, and hence one must suppose that the North is more, rather than less, sensitive to pollutants and other environmental dislocations. This is the sort of thing

upon which we need more precise information than we have at present, and which we need time to obtain.

One important ecological factor that may well be dependent both upon food supply and temperature is growth, the rate at which animals reach maturity. This is especially true of the poikilothermal animals and of plants. This means that damage done to populations of animals and plants takes a long time to repair. One may, for instance, come upon a remote lake full of arctic char, or lake trout, and thrill at the prospect of such excellent fishing. This has happened not infrequently in the North. After two years of fishing by Eskimos, or by visitors, the lake appears to be devoid of fish; the reproductive rate and the growth rate of the fish have not come near to making up for the fishing take, and it may in fact require a rest of many decades before the fish population is restored. The arctic char of the Sylvia Grinnell River, at Frobisher Bay in Baffin Island, take twelve years' growth in the female before ripe eggs are produced, and even then each female spawns only every second or third year. Small wonder that such resources are soon fished out and destroyed....

The factors of population oscillation, then, and of slow growth rates, appear to give the northern ecosystems a quality of sensitivity, a knife-edge balance. A third factor is the simplicity of the system itself, for where so few species are involved the extinction of just one must be a serious matter. Yet one cannot at the moment be dogmatic on this point, because the situation has not been experimentally tested; we do not know how much stress the systems will bear and still survive. [p. 56ff.]

In the North, a certain number of species thrive. They are tough — they have to be to survive — but at the same time they are vulnerable. And in the North, man has the capability to cause irreparable injury to the environment.

Francis Bacon wrote, "Nature to be commanded must be obeyed." The northern

environment requires us to obey its rules. Where necessary, we must establish and follow new approaches. That is why we must on this, our last frontier, proceed only with the most complete knowledge of and concern for the flora and fauna of the North, for the biomes of the forest and the tundra.

Northern Peoples

The North is the homeland of a complex of indigenous cultures. We in the South may speak airily of "native people," and thereby convey the impression that there is a single culture, a single social system that occupies the vast arctic and sub-arctic terrain. But the term "native" is an inheritance from the European colonists, who usually regarded the original inhabitants of the lands they sought to subdue and settle, as a single group unified by "primitive" customs, and by their political relationship to the colonial powers themselves. In this way, the term "native" obscures essential differences between the cultures encountered in the course of European expansion.

The landscapes of the North have been shaped only marginally by the activities of man. The northern peoples have always been hunters and gatherers, and most have lived with a high degree of mobility. Small groups travelled over large areas, hunting and gathering what they needed, but without altering the environment itself. It is not always easy to remember, as one flies over the unbroken boreal forest, the tundra, or the sea ice, that the Canadian North has been inhabited for many thousands of years. The populations that have used this great area were never large by European standards, but their skills as travellers and hunters made it possible for them to occupy virtually all of the land. Extremely slow rates of northern plant growth and of decay mean that it is possible to see almost everywhere in the North signs of ancient occupation — old house remains, tent rings, fire-cracked rocks — and for archaeologists to find, on or close to the surface, a wealth of artifacts and other evidence to show the richness, diversity and wide extent of northern aboriginal society.

In the North, there are not just "native peoples," but a network of social systems. The Indians of the Mackenzie Valley and Western Arctic are part of the Athabascan language and culture group. They are separated into the Kutchin (or Loucheux), Hare, Slavey, Dogrib and Chipewyan. The Athabascan people are one of the most widely dispersed groups of Indians in North America. In addition to the Indians of the Northwest Territories and the Northern Yukon, they include the Koyukon and Tanana of Alaska, the Tutchone of the Southern Yukon, the Beaver and Carrier of British Columbia, the Navaho and Apache of the Southwest United States, and still others in California and Oregon. All these Indians, with whatever dialectical variation in their languages, regard themselves as *the people*. To the Slavey they are the *Dene,* to the Navaho *Dine;* in Kutchin the word is *Dindjie;* in Apache it is *Nde.* Today, in the North, the Indian people collectively call themselves the *Dene.*

The native peoples of the Western Arctic also include the Eskimos or, as they are now widely known, the Inuit; they occupy part of the Mackenzie Delta and the shores of the Beaufort Sea. Although all of the Inuit, from Siberia to eastern Greenland, speak closely related dialects of the same language, regionally there are differences in technology and

social organization that even today complicate anthropological generalizations about them. Certainly the Inuit themselves perceive major differences between their various groups: the Inuvialuit of the Delta see themselves as distinct from the Copper Eskimos, who are their neighbours to the east; and the Copper Eskimos — or Qurdlurturmiut — emphasize that they are unlike the Netsilik, the Aivilik or the Igloolik people, who live still farther east. And, within each of these broad groups, there are yet finer divisions and distinctions that reflect different patterns of land use and are represented by changes in dialect and in hunting techniques.

This brief elaboration of social systems may seem to lie at the periphery of this Inquiry, but it indicates that the Dene and the Inuit — as well as the Metis, to whom I shall return — are distinct peoples in history. They have common interests in relation to the proposed Mackenzie Valley pipeline, and they therefore share many concerns. But the intensity of their feelings, no less than the vigour with which they are now expressing their hopes and fears, reflect historical and cultural depths that cannot be comprehended by the term "native." The North has become our frontier during the past few decades; it has been a homeland of the Dene and Inuit peoples for many thousands of years.

Earliest Known Migrations

The last glaciation affected occupation of the arctic regions of North America in two ways. Covered by a vast ice-sheet, much of the area was uninhabitable, but the lowered sea level exposed the continental shelf and provided a land-bridge for migrants across what is now the Bering Strait, and the interior of Alaska and parts of the Yukon remained free of ice.

The earliest of these migrations occurred probably between 25,000 and 30,000 years ago. Some of the people who crossed the land-bridge at that time seem to have continued south, giving rise to many early Indian cultures. A later migration from eastern Asia, perhaps 10,000 to 14,000 years ago, is believed to have taken place just before the final melting of the ice-sheets. These were the ancestors of the Athabascan Indians, and their later arrival is evidenced by their occupation of large blocks of land in northwestern North America. Yet a third migration, around 5,000 years ago, is thought to have brought the predecessors of the Eskimo peoples to the New World.

The people of the Thule culture, famous for their skills as whale hunters, are probably the descendants of these earlier Palaeo-Eskimo people. About a thousand years ago, they spread throughout the Arctic, displacing the Dorset culture, which had developed in Northern Canada in about 1,000 B.C. Superbly equipped for life on the barrens and on the sea ice, the range of the Thule people in what is now Canada eventually included all the coastal areas, practically all of the islands of the Arctic Archipelago, and reached as far east as the Gulf of St. Lawrence and Newfoundland. The Inuit of today are their direct descendants.

It must, of course, be recognized that all models of early Arctic occupation remain speculative, and that the full historical extent of occupation of Northern Canada is only beginning to be documented. As archaeological work advances, however, so we will more and more realize the cultural heritage of which the Inuit and Dene are a part. But it is already evident that Indians were established in the forestlands of Western and Northern Canada, and Palaeo-Eskimos inhabited the northern rim of the "New

World" some 5,000 years before Alexander Mackenzie reached the Arctic coast.

Distinctive Material and Intellectual Cultures

The specialized skills and knowledge of the Dene and Inuit corresponded, of course, to the different terrains that each people has so long inhabited. The dog team, for example, was the principal means of travel, although the sledge styles and hitches varied regionally. The relationship between these variations and the kinds of terrain in which they were used can be illustrated by a comparison between the fan-hitch of the Inuit of the Central and Eastern Arctic and the tandem- or line-hitch used by the Dene and the Inuit of the Western Arctic. The former was ideal for travel on rough ice and the barrens; the latter was suited for travel over snowy lakes and through trees. The range of each broadly corresponds to the two kinds of landscape.

Both Inuit and Dene societies used caribou skin for clothing. The density of the fur and the fact that the hairs are hollow make the skin both light and extremely effective insulation, so it is ideal for arctic garments. Despite many conventions of style and varieties of sewing, differences that have given each group or society its distinctive clothing, both the Dene and Inuit regarded the caribou as their most important source of winter clothing.

Inuit and Dene cultures are not merely a response to environmental conditions. Each society, armed with its own skills and perceptions, found and used the North in its own distinctive way. One example of a distinctive and essential element of material culture is the Inuit harpoon. This brilliantly successful device, with its detachable head and turning blade, is found throughout Inuit territory, and it evidently came with them from Asia.

The Inuit and Dene also speak different languages. Some thousands of years separate their ancestors' departures from Asia, and it is not surprising, therefore, that the Eskimoan and Athabascan languages have no more in commmon than do English and Hungarian. Indeed, the linguistic contact between them even today is so limited that virtually no words have been borrowed from one by the other, despite the fact that the hunting grounds of some Athabascan groups overlapped with those of some Inuit. Because there are no longer any Asiatic peoples (with the exception of some 1,500 Siberian Inuit, who represent a back-migration across the Bering Strait), who speak versions of either of the two language families, it is not possible to establish a link between the two even in ancient times.

The various Athabascan languages spoken in Northern Canada bear the same kind of relation to one another that exists among the Romance languages of Europe. The structure of Athabascan grammar is noted for its use of prefixes, and its vocabulary is finely tuned to descriptions of the environment. Moreover, the nature of its word-forming system equips it well for the task of inventing new terms.

The Inuit language is agglutinative and very regular. Each word-like expression is composed of several items, and a word can be as intricate as a whole sentence in English. This agglutination is found in all of the Inuit dialects and, although the dialects most remote from one another are not readily mutually intelligible, the single language, with comparatively minor variations, reaches from Siberia to eastern Greenland — a spread of some 5,000 miles.

The specialized material and intellectual culture of the Inuit and Dene obviously cannot be elaborated in this report, but I wish to emphasize that each of these peoples had its own way of hunting, of making clothes, of raising children, of dealing with one another, and of regarding the environment and the spiritual powers they saw as integral to their world. Their knowledge of the land and its life constitute distinctive ethno-scientific traditions.

The Metis

During the past 150 years, the Metis have joined the Dene and Inuit of the Mackenzie Valley as one of the groups now included in the category of "northern native people." The first Metis who moved into the North in the early 19th century settled around Great Slave Lake, and they trace their ancestry to the unions between coureurs de bois and Indian women in the early days of the fur trade. Richard Slobodin, in *Metis of the Mackenzie District*, has described their heritage:

> The Metis nationality or ethnic group ... evolved in Quebec and Ontario during a period from the late 17th to the early 19th centuries, through the activities of *coureurs de bois* and other fur trade functionaries who, with their offspring by Indian women, developed a way of life partly Indian, partly marginal European, but in time distinct from both. ... On the prairies and the high plains, the Metis way of life underwent a further ecological adaptation. It was here, among Metis centering on the Red and Saskatchewan River Valleys, that consciousness of kind was heightened to the level of incipient nationality, a tendency culminating in the declaration of Metis nationhood and the consequent insurrections of 1870 and 1885. [p. 12]

In the aftermath of the Northwest Rebellion of 1885, many Metis moved North and settled in what is now the Northwest Territories.

Indians and whites in Fort Resolution. (National Museums)

Other Metis are the descendants of unions between Hudson's Bay Company men — mainly of Scottish origin — and Dene women. The children of these unions usually intermarried with the original Dene inhabitants, so that in most native communities in the North there are close family ties between the Metis and the Dene.

The Metis culture has been patterned after that of the Dene. In *Our Metis Heritage . . . A Portrayal,* produced by the Metis Association of the Northwest Territories, we are given this account of the location of the Metis between the Dene and white worlds:

> For most Metis families in the present Northwest Territories, it would appear that the woman passed on to her children all that she knew of her own culture, which was the Indian culture, and the man's influence though significant, played a secondary role in the emergent Metis way of life. This may account in part for the fact that the Metis lifestyle was very closely patterned after the Indian.
>
> The Metis were equipped with survival mechanisms to operate in both worlds; they could hunt, trap and live off the land like their Indian ancestors, or they could take advantage of their white ancestors' technology through education.
>
> Although the N.W.T. Metis seem to have chosen to maintain the traditional relationship with the Indian, they have creatively succeeded in building and sustaining a unique way of life. [p. 95]

Discussion of the Metis brings us to changes that have occurred in recent times. These are matters to which I shall return, and they need not be more than adumbrated here. I have tried to indicate the depth and richness of aboriginal cultures; I urge that we not lose sight of their historical reality, their values, and their right to command our respect. The North has been a homeland to the native people for thousands of years; it has been a frontier only since the fur trade, and a major oil and gas frontier only since the 1960s.

The Corridor Concept

The Corridor Concept and Cumulative Impact

The concept of a pipeline corridor from the North was first enunciated by the Government of Canada in the 1970 Pipeline Guidelines. In 1972, these Guidelines were expanded. The Expanded Guidelines for Northern Pipelines (to which I shall refer as the "Pipeline Guidelines") were tabled in the House of Commons in June 1972, and they form the cornerstone of Canadian policy with regard to the construction of northern pipelines. The Inquiry is bound by Order-in-Council, P.C. 1974-641 March 21, 1974, under which it was established, to consider the proposals made by the pipeline companies to meet the specific environmental and social concerns set out in the Pipeline Guidelines.

The significance of the corridor concept to this Inquiry relates to the consideration of impact and cumulative impact. The Pipeline Guidelines assume that, if a gas pipeline is built, an oil pipeline will probably follow it, and they call for examination of the proposed gas pipeline from the point of view of cumulative impact. We must consider then, not only the impact of a gas pipeline, but also the impact of an oil pipeline — in sum, the impact of a transportation corridor for two energy systems.

The government's corridor policy is plainly spelled out in the Pipeline Guidelines:

> In view of the influence of the *first* trunk pipeline in shaping the transportation corridor system and in moulding the environmental and social future of the region, any applicant to build a first trunk pipeline within any segment of the corridor system outlined in 1. above must provide with [its] application:

> i) assessment of the suitability of the applicant's route for nearby routing of the other pipeline, in terms of the environmental-social and terrain-engineering consequences of the other pipeline and the combined effect of the two pipelines; ...
> ii) assessment of the environmental-social impact of both pipelines on nearby settlements or nearby existing or proposed transportation systems. ... [p. 10]

The assumption in 1970 was that an oil pipeline would be built first, and a gas pipeline would be likely to follow it; ever since the Pipeline Guidelines were issued in 1972, the assumption has been that a gas pipeline would come first and that an oil pipeline would be likely to follow it. Now we have before us proposals by Arctic Gas and Foothills to build a gas pipeline. The influence of a gas pipeline on the development of an energy corridor and in moulding the social, economic and environmental future of the North will be enormous. The Pipeline Guidelines call for a consideration of the environmental and social impact of a gas pipeline and an oil pipeline, as well as of the combined impact of the construction of both pipelines along the corridor. That policy ramifies throughout the Inquiry's consideration of the environmental and social issues that arise along the whole route. However, the corridor will not be simply a corridor for gas and oil pipelines. The Pipeline Guidelines envisage that the corridor may eventually include roads, a railroad, hydro-electric transmission lines and telecommunications facilities.

There are real limits to our capacity to forecast the impact of such a corridor. The Pipeline Guidelines are principally concerned with the impact that gas and oil pipelines will have in the North. The Inquiry has, therefore, largely limited itself to a consideration of the impact of these energy transportation systems. But sometimes it has been necessary to consider the impact of pipelines in relation to other transportation systems. For instance, what if a haul road had to be built along the Arctic Coastal Plain of the Northern Yukon? Or to what extent will the capacity of the existing fleet of tugs and barges on the Mackenzie River have to be augmented? Or to what extent will hunting from the Dempster Highway have to be restricted to enable the recommendations of this Inquiry to be carried out? We cannot make an intelligent assessment of the impact of a gas pipeline unless we do so in the light of the cumulative impact of the corridor.

Of course, the gas pipeline itself will be a multi-stage project involving considerations of cumulative impact. The gas pipelines proposed by Arctic Gas and by Foothills can be expected to be looped. Looping is the process of progressively increasing the amount of gas that can be transported by the pipeline system; a second (or third) pipeline is built beside the first in sections or loops from one compressor station to the next. This means that construction along the gas pipeline right-of-way can be an ongoing or repetitive process and can involve cumulative impacts over and above those resulting from the project that was originally proposed.

The importance of considering the impact of a gas pipeline in the light of cumulative impact along the corridor is obvious. This importance can be illustrated by reference to gravel, which is in short supply in the North. Arctic Gas estimate that the gas pipeline will require 30 million cubic yards of gravel and other borrow materials within Canada and North of 60. Mackenzie Valley Pipeline Research Limited estimated the gravel requirements for an oil pipeline at 42 million cubic yards. It would be foolish to consider the impact of the borrow requirements of a gas pipeline without taking into account the gravel requirements of an oil pipeline, as well as those of other regional and local projects. Substantial amounts of borrow materials will be required for gas plants and gas-gathering systems in the Mackenzie Delta, for the completion of the Mackenzie Highway and the Dempster Highway, and for airports, not to mention the needs of communities along the route. Gravel provides a quite straightforward example of cumulative impact. There are many other examples, some of them by no means as straightforward, that I shall be dealing with in this report.

The Northern Yukon Corridor and the Mackenzie Valley Corridor

It should be borne in mind that there are two proposed corridors: one across the Northern Yukon and another along the Mackenzie Valley. The following passage from the Pipeline Guidelines makes this plain:

> The Government of Canada is prepared to receive and review applications to construct one trunk oil pipeline and/or one trunk gas pipeline within the following broad "corridors":
> i)   Along the Mackenzie Valley region (in a broad sense) from the Arctic coast to the provincial [Alberta] boundary;
> ii) Across the northern part of the Yukon Territory either adjacent to the Arctic coast or through the northern interior region from the boundary of Alaska to the general vicinity of Fort McPherson, and thus to join the Mackenzie "corridor"; . . . [p. 9]

Arctic Gas propose to build a pipeline from Alaska that would use the corridor across the Northern Yukon as well as the corridor along the Mackenzie Valley. Foothills propose to build a pipeline that would use only the corridor along the Mackenzie Valley.

Arctic Gas propose to transport only Alaskan gas in the corridor across the Northern Yukon, and to transport both Alaskan and Canadian gas in the Mackenzie Valley corridor. Under the Foothills proposal, the Mackenzie Valley corridor would be used to carry only Canadian gas.

Since 1972, as mentioned above, the Government of Canada has assumed that a gas pipeline along either of these corridors would probably be followed by an oil pipeline. That assumption is a sound one: once a gas pipeline is built across the Northern Yukon, there will be every reason for an oil pipeline carrying American oil to follow the same route. You may ask, is not the trans-Alaska pipeline to carry American oil to the Lower 48? The Alyeska pipeline was built to deliver oil to the western states, but the United States still has severe shortages of oil in the midwest and the east. And there are great petroleum reserves in northern Alaska, especially in Naval Petroleum Reserve No. 4 lying to the west of Prudhoe Bay. The urgency of bringing oil from northern Alaska to the markets in the Lower 48 that need it most is obvious. If a gas pipeline and energy corridor were already in place across the Northern Yukon and along the Mackenzie Valley, it is quite likely this corridor would be the route of choice.

Once a gas pipeline is built along the Mackenzie Valley, it is likely that in the future an oil pipeline will follow. Oil has in fact been found in the Mackenzie Delta region. It is said that discoveries of oil in the

Mackenzie Delta and the Beaufort Sea do not justify an oil pipeline today. Nonetheless, while the proven reserves of oil in the Mackenzie Delta region have not yet reached threshold levels, they may do so in time. In any event, it is obvious that if present or future exploration programs reveal large reserves of oil under the Beaufort Sea, the call for an oil pipeline from the Delta to the mid-continent will be made once again.

I think all of this demonstrates the wisdom of the Pipeline Guidelines, which insist that there should be an examination of the impact of an oil pipeline along with the gas pipeline. Any attempt to dismember the policy and to assess the impacts piecemeal, along either the Northern Yukon corridor or the Mackenzie Valley corridor, should be resisted.

The United States' Interest in the Corridor

The Arctic Gas pipeline, if it is built, would provide a land bridge for the delivery of Alaskan gas across Canada to the Lower 48. The implications of this prospect, from the point of view of Canadian policy in the North, should be borne in mind.

The corridor across the Northern Yukon will be an exclusively American energy corridor. The Mackenzie Valley corridor, under the Arctic Gas proposal, will be an American energy corridor as much as it is a Canadian energy corridor. The United States will have an interest in the scheduling of pipeline construction in Canada and, when the pipeline is built, in seeing that it remains safe and secure, because it will be carrying Alaskan gas in bond to the Lower 48. It will be an energy lifeline for the United States,

Trans-Alaska pipeline and gravel haul road.
Sideboom tractors lower pipe into ditch. (Alyeska)

Stockpile of drill pipe. (NFB—McNeill)

Drill rig in the Delta. (Arctic Gas)

Mackenzie Highway right-of-way beside
Mackenzie River. (J. Inglis)

extending across the Northern Yukon, across the Mackenzie Delta, along the Mackenzie Valley, and then through Alberta, Saskatchewan and British Columbia to the Lower 48. It will supply gas to a complex of industries and urban centres in the United States. The Americans will be dependent on the continuous supply of gas, and the gas being transported from Alaska will be their own gas. Moreover, the United States wants the pipeline to begin to deliver that gas as soon as possible.

There are, of course, pipelines that cross United States territory and carry oil and gas to Canadian markets: the Interprovincial pipeline, which delivers western oil to Ontario; the Portland-Montreal pipeline, which delivers offshore oil to Quebec; and the Great Lakes Transmission Company pipeline, which delivers gas to Ontario. All of them pass through the United States. But these connections cannot be compared in magnitude or impact to the Arctic Gas proposal. They are not pipelines reaching some 2,000 miles from a distant frontier.

The consequences of such American interest in the pipeline are of special concern to the Inquiry. The impact of the pipeline, so far as northern peoples and the northern environment is concerned, will be largely within Canada (the line from Prudhoe Bay to the Alaska-Yukon border is only 200 miles long, whereas the line from the Alaska-Yukon boundary to the Northwest Territories-Alberta border is 1,000 miles long). The native people's concern over when a pipeline is built, the environmental concern over where it should be built, and the stipulations for protecting the people and the environment apply largely in Canada. The United States cannot be expected to be as concerned as Canada with the seriousness of the social and environmental impact of the pipeline along its route. This difference, coupled with the Americans' rather more urgent need of gas, might result in pressure to complete the pipeline without due regard to the social and environmental concerns in Canada. The risk is in Canada. The urgency is in the United States.

A pipeline 2,200 miles long (in Canada) is a highly vulnerable artery. What measures might have to be taken to forestall an interruption of delivery — an interruption that would affect vital Canadian interests, but even more tellingly, vital American interests? There may be real possibilities for misunderstanding and tension between our two countries, notwithstanding our long history of good relations. These considerations deserve the attention of the Government of the United States as well as of the Government of Canada. It may be that they are not at all daunting. But they should still not be overlooked.

A treaty between Canada and the United States will not cover all possibilities. It will, of course, define the rights of our two governments with regard to the pipeline and to the gas being transported in that pipeline. And it will establish the ground rules for the transportation of Alaskan gas across Canada to the United States. It cannot do more. I say this because a treaty, although it will regulate the conduct of our two governments, will not necessarily regulate the conduct of the two countries' citizens.

The implications for our relations with the United States of the building and maintenance of the proposed gas transmission system deserve careful consideration by all Canadians. We are not simply considering a proposal to build a pipeline on an isolated frontier. We are considering, in the Arctic Gas proposal, the establishment of an international energy corridor that will cross some 2,200 miles of Canadian territory, opening up wilderness areas that are among the most important wildlife habitat in North America. It will cross lands that are claimed by Canada's native people, a region where the struggle for a new social and economic order and political responsibility is taking place.

It seems to me the question of whether or not there should be a corridor to carry vital energy supplies from Alaska through the heartland of Canada to the Lower 48, is at the threshold of the decision-making process. If Canadians decide that there is to be such a corridor, then we must also consider when it should be established and what route it should follow. These are questions Canadians must decide for themselves.

Early northern development; clockwise from top:

Dawson City at the height of the Klondike Gold Rush, July 4, 1899.

A wood-stave pipe used to carry water to Klondike placer mines.

Plank road on the ice across the Peace River, part of the Alaska Highway, 1942.

US soldiers lay logs for corduroy road, Alaska Highway, 1941.

Inspector checks weld in Canol pipeline, Mackenzie Mountains, 1944.
(Public Archives of Canada)

Engineering and Construction

Transportation and Construction in the Northwest

THE EARLY YEARS

Fur-traders of the Montreal-based North West Company followed the water routes explored by the French to the western plains, then extended them north to Lake Athabasca, where they built Fort Chipewyan in 1788. A year later, Alexander Mackenzie set out across Great Slave Lake and down the long northern river that now bears his name. It proved to extend just over a thousand miles through rich new fur territory, and soon the North West Company had established trading posts along its banks at Trout River in 1796, and at sites near the present settlements of Fort Simpson, Fort Norman and Fort Good Hope in the following decade.

In the last century, the traders travelled by York boat from Methy Portage to the 16-mile stretch of rapids on Slave River above present-day Fort Smith, around which they had to portage. (This river route was shortened by the extension of rail from Edmonton to Waterways early in this century, and York boats were replaced by steamboats.) They then continued down the Slave River to Fort Resolution, across Great Slave Lake to the head of the Mackenzie, and down the Mackenzie as far as the Delta. Today, the Mackenzie River is still the principal means of transporting supplies to settlements along the Mackenzie Valley and in the Western Arctic. And it is this fleet of tugs and barges on the Mackenzie River that will have to be expanded to carry the equipment, material and supplies for the proposed pipeline.

In 1888, a Select Committee of the Senate was appointed "to inquire into the resources of the Great Mackenzie Basin and the country eastward to Hudson's Bay," but Northern Canada first came to international notice in the late 1890s, when gold was discovered in the Yukon Territory. An estimated 100,000 men and women sought the gold fields, and almost overnight Dawson City became the largest city in Canada west of Winnipeg, with a population of over 30,000.

The city was built on difficult permafrost soils. Most of its early foundations were simple mud sills of local timbers laid in gravel or sand and levelled with the same material. Wood was the primary building material for the banks, post office, hotels and dance halls and the many homes that were built. The city acquired such urban services as running water, electric lighting and telephones. On the gold fields themselves, the Yukon Gold Company built a 70-mile ditch system to provide water for a large-scale dredging operation on the Klondike River and its tributaries. This project, which included 13 miles of 42- to 54-inch-diameter wood-stave and steel pipe, was a remarkable engineering feat on an isolated frontier.

The 1920s witnessed the development of the petroleum reserves at Norman Wells. Mackenzie himself had reported oil seepages on the river bank, but it was only in 1914 that a geologist, T.O. Bosworth, staked three claims near these seepages. Imperial Oil acquired these claims in 1919, and by 1924 six wells had been drilled, three of which were producers. A small refinery was built, but the market was so small that in the same year the wells were capped and the refinery shut down. During the development of the petroleum reserves at Norman Wells, the detrimental results of thawing perennially frozen water-bearing silts and clays soon made themselves evident, and experimentation began with the installation of foundations on gravel pads.

In the early 1930s, after rich mineral deposits had been discovered at Yellowknife and at Port Radium on Great Bear Lake, the refinery at Norman Wells was reopened to supply gasoline and fuel oil for riverboats and mine machinery. Between 1937 and 1972, heavy fuel oil was barged from Norman Wells to the rapids on Great Bear River, transported by a 2-inch 8.5-mile pipeline around the rapids, then barged the remainder of the way to the Eldorado uranium mine on Great Bear Lake.

DEFENCE PROJECTS DURING AND AFTER THE SECOND WORLD WAR

During the Second World War the United States Army undertook two major construction projects in the Canadian North: the Northwest Staging Route and an associated highway, now called the Alaska Highway; and the Canol Project to transport men, materials, equipment and oil to defend Alaska against the Japanese.

The Alaska Highway connected Dawson Creek, B.C., to Fairbanks, Alaska, following the Northwest Staging Route airports at Fort St. John and Fort Nelson, B.C., Watson Lake and Whitehorse, Y.T., and Big Delta, Alaska. The construction began in March 1942, and it involved a force that totalled some 11,000 officers and men over the construction period. By the end of October 1942, a passable pioneer road, 1,428 miles long and 26 feet wide, linked Dawson Creek to Big Delta. Permafrost conditions were ignored during construction, which resulted in road failures and severe icings at many locations. During most of 1943, 81 contractors under the United States Public Roads Administration worked on an all-weather gravel road with a civilian force that totalled some 15,950 men over the construction period. The total cost of the project was $147 million. When the war ended, the United States handed over the Canadian section of the Alaska Highway to Canada.

In 1942, also, the United States Army undertook the Canol project to transport oil from Norman Wells across the Mackenzie Mountains to Whitehorse. The oil was to be refined there, then delivered to Alaska to aid the war effort. The labour force over the construction period of the pipeline involved 2,500 military personnel and approximately 22,550 civilians. A pioneer road preceded pipelaying and the building of pumping stations. Except at its southern end, the road was laid entirely over permafrost. The road performed satisfactorily during its short period of use, April 1944 to May 1945, except for icings on some stretches. The pipeline, consisting of 100 miles of 6-inch pipe and 500 miles of 4-inch pipe, was laid on the ground beside the road, and pumping stations were spaced about 50 miles apart. This project was completed in 1944 and cost $134 million. Very little oil reached Whitehorse by the pipeline, and when the war ended, the Canol road was closed and the pipeline dismantled.

Between 1955 and 1957, Canada and the United States built the Distant Early Warning Line (DEW Line), a chain of radar stations intended to detect foreign aircraft in polar regions and to relay the warning to North American Air Defence Command units. The line stretches 5,000 miles along the Arctic coast from Point Barrow, Alaska, to Cape Dyer, Baffin Island. The construction of the DEW Line involved airlifting a total of about 25,000 men and one-half million tons

of equipment by commercial aircraft. Approximately 45,000 flights averaging 720 miles each were made.

POST-WAR PERIOD

In 1954, construction began on Inuvik, a new regional administrative centre for the Western Arctic at a site on the east side of the Mackenzie Delta. All major buildings, including serviced housing, are elevated on piles. The air space between the buildings and the ground dissipates heat losses from the buildings, thus reducing the possibility of permafrost degradation and associated shifting of foundations. These buildings have performed satisfactorily; only a few of the 14,000 piles installed have shown any significant movement owing to thaw settlement.

Other new towns have been built farther south, but they did not encounter the same formidable permafrost problems. In the 1960s, Cominco's development of the rich lead-zinc deposits on the south shore of Great Slave Lake led to the construction of a large mill and the associated mining town of Pine Point. Edzo, another new town, was built at the head of the North Arm of Great Slave Lake in 1971. At Yellowknife and Hay River, there are suburbs and high-rises that would have been difficult to imagine in such settings only a few years ago. The development of the Northern Transportation Company Limited (NTCL) dry-dock and transshipment facilities at Hay River is representative of the recent growth in transportation.

TRANSPORTATION

Barge and boat transporation on the Athabasca, Slave and Mackenzie Rivers has served the transportation needs of the Northwest for more than a century. Today, water

transport northward from Hay River continues to be important, particularly for construction materials, heavy equipment and fuels. Although freight traffic on the Mackenzie River has had intermittent periods of rapid growth, its long-term annual growth rate is about nine percent. This growth peaked in 1972 at 477,000 tons; since then annual traffic has averaged around 400,000 tons.

Northern Transportation Company Limited, a crown corporation, is the largest common carrier in the Mackenzie River system, and it also serves the Arctic coast from Alaska to Spence Bay. KAPS Transport Limited, the second largest operator, is licensed to transport goods to and from exploration and drilling sites, and building and construction sites in the Mackenzie watershed.

In recent years, there have also been major air, rail and road developments in the Western Arctic. Northern air services began in the region in 1920, with float-equipped aircraft. During and shortly after the Second World War, airfields were built at several settlements on Great Slave Lake and along the Mackenzie River, including Hay River, Yellowknife, Fort Resolution, Fort Providence, Fort Simpson and Norman Wells, and both scheduled and charter flights in the Western Arctic increased steadily.

Today, there is air service to all of the Mackenzie River settlements, although its frequency varies. Pacific Western Airlines, the largest carrier operating in the Northwest Territories, has the most extensive network of routes; and chartered aircraft serve the smaller and remoter settlements. These carriers, commercial and private, are essential to the communities in the Mackenzie Valley and the Western Arctic, the territorial and federal governments, tourist

Distant Early Warning (DEW) Line site, Tuktoyaktuk. (GNWT)

Great Slave Lake Railway near Pine Point. (Canadian National)

Judge Berger at pipe stockpile in Alaska. (I. Waddell)

Inquiry staff viewing TransCanada pipeline under construction in Ontario. (G. Milne)

lodges, and construction companies, and they play a vital role in the activities related to oil and gas exploration.

The Great Slave Lake Railway, built in the early 1960s, extends from Grimshaw, Alberta, to Hay River, Northwest Territories. The railway, which closely parallels the Mackenzie Highway, was constructed primarily to ship concentrates from Cominco's mine at Pine Point, to which it is connected by a branch line. Heavy goods are shipped by rail to Hay River, then trans-shipped to barges for the voyage down the Mackenzie River.

The Mackenzie Highway between Grimshaw and Hay River was built between 1946 and 1948. In 1960, as part of the federal Roads to Resources program, it was extended 280 miles around the north end of Great Slave Lake to Yellowknife; in 1970, the highway reached Fort Simpson, and it is planned to reach Wrigley by 1979. There has been road construction between Arctic Red River and Inuvik, but it is not complete.

A second major highway project, the Dempster Highway, was begun in 1959 and is scheduled for completion in the late 1970s. It will link Dawson City to Inuvik and will connect with the Mackenzie Highway.

Recent gas and oil exploration activity in the Mackenzie Valley and Western Arctic used existing transportation systems in the region, which has helped these systems to expand to their present capacities. The nature and level of future petroleum development will clearly have an important influence on the future development of these transportation systems. Implementation of either pipeline proposal will involve major expansion in existing transportation capabilities.

The Pipeline Project: Its Scope and Scale

Two companies, Canadian Arctic Gas Pipeline Limited and Foothills Pipe Lines Ltd., are competing for the right to build a pipeline to bring natural gas through the Mackenzie Valley to markets in the South. Arctic Gas propose to build a pipeline from the Prudhoe Bay field in Alaska across the Northern Yukon to the Mackenzie Delta, to join with their pipeline extending south from the Mackenzie Delta gas fields. The Foothills proposal is for a pipeline southward from the Mackenzie Delta only.

The Arctic Gas group is a consortium of Canadian and American producers and gas transmission and distribution companies. Imperial, Gulf and Shell, the three principal gas producers in the Mackenzie Delta, are members of the consortium, as well as TransCanada Pipe Lines, Canada's largest gas transmission company. The Foothills Pipe Lines group is made up of two companies, Alberta Gas Trunk Line and West Coast Transmission, the largest gas transmission companies in Alberta and British Columbia.

The pipeline that Arctic Gas and Foothills propose to build presents quite novel problems of science, engineering and logistics. Either pipeline will be very long, and will carry enormous volumes of gas. But these are not unique characteristics: what makes either pipeline unique from an engineering point of view is that it will be buried in ice-rich, permanently frozen soil — permafrost — and the gas transported in the pipe will be refrigerated. The pipeline is to be built across our northern territories, a land that is cold and dark throughout the long winter, a land that is at present largely inaccessible by road

or rail, and through which a large infrastructure of roads, wharves, airstrips and other work sites must be built. The pipeline's impact will not, therefore, be confined to its right-of-way.

Unique Aspects of the Project

The pipeline that Arctic Gas propose to build would be longer than any pipeline in the world: it is 2,400 miles from Prudhoe Bay to the Lower 48. Pipelines have, of course, been built over great distances in the past. The 31-inch trans-Arabian pipeline (now abandoned) from Abaiq Field in Arabia to Sidon in Lebanon is 1,047 miles long; the 36-inch Colonial pipeline from Houston to New Jersey is 1,531 miles long. And pipelines have been built and are being built today across difficult terrain and in northern latitudes. The trans-Andean pipeline crosses one of the most rugged mountain ranges in the world, and the trans-Alaska pipeline crosses three mountain ranges. Some of the biggest pipelines in the world have been built in Siberia, and both these and the trans-Alpine pipelines were constructed in severe climatic conditions. But, as we shall see, there is not a great deal we can learn from the experience of the Soviet Union, the United States and other nations that is directly relevant to the design and operation of a buried refrigerated pipeline.

Normally, gas flows through a pipeline at temperatures above freezing. Compressors drive the gas through the pipe, and the process of compressing gas makes it hot. If the pipeline is buried in permafrost, heat from the gas will thaw the ground around the pipe. Such thawing could lead to severe and costly engineering and environmental problems where the soil contains any appreciable quantity of ice. Problems arising from progressive sinking of the ground, blocking of drainage, erosion or slope failure could damage or rupture the pipe. To avoid these problems, both Arctic Gas and Foothills propose to chill the gas passing through the pipeline so there will be no heat loss to melt the permafrost. Chillers will, therefore, be needed to extract the heat generated by compression before the gas goes into the pipeline and through the permafrost.

A pipeline running south from the Mackenzie Delta along the Mackenzie Valley must cross about 250 miles of continuous and about 550 miles of discontinuous permafrost. It cannot avoid long stretches of ice-rich soil in both zones of permafrost. A pipeline across the Northern Yukon would lie entirely within the zone of continuous permafrost. Thus, neither the Arctic Gas nor the Foothills proposal can avoid the problem. They must either refrigerate a pipeline through the permafrost or, at much greater cost, lay a pipeline on the ground or elevated above it. Now, if a chilled and buried pipeline passes through ground that is not frozen, it will freeze the ground around it. This change may lead to a build-up of ice in the ground around the pipe and may cause the pipe to move upward. This is known as frost heave.

Magnitude of the Project

A pipeline through the Canadian North has been likened to a string across a football field. This simile is misleading and is indicative of a utopian view of pipeline construction. Of course, the area required for the right-of-way, compressor stations, and ancillary facilities is miniscule when measured against the great mass of the Canadian North. Although Arctic Gas propose to lay 1,100 miles of pipeline across the Yukon and Northwest Territories, their total land requirement for the right-of-way and related facilities is only about 40 square miles. Such a figure gives a mistaken impression of the magnitude of the construction project. It is not just a 120-foot right-of-way.

The estimated cost of the Arctic Gas project within Canada now stands at about $8 billion. A network of roads largely of snow and ice must be built. The capacity of the fleet of tugs and barges on the Mackenzie River must be greatly increased. Nine construction spreads and 6,000 construction workers will be required North of 60 to build the pipeline. Imperial, Gulf and Shell will need 1,200 more workers to build the gas plants and gas gathering systems in the Mackenzie Delta. There will be about 130 gravel mining and borrow operations, and about 600 water crossings. There will be about 700 crawler tractors, 400 earth movers, 350 tractor trucks, 350 trailers and 1,500 trucks. There will be almost one million tons of pipe. There will be aircraft, helicopters, and airstrips. Arctic Gas propose to use about 20 wharf sites; and plan to build about 15 STOL airstrips of 2,900 feet each and five airstrips of 6,000 feet each. Carson Templeton, Chairman of the Environment Protection Board, has likened the building of a pipeline in the North in winter to the logistics of landing the Allied forces on the beaches of Normandy. The pipeline's effects will be felt far beyond the area of land across which it is built.

I have visited the trans-Alaska pipeline project, and it has given me some idea of the scale of activity that construction of a pipeline in Northern Canada would entail. Construction of the trans-Alaska oil pipeline began officially in April 1974. To transport oil from Prudhoe Bay on the northern coast of Alaska to the southern Alaskan port of Valdez has required, in addition to the construction of an 800-mile-long, 48-inch diameter pipe, the construction of a 360-mile-long gravel road, bridges over 20 major streams, a 2,300-foot bridge over the Yukon River, three permanent airfields, eight temporary airfields, 15 permanent access roads, numerous temporary access roads, 19 construction camps, 12 pump stations, and oil-storage and tanker-loading facilities. The project is expected to cost approximately $8 billion, and the estimated completion date is mid-1977.

Flying low along the route of the trans-Alaska pipeline, south from Prudhoe Bay, you can see the extent of activity: construction spreads, pump station sites, hovercraft on the Yukon River, trucks on the haul road, the right-of-way itself. At Prudhoe Bay, the oil wells and gathering facilities stretch outward for miles, and they give you some idea of how similar facilities would alter the landscape of the Mackenzie Delta.

The Mackenzie Valley pipeline, according to the proposal of Arctic Gas, would be the greatest construction project, in terms of capital expenditure, that private enterprise has ever undertaken, anywhere. We have been told by Vern Horte, President of Arctic Gas, that if the pipeline is built, it is likely that it will be fully looped over time — that is, by building loops between compressor stations, a second gas pipeline would ultimately parallel the original one. But looping would not begin until the original system is fully loaded, and that, we were told, will not happen until its fifth year of operation.

Twelve-hundred man construction camp on the trans-Alaska pipeline. (Alyeska)

Welding pipe on the trans-Alaska pipeline. (E. Weick)

Pipe being laid in ditch, trans-Alaska pipeline. (Alyeska)

Bunkhouses for workers at the Valdez terminal of trans-Alaska pipeline. (E. Weick)

Pipe Size and Pressure

The Arctic Gas pipeline, by tapping both the Prudhoe Bay and Mackenzie Delta gas fields, would carry much more gas than the Foothills pipeline. The Arctic Gas proposal is, therefore, for a larger pipe than that proposed by Foothills, and it will be operated at a higher pressure.

To carry very large quantities of gas, Arctic Gas propose to use 48-inch diameter pipe made of steel 0.720 inches thick and operated at a maximum pressure of 1,680 pounds per square inch. At this pressure, the pipe can carry 4.5 billion cubic feet of gas per day, which is more gas than Canada at present consumes each day. This pipe is bigger in diameter than any existing gas pipeline in North America, although there are 48-inch and 56-inch gas pipelines in the Soviet Union. There are oil pipelines of this size in North America: both the Alyeska oil pipeline and loops on the Interprovincial oil pipeline are 48 inches in diameter. The pressure of 1,680 pounds per square inch is substantially higher than that of ordinary gas pipelines in Canada, and even the 48-inch and 56-inch gas pipelines in the Soviet Arctic reach pressures of only about 1,000 pounds per square inch. Of course, the pipe to be used by Arctic Gas is designed to withstand this high pressure, and the pressure complies with Canadian standards for the maximum operating pressure in such pipe. Nonetheless, Arctic Gas are sufficiently concerned by the possibility that the pipe might crack under pressure, that they plan to surround the pipe with steel reinforcing bands or "crack arrestors" at intervals of about 300 feet.

Foothills say that the system proposed by Arctic Gas is novel and untried, whereas the system they propose will use conventional techniques. Foothills propose to use 42-inch diameter pipe made of steel 0.520 inches thick and operated at a pressure of 1,220 pounds per square inch, although that pressure can (and might) be raised to 1,440 pounds per square inch. The higher pressure is the maximum operating pressure for this 42-inch pipe, according to Canadian standards, and Foothills say they will use the lower pressure for safety. Pipe of the size chosen by Foothills is already used by TransCanada Pipe Lines and Alberta Gas Trunk Line in sections of their gas pipelines, but at pressures lower than that proposed by Foothills.

Existing Pipelines in Permafrost Areas

Pipelines have been built across permafrost areas of Alaska and the Soviet Union, and short sections of the Pointed Mountain pipeline on the British Columbia-Yukon-Northwest Territories boundary cross permafrost. Although we can learn about permafrost and northern construction from these projects, they are of little help in assessing the proposals before this Inquiry to bury a refrigerated gas pipeline in ice-rich permafrost soils.

Let us look first at the Soviet experience. Gas pipelines in the Soviet Union are usually buried, but in permafrost regions they may also be elevated on piles or placed on the ground surface in a sand mound or berm. Elevated-pile construction is used across ice-rich permafrost terrain, berm construction is used where the permafrost terrain has moderate-to-low ice content, and burial is used only where the soil is sandy and dry or unfrozen.

There are three pipeline systems in the Soviet sub-Arctic, but none has yet been built north of the tree line. The oldest of these pipelines was built between 1966 and 1968 from Tas Tumus to Yakutsk in Eastern Siberia; it is 300 km (190 miles) long and 500 mm (20 inches) in diameter. The northern half of it crosses what appears to be ice-rich permafrost terrain and is built on piles; the southern half is buried. The line was later extended about 100 km south to Bestyakh and Pokrovsk; this section is apparently almost entirely elevated.

The Messoyakha-Norilsk system in the north part of West Siberia comprises two 730-mm (29 inches) lines, each 265 km (165 miles) long. The first was built between 1968 and 1970, the second between 1971 and 1973. The system crosses an area of discontinuous permafrost and is elevated on piles. In 1972, a 730-mm (29-inch), 35-km (22-mile) extension was built on piles from the Soleninskoye to Messoyakha gas fields.

The most recently built trunk pipeline system in the Soviet Union — the line between Medvezhye and Punga in northwestern West Siberia — is the largest in the Soviet Union in terms of pipe size. It comprises 670 km (420 miles) of 1,420-mm (56-inch) and 1,220-mm (48-inch) diameter pipe. The northern part of this pipeline passes through a region of discontinuous permafrost, where it is partly on the ground in a berm and partly buried. In many places the route of this pipeline avoids potentially troublesome areas of ice-rich permafrost by crossing dry sand plains, where the pipeline is buried. The Medvezhye pipeline, like the others, is operated at temperatures above freezing, but it is planned to refrigerate a short section of it as an experiment.

There is not a great deal that we can learn from the Russian experience. The Yakutsk and the Messoyakha-Norilsk systems are

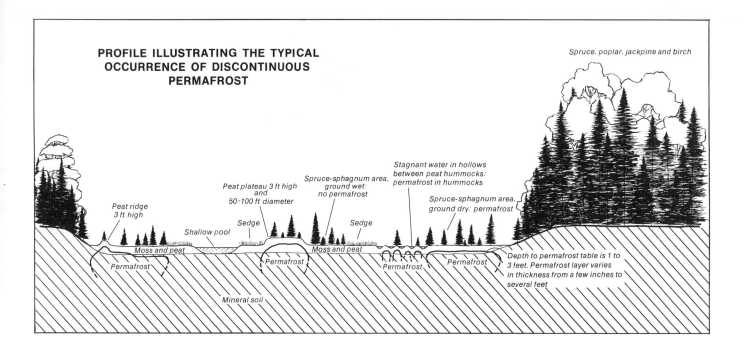

PROFILE ILLUSTRATING THE TYPICAL OCCURRENCE OF DISCONTINUOUS PERMAFROST

Spruce, poplar, jackpine and birch

Peat plateau 3 ft high and 50-100 ft diameter

Spruce-sphagnum area, ground wet: no permafrost

Stagnant water in hollows between peat hummocks: permafrost in hummocks

Spruce-sphagnum area, ground dry: permafrost

Peat ridge 3 ft high

Shallow pool

Sedge

Sedge

Moss and peat

Moss and peat

Permafrost

Permafrost

Permafrost

Permafrost

Permafrost

Depth to permafrost table is 1 to 3 feet. Permafrost layer varies in thickness from a few inches to several feet

Mineral soil

built on piles above ground, and they are not large-diameter pipelines. Where the Medvezhye pipeline has been buried, it has been routed to avoid permafrost. The Soviet Union, so far, has been able to avoid the vital questions that we must consider in Northern Canada: How can the permafrost be kept from melting? And how can we overcome the problem of frost heave?

What about the trans-Alaska oil pipeline? Alaska, after all, has a permafrost distribution very similar to Canada's, and the problems to be overcome would seem to be similar. But, once again, the experience is of limited usefulness for us. The Alyeska pipeline will carry oil, and oil can be transported in a pipeline only when it is hot. Obviously, such a pipe cannot be buried in permafrost without melting the ice in it, and therefore the trans-Alaska pipeline is elevated wherever it crosses ice-rich permafrost terrain. Elsewhere it is either bermed or buried, depending upon the ground conditions.

The proposed Mackenzie Valley pipeline is a new kind of pipelining venture that will entail innovations in engineering design, construction and operation. Canadian engineers and pipeline contractors have as much northern experience and expertise as their counterparts in any country. Nevertheless, the proposed pipeline will confront engineers and builders with major challenges of engineering and logistics.

Buried Refrigerated Pipeline: Frost Heave

Where the pipeline crosses permafrost, both Arctic Gas and Foothills propose to refrigerate their buried pipeline by chilling the gas to a temperature below freezing. Unfortunately, because permafrost is discontinuous along parts of the route, this ingenious solution to the problem of thawing of frozen ground would create other problems in previously unfrozen ground. The creation of artificial permafrost around the refrigerated pipe could cause upward movement of the ground by a process called frost heave. This movement, if it exceeded certain limits, would damage the pipe.

A great deal was said at the Inquiry about the plans of Arctic Gas and Foothills to prevent, avoid, reduce or control frost heave and its effects, and the two companies were not in agreement on the problem nor on its treatment. I have, as well, heard a great deal of criticism of their plans to control frost heave and I have heard many expressions of concern about the environmental consequences likely to result from inadequate control of this problem. Moreover, in the last weeks that the Inquiry heard evidence, Arctic Gas revealed that, through a laboratory error, they had underestimated the magnitude of the forces causing frost heave, and I learned that they will have to modify the procedures proposed for controlling frost heave.

How important is this specific problem of engineering, a problem that involves concepts of physics about which the experts do not agree? From the beginning, refrigeration of the gas has been regarded as the key to design of the Mackenzie Valley pipeline.

This technique, it was claimed, would solve the problems created by the thawing of permafrost and the settling of ground that had forced Alyeska to adopt the expensive elevated construction mode. But the refrigerated buried gas pipeline is an innovation that lacks engineering precedent. Arctic Gas and their engineering consultants have discussed their plan to refrigerate and bury the pipeline with optimism and assurance. I think, however, my own approach should be conservative. I must consider the impacts that can be expected to arise from the construction, operation, maintenance and repair of a buried refrigerated pipeline that must be protected from frost heave.

In my view, the controversy and uncertainty that surround the subject of frost heave and its control reflect adversely on the proposals brought before this Inquiry by both companies. I recognize, of course, that these proposals were in a preliminary, conceptual stage, not in their final design stage. I recognize, too, that important improvements will appear in the final design. Arctic Gas filed their application for a right-of-way in March 1974. They insisted then, that it was essential that the right-of-way be granted within the year. Yet now, three years later, we are still faced with basic uncertainty about this fundamental aspect of their design.

Frost Heave and the Frost Bulb

A refrigerated pipeline will experience frost heave and related effects principally in the zone of discontinuous permafrost, which extends southward from Fort Good Hope to the general vicinity of the Alberta border, a distance of about 550 miles. In this zone, the pipeline will repeatedly pass through sections of unfrozen ground that alternate with

Ice in soil in permafrost area, Inuvik. (R. Read)

Carson Templeton. (Native Press)

Thawing of permafrost caused the soil to liquify and flow, Dempster Highway near Fort McPherson. (GSC–A. Heginbottom)

sections of permafrost. Heave may occur wherever the pipe passes through unfrozen wet ground and the gas in it is kept at a temperature below the freezing point of water. Foothills argued at the Inquiry that the "southern limit of chilling" should be in the neighbourhood of Fort Simpson, but Arctic Gas argued that it should be near the Alberta border. North of Fort Good Hope, in the zone of continuous permafrost, the pipeline would pass through unfrozen ground in relatively few places, principally beneath river channels. The problem of frost heave is not, therefore, widespread in this zone, but it may be serious at river crossings: Arctic Gas say that their present proposed route passes through 17 miles of unfrozen ground beneath the channels of the Mackenzie Delta.

Where the refrigerated pipe passes through unfrozen ground, it will surround itself with a frost bulb, a zone of frozen soil, that will grow outward at first rapidly, then more slowly, over a period of years. It could extend 20 feet or more below the pipe. The frost bulb will cause frost heave in varying degrees, depending on local conditions in the ground, including the nature of the soil, temperature, pressure and availability of water. When soil freezes, two things happen that cause it to expand and the ground to heave. First, water in the soil expands by about ten percent in changing to ice. Second and more important, water in fine and fairly fine soils such as silt or clay may move progressively to the freezing soil, so that the amount of water, as ice, increases in the frozen soil generally in layers. The expanding soil would heave the pipe upward by a distance approximately equal to the sum of all the ice layers that have grown beneath it. If this heave should be uniform all along the pipe, it would raise both the pipe and the

ground surface, but it would not buckle the pipe. However, where the amount of heave varies within a short distance, the pipe could buckle or even rupture.

The effects of the growing frost bulb are not limited to frost heave. Carson Templeton of the Environment Protection Board referred to the frost bulb as a wall. It would be a continuous frozen underground barrier that would be created along the length of each section of refrigerated pipe that passes through unfrozen ground. This barrier would block movement of groundwater across the pipeline's route. Ponds or surface icings might be created, or water might begin to move along the pipe or parallel to it. This movement of groundwater on sloping terrain could lead to erosion or slope instability. Also, many river and stream beds are not frozen in winter: when a buried chilled pipeline crosses under a stream that has only a little water flowing in it, the frost bulb could block or divert that flow or create icings.

Controversy over Heave Forces and Control

The processes that cause frost heave are understood in general terms, and so are the soil types, temperature, pressure, and water availability that are conducive to frost heave. Moreover, highway engineers and others have had practical experience in reducing the amount and rate of frost heave by putting a load – gravel perhaps – on the surface to counteract the upward heaving force. Experience in controlling frost heave, however, is limited to situations in which frost builds up during the winter months and then melts in spring and summer. This experience is no precedent for a situation in which frost will build up continuously from

year to year. Moreover, there is no unanimity about details of the frost heave process, the magnitude of the forces that are generated, the range of situations in which the problem may be encountered, and – especially – the magnitude of the differential forces to which the pipe might be subjected. Finally, the engineering procedures to reduce or avoid the heaving of a buried refrigerated pipeline over the years are still in a conceptual stage. There has been no practical demonstration of these procedures under the conditions that will prevail in this project.

Arctic Gas have given much attention to frost heave and its related effects on a buried refrigerated pipeline. More than $1 million has been spent on their Calgary test site and on associated experiments. The impressive panel of geotechnical experts brought before the Inquiry in the spring of 1975 by Arctic Gas indicated that they fully understood the frost heave phenomenon and its effect on the pipeline, and that they had complete confidence in the methods they proposed for its control. They gave assurances that frost heave could be reduced to an acceptable level by loading – either by deep burial or by a built-up berm or by both – without substantial environmental impact. Dr. Ken Adam, on behalf of the Environment Protection Board, and Dr. Peter Williams, of Carleton University, who was called by Commission Counsel, disagreed with the opinion of the Arctic Gas panel. Williams in particular disputed the theoretical and experimental basis of the analysis made by the Arctic Gas experts, and he indicated that the magnitude of the heave forces had been underestimated:

In my opinion, the maximum shut-off pressures that would be required to prevent deleterious heaving during the life of the pipe are greater than those that have been stated. Correspondingly, at problem sites, such as

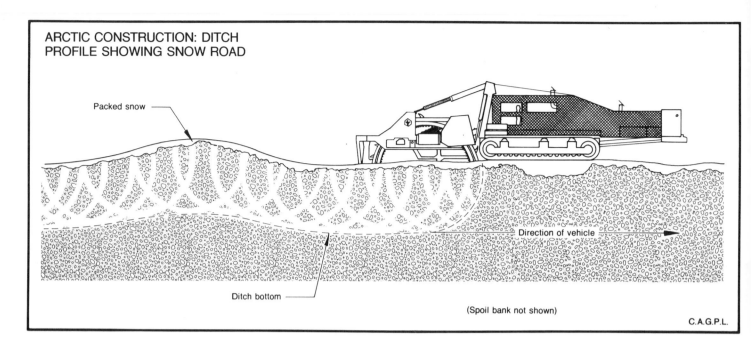

ARCTIC CONSTRUCTION: DITCH
PROFILE SHOWING SNOW ROAD

Packed snow

Direction of vehicle

Ditch bottom

(Spoil bank not shown)

C.A.G.P.L.

transitions between different types of materials where the possibilities of differential heave damaging the pipe are greatest, conditions will be more difficult than that described by the Applicant's witnesses. Particularly in the region of discontinuous permafrost, it appears that freezing induced by the cold pipeline could give rise to pipe deformations greater than the Applicant's maximum permissible curvature of the pipe. [Summary of evidence, filed July 8, 1975, p. 2]

Arctic Gas disagreed fundamentally with the position taken by Williams, which their counsel summarized as follows:

Dr. Williams' thesis is that a chilled pipeline, such as that proposed by Arctic Gas, is going to produce many times more heave than our evidence predicts, and that we will not be able to suppress this heave with types of burial or surcharging that we propose. [F10825]

Arctic Gas then brought forward another panel that strongly challenged Williams' thesis and emphasized that the position of Arctic Gas remained unchanged. Williams in turn maintained his position.

About a year later, in October 1976, Arctic Gas informed the Inquiry that there had been a continuing malfunction in the test apparatus they were using to determine frost heave. This discovery, which had been made by the Division of Building Research of the National Research Council, indicated that the measurements of frost heave pressures upon which Arctic Gas had relied were erroneous: the pressures that had been measured were, in fact, less than the correct pressures. At that date, Arctic Gas did not know the magnitude of the heave forces that the refrigerated pipeline would encounter under severe conditions, and they admitted that, in some situations, burial or surcharge would not be able to suppress heave. Counsel for the company stated:

Arctic Gas believe that there are some soils in

which the heave pressure is larger than can be controlled by deep burial and/or surcharge. [F31491]

Counsel went on to list five other methods that are available to control the problem: insulation of the pipe, insulation of the pipe with heat trace (heating cable), operation of the pipe at temperatures close to 32° Farenheit, replacement of frost-susceptible soil, and placement of the pipe with insulation in a berm on the ground surface.

Thus, at the end of the hearings, Arctic Gas had withdrawn from the position they had held so strongly regarding frost heave and its control. The surcharge method they had relied on as the principal means of controlling frost heave was admitted to be inadequate in severe conditions. The five alternative methods of frost heave control were not described in any detail.

The evolution of the plans of Arctic Gas to control frost heave of the refrigerated twin pipes they propose to bury beneath Shallow Bay, a four-mile crossing in the Mackenzie Delta, provides a graphic illustration of the uncertainties in frost heave control. At Shallow Bay, and at river crossings in general, it is obvious that a berm cannot be used to control heave. In March 1976, the design proposed for the Shallow Bay crossing indicated that burial of the pipeline 10 feet below the bottom would satisfy frost heave requirements. But further studies led to an increase in the depth of burial: 35 feet was then thought to be required to achieve the necessary overburden pressure. Arctic Gas presented this information to the National Energy Board in June 1976. After the fault in the test equipment was discovered, Arctic Gas told this Inquiry in November 1976 of yet further changes to their plans for Shallow Bay:

This [fault] indicated a need for even greater

burial depths and gravel borrow if the surcharge method were employed. Further assessment of the data is required to determine the feasibility of this technique. If the surcharge method of design proves to be not feasible, alternative designs as put before the Berger Commission on October 15, 1976, will be applied. Two alternatives are feasible: one involving the use of insulation and replacement of frost-susceptible soil . . . and the other . . . insulation of the pipe with heat trace. [Exhibit F891, p. B-13]

In view of these uncertainties, it is not surprising that counsel for Arctic Gas said that this Inquiry is not in a position to offer any specific findings in this regard.

In February 1977, Arctic Gas filed with the National Energy Board further evidence regarding their plans for controlling frost heave in which they conceded that, for virtually all soils to be crossed by the refrigerated buried pipe, the depth of burial and the height of the berm required to control frost heave would exceed practical limits. They had found that they could not, as a practical matter, bury the pipe deep enough nor build a berm high enough to control frost heave. Moreover, Arctic Gas indicated, for the first time, that frost heave would be a problem wherever the refrigerated pipe passes through shallow permafrost. According to their new plans, presented with this evidence, insulated pipe with heat trace would be used in all of the overland sections where the ground is unfrozen or where permafrost is less than 15 feet deep. Heat probes would be used to prevent the build-up of ice lenses where permafrost is 15 feet or more thick. At river crossings, in frost-susceptible soils, a heavy casing would be placed around the insulated pipe and heating cables would also be used.

To reduce the length of pipe requiring frost heave control, the southern limit of

Above-ground section of trans-Alaska pipeline.
(Alyeska)
Pipeline ditching machine. (E. Owen)
Pipe in ditch with saddle weights to prevent it from floating, Pointed Mountain. (E. Owen)

refrigeration of the pipe would, according to this modified plan, be moved northward about 160 miles to a point north of Fort Simpson. This 160-mile section would be kept above rather than below freezing, and it would thaw any permafrost that it encounters. To maintain pipe stability when such a thaw occurs, Arctic Gas now propose deep burial of the pipe and, in critical locations, support of the buried pipe on piles fixed in stable material beneath the thawed zone.

Throughout the uncertainties and changes associated with frost heave, Arctic Gas have strongly opposed the use of above-ground pipeline construction. In 1975, Dr. Hoyt Purcell, a witness for Arctic Gas, summarized the company's position as follows:

> After reviewing the pros and cons of above-ground versus buried construction, the Arctic Gas engineers continued to use the buried mode as their prime design technique, and put the above-ground mode on the shelf to be used only in the event insuperable problems with the buried mode emerged. [F3764]

Purcell also said that the cost of a section of pipeline would be increased by 60 percent if two-thirds of its length were built above ground on piles instead of being buried. Arctic Gas told the Inquiry in November 1976 that they do not consider above-ground construction a viable alternative. In February 1977, they still maintained that above-ground construction is greatly inferior to an insulated, heat-traced pipeline buried in frost-susceptible terrain.

Despite the strength of their statements against above-ground construction of the pipeline, Arctic Gas have admitted the possibility of placing short sections of insulated pipe on the ground within a berm to avoid frost heave. Counsel for Arctic Gas referred to this possibility in October 1976; it was raised again before the Inquiry in November 1976, and again before the National Energy Board in February 1977.

Implications

I have reviewed the problem of frost heave in some detail to illustrate two problems: first, the inadequacies in some aspects of the pipeline proposals; and second, inadequacies in the knowledge that is available to the Inquiry and to the government on which an assessment of precedent-setting or innovative aspects of the pipeline engineering must be based.

In considering the original pipeline proposal made by Arctic Gas, the Pipeline Application Assessment Group stated in their report, published in November, 1974:

> The application provides principles and theory but in many respects lacks specifics of the *modus operandi;* it contains frequent assurances that the subject being considered is adequately understood, that designs will be developed to cope with the situations of concern, or that additional studies already planned will remove any uncertainties. [*Mackenzie Valley Pipeline Assessment,* p. 5]

Now, more than two years later, this comment is still applicable. Critical questions remain unanswered. Company officials and consultants continue to express confidence in proposed engineering designs and construction plans and to give assurances that major and precedent-setting aspects of the project are well in hand. The question of frost heave illustrates these unsatisfactory aspects of the present design proposals. The section of this chapter on construction scheduling will provide a comparable illustration. I recognize that the project proposals are still in a conceptual, and not a final, design stage. I also recognize that improvements in them will continue to be made. My concern about the engineering and scheduling aspects of construction relates to my duty to assess and judge the proposals as they now stand. Arctic Gas, at the close of the hearings, argued that the Inquiry was not in a position to make any specific finding with regard to frost heave. I agree. I am not, therefore, in a position to say that the proposals made by Arctic Gas to control frost heave are sound. But I can say something about the reasons why the Inquiry is in this position.

In dealing with frost heave and with other questions of innovative design or construction planning, it has become apparent that much of the specialized knowledge and expertise that is relevant to these matters is tied up with industry and its consultants. This situation is untenable when faced with the need to make an objective assessment of the project. Government cannot rely solely on industry's ability to judge its own case; rather, with respect to questions of fundamental design, government must have the knowledge to make an independent judgment. A contrast has been clearly apparent at the Inquiry between biological issues, where the Environmental-Social Program, the Beaufort Sea Project and related ongoing federal research have provided knowledge and expertise, and engineering issues, where the knowledge and expertise is largely confined to the industry itself. This is in no way a criticism of the advice and information that the Inquiry has received on technical matters. Indeed, it is this advice that has enabled the Inquiry to assess the magnitude and the implications of the frost heave question. But I urge the government to make itself more knowledgeable in matters involving major innovative technology, such as frost heave and other questions related to the burial of pipelines in permafrost, which are and will be involved in northern oil and

ARCTIC CONSTRUCTION:
RIGHT—OF—WAY CONFIGURATION

Stripped organic layer
(where applicable)

Spoil pile

Ditch

Packed snow

Packed snow

Working surface

Traffic lane
(Snow road)

10′   25′   2′ 7′ 11′   35′   30′

120′

C.A.G.P.L.

gas exploration and development proposals for years to come. Acquisition of this knowledge will necessitate ongoing research and expert scientific staff. Industry proposes, the government disposes. Without such a body of knowledge, the government will not be able to make an intelligent disposition of industry's proposals now or in the future.

The question of frost heave is basic to the theory and design of the pipeline project. If the pipe is to be buried, the gas must be chilled. If the gas is chilled, the result — frost heave — has to be overcome. The pipeline companies are obviously having trouble in designing their proposal to deal with frost heave, and they are making fundamental changes in the methods proposed for heave control. Their methods seem to be getting more complex, and the conditions for success more restrictive. There is every likelihood that the companies will make yet further changes in their proposals, changes that are likely to increase costs further and to alter substantially the environmental impacts that we have been trying to assess. The possibility that for some sections of the pipe, the buried refrigerated mode will be replaced by above-ground berm construction or above-ground pile construction brings with it a host of attendant problems. It seems to me unreasonable that the Government of Canada should give unqualified approval to a right-of-way or provide financial guarantees to the project without a convincing resolution of these concerns.

The Construction Plan and Schedule

Large-scale engineering projects are not unprecedented in the arctic and sub-arctic regions of North America. I have mentioned the large defence-oriented projects that have already been constructed in these regions, such as the Alaska Highway, the Canol Pipeline and the DEW Line. More recently, we have seen the Churchill Falls hydro-electric project in Labrador, the James Bay hydro-electric project in Quebec and, of course, the Alyeska oil pipeline in Alaska. These are all huge multimillion dollar projects in frontier settings. Now we have before us the Mackenzie Valley pipeline proposals of Arctic Gas and Foothills. Why are we so concerned by these proposals?

At the outset, we must bear in mind that the pipeline as proposed is not a simple extension of past defence- and energy-oriented frontier construction projects, nor simply an extension of tested technology to a far northern setting. In my discussion of frost heave, I have already sought to demonstrate the novel engineering aspects of the project. But the innovations — and problems — are not confined to design: the construction plans and proposed schedules for building the pipeline also involve techniques that lack precedent. Even now, before the project is underway, a number of scheduling problems can be discerned that may well compound one another in ways that have not yet been adequately considered by either Arctic Gas or Foothills. The natural and logistical constraints that the project will encounter could make the present approach to its construction optimistic and, in some respects perhaps, unrealistic.

The environmental, social and economic assessments made by the pipeline companies were carefully predicated on the assumption that the project would, in fact, be built as proposed. However, it should be plain to anyone that every substantial modification in the schedule or in the methods of construction will alter these impacts.

Let me outline some of the features of the construction plan that are novel and that may pose problems. Each of them could lead to difficulties in adhering to the construction schedule. Each of them could force changes in the project. When taken together, these changes could present us with a project that has become so different from the one originally proposed that we should question the basis of the present assessments of impact. This concern is greatest along the Arctic Gas route across the Northern Yukon where the schedule is likely to be most susceptible to upset and where the environment is highly sensitive to impact.

Snow Roads

Except for pre-construction activity, and for construction of major water crossings and compressor stations, the companies intend to build the pipeline in winter. Winter pipeline construction is not new: it is now almost standard Canadian practice because it allows heavy equipment to be moved along a right-of-way when the ground is frozen, making the construction of all-weather roads unnecessary. Such roads are expensive and could result in greater environmental and social impact than the pipeline itself.

This pipeline project is different because the continuous or discontinuous permafrost that underlies its entire route North of 60 precludes the standard approach to winter

Arctic Gas snow road test loop. (W. Sol)

Les Williams, Northern Engineering Services. (Arctic Gas)

Snow road construction at test site. (K. Adam)

grading and right-of-way preparation. Measures must be taken to protect the ground surface from damage that would lead to thermal degradation of the permafrost. To protect the ground surface, both companies propose to use snow roads and snow working surfaces, which are subtle but important variations on winter road construction practices that are common in Northern Canada. Winter roads are of snow pack or ice construction or are cleared rights-of-way along frozen waterbodies. The Denison Ice Road, which runs from the Mackenzie Highway near Rae north to Great Bear Lake, the winter road that used to run northward along the Mackenzie Valley from Fort Simpson in the early 1970s, and the roads the oil companies and their contractors have recently been using in their Delta exploration programs are examples of conventional winter roads.

The snow roads proposed for the pipeline project are a more sophisticated version of these common winter roads, and are designed to protect the vegetation, and hence the permafrost, from heavy traffic. Access roads from stockpile sites, water sources, borrow pits and camps to the pipeline right-of-way are expected to have as many as 45,000 vehicle passes in one season, and haul roads along the right-of-way will have about 29,000 passes. This volume of traffic requires a higher standard of construction than is necessary on conventional winter roads. Thus the proposed snow roads will consist of a densely compacted snow pavement over the naturally frozen but undisturbed ground surface. Adjacent to the snow road on the right-of-way there will be a snow working surface along the ditch line; it will be similar to the snow road but its pavement will be less densely packed because it will need to sustain only a few passes of slow-moving equipment.

Both Arctic Gas and Foothills propose to build hundreds of miles of snow roads, and the whole pipeline construction schedule will depend on their availability. Yet lack of experience with them has led to a number of criticisms about their potential usefulness, particularly in tundra areas.

Arctic Gas undertook at an early stage to verify the practicability of the snow road concept. Preliminary tests at the Sans Sault Rapids and Norman Wells test sites were, as Les Williams, Director of Field Services for Northern Engineering Services Company Ltd., said, "not too successful" and were "not completely valid." [F4306] In 1973, Northern Engineering Services built an experimental snow road at Inuvik to verify the viability of the scheme in the more northern latitudes where the problems would be greater. A test section about three-quarters of a mile long was prepared but, because of low snowfall, snow had to be harvested from a nearby lake and hauled to the site. Snow manufacturing also was tried with some success. Once in place, the snow was compacted to achieve the necessary pavement density, and trafficability tests were conducted in winter and spring by making successive passes with a loaded truck. Follow-up observations made on the vegetation beneath the road revealed that the ground surface was relatively undisturbed.

Arctic Gas concluded that densely packed snow roads will be able to withstand heavy traffic and to protect sensitive terrain from disturbance. But not everyone shared their view. Walter Parker, Commissioner of Highways for the State of Alaska, and Dr. Robert Weeden of the State Governor's Office told the Inquiry that, despite the results of the test at Inuvik, they did not think the feasibility of snow roads had been demonstrated, particularly for use on the Arctic Coastal Plain. In their opinion, snow roads should be regarded as operationally unproven. Others, such as Dr. Ken Adam of the Environment Protection Board, and Paul Jarvis, a witness for Foothills, also expressed reservations, although they did not criticize the concept as severely.

In my view, the issue is not whether snow roads, once in place, will work. Canadian engineers have had ample experience with winter roads, airstrips and snow-surfaced work areas. Rather the dispute hinges on two questions. The first relates to timing, and the second to the sufficiency of snow.

The timing question is this: can the snow roads be ready early enough and can they be used long enough to enable the construction to be completed on schedule? After all, they must be prepared before pipeline construction can begin, and construction cannot continue after the roads begin to melt. There is a definite "window" for winter construction, limited on each side by freezing and thawing temperatures. The construction season cannot be extended beyond it: additional men and equipment would be of no help once the season has ended.

If the pipeline company tries to adhere to a fixed schedule in preparing snow roads, there could be considerable unnecessary damage to terrain and disruption of construction plans. Schedules must take into account regional and annual variations in climate, snowfall and frost penetration. Before snow roads can be prepared in the fall, the ground must be frozen deep enough to support heavy vehicles and there must be sufficient snow to protect the surface vegetation. Frost penetration varies from place to place and from year to year. Streams, drainage channels and wet areas will delay road preparation because they freeze more slowly than intervening areas. If it is impossible to wait until the frost has gone deep enough in wet areas to support the movement of vehicles, temporary crossings will have to be built.

Construction activity in the spring will also be of great environmental concern. There will be compelling reasons to try to extend the use of snow roads as long as possible, particularly if the work is running behind schedule. But the shut-down date of a snow road is completely dependent on the spring weather, which varies substantially from year to year. Construction activity must be able to stop at short notice without harm to the environment.

If scheduled work cannot be accomplished in the period prescribed by nature, it will either have to be postponed until the next season or, as in Alaska, a permanent gravel road-and-working surface will have to be built to permit summer construction. Either way, the schedules and costs of construction would be changed, and the impact of the project would be increased. Arctic Gas maintain that such alterations will not be necessary. Foothills dispute that claim; late in the Inquiry, they told us they propose to build 50 miles of gravel road along the northern end of their right-of-way, to enable them to proceed whether or not temperature and snowfall allow construction of snow roads early in the season.

The second question about snow roads is this: will the snowfall early in the season be adequate for building the roads, and, if not, can sufficient snow be gathered or manufactured in an environmentally acceptable manner? The farther north you go along the proposed pipeline route, the less snow there is. The average annual snowfall of the Arctic Coastal Plain of the Yukon is less than half

that of Northern Alberta. So, at the northern end of the pipeline route, the longer winter construction season is offset by lack of snow.

Thus, construction of snow roads will be most difficult in the tundra regions, mainly because of the light snowfall there. The proposed Arctic Gas Coastal Route across the Northern Yukon is the principal area of concern in this regard. Arctic Gas say that, in such regions, they will supplement natural snowfall by using snow fences to catch snow, by harvesting snow from lakes and hauling it to the road bed, and by mechanically manufacturing snow and blowing it onto the roads and work surfaces. But the winter winds sweeping across the treeless landscape will further complicate the harvesting and accumulation of snow for roads.

Along the Coastal Route snow will have to be harvested from a multitude of lakes and then hauled to where it will be used — an activity that will require extensive movements of equipment and networks of secondary snow roads (and thus even more snow). Vehicles and equipment will have to be kept in the area over summer to be available on site in the fall, and snow fences will have to be strung in the fall. Snow fences have not yet been tested on a scale and in locations similar to those proposed, nor has there been any field research on their potential effects on wildlife.

The plans for manufacturing snow also involve uncertainties. Snow making is common practice on ski slopes, and it has been used to a limited extent to make snow surfaces on airstrips, but it has never been used on the scale proposed by Arctic Gas. The experimental snow road in Inuvik used what Les Williams described as a "gerry rigged apparatus." The snow-making equipment to be used on the Arctic Gas Coastal Route does not yet exist — we were simply

shown an artist's conception of a large vehicle, with a big compressor and up to six snow-making nozzles. This machine will be fed by fleets of tanker vehicles, which will in turn require an extensive network of snow roads to acceptable water sources. The snow-making machine will require up to 1,000 Imperial gallons of water per minute. Williams said that if the snow road and working surface had to be fully manufactured, about 1.75 million Imperial gallons (50,000 barrels) of water per mile of right-of-way would be needed.

This program of harvesting and manufacturing snow for roads and work surfaces is obviously a very extensive operation and Arctic Gas have tended to understate the problems involved. Quite understandably, they hope for an early and abundant snowfall during the winter they build the pipeline from Prudhoe Bay to the Mackenzie Delta. Although they have outlined techniques for harvesting and manufacturing snow, they have not presented a comprehensive plan for the whole range of activities that will be required if conditions are less than favourable.

Our greatest concern about the snow roads centres on the Northern Yukon. There the project faces the greatest environmental sensitivity; there adherence to schedules is most critical. If the snow roads across the Northern Yukon cannot be built according to plan, there could be massive disturbance that would have far-reaching geotechnical and environmental consequences.

Productivity

I began this discussion of the planning and scheduling of construction with snow roads because they determine the length of the winter construction season. Productivity

Machines in darkness of arctic winter day. (DIAND)

Alan Hollingworth and Reginald Gibbs, Q.C.,
counsel for Foothills. (Native Press)

Vern Horte, President of Arctic Gas. (Arctic Gas)

Pierre Genest, Q.C. and Jack Marshall, counsel for
Arctic Gas. (Native Press)

within that season will dictate the success of the schedule. The duration of the construction season lengthens from south to north because of earlier freeze-up and later break-up. But other factors such as cold and dark that affect productivity are more severe farther north. Assuming that the snow roads can be built and used in the time proposed, can the amount of work that each construction spread must accomplish be done during the winter construction season?

The schedule that Arctic Gas propose is based on a winter construction season substantially longer than that proposed by Foothills. According to Arctic Gas, the preparation of snow roads and snow working surfaces across the Northern Yukon can begin in October, and pipelaying can start in early November. Foothills disagree; they say that December is the earliest starting date, but because of the cold and darkness and because the construction crews will insist on a Christmas break, it would be impractical to start work on that segment before the end of January. Arctic Gas say that darkness can be overcome by floodlighting the construction spread. In addition, they will shorten the Christmas break and pay people to stay on the job. Cold and adverse weather such as ice fog, blowing snow and whiteouts will, they agree, pose problems, but they have allowed for some delays in their schedule. They maintain, and so do the union representatives who testified, that the workers can and will work throughout the northern winter.

I heard a great deal of evidence about start-up dates, productivity, shut-down dates, downtime, the effects of cold and darkness, the practicability of lighting an entire construction spread, the working conditions the unions would insist upon, and so on. Out of it all, several main themes emerge that underline the uncertainties in planning and scheduling the pipeline project.

Winter conditions, of course, will affect productivity. Arctic Gas estimate that, along the Yukon Coastal Plain, winter productivity will be only 60 percent of what it is for summer pipeline construction on the prairies, although in the southern part of the Northwest Territories, productivity will reach about 90 percent. In preparing their construction schedules, they allowed for break-up, freeze-up, holidays, bad weather, darkness, low temperatures and downtime for environmental reasons. But, as Williams pointed out, their downtime evaluations did not include allowances for wind chill and limited visibility.

The unions and the workers will also have something to say about productivity. The labour representatives who appeared at the Inquiry said that there will be a no-strike no-lockout agreement. They said that work in severe weather can be undertaken, and specific conditions will be on a business-like basis with the contractor on the job — but unresolved and unquantified is the whole issue of downtime caused by labour disputes. Despite assurances from the company and the unions, it seems obvious that there are limits beyond which the workers will not go.

Innovations in equipment will also be required. The ditching machine, for example, is still being developed and so are some of its components such as the ditcher teeth. There is only one large ditcher in existence, the 710. Arctic Gas say that this ditcher can do 60 percent of the ditching. But this machine has not been used in permafrost, and its teeth appear to be unsuitable for permafrost work. A new ditcher, the 812, is therefore being developed, and new teeth for it are being tested to meet Arctic Gas' requirements. No prototype has yet been built.

Changes in the design of the project could also have an adverse effect on productivity. For instance, the uncertainties about frost heave referred to in the preceding section and the requirements for installing crack arrestors around the pipe have both arisen since Arctic Gas prepared their schedule.

Foothills criticized Arctic Gas' proposal to illuminate artificially a winter construction spread that will involve up to 500 men and 50 pieces of equipment deployed over a two-or-three mile stretch of confined right-of-way. They maintain that work under these conditions would be hazardous to workers — even if it were feasible. The lighting of a moving pipeline spread of this magnitude is in itself novel and quite different from the lighting of fixed and confined operations such as drilling rigs.

Although Foothills have raised important questions about the Arctic Gas proposal, they have not vindicated their own construction plan. As Arctic Gas pointed out, the most significant difference between the two plans lies in the start-up dates of fall construction, not in the productivity per spread. Recently, Foothills have modified their plans for the northern end of their pipeline to include the construction of an all-weather gravel road so that pipelaying can be carried out in the fall, too. This change in itself is of great environmental concern, and it is perhaps an indication of the way in which we might expect the construction plans of either company to evolve.

The schedules of both companies are unproven. There are no precedents by which to judge the winter construction schedule for the northern part of the line. Even if there were, the many unique elements of design would make any comparison doubtful. It has been said that the trans-Alaska pipeline is a precedent — but that pipeline is a hot oil pipeline built in summer and is fundamentally different in design from the buried chilled gas pipeline that is proposed for the Mackenzie Valley. In fact, Arctic Gas told the Inquiry that the trans-Alaska project is so different from their proposal that any comparison between the two is meaningless.

The Schedule in the Northern Yukon

The problems of snow roads and of productivity will be especially acute on the north slope of the Yukon, and it is right to ask whether Arctic Gas can build a pipeline from Alaska across the Northern Yukon in one season. Arctic Gas have said that, if experience during the first two years of pipelaying in the Mackenzie Valley indicates that they will encounter greater difficulty on the north slope than they now envisage, and if they think the pipeline from Alaska could not be built on schedule, they will establish two additional construction spreads, one in Canada and one in Alaska. But this approach — overcoming the forces of nature with more money, more men, and more equipment — clearly has limits. The extreme environmental sensitivity of the Northern Yukon that I will describe in a subsequent chapter will impose severe limits on any *ad hoc* response to construction problems.

If the pipeline across the Northern Yukon cannot be built in one winter season, there will be great pressure to extend the work into summer and to build a gravel road rather than to postpone further construction until the following winter. Only by this means will a heavy financial penalty be avoided. But once a permanent road is in place, the likelihood is that it will be used for maintenance and repairs and will form an integral part of corridor development. This will open up the wilderness of the Northern Yukon, exposing caribou, snow geese and other species to impacts that will go well beyond the impact of pipeline construction itself.

Logistics

The Arctic Gas project will require approximately two million tons of materials to be transported from southern supply points to northern stockpile sites scattered along the pipeline route. Summer barging on the Mackenzie River and, to a lesser degree, along the Arctic coast will be relied upon to deliver the material. The deluge of construction materials — pipe, fuel, camps and equipment — will require a doubling of the capacity of the river barging system. Virtually a whole infrastructure of wharves, stockpile sites, staging areas, haul roads, camps and communication systems must be installed by the company before the pipeline can be built.

Winter construction will depend, therefore, on a short summer shipping season. If there are delays in summer transportation, the winter construction program may well be disrupted, forcing the companies to ship goods by the Dempster Highway, or by winter road from Fort Simpson to Inuvik, or by aircraft. These alternatives would be of only limited value in major freight movements, and they could involve substantial social and environmental impacts.

The vulnerability of the construction schedule goes right back to the suppliers involved. Delays in delivery caused by strikes or slowdowns by southern transportation facilities, such as railways, ports and trucking operations, could seriously impede the construction program. This dependence on suppliers and on logistics is common to all construction projects — so why the great concern here? The answer is that the construction plan and schedule of this particular project are based on a "winter-only" construction program. And its success depends on the shipment of supplies from the South during a short, inflexible "summer-only" transportation season.

All large construction projects operate according to definite schedules, and there is every reason to believe that this project would use the most sophisticated techniques of planning and management to assure success. But there are limits to what any one company or union — or even government — can do. A series of relatively small, unforeseen, and uncontrollable logistical problems could cause the break-down of the whole supply program.

The logistics plans of both companies include the use of many non-company facilities. For example, they have made various assumptions about the Mackenzie Highway, the Dempster Highway, the Fort Simpson-to-Inuvik winter road, the use of wharf sites and airstrips near communities, and the use of trans-shipment facilities at Hay River. Also, they say that a proposal they both have made to establish a new major trans-shipment facility at Axe Point, near Mills Lake on the Mackenzie River, will extend the barging season and will relieve the pressure on the existing facilities at Hay River. Over the course of the Inquiry, there has been a steady modification of all these plans, partly in reaction to the attitudes of local people, and partly in response to specific requirements as the designs and plans have evolved. It should not be assumed that the approval of a right-of-way would

Barge on the Mackenzie River. (NTCL)

Building materials being loaded into aircraft.
(N. Cooper)

*Forty-eight-inch diameter pipe at Sans Sault Test
Site.* (Canadian Press)

Trucks passing on northern highway. (Native Press)

automatically carry approvals of all the logistical details advanced by the companies. For example, it will be necessary to decide if the proposed new facility at Axe Point will serve the immediate and long-term needs of the region. If the Axe Point facility is not approved, how will the limited summer shipping schedule be affected?

Implications

Throughout this Inquiry, we have heard a great deal about the ways the construction schedules could go wrong. In this section, I have reviewed at some length some criticisms of the proposals because of the consequences that a break-down in the construction plans and schedules would have. Scheduling failures will have serious financial implications for the company, its contractors, sub-contractors and workmen; for suppliers, shippers and the whole logistics infrastructure; and for local people and local communities. If the government has guaranteed cost overruns, then the government too will have an important financial stake in ensuring that the project adheres to the planned schedule. If there were a schedule failure and plans had to be changed, all of the parties concerned would react in a way dictated by their own interest. Such reaction could lead to *ad hoc* solutions, loss of quality control, an increase in accidents, and it might become impossible to protect the environment, the local people, and the local economy as originally planned.

I am not confident that the pipeline can be built in accordance with the present plans and schedules. Particularly, I am concerned that scheduling problems in the Northern Yukon could lead to a need for summer construction and a gravel road along the Coastal Route. The environmental impact of this change would be very severe. The project would then have to be completely reassessed, because the premises that were basic to all planning, environmental, social and economic assessments would have changed.

I recognize that the present stage of the companies' planning is preliminary and that, by the time final design and final plans are ready, there may be answers to the scheduling problems that concern us now. But my task is directed to assessment of the proposals in their present form and to the decision that government must make about them now. In this context, it seems unreasonable to me that Canada should give unqualified approval of the pipeline right-of-way or financial guarantees to the project without a convincing resolution of the fundamental concerns over the schedules.

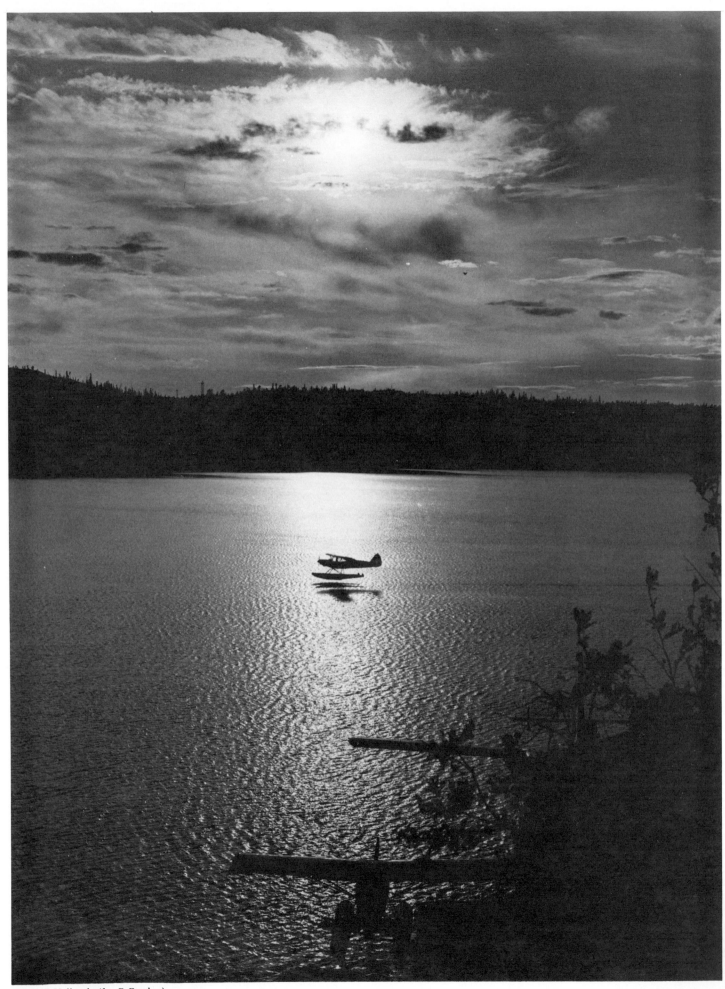

(DIAND Yellowknife—B. Braden)

The Northern Environment

Environmental Attitudes and Environmental Values

The history of North America is the history of the frontier: of pushing back the wilderness, cultivating the soil, populating the land, and then building an industrial way of life. The conquest of the frontier in North America is a remarkable episode in human history, and it altered the face of the continent. The achievement was prodigious, and there is no need here to tell how transportation networks were evolved, cities founded, industries established, commerce expanded, and unparalleled agricultural productivity developed. The superabundance of land and resources gave rise to a conviction that the continent's resources were inexhaustible. Land on the eastern seaboard was abandoned almost as rapidly as it had been cleared. Thomas Jefferson wrote, "We can buy an acre of new land cheaper than we can manure an old one."

Cultivation of agriculturally unsuitable soils left a legacy of abandoned farms, rural poverty, ruined landscapes and silt-choked streams. Soil erosion and pollution by countless sources of domestic and industrial wastes choked many of our rivers, reducing a once bountiful fishery. The buffalo herds, estimated to number about 75 million, were reduced in only a few decades to a few hundred survivors. The prairies were ploughed and overgrazed, setting the stage for the disastrous dust-bowl conditions of this century. In *Democracy in America,* Alexis de Tocqueville wrote of the United States he visited in 1831:

> The Americans themselves never think about [the wilds], they are insensible to the wonders of inanimate nature ... their eyes are fixed upon another sight, [they] march across these wilds, draining swamps, turning the course of rivers, peopling solitudes, and subduing nature. [p. 47]

We should recognize the links between attitudes to environment and attitudes to native peoples. The assault upon the environment was also an assault on their way of life. To be sure, it was often an assault carried out under the banners of benevolence and enlightened progress, but it was nonetheless an assault. The native peoples and their land were, and to some extent continue to be, under siege.

We have observed the passage of the white man from the eastern seaboard of North America into the great plains and yet farther west. He has penetrated the North, but his occupation of the North is not yet complete. There are those with an abiding faith in technology, who believe that technology can overcome all environmental problems. They believe there is no point at which the imperatives of industrial development cannot be reconciled with environmental values. But there are others who believe that industrial development must be slowed or halted if we are to preserve the environment.

Different views of the North can be distinguished by the emphasis placed either on the achievement of industrial development at the frontier or on its cost. A particular idea of progress is firmly embedded in our economic system and in the national consciousness; but there is also in Canada a strong identification with the values of the the wilderness and of the land itself. No account of environmental attitudes would be complete that did not recognize this deeply felt, and perhaps deeply Canadian, concern with the environment for its own sake. The judgment of this Inquiry must, therefore, recognize at least two sets of powerful, historically entrenched — but conflicting — attitudes and values.

In recent years, we have seen the growth of ecological awareness, and a growing concern for wilderness, wildlife resources and environmental legislation that parallels — although it does not match — the increasing power of our technology, the consumption of natural resources, and the impacts of rapid change. There are situations in which the two sets of attitudes and values simply cannot be reconciled. The question then turns on the depth of our commitment to environmental values when they stand in the way of technological and industrial advance.

This opposition of views is particularly clear in the North. The northern native people, along with many other witnesses at the Inquiry, insisted that the land they have long depended upon will be injured by the construction of a pipeline and the establishment of an energy corridor. Environmentalists pointed out that the North, the last great wilderness area of Canada, is slow to recover from environmental degradation; its protection against penetration by industry is, therefore, of vital importance to all Canadians. It is not easy to measure that concern against the more precisely calculated interests of industry. But we must accept the reality of this opposition, and we must try and face the questions that are posed in the North of today: Should we open up the North as we opened up the West? Should the values that conditioned our attitudes toward the environment in the past prevail in the North today and tomorrow? Perhaps we can see the force of, and even some answers to, these questions by examining the concept, as it has developed, of preserving the wilderness on this continent.

Wilderness

Wilderness is a non-renewable resource. If we are to preserve wilderness areas in the North, we must do so now. The available areas will diminish with each new industrial development on the frontier. We have not yet in Canada developed a legislative framework for the protection of wilderness, but a model exists in the United States.

A century ago, for the first time in history, a tract of land in its natural state was set aside for its own sake, for its intrinsic values, not for the resources it might later provide. That was Yellowstone National Park, and it marked the beginning of the national park system. This idea of preserving unexploited and superb examples of nature was adopted within 15 years in Canada, and it rapidly spread to other nations.

Initially, Canadian and American parks seemed to be designated to preserve natural geological features found in magnificent settings, such as geysers (Yellowstone, 1872) and hot springs (Banff, 1885). In a few years, concern for the giant trees of the Sierra Nevada led to the establishment of Sequoia National Park, and plant life came to be regarded as a valuable component of land in its natural state. Then wildlife was accorded recognition. The idea of preserving wilderness itself continued to develop, culminating in the passage by the United States in 1964 of the Wilderness Act. This Act, in defining wilderness, called it a place:

> where the earth and its community of life are untrammeled by man, where man himself is a visitor who does not remain. [p. 1]

I rely here on American experience because I see no difference between the United States and Canada in the perception of environmental values. I have heard witnesses from Alaska and the Lower 48. What they said about wildlife and wilderness did not distinguish them from Canadians, but rather reinforced my impressions of the values that Canadian society now embraces.

Let me be clear about the importance that is hereby accorded to wilderness. No one seeks to turn back the clock, to return in some way to nature, or even to deplore, in a high-minded and sentimental manner, the real achievements of modern-day life. Rather, the suggestion here is that wilderness constitutes an important — perhaps an invaluable — part of modern-day life; its preservation is a contribution to, not a repudiation of, the civilization upon which we depend.

Wallace Stegner wrote in 1960:

> Without any remaining wilderness we are committed ... to a headlong drive into our technological termite-life, the Brave New World of a completely man-controlled environment. ... We simply need that wild country ... [as] part of the geography of hope. [cited in W. Schwartz, *Voices for the Wilderness*, p. 284ff.]

The difficulty in describing the importance of wilderness is that you cannot attach a dollar value to it or to its use and enjoyment, any more than you can to the rare and endangered species, or to archaeological finds. The value of wilderness cannot be weighed in the scale of market values. It is a national heritage. Many who sense change everywhere, recognize that our northern wilderness is irreplaceable.

Sigurd F. Olson, an American naturalist, writing of the Canadian North in *The Lonely Land,* said:

> There are few places left on the North American continent where men can still see the country as it was before Europeans came and know some of the challenges and freedoms of those who saw it first, but in the Canadian Northwest it can still be done. [p. 5]

Wilderness implies to all of us a remote landscape and the presence of wildlife. I think there are three kinds of wilderness species. The first are species that, because of their intolerance of man or their need for large areas of land, can survive only in the wilderness. Such are caribou, wolf and grizzly bear. These species require large areas of wilderness to protect the integrity of their populations and preserve their habitat. Second are the species that conjure up visions of wilderness for every Canadian, although they are often seen in other areas, too. I do not believe there can be a Canadian anywhere who does not think of wilderness on hearing the call of a loon or of migrating geese. Third are the rare and endangered species that do not inherently require a wilderness habitat, but, because they are tolerant of man, have been driven close to extinction. The peregrine falcon, trumpeter swan and whooping crane are well-known examples of species that are abundant (if abundant at all) only in wilderness areas. Our concern is that the process of adaptation and evolution through millenia of each of these species should not be ended. We cannot allow the extinction of these species, if it can be prevented. These species, like wilderness itself, need protection in the North today.

Wilderness is a resource that can be used by both public and private interests, in both a consuming and a non-consuming way. A consuming use of the wilderness destroys or degrades it, and so decreases its value for other users. Industrial and commercial interests are almost invariably consumers; they do not use the wilderness itself, but some aspect of it. Non-consuming use is represented by the traditional pursuits of the

Whistling swans in the Delta. (C. & M. Hampson)

Arctic tern on nest. (C. & M. Hampson)

Ermine. (NFB—Cesar)

Red-throated loon on nest. (W. Campbell)

native people, and by certain recreational activities.

To some people, the notion of preserving a wilderness area inviolate from industry is anathema — as though we were on the brink of starvation and could not survive without exploiting the resources of every last piece of ground in our country. They would argue that the urge to develop, to build, to consume, is fundamental to man's very nature and that this urge ought not to be checked; even if, were we to follow this urge, it would produce no more than a marginal — perhaps even an illusory — increment to our material well-being. But this argument would apply to northern wilderness areas only if there were no other way in which, and no other area where, man could satisfy this urge. This manifestly is not the case.

Wilderness and Northern Land Use

If we decide to preserve the wilderness, then we must withdraw from industrial use the land designated as wilderness. This decision would have certain implications in respect of land use and land use regulations in the North.

Wilderness parks in the North would be a logical extension of our national park system. In fact, some of the provinces have already established wilderness areas. There have been many intrusions into the great national parks along the Alberta-British Columbia boundary. Two national railways run through these parks (although both were there when the parks were created). The Trans-Mountain oil pipeline from Edmonton to Vancouver and the Trans-Canada Highway cross Jasper National Park. But these national parks are not — and were never intended to be — wilderness parks. In the North, certain ecosystems and certain migratory populations can be protected and preserved only by recognizing the inviolability of wilderness. Our national parks legislation, as it now stands, is not adequate to preserve northern wilderness areas, which, if they are to be preserved, must be withdrawn from any form of industrial development. That principle must not be compromised. It is essential to the concept of wilderness itself as an area untrammeled by industrial man.

Virtually any northern development must involve land, and in areas such as the Mackenzie Delta there has been, during recent years, a dramatic increase in the number of competing uses to which the land is put. The potential for chaotic development, degradation of environmentally important areas, the overwhelming of native people's interests, or even a stalemate in the conflict of interests, is great.

The Mackenzie Valley and the Western Arctic are still at an early stage of industrial development, and the latitude of choice that can be exercised for the future of these areas is still considerable — at least in comparison with most parts of Canada. Nevertheless, with each passing season, and with each decision by the public and private sectors concerning townsite development, transportation facilities, municipal or industrial use of land, or resource development, the number of options is decreased.

We should recognize that in the North, land use regulations, based on the concept of multiple use, will not always protect environmental values, and they will never fully protect wilderness values. Withdrawal of land from any industrial use will be necessary in some instances to preserve wilderness, wildlife species and critical habitat. Parliament contemplated that withdrawals of land in the North would be made. The Territorial Lands Act provides for lands to be reserved for special purposes such as recreation sites and public parks (under Section 19[b]), for the general good of native people (Section 19[d]), and for use as national forests or game preserves (Section 19[e]). Despite these provisions, no attempt has yet been made to preclude industrial development in any part of the Territories; instead the policy of multiple use has been followed.

In two recently prepared studies on land management North of 60, *Land Management in the Canadian North* by Kenneth Beauchamp and *Land Use and Public Policy in Northern Canada* by John Naysmith the authors argue that we must confront the question of land withdrawal versus its regulation for multiple use. I think they are right.

We should include in our National Parks Act a provision for a new statutory creation: a wilderness park. It would consist of land to be preserved in its natural state for future generations. In chapter 5, I shall recommend that such a wilderness park be established in the Northern Yukon.

THE COASTAL ROUTE AND THE CARIBOU: GENERALIZED MOVEMENTS OF THE PORCUPINE CARIBOU HERD IN MAY, JUNE AND JULY

General area of the post-calving aggregation along the coast

Principal calving area ....
Spring migration ....
Post-calving movement ....
Arctic Gas Coastal route ....
Compressor station .... ■
Wharf/staging area .... ▲
Boundaries of existing Arctic National Wildlife Range in Alaska and proposed Northern Yukon Wilderness Park ....

Prudhoe Bay

Kaktovik

Richards Island

Canning River

ALASKA

Inuvik

Aklavik

N.W.T.

Arctic Village

YUKON

Old Crow   River

Porcupine

Fort McPherson

Kilometres 0 — 150
Miles 0 — 100

THE INTERIOR ROUTE AND THE CARIBOU: GENERALIZED MOVEMENTS OF THE PORCUPINE CARIBOU HERD FROM AUGUST TO APRIL

Prudhoe Bay

Kaktovik

Richards Island

Tuktoyaktuk

Canning River

BROOKS   RANGE

N.W.T.

ALASKA

Old Crow Flats

Inuvik

Aklavik

Arctic Village

Arctic Red River

Mackenzie River

Fort McPherson

Porcupine   River

Old Crow

YUKON

Peel River

Highway

Dempster

Arctic   Circle

Fort Yukon

Circle

Yukon   River

Spring migration ....
Fall migration ....
Principal over wintering areas ....
Arctic Gas Interior route ....
Arctic Gas Coastal route ....
Compressor station complex .... ■
Boundaries of existing Arctic National Wildlife Range in Alaska and proposed Northern Yukon Wilderness Park ......

Kilometres 0 — 100
Miles 0 — 50

The Northern Yukon

A Unique Heritage

My first view of the Northern Yukon was from a helicopter, flying along the Arctic coast in June 1975. The ice had not yet left the shore, and two tugs were still frozen in at Herschel Island. Seals were everywhere on the ice. As we turned away from the ocean, I could see three grizzlies on the tundra. Then, as we left the coast and headed across the British Mountains, I saw hundreds of caribou, part of the Porcupine herd. They had already been to the coast to calve, but they had not yet come together in their magnificent annual aggregation, when tens of thousands of animals move together across the land. Caribou were scattered on the coastal plain, in the foothills and in the mountains.

At the coast, the tundra was still brown but as we went up the Firth River we began to see trees. At first there were just a few, then more and more until, by the time we reached Old Crow Flats, there were trees everywhere and the earth was green.

Old Crow Flats lie on an alluvial plain with mountains in the far distance on all sides. The Flats comprise a multitude of lakes, through which the Old Crow River meanders. I saw caribou, moose and thousands of waterfowl on the Flats, and there, too, I met the people of Old Crow.

I visited a dozen camps on the Flats, where people from Old Crow were out hunting muskrats. They go out "ratting" in the middle of May, when the ice still covers the lakes, and come back in mid-June, when the ice has gone. They trap muskrats on the ice until it thaws; after that they hunt them with rifles along the shore, travelling by canoe. At each camp there were two or three tents, and there were muskrats everywhere.

The people hunt at night under the midnight sun, and during the day they skin their catch. The pelts are put on stretchers to dry, and the meat is hung on racks.

The native people came here long ago from the Old World, across the Bering Strait. A fleshing tool, made from a caribou leg bone and notched by man, has been found by archaeologists on Old Crow Flats. This implement, used to scrape the flesh from hides, is estimated to be about 30,000 years old, and it may be the oldest evidence we have of the entry of man into the western hemisphere.

The Yukon interior is the only substantial region of Canada that was not overrun by glaciers during the Pleistocene Epoch. Only here in the Yukon and in adjoining parts of Alaska can we obtain a relatively complete and continuous record of human occupation of the tundra and the boreal forest.

Like Columbus thousands of years later, the people who came from Asia to the western hemisphere did not realize they had set foot upon a new continent. In small family or kinship groups, they crossed the land-bridge that once linked Asia with North America. They lived by hunting large mammals — mammoth, bison, horse and caribou; of these, only the caribou has survived in this region.

The caribou have been the mainstay of the native people of Old Crow for thousands of years. Today these people are apprehensive, because they fear that the caribou, and thus they themselves, are threatened. They know the power of the white man. They know that elsewhere the great animal herds have died off with the advance of agriculture and industry. They have seen the white man come and dominate them and their land. Exploration crews, bulldozers and the airstrip that crowds their village against the

Porcupine River are continuing reminders of this encroachment. These people fear that the white man may destroy their land and the caribou. They and the caribou have made a long journey together across time and the continents. Is this journey to end now?

The caribou go to the Arctic Coastal Plain of the Yukon in summer to have their young. Many factors combine to create a uniquely favourable habitat for their calving grounds there. Good forage provides the high levels of energy that the caribou need to bear and nourish their young, then to migrate southward, and to survive the winter. In summer, when the sun never sets, the coastal plain seems never to sleep. It is a place of growth and productivity, of movement and sound. But the summer lasts for only a short time. Winter, which lasts some eight months of the year, is bitterly cold and, but for the wind, silent.

Once fed and fattened, the caribou gather in their tens of thousands and travel in a great herd through the foothills and the mountains far southward into the boreal forest. The native people of Old Crow have always taken caribou as they migrate southward, and the energy that the animals stored up while grazing on the coastal plain nourishes the people through the winter. These animals are the last link in a food chain that transfers energy from the sun, through plants, then through the caribou, to man. And the people of Old Crow need only a very small proportion of the herd for their food.

In the old days, but still within living memory, the Old Crow people intercepted the caribou on their migration in late summer and fall by driving them into huge corrals, the outlines of which can still be seen. They consisted of poles lashed together with willow roots to form a fence and were placed along the herd's main migration routes. Because they stood among the trees, they were not readily visible. Some fences had wings up to three miles long, and an inner pocket one-quarter to one-half mile deep. Once inside the fences, the caribou were caught with snares and speared. The corrals illustrate the technological ingenuity of the native people.

About the turn of the century, the people began to obtain rifles and, within a year or two, the caribou fences were abandoned. Today only their outlines can be seen: so quickly may one technology displace another. The native people welcomed that change, for it enabled them to harvest caribou more effectively. But they do not see the technology that Arctic Gas propose to introduce into the Northern Yukon in the same way. They see it as a threat, and they are deeply concerned about what its effects may be on their environment, their way of life and their community.

The Northern Yukon is an arctic and subarctic wilderness of incredible beauty, a rich and varied ecosystem: nine million acres of land in its natural state, inhabited by thriving populations of plants and animals. This wilderness has come down through the ages, and it is a heritage that future generations, living in an industrial world even more complex than ours, will surely cherish.

In late August, thousands of snow geese gather on the Arctic Coastal Plain to feed on the tundra grasses, sedges and berries, before embarking on the flight to their wintering grounds. Just as the caribou must build up an energy surplus to sustain them, so must the geese and, indeed, all other arctic waterfowl and shorebirds store up energy for their long southward migration to California, the Gulf Coast, or Central and South America.

The peregrine falcon, golden eagle and other birds of prey nest in the Northern Yukon. These species are dwindling in numbers because of the loss of their former ranges on the North American continent and because of toxic materials in their food. Here in these remote mountains they still nest and rear their young, undisturbed by man.

One-fifth of the world's whistling swans nest along the Arctic coast of the Yukon and in the Mackenzie Delta region. The Old Crow Flats, the Delta and the Arctic coast provide critical habitat for other waterfowl, including canvasback, scaup, scoter, wigeon, old squaw and mallard. These northern wetlands are particularly important during years of drought on the prairies. Then the waterfowl flock North in much larger numbers than usual, and are thus able to survive to breed again in the South in more favourable years.

You will find polar bear on the ice along the coast, the barren-ground grizzly on the open tundra, and the black bear around Old Crow Flats. You will find moose and Dall sheep, wolf, fox, beaver, wolverine, lynx and, of course, muskrat.

But of all the species of the Northern Yukon, the barren-ground caribou is the most important to the people of Old Crow. On this animal they have always depended for a living. The Porcupine herd, which now stands at about 110,000 animals, is one of the last great herds of North America.

The Northern Yukon is a place of contrasts: of an explosively productive but brief summer and of a long, hard winter; of rugged mountains and stark plains. Its teeming marshes and shorelands give it a beauty equalled by few other places on earth. The ecosystem is unique and vulnerable.

This is why the proposal by Arctic Gas to build a pipeline across the Northern Yukon, to open up this wilderness, poses a threat.

This ecosystem, with its magnificent wildlife and scenic beauty, has always been protected by its inaccessibility. With pipeline construction, the development of supply and service roads, the intensification of the search for oil and gas, the establishment of an energy corridor, and the increasing occupation of the Northern Yukon, it will no longer be inaccessible to man and his machines.

The proposal by Arctic Gas to build a pipeline across the Northern Yukon confronts us with a fundamental choice. It is a choice that depends not simply upon the impact of a pipeline across the Northern Yukon, but upon the impact of the establishment of a corridor across it. Opening up this country to industrial development will have lasting effects on the great wilderness and on the native people who live there.

In this chapter, I shall try to outline the full nature and consequences of that choice. Arctic Gas have proposed two possible routes through the Northern Yukon: the Coastal Route and the Interior Route. I have concluded that there are sound environmental grounds for not building the pipeline on the Coastal Route. There are also sound environmental grounds for not building it on the Interior Route, but they are not as compelling as they are in the case of the Coastal Route. However, the social impact of a pipeline along the Interior Route would be devastating to the people of Old Crow. I recommend, therefore, that no pipeline be built across the Northern Yukon along either of the proposed routes. If a pipeline must be built to carry Alaskan gas through Canada to markets in the Lower 48, then it should follow a more southern route.

Yukon Coastal Plain and British Mountains.
(E. de Bock)

Coastal tundra near mouth of Firth River.
(I. MacNeil)

*Babbage River flowing from mountains onto
Yukon Coastal Plain.* (GSC–P. Lewis)

Brooks Range. (ISL–G. Calef)

The Pipeline and the Corridor

The pipeline that Arctic Gas propose to build across the Northern Yukon would carry gas from Prudhoe Bay in Alaska to markets in the United States. This pipeline would extend eastward from Prudhoe Bay to join the Mackenzie Valley pipeline in the Delta area.

Coastal Route and Interior Route

Arctic Gas would like to build their pipeline from Alaska along the Arctic Coastal Plain of the Yukon. If they are not allowed to use the Coastal Route, they want to use a route that would bring the pipeline close to Old Crow and Old Crow Flats. This they call the Interior Route.

The Coastal Route runs from Prudhoe Bay 195 miles across Alaska to the international boundary, and 131 miles from there across the Yukon. This route is entirely on that part of the Arctic coast referred to as the north slope or the coastal plain. Arctic Gas propose to build the pipeline along the Coastal Route in winter, using a packed snow working surface and snow roads: they say they will not build a permanent, gravel road along the route. Pipe, construction materials and equipment will be shipped to wharf and stockpile sites along the Arctic coast during the summer by barge. Snow roads will be needed in winter to transfer the materials to construction sites along the right-of-way. There are two DEW Line stations on the Arctic coast of the Yukon. Some native people, most of them from Aklavik, use the

area seasonally to hunt and fish, but there are no communities.

In Alaska, the Coastal Route would cut across 133 miles of the Arctic National Wildlife Range. Because the Government of the United States may not permit Arctic Gas to build a pipeline across the Wildlife Range, the company proposed the Interior Route as an alternative to the Coastal Route. This route skirts the southwestern margin of the Wildlife Range, then swings eastward across the Yukon Territory to the Mackenzie Valley. In crossing the Brooks Range in Alaska, it passes through some 80 miles of steep-sided narrow valleys, and here construction would have to take place in summer. It would involve trenching in rock and across steep unstable talus slopes. In 1974, Arctic Gas estimated that a pipeline along the Interior Route would cost about $500 million more than one along the Coastal Route and around the Delta.

Throughout most of its length in Alaska and the Yukon Territory, the Interior Route is remote from other transportation routes. Arctic Gas propose to transport pipe, construction materials and equipment to the right-of-way by temporary winter roads from the Dempster Highway in Canada and from the Alaska State road system at Circle. Some of these access roads would be more than 100 miles long. Most of the Interior Route would be built in winter using snow roads for access; it would not require permanent gravel roads or gravel working surfaces. But the section of the route that passes through the Brooks Range, and possibly short parts of it through the Richardson Mountains, would be built from a gravel pad in summer, and Arctic Gas propose to make one of the access roads to the pipeline from the Dempster Highway a permanent road. The pipeline will, therefore, encroach in a

major way on the hunting, trapping and fishing territory of the Old Crow people. The proposed route also passes close to Fort McPherson and through hunting areas in the Yukon and the Northwest Territories that are used by native people from Fort McPherson and Aklavik.

Energy Corridor Across the Yukon

If Arctic Gas build a pipeline across the Northern Yukon along either the Coastal Route or the Interior Route (or any other route), we cannot assume that no other energy transportation systems will follow. The Pipeline Guidelines foresee that, once a gas pipeline is built across the Yukon, an energy transportation corridor will have been established and another pipeline will follow. That is why the Pipeline Guidelines insist that, in assessing the impact of the first pipeline, it is necessary to consider also the cumulative impact of a second pipeline and any other industrial development along the route. Nonetheless, Arctic Gas based their case on only the initial gas pipeline. In my opinion, this approach is unrealistic. Once an overland route has been approved for a gas pipeline from the north slope of Alaska to markets in the Lower 48, oil and gas exploration in the North will be intensified. Oil and gas exploration and development in Northern Alaska is only just beginning, and the petroleum potential of the Alaska North Slope province is very large. Even at Prudhoe Bay, present planned production of oil and gas is based on incomplete knowledge of the full extent of the field. Dr. Robert Weeden, speaking for the Government of Alaska, said:

The location of the proposed pipeline corridor

facilities could in turn lead to the development of oil and gas within the Arctic National Wildlife Range, as well as the Beaufort Sea Offshore Province specifically, and could influence the development of the entire Alaskan arctic coastal area including Naval Petroleum Reserve Number 4, which lies to the west of the Colville River and encompasses approximately 23 million acres. [F7462]

Moreover, construction of a pipeline along either the Coastal or the Interior Route would accelerate oil and gas exploration and development in the Yukon Territory. Thus, if the Coastal Route is used, exploration may be expected on the coastal plain and offshore, beneath the shallow waters of the Beaufort Sea. On the other hand, if the Interior Route is chosen, it would spur oil and gas exploration on the Old Crow Flats and the Eagle Plains. The latter area has already been extensively explored and some petroleum discovered.

I consider that, once a gas pipeline is built across the Northern Yukon, increased exploration is inevitable. There will be demands for a second gas pipeline and, later, a hot oil pipeline. Vern Horte, President of Arctic Gas, told the Inquiry it is likely that the whole Arctic Gas pipeline system would be looped. An oil pipeline, for at least part of its length, would be elevated rather than buried in the ground to avoid the adverse effects of the hot oil pipe in ice-rich permafrost. Also, a permanent road or roads would probably be built to service the oil pipeline and other facilities and to provide access to the energy corridor.

Man and the Land: Old Crow

The people of Old Crow are the only people who live permanently in the Northern Yukon. What does the land mean to them? When I took the Inquiry to their village, they told me that, in their view, the construction of a pipeline across the Northern Yukon would change their homeland and their way of life forever.

The Arctic Gas pipeline on the proposed Interior Route would pass between the village of Old Crow and Old Crow Flats. If this route were followed, a construction camp of 800 workers would be established near the village. The people of Old Crow do not look forward to that prospect, but, at the same time, they oppose a pipeline along the Coastal Route, because of the threat it represents to the calving grounds of the Porcupine herd on the coastal plain: they believe that the decline of the herd would undermine their way of life. Whichever route the gas pipeline takes, it may be followed by an oil pipeline, and by increased gas and oil exploration and development along the route. The people of Old Crow realize the implications of this.

The whole village told me they were opposed to the pipeline. I heard 81 people testify; virtually everyone, man and woman, young and old, spoke and they spoke with one voice. Here are the words of 21-year-old Louise Frost, who expressed the feelings of her people:

> I can see our country being destroyed and my people pushed on reservations, and the white men taking over as they please. ... The pipeline is only the beginning of all this. If it ever does come through, there will be a time when other companies will want to join in on this. Any major development that has taken

place in the North has been of a rapid nature. Their only purpose in coming here is to extract the non-renewable resources, not to the benefit of northerners, but of ... southern Canadians and Americans. To really bring the whole picture into focus, you can describe it as the rape of the northland to satisfy the greed and the needs of southern consumers, and when development of this nature happens, it only destroys; it does not leave any permanent jobs for people who make the North their home. The whole process does not leave very much for us to be proud of, and along with their equipment and technology, they also impose on the northern people their white culture and all its value systems, which leaves nothing to the people who have been living off the land for thousands of years. So to put it bluntly, the process of the white man is destroying the Indian ways of life. [C1569ff.]

To assess the environmental and social impact of a pipeline across the Northern Yukon, we must understand the relation between the people of Old Crow and the land and animals.

The fall caribou hunt, when the animals migrate southward to their winter range, after they have fed and fattened on the coastal plain and the nearby mountains, has always been the most important event in the yearly cycle of the Old Crow people. They believe the pipeline will interfere with the caribou migration and break what they see is the essential link between their past and their future. Peter Charlie told the Inquiry about the caribou migration:

> People used to travel back and forth ... and in the fall after the freeze-up, the caribou would migrate up around Driftwood River, and they crossed the river there, and when the caribou does that, that means that there's going to be caribou amongst the timber country. And when they hear that, it makes the people very happy that the caribou have migrated into the timber country. Now, this migration that I am telling you about happened many, many

The village of Old Crow. (I. MacNeil)

Louise Frost. (J. Falls)

Father Jean-Marie Mouchet. (J. Falls)

Old Crow. (E. Peterson)

years ago. Now today, the caribou still migrate the same way. Every fall, my children go up the river, and they get the meat from where these caribou migrate. Now today, I hear about the pipeline that is going through, it's going to spoil all these routes where the caribou migrate. It really makes me sad to hear about the pipeline. [C1390ff.]

The Old Crow people fear that the proposed pipeline, whether it follows the Interior or the Coastal Route, would adversely affect the Porcupine caribou herd and therefore their way of life. A pipeline on the Coastal Route would disturb the caribou on their calving range and could reduce the size of the herd. A pipeline along the Interior Route could interfere with the herd's migration pattern and thus with the people's ability to hunt them. If the herd's migration routes were altered, the people of Old Crow might be as effectively deprived of caribou as they would be if the herd were diminished.

The people of Old Crow are also concerned about the impact of the Interior Route on the Old Crow Flats and on the animal and fish populations there. Peter Lord explained:

> The Crow Flats is the migrating ground for caribou, and also it's a breeding ground for moose in summer. . . . Also, we use it for muskrat. It is a good breeding ground for muskrat and . . . for furbearing animals, such as fox, lynx, mink and sometimes marten [and] wolverine. . . . Its many streams . . . all carry fish, and it's a very good spawning place for fish in the summer. All fish go up Crow River and into the little creeks and up to the little lakes. [C1284]

The spring muskrat hunt on Old Crow Flats is an event of cultural and economic significance to the people of the village. It provides meat, cash from the sale of fur, and an opportunity for the whole family to get out onto the land.

The people fear not only the impact of the Interior Route on Old Crow Flats but also the gas and oil exploration that they believe would follow the grant of a right-of-way and the designation of an energy corridor. The threat of the Interior Route is obvious and immediate. Alfred Charlie, speaking through an interpreter, put it this way:

> One time he went to Whitehorse to a meeting about this Crow Flats, and there were a lot of people in that meeting from different places. . . . He told those people that if people start to come to Crow Flats to drill for oil and do their seismic in Crow Flats, they will probably mess up the place, and then probably if they strike oil under Crow Flats, everything will be messed up. . . . He told those people, some of you are working, some of you are government people; you make money, you put money in the bank. He said [Old Crow] people don't do that; they don't put money in the bank, but when they want to make money, they use Crow Flats for a bank, they go back there to trap and hunt muskrat so they use it as a bank. . . .

> He heard lots of good things about the pipeline from different people from the oil companies . . . but we don't hear no bad things, everything is going to be perfect. But there's going to be trucks, there's going to be bulldozers and other vehicles that travel over the land, and all these travel by power, oil power and gas power, and they will be refuelling different places and they are going to spill a lot of oil on the ground. . . . They will pollute the water with it. Perhaps fish will get sick from this, too. Suppose we eat fish like that and people don't expect to live healthy with that kind of food. Our main food in Crow Flats is muskrat . . . and supposing we eat sick muskrat from this polluted water. [C1358ff.]

These concerns are shared by all generations at Old Crow. Lorraine Netro, 19 years old, testified:

> I was born and raised in Old Crow. . . . The proposed pipeline route is supposed to be put through the most important piece of land to the Old Crow people, the Old Crow Flats. I do not agree with this pipeline route at all. . . . The young people, my generation now, will need this land for our future, and also for the future of our children. We depend on this land as much as our parents do. . . . If the pipeline comes through, what will become of our future? . . . Are we going to look forward to dead or sick muskrats floating around in the polluted lakes, or forests with no birds singing? I do not think any . . . person will even go out into this kind of country to try to hunt in that kind of hunting ground. All that they could do is to remember how beautiful and rich this land used to be. I do not want to see this happen to our land, and to our people. . . . I hope we can keep on living the way we are today, for tomorrow and forever, developing in our own way for generations to come. I do not want the proposed pipeline route through our country. [C1560ff.]

The Old Crow people expressed deep concern about the impact the construction of the pipeline would have on the social fabric of the village. They feel that, whichever route the pipeline follows, new people and new influences will come to undermine the traditional values of the village. When the development cycle has run its course, the Old Crow they know today will no longer exist. Marie Bruce testified:

> Meaningful existence means a lot to the people of Old Crow. It is probably the most important thing in a person's life. I [would] like Old Crow to be the way it is today. . . . Old Crow will end up deserted like Dawson City . . . in 1898, there was a gold rush in Dawson and people from all over the world went there. When it was over, everyone left Dawson City. This also will happen to Old Crow. It will be very hard to go back to your own way of life after this happens. . . . It is a good feeling when you have nothing or no one to fear in Old Crow. Everyone knows each other here, and they all help make it a better place to live. . . . You can still go to bed here without locking your doors, and you can still walk alone at night without any fear. [C1529ff.]

James Allen is an Indian employed at Old Crow by the Yukon Lands and Forest Service. He had this to say:

> If the pipeline moved a camp of 800 men near Old Crow, I think it would be disastrous for the community as a whole. Many of the social diseases which have destroyed many Indian communities in the South would move in, such as alcoholism, child abuse, mental and physical health, broken homes, broken marriages, and many other points that break down a healthy society. Also, where there are 800 men, some sort of liquor outlet soon follows. Liquor would become easily obtainable in the village. The white people say money is the root of all evil, but in our Indian communities today, liquor is the root of all evil. [C1559ff.]

The white people who live in Old Crow feel the same way. The Anglican minister, the Reverend Mr. John Watts, told the Inquiry that, although the church is still important in the lives of the villagers, he feared the situation would change with pipeline construction and the presence of many outsiders. The serious impact of the Alaska Highway on native communities in the Southern Yukon, a generation ago, undermined native values and community life there; he feared that this history may be repeated in Old Crow.

Father Jean-Marie Mouchet, the Roman Catholic priest at Old Crow, told the Inquiry of the code that governs life in Old Crow: it is a complex web of shared understanding and experience within which people carry on their lives. Father Mouchet expressed the fear that outsiders, attracted to the region by the pipeline, would neither understand nor respect this code.

Herta Richter, a nurse in Old Crow, opposed the pipeline:

> ... the pipeline will certainly be a great disaster to this area, and I'm not sure if I could tolerate to stay here after it comes. It would be too painful to see the change in these people and in the surroundings. [C1579]

The people of Old Crow have expressed their fears about a pipeline along the Interior Route, which would be, of course, an immediate threat to their village. But they know, also, that a pipeline along the Coastal Route would threaten the calving grounds of the Porcupine caribou herd, and, if a pipeline along the Coastal Route were to lead to the loss of the herd, the impact of its loss on their village and on their way of life would be great. The choice we have to make is not, therefore, between the Coastal Route and the Interior Route. The choice is whether or not we should build a pipeline across the Northern Yukon at all. The preservation and maintenance of the Porcupine caribou herd are of fundamental importance to the survival of the people of Old Crow.

To the people of Old Crow, the pipeline is symbolic of the white man's ways and his values. Their opposition to the pipeline is so strongly and deeply felt that a decision to proceed with it in the face of their opposition will be to them the clearest affirmation that their way of life and everything they cherish as valuable is, in the eyes of the white society, worthless. It would mean the end of Old Crow as the people know it.

I will turn later to the views of social scientists on this subject, but the people of Old Crow have summed up the situation for themselves. Indeed, there is as much wisdom in Old Crow as there is in Ottawa. In the words of Alice Frost:

> Do [the white people] have a right to ask us to give up this beautiful land of ours? Do they have a right to spoil our land and to destroy our wild game for their benefit? Do they have any right to ask us to change our way of life, that we have lived for centuries? Do they have any right ... to decide our future? We live peacefully ... in harmony with nature,

here in Old Crow. You won't find very many places like this left in this world. [C1566]

Porcupine Caribou Herd

Sensitivities and Concerns

The Porcupine caribou herd, comprising 110,000 animals or more, ranges throughout the Northern Yukon and into Alaska. It is one of the last great caribou herds, and it accounts for about 20 percent of the caribou in North America. The Porcupine herd has flourished until now because of the isolation of its range. The only communities within it are Old Crow in the Yukon and Kaktovik and Arctic Village in Alaska. The herd is vulnerable to the changes that will accompany industrial development and increased contact with man.

A caribou "herd" is defined as a group of animals that calve in a traditional area different from that used by other groups. The calving grounds of the Porcupine herd are on the Arctic Coastal Plain — on the tundra near the shore of the Beaufort Sea in Northwestern Yukon and Northeastern Alaska. Every spring the Porcupine herd leaves the spruce forests of the interior of the Yukon — the Ogilvie Mountains, the Eagle Plains and the Richardson Mountains — where they have wintered, to travel hundreds of miles north to calve. They begin their journey, which may cover 800 miles, in March. At first they move slowly, and they usually reach the Porcupine River late in April. We still do not know how the caribou learn to follow their migration routes, but we do know that in their migration to the coast they leave behind most of the wolf population — a major predator — which dens during April

Caribou herd. (G. Calef)

Caribou calf harassed by biting insects. (C. Dauphiné Jr.)

Little Bell River, Yukon Territory. (ISL—G. Calef)

Caribou on winter range. (G. Calef)

and May. The arrival of the herd at the calving grounds in late May or early June, before the blood-sucking insects emerge, is predictable.

Calving takes place between late May and mid-June on the sedge meadows and the ridges of the coastal plain and the foothills from Babbage River in the Yukon to Camden Bay in Alaska. After the calves are born, the animals come together to escape the impact of the mosquitoes and botflies and begin to move eastward along the coast. This post-calving aggregation of a large part of the Porcupine herd within a few square miles is one of the last remaining marvels of the natural world in North America. It may be compared to the massing of buffalo, a sight that will never be seen again.

The herd continues its post-calving migration eastward along the coastal plain through July, but by August it begins to migrate southward towards the fall and winter range. In September large numbers of caribou pass through Old Crow Flats, crossing the Porcupine River later in the same month. The rut occurs in mid-October in the mountains.

Most of the Porcupine caribou herd spends nine months of the year in the interior of the Yukon and Alaska. This country offers both open habitat and forest, and in it caribou can move from low areas to higher ground to locate favourable plant or snow conditions, or relief from insects. This herd may be in a better position than other Canadian herds to avoid sudden losses by the failure of a given plant food, or unfavourable weather.

Most of the biologists who gave evidence at the Inquiry regard continued use of the calving grounds as essential to the survival of the herd: any interference with them or with the post-calving aggregation could be critical. They argued, therefore, against

building the pipeline along the Coastal Route through the calving grounds. If the pipeline is to be built, most thought it should follow the Interior Route. But they were not unanimous. Dr. Frank Banfield, a consultant to Arctic Gas, said that the animals are, in fact, more vulnerable on their winter range, when they are widely dispersed foraging for food in the snow. He thought that pipeline construction during the winter along the Interior Route, through the midst of the herd's winter range, would disturb the herd when the pregnant females are vulnerable. He thought that a pipeline should be built along the Coastal Route.

The crux of the dispute among the experts centres on the question, which is more important to the caribou, their limited calving grounds or their vast winter range? The calving grounds cover about 4,000 square miles on the coastal plain; the winter range covers about 60,000 square miles.

I think the calving grounds are absolutely vital to the herd during the calving season, and interference with the herd at that time and at that place must be avoided. Caribou are more sensitive to disturbance when they are calving and immediately afterward than they are at other times of the year. Disturbance could prevent or delay movement of pregnant cows to the calving grounds, forcing them to calve in unsuitable areas where predation or other factors may cause a very high loss of newborn calves. The first 24 hours of the calf's life are crucial: it is then the cow and the calf learn to know one another, so that when they join the herd of thousands of animals they will be able to find each other. The females seem to require a short sedentary period to learn to recognize their calves. When the herds are disturbed, females and young are frequently separated. For example, a helicopter forced by fog to fly

low across the calving grounds would be a serious disturbance to the caribou — and fog is common along the north coast. A single such flight could cause the loss of many calves.

Once the calves begin to nurse, the cows join together in small groups and, when the mosquito season arrives, the herd gathers to limit the impact of these insects. The animals are thin when they arrive on the coast in June, but they are sleek and fat by the end of August. The herd is under great stress after calving, for mosquitoes and other insects attack them relentlessly. At this time, also, the animals' energy demands for nursing and for antler growth are at their maximum. The greatest loss of calves occurs at this season, and the herd may go for several years before enough calves survive to replace the natural losses among the adults, but over the years the delicate balance of the herd is maintained.

The Porcupine herd has not been subjected to any great slaughter since the days of whaling at the turn of the century, when significant numbers of caribou were killed every year to feed the crews overwintering on the Arctic coast. Today animals from this land are taken principally by native people from Old Crow, Aklavik and Fort McPherson in Canada and Kaktovik and Arctic Village in Alaska. Each of these communities takes some 500 animals each year, and the total annual kill is about 4,000 animals, a tolerable level given the present condition and size of the herd. But this picture is changing. The Dempster Highway now crosses part of the winter range of the herd, and already hunters on it may be taking 500 caribou annually. Obviously this new harvest will have to be watched with care.

Caribou are disturbed by any unfamiliar sight or noise. Low-flying aircraft may cause the herd to run and even to stampede, frights that use up great amounts of energy. The animals are disturbed by people, machinery and sudden noises, such as blasting, and when these annoyances are repeated, they can be driven from their ranges. Dr. Peter Lent, a biologist from the University of Alaska, explained that the migratory barren-ground caribou is a wilderness species that can survive only in a wilderness where it has virtually untrammelled access to a vast range. Lent said that when other caribou populations have shrunk, they retreated from peripheral ranges, but they persisted in returning to the same calving grounds. He therefore urged the protection of the calving grounds and the post-calving area on the coast.

Dr. George Calef presented to the Inquiry an analysis of recorded changes in the size of various caribou herds during their contact with industrial man. The Fortymile herd used to roam the Yukon Territory and east central Alaska. In 1920, Olaus J. Murie estimated this herd to be 568,000 animals, but its population stands today at something like 6,000 animals. The Nelchina herd of Southeast Alaska consisted of 70,000 animals in 1962; by 1973, it had been reduced to only 8,000 animals. The Kaminuriak herd used to winter in Northern Manitoba. Although the Hudson Bay Railway, built in the late 1920s, crossed their winter range, the herd continued to use it for many years. By the early 1960s, however, the caribou had stopped crossing the railway, and they no longer foraged south of the Churchill River. The herd stood at 149,000 in 1955 and at 63,000 in 1967. Dr. David Klein has written about the gradual abandonment of ranges in Scandinavia by reindeer, after their migration routes had been interrupted by rail or highway traffic.

Calef said that there is not sufficient evidence to prove that the decline of any given herd can be attributed to the presence of man and his works. He was careful to say that we do not know exactly what caused the decline of these herds. Nonetheless, it is clear that a number of herds have abandoned parts of their ranges and they have decreased in numbers after they came in contact with industrial man. In my judgment the evidence, though circumstantial, is compelling. Increased access to the Porcupine herd and increased human and industrial activity can be expected to have major adverse impacts on the herd.

Coastal Route
Impacts on Caribou

More than 300 miles of the Coastal Route proposed by Arctic Gas lie within the range of the Porcupine caribou herd. Moreover, 200 miles of the route crosses the herd's principal calving range. Although only a small part of the herd winters near the Coastal Route during some years (for example, 5,000 animals wintered along the Arctic coast of the Yukon in 1974), most of the herd occupies ground along it during early summer. Each year, in May, June and July, virtually the whole herd moves onto the north slope for its migration to the calving grounds, the calving itself, the post-calving aggregation, and the post-calving migration. The massed herd is highly vulnerable to disturbance throughout these stages of its annual cycle.

The Arctic Gas proposal is to build this section of the pipeline in winter, when there are normally few if any caribou in the area; to cease work if caribou approach any area of pipeline construction; to limit and control

construction-related activities and operational or maintenance activities in the summer, when caribou are in the area; to control the altitude of aircraft over caribou; and to prevent construction personnel from hunting. On the basis of these elements of the proposal, both of the wildlife consultants retained by Arctic Gas, Banfield and Ronald Jakimchuk, testified that the project will not have a significant impact on the Porcupine caribou herd. This must be considered an optimistic view of the project.

Notwithstanding the emphasis on winter construction, there will be summer activities at wharves and stockpile sites along the coast, barge activity, traffic on roads, construction at compressor and camp sites, aircraft and helicopter flights and many related activities as well as workers moving about in construction areas and probably elsewhere. After completion of the pipeline, some of these summer activities would continue; there would be compressor and other noises peculiar to pipeline operation; and there may be summer maintenance or repairs. It is worth noting that the time of maximum concern for caribou along the Coastal Route — the calving and post-calving period — coincides with the time of snow melt and river break-up, when the pipeline will need to be checked frequently and when emergency repairs may be required. The United States Department of the Interior, in reviewing concerns over the impact of the Arctic Gas project on the calving herd, in the context of the measures proposed by Arctic Gas to mitigate these impacts, concluded:

Increased access, disturbance by aircraft and ground vehicles on the calving ground, summer borrow activities, and shipping activities all will act adversely on the herd. Disturbance

Arctic Gas' environmental panel (background) at the formal hearings, Yellowknife. (T. Chretien)

Caribou cows and calves. (ISL—G. Calef)

Caribou crossing Porcupine River. (G. Calef)

Caribou carcasses on the bank of Porcupine River near Old Crow. (G. Calef)

factors associated with material staging, construction, and operation of the compressor stations will add to the adverse, long-term impact on the herd. It is probable that these impacts will result in some reduction in herd numbers. If the animals abandon the traditional calving grounds and portions of their summer range, a major reduction (more than 50 percent) in herd size could result. [Final Environmental Impact Statement, Alaska Volume, p. 421]

Arctic Gas have assumed that all of their construction plans and schedules will be met, and that no activities planned for winter will spill over into the calving and post-calving period. But the Inquiry also heard a great deal of testimony about possible delays in construction scheduling on the north slope caused by snow road problems and by worker productivity problems in the dark and extreme cold. Any delays of this nature would increase work pressures at the end of the construction season, with the likelihood that certain activities would be carried over into the period when the calving herd has reached the north slope. Moreover, it could become necessary to transfer some activities from winter to summer, with associated increases in summer movements of men, machinery and aircraft, and consequent increases in impact on the herd.

In view of the above, I cannot share the opinion of Arctic Gas and their consultants that the gas pipeline along the Coastal Route would have little detrimental effect on the Porcupine caribou herd. Rather, it is clear that the pipeline could have highly adverse effects on the caribou during the calving and post-calving period. Thus, it is not surprising that the caribou biologists — except for those retained by Arctic Gas — have taken the position that no pipeline should be built along the Coastal Route through the calving grounds.

The case made by Arctic Gas in favour of the Coastal Route, and the support of this case by their biological consultants (except for Dr. William Gunn, their ornithological consultant), is based upon a consideration of the pipeline in isolation from other corridor developments. In fact, Jakimchuk said that he would not countenance an oil pipeline along either the Coastal Route or the Interior Route. But we cannot consider the gas pipeline in isolation; rather we must consider the pipeline together with the other developments that can be expected to follow it along the energy corridor.

It is really not practical to say that the gas pipeline should be approved, but that no other development should be permitted later. Construction of the gas pipeline would probably be followed by looping of the gas line, construction of an oil pipeline, and a road or roads to service the oil pipeline and perhaps the other developments. Approval of the initial development by Canada and the United States would spur petroleum exploration on the coastal plain and the adjacent offshore region, which could lead to development of producing fields feeding into the energy corridor. These activities could not fail to aggravate the adverse impact on the calving herd that has been postulated above for the gas pipeline alone. Each new development in the corridor would bring additional workers, aircraft, barge traffic, vehicles, machinery, and destruction of habitat. Disturbance would inevitably increase during the calving period. Multiple facilities would be much more likely to deflect migratory caribou than a single buried gas pipeline, even though overpasses and underpasses might be provided at intervals along above-ground structures. An oil pipeline would be elevated for part or all of

its length across the Northern Yukon, as would feeder lines from producing wells.

What would be the effect on the Porcupine caribou herd of these multiple and sequential developments taking place on the calving grounds? The effect certainly would be much more severe than that of the gas pipeline alone, which the United States Department of the Interior concluded could cause a "major reduction (more than 50 percent) in herd size," should the animals "abandon the traditional calving grounds and portions of their summer range." [op. cit., p. 421] The evidence brought before me concerning decreases in the population of various caribou herds following the entry of industrial activity into their range is complex and circumstantial, but I find it compelling. I think it is likely that industrial development in the coastal calving and post-calving grounds would reduce the Porcupine caribou herd to a remnant.

Interior Route
Impacts on Caribou

Throughout most of its length from Prudhoe Bay to the eastern border of the Yukon Territory, the proposed Interior Route traverses ranges used by the Porcupine caribou herd during winter and during the spring and fall migrations. Thus, caribou are found at various places along the proposed route from August until early March. Construction during winter, as proposed by Arctic Gas, would encounter caribou not only during winter but also during the early stages of their northward spring migration in April and early May. Such encounters would occur not only along the route itself but also along the long access roads that Arctic Gas propose to build to transport pipe, fuel and other supplies required for construction. Three such roads in the Yukon would connect the pipeline route to the Dempster Highway.

Construction and operation of the gas pipeline along the Interior Route could have impacts on caribou caused by the presence of people, operation of machinery and vehicles, aircraft noise, and destruction of habitat by fire. Migrating caribou could be deflected from their normal migration routes by construction or other activities along the pipeline or access roads, and, in the absence of disturbing activities, caribou might follow the cleared right-of-way or roads. These departures from normal migration patterns could have adverse effects on the herd itself, and could cause difficulty for the native people who hunt the caribou according to their traditional migration patterns. A gas pipeline along the Interior Route and access routes from the Dempster Highway to the pipeline would open up to hunters from outside the area large parts of the fall and winter range of the Porcupine herd that are now accessible only to the people of Old Crow. If there were a substantial increase in the number of caribou killed by outsiders, caribou harvesting by the Old Crow people could be affected and, over the long term, the overall size of the herd could be reduced.

In the paragraphs above, I have considered the potential effect of a gas pipeline on the Porcupine caribou herd along the Interior Route, but, as in the case of the Coastal Route, we should not consider the gas pipeline in isolation. We are bound to consider the cumulative impact of the gas pipeline, the looping of the gas pipeline, an oil pipeline and probably a road or roads. A gas pipeline along the Interior Route would also spur petroleum exploration (perhaps leading to production) in the Eagle Plains part of the

herd's range, and would lead to pressure on the government to permit exploration in the Old Crow Flats. This complex of industrial development, even if it were kept under the strictest control, would magnify many times the adverse effects on the Porcupine herd.

What then are the implications of the Interior Route for the caribou? We have seen that combined pipeline and corridor development along the Coastal Route would have a devastating impact on the whole herd by causing disturbance during the calving and post-calving periods. I have reviewed the arguments of the biologists that the caribou are less vulnerable in winter and along the Interior Route, but have noted Banfield's statement on the importance of overwintering conditions in maintaining the caribou population and Jakimchuk's conclusion that "the migratory periods are the most vital elements in the life cycle of the barren-ground caribou, the weakest link in the chain." [F13480]

Taking all the evidence into consideration, I think that a gas pipeline by itself along the Interior Route would not drastically reduce the herd, and that carefully controlled development along the Interior Route would have a less severe effect on the herd than development along the Coastal Route. Nonetheless, the cumulative effect of multiple facilities following the initial gas pipeline along an interior energy corridor, combined with the effect of the Dempster Highway, would undoubtedly be highly detrimental to the herd. It could substantially reduce the herd's numbers and, of course, it would undermine the caribou-based economy of the Old Crow people.

Dempster Highway
Impacts on Caribou

Upon completion, the Dempster Highway will connect Mackenzie Delta and Dawson City in the Yukon. It crosses the wintering grounds and migration routes of the Porcupine caribou, and this, it is said, represents a great threat to the herd. In determining the impact of a pipeline along either route, and in recommending terms and conditions to ameliorate its impact, we must consider the impact of the Dempster Highway as well.

The highway passes through more than 250 miles of caribou winter range. During migration, the highway and its traffic could deflect the animals from their normal migration routes or disrupt their normal migration schedule. Migrating caribou are subject to disturbance by men and machines. To a degree, they can tolerate the close presence of men, if they have not learned to associate men with harassment and injury. We know from experience at Prudhoe Bay and elsewhere that caribou in small groups can become used to vehicular traffic. In general, however, any road along which vehicles pass frequently is almost impassable for herds of caribou. The Dempster Highway will form a barrier to passage of the herd and, much more important, it will increase the access to the herd by hunters. With regard to the Dempster Highway, Jakimchuk said:

> I feel that there is a distinct threat to the Porcupine herd. This threat constitutes human access through their winter range and through one of their major spring migration routes. [F14326ff.]

At present, only about 4,000 animals are taken by hunting each year from the Porcupine caribou herd in the Yukon and Alaska. This a is tolerable level. But unrestricted

Dempster Highway construction. (J. Inglis)

Muskrat feeding. (CWS)

Wolverine. (NFB–Hoffman)

Timber wolf. (C. & M. Hampson)

access for other hunters via the Dempster Highway would lead to intolerable pressure on the herd. Jakimchuk and other biologists highlighted the need to develop and implement controls over hunting along the highway to avoid this threat to the herd. Such controls are needed, not only along the highway itself, but also on hunting from winter roads, seismic lines and other access routes that have been and will be open to people travelling along the highway. The impact of the Dempster Highway can, I think, be limited, if appropriate measures are taken. I intend to set out my recommendations in that regard in Volume Two of this report. They will include restrictions on hunting along and near the highway.

The Dempster Highway is near completion, but Jakimchuk and Arctic Gas have estimated the impact of the gas pipeline on caribou without taking into account the impact of the completed highway. In my opinion, this is not realistic. The completed highway and its traffic, as well as hunting from it, will have placed the herd under stress before any pipeline is built. Therefore, a pipeline and an energy corridor along either the Coastal or the Interior Route would affect the herd already under pressure from the highway, not the herd as it exists now.

But the Dempster Highway's impact on the herd will be nothing like as great as that of a pipeline along the Coastal Route because the highway does not go near the calving grounds. It impinges on the winter range, but not in a way that is likely to deprive the animals of significant habitat. The herd can survive the loss of part of its wintering range, but it could not survive the loss of its calving grounds.

Other Environmental Concerns

The most obvious and important environmental impacts of a pipeline and an energy corridor across the Northern Yukon would be on the Porcupine caribou herd and on the fall staging snow geese. But, the overall effect of the proposed pipeline and corridor would involve virtually all components of the environment — birds, mammals, fish, and the landscape itself. These incremental effects taken together would bring about fundamental changes in the ecosystem, destroy the wilderness character of the region, reduce the populations of some species, and reduce the potential harvest of renewable resources. Some of these effects would be greater along one route than the other, and some would affect both routes equally.

Mammals

Various mammal populations, in addition to the Porcupine caribou herd, would decline as a consequence of pipeline and energy corridor development. The grizzly bear population and the small wolverine population, for instance, may be expected to decline following human encroachment on their ranges along either route. Wolves would be more vulnerable in the tundra region along the Coastal Route than in the forest. Polar bears occur only along the coast, and would be adversely affected by development there. Dall sheep would be affected along the Interior Route where it passes through the Brooks Range in Alaska and also along the Coastal/Circum-Delta Route where it skirts the base of Mount Goodenough. Muskrats

are not highly susceptible to the kinds of disturbance associated with a gas pipeline and an energy corridor, but a pipeline along the Interior Route close to the Old Crow Flats could cause short-term decreases in the muskrat population in some parts of the Flats, and some disruption of muskrat harvesting by the Old Crow people.

Fish

The Inquiry heard extensive testimony regarding the serious disturbance to local fish populations (particularly arctic char) that would accompany pipeline construction along the Coastal Route. Removal of water from streams and lakes during winter would harm overwintering fish or eggs. Moreover, winter construction of river crossings and the growth of a frost bulb around pipe buried under a riverbed may impede the flow of water into ponds used by overwintering fish. Gravel removal from river channels would be a hazard to spawning and migration of fish.

These and similar impacts can be limited through remedial or ameliorative measures, but uncertainties over adherence to construction schedules and over plans for snow roads leave in doubt the effectiveness of such measures. Even under well-regulated conditions, construction along the north slope might damage fish populations overwintering in confined spring-fed pools by a lowered water level, siltation, chemical pollution (for example, fuel spills) and increased fishing. The development of an energy corridor with an oil pipeline, a road, and perhaps other facilities, would greatly increase these hazards. Thus Dr. Norman Wilimovsky, of the Environment Protection Board, told the Inquiry that:

in carrying out an impact assessment of the

aquatic environment, one must plan for the greatest impact ... [and] if one rates a gas pipeline as one level of danger, an oil pipeline would be three to five times greater, and in my estimation, a road six to ten times more dangerous than an oil pipeline. [F6168]

The consensus of the biologists who appeared before the Inquiry was that a gas pipeline along the Interior Route in Canada would be a greater threat to fish than a gas pipeline along the Coastal Route because of the diversity of fish in the Porcupine River drainage, the importance of fish to the Old Crow people, and the international importance of the Porcupine River salmon runs. These risks would be multiplied many times if an oil pipeline or a road or both followed the same general route.

Birds

Both the Coastal and Interior Routes have the potential for major impacts on birds, but the magnitude and number of anticipated impacts are greater along the Coastal Route because it crosses an area of critical importance for migratory birds. There is a special concern for the fall staging snow geese on the Coastal Route, which will be discussed more fully below.

Among the many species of birds that summer along the pipeline route in the Northern Yukon, two groups are of particular concern. The first group includes species that are rare and relatively rare, especially birds of prey such as the peregrine falcon and the golden eagle. Birds of prey nest along both routes, and along any other route that could be chosen across the Northern Yukon, but impact on them appears likely to be greater along the Interior Route.

The second group includes populations of waterfowl, which congregate in large flocks in relatively confined areas or within limited ranges during some critical parts of their life cycle. Such concentrated populations are found on the Old Crow Flats, north of the Interior Route, and along the full length of the Coastal Route in the Yukon and Alaska.

Old Crow Flats are a waterfowl-production area of continental importance, with breeding populations of ducks of up to 170,000. Fortunately, the Interior Route avoids this critical area but the bird populations could still be adversely affected by frequent aircraft overflights at low level, increased human access, fuel spills into creeks that drain into the Flats, and exploration activities. If an oil pipeline follows the gas pipeline, a pipe failure could cause oil to leak into the Old Crow Flats and become a very serious threat to these large populations of migratory waterfowl.

The coastal plain of the Yukon and Alaska is an important nesting and moulting area for ducks, geese, swans, loons and various shorebirds. It is the fall staging area for snow geese, which in some years number in the hundreds of thousands. The nearshore waters are used for moulting by thousands of ducks, and the coastal area in general serves as a migration corridor, both eastward and westward, for millions of waterfowl and shorebirds.

Although Arctic Gas propose to carry out their main construction activities along the Coastal Route in winter, when there are few birds in the area, they cannot eliminate all concern for the project's impact on birds. During summer, in the construction period, there will be aircraft and barge movements; activities at the coastal stockpile sites, compressor sites and airfields; and perhaps gravel operations and other activities along the pipeline route. During operation of the pipeline, there will be noise from compressors and from blow-down, aircraft and barge movement, vehicles, and probably repair and maintenance work. During both construction and operation, fuel could be spilled into coastal waters from onshore storage tanks or from barges or barge-unloading. The birds could be adversely affected if the lakes they use for nesting and feeding are contaminated or made turbid, or if the removal of water from them during winter for snow roads or pipe testing caused lower water levels to persist into the summer. Finally, there could be physical disturbance of the coastal beaches, bars and spits that are of critical importance to the birds.

Arctic Gas have proposed various measures to reduce or to avoid adverse impacts on birds, and Volume Two of this report will recommend measures to protect bird populations. Nonetheless, adverse effects on them would be an inevitable complement to a gas pipeline on the Coastal Route. Our basic concern for these birds, and our objective in protecting them, is to permit these international migratory populations to continue to use this region year after year without having their numbers progressively diminished. I have heard various opinions on whether or not the gas pipeline by itself would cause an unavoidable or substantial reduction in the bird populations that use the coast, but it is significant that all of the bird specialists would prefer that the pipeline should not follow the Coastal Route. And, if we consider the gas pipeline, not in isolation but as the first step in the development of an energy corridor along the Coastal Route, then it appears that the cumulative effect of these developments would inevitably lead to progressive decline in some bird populations.

Snow geese. (C. & M. Hampson)

Whistling swan protecting young.
(C. & M. Hampson)

Yukon coast showing spits, islands and bays used
by shorebirds and waterfowl. (I. MacNeil)

Newly hatched whistling swans. (C. & M. Hampson)

Snow Geese

In late August, great flocks of snow geese gather on the Yukon Coastal Plain, the adjacent coastal plain in Alaska, and the outer parts of the Mackenzie Delta. For about a month, they graze near the proposed Coastal Route, building up energy for their long southward flight. Disturbance of the birds during this highly critical period of energy build-up could mean that some of them, both juveniles and adults, might not have the stamina to complete their southward migration. In the long term, pipeline and corridor development could lead to decline of this internationally important goose population.

The lesser snow geese of the Pacific Flyway winter primarily in the Central Valley of California. In spring, they fly north to nest in large colonies in the western Canadian Arctic and on Wrangel Island off the coast of northeastern Siberia. The Pipeline Application Assessment Group has described the Canadian population of these geese as follows:

Each spring, thousands of birds return from their wintering areas in the southern United States by way of the Mackenzie River Valley. They require open water, and they rest, feed and mate on the partly flooded river islands and on nearby lakes after the break-up of the river ice. Their destinations are the few suitable nesting areas at the mouths of the Anderson and Smoke Rivers (Northwest Terriories), Banks Island, and a few small scattered sites near the marine interface of the Mackenzie Delta. Snow geese are colonial nesters, returning each year to the same areas. Such areas have extensive brood-raising capabilities.

By mid-August the geese gather on the islands of the Delta in flocks of some 20,000 to 50,000 birds, totalling 500,000 in some years. They then fly westward to the North Slope of the Yukon Territory and Northeast Alaska.

Here they feed intensively on berries and sedges for four to six weeks to prepare themselves for the long migration to the wheat fields of southern Alberta and beyond. They usually fly non-stop the 800 miles between the North Slope and Hay Lake in northern Alberta. [*Mackenzie Valley Pipeline Assessment*, p. 296]

During their stay on the staging grounds, snow geese are highly sensitive to human presence, noise, and aircraft. Dr. William Gunn, an ornithological consultant to Arctic Gas, described to the Inquiry experiments to test the sensitivity of snow geese. In one such experiment, the geese would not feed any closer than 1.5 miles from a device simulating the noise made by a compressor station, and birds flying over it diverted their course by 90 degrees or more. Gunn also reported that snow geese are sensitive to the presence of aircraft and they show evidence of being disturbed by flushing at a mean distance of 1.6 miles from small aircraft, 2.5 miles from large aircraft, and 2.3 miles from small helicopters. They also flushed in response to aircraft flying at altitudes of 8,000 to 10,000 feet, the maximum height at which the test flights were conducted. Deliberate harassing of flocks of geese in an area approximately five miles by ten miles cleared them out of the area in 15 minutes.

On the basis of data on the rates of disturbance at a time when the birds, especially the juveniles, needed to build up their energy reserves for migration, Gunn concluded that a potentially severe problem could arise if the present frequency of aircraft flights in the region were to double.

Jerald Jacobson, in Volume 4 of the *Environmental Impact Assessment* published in 1974 by the Environment Protection Board, generalized the available information on the response of snow geese to various human and industrial activities, and he inferred that geese may avoid an area as large as 20 square miles around an operating drill rig, 28 square miles around an operating compressor station, and 250 square miles around an airstrip during takeoff and landing of aircraft. He also drew the following conclusions regarding the effect of aircraft:

The use of airstrips and general operation of aircraft for construction and operation activities from 15 August to 15 October on the Yukon coast is a major conflict, and could seriously degrade or even destroy the integrity of the area for fall staging snow geese....

Because "There is no practical flight altitude that does not frighten snow geese" (Salter and Davis 1974b), unrestricted aircraft traffic on the Yukon coast from 15 August to 15 October could be expected to disturb snow geese on 100 percent of the staging area. Any increase in aircraft traffic will result in increased disturbance to snow geese and reduce the suitability of the area up to some unknown threshold level, when it may become unacceptable to fall staging snow geese. There are no data available on the cumulative and long-term effects of aircraft disturbance to snow geese, or on their accommodation to aircraft disturbance during this stage of their life cycle. [p. 139]

Of course, Arctic Gas propose to schedule their principal construction activities in winter after the geese have flown south, and to restrict noisy activities during both construction and operation of the pipeline when the geese are feeding before going south. Nevertheless, aircraft flights, shipping, activities at wharf and storage sites and construction at camp and compressor sites appear to be inevitable during the construction phase even when the geese are on their staging grounds. Similar potentially disturbing activities at this season would take place throughout the operating life of the pipeline.

The gas pipeline's impact on the fall staging snow geese would not be limited to

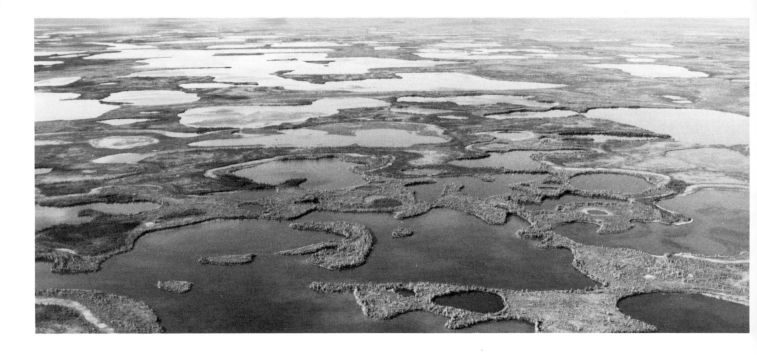

the Yukon and Alaska Coastal Plain. If the Arctic Gas Cross-Delta Route is followed, the impact would spread to the outer parts of the Mackenzie Delta that are used by fall staging snow geese. Particular concern has been expressed before the Inquiry over construction activities at the Shallow Bay and other Delta channel crossings during this season. They include the effects of shipping, aircraft and especially hovercraft noise, the effects of waterborne fuel spills on the wetlands in the Delta, and the effects of a compressor station or other long-term facilities on the outer Delta.

After considering these potential effects on the fall staging snow geese and the measures proposed by Arctic Gas to mitigate them, the United States Department of the Interior concluded:

> the entire population of snow geese could be adversely affected if repeated aircraft flights, such as might be expected with a major repair of the pipeline system, were required to cross critical staging habitat areas while geese are present. [p. 284]

> Snow geese, while on the fall staging and feeding areas, will be affected more than other geese species. If disturbance is severe and long-term, it could cause the geese to seek other less suitable areas for staging and feeding. In any case, the population of snow geese will be reduced. [Final Environmental Impact Statement, Alaska Volume, p. 422]

This forecast is based on the assumption that Arctic Gas would build a pipeline in the manner and following the schedule at present proposed by the company, and it considers the gas pipeline in isolation from other developments. My assessment of impact cannot be based on these premises. The possibility that Arctic Gas will have to modify their plans and schedules is discussed in another chapter of this report, and I have already explained why I am forced to look at the gas pipeline as the trigger for multiple developments along an energy transportation corridor.

What would be the effect on the snow geese of the pipeline, the energy corridor, and related industrial development throughout their fall-staging grounds? These disturbances would inevitably involve a progressive increase in the numbers of people, of aircraft, barge and vehicle movement, and machinery noise. From the evidence before me, it appears that this population of snow geese would certainly dwindle, and it could decline drastically if the stresses imposed by industrial development on their fall staging grounds were continued through a succession of years when spring was late or snow came early.

A National Wilderness Park for the Northern Yukon

The Northern Yukon has been described by Dr. George Calef as:

> ... a land richer in wildlife, in variety of landscape and vegetation, and in archaeological value than any other in the Canadian Arctic. Here high mountains, spruce forests, tundra, wide "flats" of lakes and ponds, majestic valleys, ... and the arctic seacoast come together to form the living fabric of the arctic wilderness. Altogether there are nine million acres of spectacular land in its natural state, inhabited by thriving populations of northern plants and animals including some species which are in serious danger elsewhere. [*The Urgent Need for a Canadian Arctic Wildlife Range*, p. 1]

If this unique area of wilderness and its wildlife are to be protected, the Arctic Gas pipeline should not be built across the Northern Yukon. The region should not be open to any other future proposal to transport energy across it, or to oil and gas exploration and development in general. This summarizes my approach in the earlier parts of this chapter. But now we must go further. It seems to me that, if this kind of protection of the land, the environment and the people is to be effective, the Northern Yukon must be formally designated as an area in which industrial development of any kind is to be totally and permanently excluded. I therefore urge the Government of Canada to reserve the Northern Yukon as a wilderness park.

The park that I propose for the Northern Yukon should be set up under the National Parks system, but it would be a new kind of park — a wilderness park. It would afford absolute protection to wilderness and the environment by excluding all industrial activity within it. Of course there would have to be guarantees permitting the native people to continue to live and to carry on their traditional activities within the park without interference. In my opinion, there should be an immediate withdrawal of the land and water areas needed for this park which could be effected by designating it as a land reserve under Section 19(c) of the Territorial Lands Act. This action would serve as a clear indication of intent and as the starting point for the planning of the park and negotiations with the United States regarding its relationship to the Arctic National Wildlife Range in Alaska.

The wilderness park that I am proposing would comprise all land between the Alaska-Yukon border and the Yukon Northwest Territories border from the Porcupine River northward to the coast, including Herschel Island and all other islands adjoining the coast. Its northern boundary would be three miles offshore. This par

Old Crow Flats. (I. MacNeil)

Canada geese. (C. & M. Hampson)

Grizzly bear. (C. & M. Hampson)

Bald eagle. (NFB—Cognac)

would cover approximately the same area as the Canadian part of the proposed International Wildlife Range, and would adjoin the Arctic National Wildlife Range in Alaska.

The size and boundaries of the proposed park would protect important habitats of migrating birds, the Porcupine caribou herd, and various other mammals; they would also protect the most important hunting and trapping areas of the Old Crow people and the unique wilderness area of the Northern Yukon. The park would include the Yukon Coastal Plain and the Old Crow Flats. The Canadian sector of the Porcupine caribou herd's spring and summer range and the critically important calving range of the herd would lie within it. But the area represents a compromise: the main wintering range of the caribou herd lies south of the Porcupine River and south of the proposed wilderness park. The Dempster Highway and extensive oil and gas exploration on the Eagle Plains render this part of their winter range unsuitable for reservation as a wilderness area.

The proposal to establish a wilderness park is entirely in keeping with the priorities for the North set out in the *Statement of the Government of Canada on Northern Development in the 70's*:

> To maintain and enhance the natural environment, through such means as intensifying ecological research, establishing national parks, ensuring wildlife conservation. [p. 29]

It is also consistent with the policy laid down by the Pipeline Guidelines. Corridor Guideline No. 4 reads as follows:

> In relation to the pipeline corridors ... the Government will identify geographic areas of specific environmental and social concern or sensitivity, areas in which it will impose specific restrictions concerning route or pipeline activities, and possibly areas excluded from pipeline construction. These concerns

and restrictions will pertain to fishing, hunting, and trapping areas, potential recreation areas, ecologically sensitive areas, hazardous terrain conditions, construction material sources, and other similar matters. [p. 11]

Wildlife Range in Alaska

The wilderness does not stop, of course, at the boundary between Alaska and the Yukon. The northeast part of Alaska, contiguous to the Northern Yukon, is a part of the same wilderness. In fact, the calving grounds of the Porcupine caribou herd extend well into Alaska, along the coastal plain as far as Camden Bay, 100 miles to the west of the international boundary; the area of concentrated use by staging snow geese, by nesting and moulting waterfowl and by seabirds also extends far into Alaska.

So a wilderness park in the Northern Yukon would not, by itself, altogether protect the caribou herd and the migratory birds. We shall need the cooperation of the United States to ensure complete protection for the herd. But I believe that cooperation will be forthcoming, for the United States is, in fact, well ahead of us in protection of the herd. A movement to protect the eastern section of the north slope and the Brooks Range began in Alaska during the 1920s. In 1960, the Secretary of the Interior issued a Public Land Order to establish the Arctic National Wildlife Range, under authority delegated by Executive Order 10355. This is a land withdrawal mechanism remarkably similar to that available to the Minister of Indian Affairs and Northern Development under Section 19 of the Territorial Lands Act. The eastern edge of the Arctic National Wildlife Range borders on the Yukon, a political, not an ecological boundary.

The movement to include this range in the

United States National Wilderness Preservation System continues. The range, as established in 1960, is within a land use category less restrictive than a national park. In 1972, 8.8 of its 8.9 million acres was recommended for inclusion in the United States National Wilderness Preservation System and, more recently, Senate Bill 2917 provided for more than 80 million acres of conservation lands in Alaska, including a 3.76 million-acre extension of the Arctic National Wildlife Range. Although these proposals have not yet been acted upon, they reflect a view, widely held in the United States, that it would be in the public interest to designate the Range as wilderness.

Dr. Robert Weeden, a biologist from Alaska, says that if no pipeline is built, and no oil and gas development occurs, the Arctic National Wildlife Range will serve as an ecological reserve and as an ecological base from which to monitor changes brought about by future developments in Alaska. But the existing Arctic National Wildlife Range is not inviolate to oil and gas exploration and development. If the wilderness, the caribou herd and the snow geese on the Alaskan side of the border are to be protected, the Range must be elevated to wilderness status.

International Wildlife Range

The international movements of caribou, waterfowl, bears and other animals have led, of course, to consideration of a wildlife range in the Northern Yukon to adjoin and complement the wildlife range in Alaska. Impetus for an Arctic International Wildlife Range came from a conference of conservationists in Whitehorse in October 1970. The conference submitted a resolution to the Governments of Canada and of the Yukon Territory

Map labels: Great Bear Lake · Great Slave Lake · Richards Island · **Coastal route** · *from Prudhoe Bay* · NORTHWEST TERRITORIES · Mackenzie Valley route · Mackenzie River · ALTA. · **Interior route** · *from Prudhoe Bay* · Circle · Arctic · Mackenzie · **To Caroline** · ALASKA · YUKON · B.C. · Kilometres 0 200 · Miles 0 100

CANADIAN ARCTIC GAS PIPELINE LTD. SYSTEM MAP

for the establishment of an "Arctic International Wildlife Range, (Canada)." The Honourable Jean Chrétien, then Minister of Indian Affairs and Northern Development, endorsed the action of the conference and promised to support it. In June 1971 the Arctic International Wildlife Range (Canada) Society was formed. The proposal for an International Range has been endorsed by the Canadian Wildlife Federation, the International Union for Conservation of Nature and Natural Resources, and the Environment Protection Board. Many witnesses spoke to the Inquiry in favour of an Arctic International Wildlife Range, consisting of a major portion of the Northern Yukon and the existing Alaskan Wildlife Range.

The wilderness park that I am proposing here would cover approximately the same area as the Canadian part of the proposed Arctic International Wildlife Range, and it would adjoin the nine-million acre Arctic National Wildlife Range in Alaska established to protect its unique wildlife, wilderness and recreational values. Together, these two areas would constitute a magnificent area of 18 million acres spanning the international boundary, an area large enough to provide for the long-term well-being of its wildlife, and especially of the Porcupine caribou herd and the snow geese. It would be one of the largest wilderness areas in the world.

There is a precedent in the Glacier-Waterton International Peace Park in Alberta-Montana. Management of major transboundary resources such as the Porcupine caribou herd might require formal international agreements instead of the informal cooperation that now works so well in Glacier-Waterton Park, where trans-boundary movements of the populations are not significant.

A pipeline across the Northern Yukon would not only destroy the possibility of establishing a true wilderness park there, but it would undermine efforts in the United States to convert the Arctic National Wildlife Range to wilderness status. Weeden, speaking for the State of Alaska, said:

> The State has taken the position that such an intrusion upon an untouched area is irreversible and tragic, whatever steps are taken to mitigate its effects. [F7545]

The largest wildlife refuge in the United States would be in jeopardy and the possibility of combining it with a Canadian range to form one of the largest wildlife refuges in the world would be thwarted.

Oil and Gas Potential

If we create a wilderness park in the Northern Yukon, shall we be denying ourselves indispensable supplies of gas and oil? Will it become necessary, in any event, to invade this wilderness? No one can say for sure, but no evidence brought before me indicated or even suggested that the Northern Yukon is a first-priority oil-and-gas province. There has been extensive exploratory drilling east of it in the Mackenzie Delta area and west of it in Alaska. In these areas, the coastal plain and the offshore continental shelf are considerably wider than they are in the Yukon. The zone of potential oil and gas exploration along the north coast of the Yukon is narrow, and the area has not achieved any prominence in exploration strategy so far. It is also noteworthy that the three deep exploratory test wells drilled near the Yukon coast were dry.

Native People and the Wilderness Park

My proposal for a wilderness park is specifically designed to benefit the native people by protecting their renewable resources and by preserving the land in its natural state, thus ensuring the physical basis for their way of life. This benefit extends to the Old Crow people, who live within the area of the proposed park, the Indians from Fort McPherson and Aklavik, who hunt in the eastern part of the proposed park, and the Inuit, largely from Aklavik, who hunt and fish along the Yukon coast. All of these people depend on the Porcupine caribou herd, the protection of which is one of the principal purposes of the proposed park.

The rights that the native people of Old Crow and the Mackenzie Delta would enjoy throughout the area covered by the park would have to be negotiated between the Government of Canada and themselves as part of a comprehensive settlement of native claims, but I do not think the dedication now of the Northern Yukon as a park would prejudice those claims.

Preservation of the wilderness and of the caribou herd is plainly in keeping with the desires of the native people. But, there are certain essential conditions that would have to be observed: the native people must be guaranteed at the outset their right to live, hunt, trap and fish within the park, and to take caribou within its boundaries; and the people of Old Crow must play an important part in the management of the park and, in particular, of the caribou herd. It is my judgment that the establishment of the park and of a management plan in cooperation with the native people, building both upon their knowledge and experience and that of the scientists who have studied the caribou

Phillips Bay, Yukon coast; breeding and staging area for waterfowl. (I. MacNeil)

Porcupine River. (ISL–G. Calef)

Alaska North Slope. (ISL–G. Calef)

and the Northern Yukon biota, can be consistent with and complementary to these principles.

We have already some experience in the establishment and management of parks (although not wilderness parks) in the North and have seen their effects on the interests of the native people. At Nahanni Butte the Inquiry was told that the Dene play no part in the management of the South Nahanni National Park. This experience must not be repeated in the wilderness park for the Northern Yukon that I am urging upon the Government of Canada. The conditions I have outlined will, in my judgment, avoid such a repetition and will avoid prejudice to native claims.

In *Runes of the North,* Sigurd Olson, an American naturalist, wrote:

> It may well be that with [the help of the native people] the Canadian north, with its vast expanses of primeval country, can restore to modern man a semblance of balance and completeness. In the long run, these last wild regions of the continent might be worth far more to North Americans from a recreational and spiritual standpoint than through industrial exploitation. [p. 156]

It may be said that no one will visit the park because it is too remote. Only the wealthy, it may be argued, will have the opportunity to see the caribou and to enjoy the solitude and the scenery. But Canadians of ordinary means and less are there now, enjoying these wonders of nature. I speak, of course, of the native people. Is that not enough? Canadians from the provinces do not have to visit the wilderness or see the herd of caribou to confirm its existence or to justify its retention. The point I am making here is that the preservation of the wilderness and its wildlife can be justified on the grounds of its importance to the native people. But the preservation of wilderness

can also be justified because it is there, an Arctic ecosystem, in which life forms are limited in number, and where, if we exterminate them, we impoverish the frontier, our knowledge of the frontier, and the variety and beauty of the earth's creatures.

An Alternative Route Across the Yukon

I have recommended that no pipeline be built and no energy corridor be established across the Northern Yukon along either of the routes proposed by Arctic Gas. This means that, if gas from Prudhoe Bay and, subsequently, gas and oil from other sources in Alaska must pass overland to the Lower 48, the pipeline will have to be routed through the southern part of the Yukon Territory. The only overland route that has been seriously advanced as an alternative to the routes proposed by Arctic Gas is the Alaska Highway Route (also known as the Fairbanks Route) which is the route proposed for the Alcan Pipeline. This route would follow the trans-Alaska pipeline from Prudhoe Bay to Fairbanks, the Alaska Highway to the eastern border of Alaska and then cross the Southern Yukon into British Columbia and Alberta.

At Whitehorse, I heard evidence from Arctic Gas and from other participants in the Inquiry, comparing this route with the Coastal and Interior Routes. On the basis of that evidence, many of the concerns that led me to reject the pipeline routes across the Northern Yukon do not appear to apply to the Alaska Highway Route.

No major populations of any wildlife species appear to be threatened by the construction of a pipeline paralleling the

Alaska Highway, either in the Yukon or in Alaska. The route follows an existing corridor along the trans-Alaska pipeline north of Fairbanks and along the Alaska Highway south and east of Fairbanks. Like the trans-Alaska pipeline, this route would come into contact with only small numbers of caribou south of Prudhoe Bay. Elsewhere, although there are important wildlife populations in the area traversed by the proposed route, they apparently would not have major contact with the corridor.

The concerns that I have expressed about the scheduling and logistics of building a pipeline across the Northern Yukon would not apply (or would be much less important) if a pipeline were built along the Alaska Highway Route. The Arctic Gas pipeline would have to be built in the cold and darkness of winter north of the Arctic Circle, from a snow working surface. It would depend upon a limited shipping season, and a whole infrastructure would have to be established to bring in material, equipment and supplies. In contrast, a pipeline following the Alaska Highway Route in Canada could probably be built in either winter or summer, and it would cross an area with less extreme winter weather, and follow a main highway that has a short connection to the Pacific coast.

Within Canada, only short sections of the Alaska Highway Route would encounter permafrost, and the problems of pipeline construction and operation across permafrost and of controlling frost heave would be of little concern. Of course, permafrost does exist throughout most of the Alaska portion of this proposed route.

I have not examined the social and economic impact of a pipeline along the Alaska Highway Route. Neither have I considered the question of native claims in the Southern

Content of the map image includes the following labels:

ALTERNATE ROUTES AND CORRIDORS PROPOSED BY ARCTIC GAS

Kilometres
0   400
0   200
Miles

Great Bear Lake
Great Slave Lake
N.W.T.
ALBERTA
Richards Island
Mackenzie River
Caroline
circle
Prudhoe Bay
Arctic
YUKON
B.C.
U.S.A.
ALASKA

Mackenzie Valley route ....
Coastal-Cross Delta route ....
Interior route ....
Circum-Delta route ....●●●●●●●
Fairbanks corridor ....
Fort Yukon corridor ....
Dempster Highway corridor ....
Offshore corridor ....●●●●●●●●●●

Yukon. The Council of Yukon Indians have advised that native claims must be settled in the Southern Yukon before any pipeline is built. These matters would be of fundamental importance in any decision to build a pipeline across the Southern Yukon and they must be assessed carefully before any recommendation is made for a pipeline along the Alaska Highway. Certainly, I am in no position to make such a recommendation.

If a decision should be made in favour of a pipeline along the Alaska Highway Route, or over any other southerly route across the Yukon Territory, I recommend that any agreement in this regard between Canada and the United States should include provisions to protect the Porcupine caribou herd and the wilderness of the Northern Yukon and Northeastern Alaska. By this agreement,

Canada should undertake to establish a wilderness park in the Northern Yukon and the United States should agree to accord wilderness status to its Arctic National Wildlife Range, thus creating a unique international wilderness park in the Arctic. It would be an important symbol of the dedication of our two countries to environmental as well as industrial goals.

The Mackenzie Delta—Beaufort Sea Region

In the preceding chapter, I dealt with the impacts of a pipeline carrying Alaskan gas destined for American markets across the Northern Yukon to the Mackenzie Delta region. In this chapter, I intend to deal with the impact of a pipeline across the Mackenzie Delta and in the Delta region, and the related impact of oil and gas exploration and development in the Delta itself and offshore in the Beaufort Sea.

The Mackenzie Delta and the Beaufort Sea together constitute an area of great importance and sensitivity for wildlife, birds and fish, an area where the land, the water and their renewable resources are still necessary to the life and culture of many native people. The impact of the construction of the pipeline across the Delta will be significant, but even more significant will be the oil and gas exploration and development that will be associated with, and that will follow, the pipeline. There appears to be a major petroleum province in the Delta-Beaufort area. What we do now will largely determine the impact that the development of this province will have on the environment of the region.

I intend, therefore, to discuss at some length the impact that the pipeline and related activities will have on the Delta-Beaufort region, because here the exploration and development activity generated by the pipeline will be most intense.

Arctic Gas propose to lay the pipeline from Alaska across the outer part of the Mackenzie Delta. Both Arctic Gas and Foothills propose to build a pipeline southward from the Richards Island area. Whatever route the pipeline follows will cause major environmental concerns in the Mackenzie Delta region.

The gas plants and the gas gathering lines associated with them will be built in the Delta area by the producer companies, Imperial, Gulf and Shell, not by the pipeline companies, but these plants and gathering lines are so obviously part of the pipeline system that any consideration of the impact of the pipeline must include them as well. After all, if the right-of-way for the gas pipeline is not granted, the gas plants and gas gathering systems will not be built.

The Pipeline Guidelines foresee a whole group of activities within a corridor. If there are pipelines running along an energy corridor from the Arctic to the mid-continent, then there will be a further extension of oil and gas exploration and development into the Beaufort Sea. In fact, Robert Blair, President of Foothills, told us that if a pipeline is built, its principal long-term result will be enhanced oil and gas exploration activity. Roland Horsfield, a spokesman for Imperial Oil, agreed. The Pipeline Guidelines require us to assume that an oil pipeline would follow a gas pipeline across the Northern Yukon, across the Delta, and from the Delta to the South.

The Department of Indian Affairs and Northern Development will assess proposals to build gas gathering lines and gas plants and will determine the extent to which drilling for oil and gas should be allowed in the Mackenzie Delta and the Beaufort Sea. It is up to the National Energy Board to determine the extent of the reserves of oil and gas in the Delta and the Beaufort Sea. But this Inquiry, if it is to do its job, must assess the impact of exploration and development that would follow approval of a pipeline, and explore the penumbra of environmental and social issues that surround such activities. It is from this perspective that the Inquiry must determine the impact that a gas pipeline would have and recommend the terms and conditions under which

a right-of-way should be granted, if a pipeline is to be built.

The pipeline cannot be considered in isolation. The environment of the North, the ecosystems of the North, are continuous and interdependent. They cannot be divided. Similarly, we cannot understand the consequences industrial development would have by hiving off a convenient component of it, and examining it in detail, while ignoring the broader implications of the whole range of its effects.

Canada has chosen to pioneer offshore oil and gas exploration in the Arctic. We are in advance of other circumpolar nations on this geographical and technological frontier. The pipeline, once built, will stimulate yet more oil and gas exploration offshore and it will lead toward full-scale development and production in the Beaufort Sea itself.

Canadians have a grave responsibility in this matter. There can be no doubt that the other circumpolar powers — the United States, the Soviet Union, Denmark and Norway — will follow us offshore. What we do there — the standards we set and our performance — will be closely watched.

Man and the Land

The Inquiry held its first community hearing in Aklavik. We went there in early spring, when the nights were still dark and the days were crisp and clear with cold.

While we were at Aklavik, I visited Archie Headpoint's camp, six or seven miles out of town. To get there we drove along the West Channel of the Mackenzie River. (Once the channels have frozen, one pass with a bulldozer will clear an ice road.) Headpoint's cabin was just above the bank of the Mackenzie. Out on the ice, in the middle of the channel, we could see one of Shell's seismic exploration camps, a series of trailers on runners.

Archie Headpoint's camp is a collection of small, cluttered buildings. In his log cabin, where he and his family have lived for a long time, the skins of muskrats hung to dry. We sat there for a while, talking and drinking tea.

The contrast between the old Arctic and the new, between the northern homeland and the northern frontier, could be seen in the few acres around that cabin. There, the landscape is crisscrossed by seismic trails and vehicle tracks that seem to come from nowhere and to go nowhere — all this right alongside the ponds where the Headpoints have always hunted muskrats in the past. The Headpoints complained that the land was no longer as productive as it had been, that the seismic trails extending from the West Channel up into the foothills of the Richardson Mountains had blocked the streams and polluted the ponds.

Following our visit to Headpoint's camp, we had lunch at the seismic exploration camp. There we met engineers and technicians, men devoted to the task of finding oil and gas — men seeking to make the northern frontier productive for the South. The camp was laid out in neat rows. Its colour — bright orange — contrasted sharply with the cold blue-white of the landscape.

There, above the Arctic Circle, just half a mile from each other, were the two Norths side by side — the North of Shell Canada, with its links to the South and the markets of the world, and the North of Archie Headpoint, with its links to the land and to a past shared by the people who have always lived there.

Can these two Norths coexist in the Mackenzie Delta and the Beaufort Sea? Or must one recede into the past, while the other commands the future? This issue confronted us in the Delta communities — Aklavik, Inuvik and Tuktoyaktuk — and at Fort McPherson and Arctic Red River. And the same issue confronted us at the Inuit settlements on the shores of the Beaufort Sea. I held hearings in all of these places, too: Sachs Harbour, Holman, Paulatuk and North Star Harbour. These settlements are far from the route of the proposed pipeline, but oil and gas exploration in and around the Beaufort Sea concerns the people who live there, because they depend on the fish, seals, whales and polar bears for which the Beaufort Sea is vital habitat.

We may sometimes think that the history of the Delta began with Mackenzie's arrival in 1789, or with the establishment of Inuvik in 1955, or even with the coming of oil and gas exploration in the 1960s. But there were native people in the Delta region when Mackenzie arrived — and they had been there for thousands of years.

Mackenzie's expedition extended the fur trade down the whole length of the Mackenzie River, but the fur trade was conducted on a regular basis in the Delta region only after the establishment of Fort McPherson, on the Peel River in 1840. First the Dene and later the Inuit traded there.

The Dene of the region hunted and trapped during the winter in the Richardson and Ogilvie Mountains, then brought their furs to Fort McPherson in June. They spent the summer at fish camps in the Delta, then returned to Fort McPherson in the fall to trade their dried fish; after that they went back to the mountains for the winter.

It is estimated that there were about 2,000 bowhead whales in the Beaufort Sea before the turn of the century. In 1889 the American whaling fleet, sailing from San Francisco, entered the Beaufort Sea, and they returned each year until 1912. During those 23 years, about 1,500 bowhead whales were killed in Canadian waters. The stock of whales in the Beaufort Sea was virtually exterminated and today only 100 or 200 bowheads summer there.

The Eskimos supplied the whalers with meat, which brought very great pressure to bear on the caribou. Dr. Arthur Martell of the Canadian Wildlife Service believes this pressure drove the Bluenose caribou herd away from the Delta. According to Knut Lang, after the whaling period the native people of the Delta had to travel far inland to hunt caribou. In the late 1920s, caribou began to reappear in the foothills west of the Mackenzie Delta. Until about 10 years ago, the Bluenose herd used to stay east of the Anderson River, but now it appears to be returning to the range it used to inhabit in the Delta region. Since the 1960s, the herd has been expanding westward toward the Mackenzie River.

Not only the caribou of the Delta were affected by the Eskimos, hunting for the whalers. By the early 1900s, the muskoxen were extirpated from the Delta region, and the western boundary of their range lay to the east of the Anderson River.

With the collapse of the whaling industry — and with the disappearance of the bowhead, muskox and Delta caribou — the fur trade resumed its role as a vital part of the Inuit economy and the source of guns, ammunition and other trade goods on which they had come to rely. With the rising prices for fur, particularly for white fox, and the emergence of muskrat as an important commercial fur, the Mackenzie Delta became an important centre of the fur trade. In 1911,

The traplines (————) and principal hunting and fishing areas (------) of Ishmael Alunik, in the Northern Yukon and Mackenzie Delta.

The whaling vessel S.S. Belvedere in Franklin Bay, NWT, 1912. (Public Archives)

Baleen on board schooner North Star, Bernard Harbour, NWT, 1915. (Public Archives)

Herschel Island Harbour, 1930. (Public Archives)

Aklavik was established at a natural camping place in the Delta, which further encouraged the harvesting of muskrats. By the early 1920s, the prices of both muskrat and white fox had increased 20-fold over what they had been at the turn of the century. The Delta trappers, harvesting muskrats by the hundred thousands, attained unprecedented prosperity. Many families bought their own schooners. But in the mid-twenties, high fur prices and an increasing number of both white and Alaskan Inuit immigrant trappers led to overharvesting in the Delta and an expansion of the Inuit trapping areas. Some Inuit moved to Banks Island, where white fox were abundant, and established what has since become the thriving trapping community of Sachs Harbour.

The Delta people remember the 1920s as a period of good times, when the relationship between man and the land was productive. We must remember that, although trapping fur for sale was important, it was, and is, only a part of the native economy. Then, as now, country food — caribou, seal, whale, polar bear, fish, goose — constituted a vital part of the native people's diet.

In pursuit of both fur and food, the people of the Delta travelled long distances. It may sometimes be difficult for us in the South to comprehend the vastness of the areas covered by a hunter-trapper and his family in the North. Ishmael Alunik, President of the Hunters and Trappers Association of Inuvik, described for the Inquiry his use of land during this period. It is representative of the experience of many Delta Inuit:

> I was born in the Yukon, and that country we always call it "Myloona;" that means "where I hunted." ... I used to go to the Crow Flats and I used to hunt rats. I was quite a small kid ... but I started hunting when I was about four years old. Not very big, you know, could just pack a trap; then my grandparents used to

come to the Crow Flats. This is the way they used the land before my parents, and my parents used the land there too. ... We made friends with the Indians. Because I was born there, I was just like one of them. I hunted all along [the Yukon] coast for white foxes, some place along there we hunted seals. ... There was another river that is called Malcolm River. I hunted caribou around there and I used this Firth River quite a few times to go to hunt [and to] fish. They call it Fish Hole there. ... I went back to Aklavik to go to school in 1936. After I got married I went down there [along the Yukon coast]. I had a camp around King Point and I hunted all along this coast and right here [at Shingle Point]. I trapped out in the sea where the ice doesn't go away; and then all around them years I was hunting right close to the mountains, right to Babbage River where the Fish Hole was, and then this part here, where the mountains are. It looks like it was an unwritten boundary, you know, unwritten law where the Indians and the Eskimos hunted long ago. The Eskimos, the way my grandparents told me, they used to hunt up that way but they don't go across the mountains where the Indian people live. It was just like an unwritten law in between there....
>
> We hunted rats on the west side right to Aklavik.... We used these rivers in summertime for most all them rivers in the Delta got fish in them, and we used them rivers just only in summertime mostly when we travelled from Kendall Island. I went there about two years and I hunted down there to [Pelly] Island.... I hunted geese around here.... We went up by the East Channel, and from there again the hunting places they used this for hunting whales. Then another part around there we hunt rats along there inland across Tununuk. Finally in later years I had a cabin right here before I moved to Inuvik. Then from there I hunted from Reindeer Station. I used this trail ... I trapped way up here for marten. While I was at Reindeer Station, I put fish nets along some lakes, there, right to Parsons Lake, I get whitefish, crooked backs and other little blue herrings. Then from there

I went hunting caribou [in the Richardson Mountains, near] Fish Hole. [C3769ff.]

Land use patterns have changed in the last 20 years, as the people moved from their camps into settlements, but there is a clear continuity between past and present native land use. Muskrats are still important. At Fort McPherson and Arctic Red River, the spring "ratting" season pulls everyone down to the Delta or the Travaillant Lake area. In spring, Aklavik is nearly abandoned because its people are out hunting muskrats, and many wage-earners in Inuvik leave their regular jobs to participate in the hunt. As Annie C. Gordon said at Aklavik:

> At this time of the year [April], the people go out trapping muskrats, and in May and June the people go out to their spring camps. Some stay until June 15 and some come back early. At this time when they are out, they hunt muskrats. It's a good thing, it is a good living, it is good living out there. Every year we go out with the children. We always say that we are going to stay in town for the spring, but when spring comes we always end up going out. We take the whole family out, and sometimes we take other children to enjoy it with our family. It's fun out there. Sometimes we take the whole family out on a hunt, just to go out for fun, and they enjoy doing it. The country is so nice in the spring, it's so quiet. It's hard work when the hunters come back, when you're skinning muskrats. But I enjoy doing that kind of work, and it's fun when you go out and shoot muskrats all night. [C122ff.]

The Delta area is still extremely important for domestic fisheries. An important commercial fishery is located at Holmes Creek on the East Channel, and most of the catch is sold in Inuvik. Native families have fishing camps throughout the Delta, especially around Aklavik. I visited many of these camps, where families spend the summer, catching fish and drying them for winter use.

I visited Whitefish Station, where native families, many of them from Inuvik, spend the summers harvesting the white whales and preparing the meat for the winter. I visited Holman in winter and watched some recently killed caribou being divided up. At Paulatuk I saw frozen char and caribou stored on the roof of every house.

The Inuit of Tuktoyaktuk, Paulatuk, Sachs Harbour, Holman and Coppermine hunt ringed and bearded seals in the Beaufort Sea, Amundsen Gulf and Coronation Gulf. At Holman — which alone takes as many as 8,000 seals a year — Jimmy Memorana spoke of the importance of the seals to the Inuit:

... they are the food of the people and they are the income of the people, and they use [those] seals all year around, for food and for cash. [C3986]

Frank Elanik of Aklavik spoke of the importance of the caribou to the native people, Inuit, Dene and Metis:

My family eat about 30 caribou a year.... If I had to buy from the Bay, I don't know how I would live. [C24]

Mark Noksana of Tuktoyaktuk spoke of the importance of the whales in the Inuit diet:

... the muktuk we [have] eating whales, we can't go without it. If we go without it ... we can't feel good. [C4398]

There is, then, in the Delta, a concentration of concerns, a compression of the social, environmental and economic forces at work elsewhere along the route of the pipeline and the corridor. There in the Delta, and extending into the Beaufort Sea, is a uniquely productive ecological system, a system that is vital to the native people.

Region and Environment

To understand the impact of pipelines and of oil and gas exploration and development in the Mackenzie Delta and the Beaufort Sea, we must have some knowledge of the geography of the three areas in the Delta-Beaufort region: the Mackenzie Delta itself, the Delta region, and the Beaufort Sea.

The Mackenzie Delta (hereafter referred to simply as the Delta) is a maze of islands, channels, lakes and swamps. It is forested except for tundra areas along the coast. In spring, the flood waters of the Mackenzie River cause break-up in the Delta and around the channel mouths earlier than in adjacent parts of the Beaufort Sea. In summer, the warm, turbid river water flows out beyond the Delta in a layer over the colder and denser sea water. Thus, the Delta region has a warmer summer and longer season of open water than the areas just east and west of it. The Delta itself may be likened to a huge, wet sponge. It is one of the most productive areas for wildlife in the Canadian Arctic, supporting innumerable muskrats and substantial populations of other furbearers, such as beaver, mink and marten, as well as fox, bear, moose, and a variety of small mammals. The channels and lakes of the Delta abound with fish. In summer, many thousands of waterfowl and other birds pass through the Delta or nest there. White whales calve in its warm waters. Because of these natural features, the Delta is of special significance to the native people of Aklavik, Fort McPherson and Inuvik, and even of Arctic Red River and Tuktoyaktuk, for trapping, hunting and fishing. The entire Delta lies within a few feet of river level or sea level, and much of it is subject to periodic

flooding. The sponge-like nature of the Delta means that waterborne pollution would have far-reaching effects on the Delta, its wildlife, and its people.

The area described here as the Delta region is a largely treeless lowland extending some 100 miles eastward from the Mackenzie Delta, and it includes the area around Tuktoyaktuk, the Eskimo Lakes and Cape Bathurst. This area, which is used extensively by the people of Tuktoyaktuk, supports Canada's only reindeer herd. The Bluenose caribou herd at the northwestern limit of its present range occupies the southern fringe of the area. Arctic fox is an important furbearer in this area, and the coast of the Delta region, like the Delta itself, supports tens of thousands of migratory waterfowl and shorebirds in summer. There are freshwater fish in coastal bays, and white whales spend the summer in the warm waters that border the Delta region and particularly the Delta itself.

In winter, the Beaufort Sea is completely ice covered. A zone of land-fast ice extends outward from the shore for some tens of miles, and is separated from the moving polar pack ice by a narrow shear zone characterized by rapidly deforming, heavily ridged and irregular ice. This zone contains leads of open water in winter, and in spring becomes a belt of discontinuous open leads hundreds of miles long. In summer, the land-fast ice melts, and the polar pack retreats farther offshore, in some seasons to the general vicinity of the edge of the continental shelf. Within the Beaufort Sea region, the principal area of environmental concern is the shear zone and the open leads at the edge of the land-fast ice. This area provides critical habitat for migrating birds in the spring and for polar bears and seals in both winter and spring.

Inuit schooners and whale boats at Kittigazuit, NWT, 1923. (Public Archives)

Flock of shorebirds. (G. Morrison)

Ibyuk Pingo near Tuktoyaktuk. (D. Mackay)

White whale hauled ashore for butchering. (W. Hunt)

Wildlife

FISH

Although fish are present in the streams, lakes and coastal waters throughout the Delta region, they are most abundant and most important for local people in the Delta itself. Native people catch fish for domestic use at many locations within the Delta and in the streams and lakes tributary to it. As some indication of the importance of this resource, the community of Aklavik consumed approximately 294,000 pounds of fish in 1973. The largest commercial fishery in the lower Mackenzie Valley is at Holmes Creek in the Delta.

About a dozen species of fish occur in the Delta, including broad and humpback whitefish, inconnu, cisco, pike, chub, burbot, sucker, grayling, lake trout and arctic char. They live in the main river channels, bays at the river mouth, and small channels and lakes throughout the Delta. Some populations of fish simply pass through the Delta on their way to the sea or to locations back upstream. Others spend most of their life cycle in the Delta. Unfortunately, because of the turbidity of the water, the multitude of channels and small waterbodies, the large size of the main channels and the long period of ice cover, there are critical gaps in our information about these fish resources, and we need that information to assess properly the impact of industrial development on the Delta. There are few details available concerning the location and timing of critical life situations, such as spawning, overwintering and migration, in which the fish populations are at greatest risk from industrial activities.

BIRDS

The Delta, the coast of the Delta region, the coastal waters and the offshore leads of the Beaufort Sea are of very great importance for migratory birds. Every spring millions of geese, swans, ducks, gulls, terns and many other species converge on the Delta-Beaufort region from wintering grounds in Southern Canada, the United States, South America and even the Antarctic. They are an international renewable resource that nature, political boundaries and treaties have made the responsibility of Canada.

In its ornithological relationship to other regions in the Western Arctic, the Delta has been described as a huge funnel. It attracts birds from literally every point of the compass, from Banks Island, Anderson River, Liverpool Bay, the north slope of the Yukon and Alaska, and by way of the Mackenzie Valley from the prairies and Central and South America. Although the Mackenzie Valley is a major flyway, birds also migrate east and west along the Arctic coast of the Beaufort Sea. For example, there is a spectacular spring migration of ducks from the Pacific Ocean, along the south shore of the Beaufort Sea and past the Delta, following the leads in the ice. These leads of open water are crucial habitat for resting and feeding. The coastal bays and lagoons, barrier beaches and islands offer vital nesting and moulting grounds for the birds arriving from all directions.

Dr. Tom Barry of the Canadian Wildlife Service estimates that two million migrating seabirds and waterfowl, representing about 100 species, frequent the Beaufort Sea and its coastal margins. The Mackenzie Delta itself offers nesting ground for a waterfowl population that ranges from 80,000 to 350,000. As I described in the preceding chapter, several hundred thousand snow geese pass through the area in spring and fall, and in some years they use the outer Delta for staging. Spring leads in the ice of the Beaufort Sea at places like Cape Dalhousie may be occupied by 50,000 or more birds at a time. A week later those birds will have moved on, and tens of thousands more will be occupying the same lead. During one fall migration period, from July 10 to September 17, 1972, 240,000 birds, representing more than 50 species, were recorded passing Nunaluk Spit on the north coast of the Yukon. The vitality of the whole region is obvious.

Another area of critical importance for waterfowl and other birds is the outer, treeless part of the Mackenzie Delta, including its bordering bays, inlets and channel mouths. This area is used extensively by nesting and moulting ducks, swans, cranes and various other species, including a small colony of snow geese. In some years, when there is early snow on the Yukon Coastal Plain, the Delta edge serves as the principal fall staging area for the migrating snow geese. I will recommend that this entire area be protected by bird sanctuaries.

MAMMALS

The variety of habitat in the Delta-Beaufort region supports a broad range of mammals, from lemmings to whales. These varied animals have a correspondingly varied sensitivity to industrial development. Many of the mammals could tolerate industrial intrusion, but for others, such activities would be intolerable, and a serious decline in these populations could be anticipated. Perhaps I can explain this diversity by citing a few examples.

The white whales of the Beaufort Sea depend on the warm, shallow waters of Mackenzie Bay. Every summer the whales concentrate there to give birth to their young. These mammals are wary of man, and if they are disturbed at this time, a year's calves could be endangered or lost. Offshore oil and gas activities within the whale concentration areas during the summer could ultimately lead to a decline in the whale populations. I therefore give special attention to them in this chapter and recommend that a whale sanctuary be established to protect their principal calving area.

Grizzly bears and polar bears are widely distributed in the Delta-Beaufort area. Although their numbers are relatively small, they range over large areas. They are attracted by camps and waste disposal sites, and encounters with man often result in the death of the bear. This kind of encounter, together with the disturbance of denning sites in winter, are threats to the bear populations of this region.

The muskrat is the most important economically of the aquatic furbearers in the Delta region. I have already described the importance of these animals to the native people. The Delta provides abundant habitat for muskrats, so disturbance would have to be widespread before it affected the whole population. Although locally vulnerable, these aquatic furbearers have the potential for relatively rapid recovery and will recolonize disturbed habitats that have not been permanently spoiled. Because of these adaptive features, there appears to be no need for concern over their long-term welfare, so long as short-term damage to habitat is corrected. However, in some areas where they have been traditionally harvested, short-term and local depletion could affect the economic well-being of trappers.

A semi-domesticated reindeer herd ranges east of the Delta. This herd was introduced into the area in 1935, and now its 5,000 animals are managed by local native people

as a renewable resource. The herd's range and its seasonal movements have been manipulated by man, so the effects of industrial development may be expected to be less critical to the reindeer than to caribou.

The Bluenose caribou herd ranges east and south of the Delta region. Present oil and gas activity touch only the edge of this herd's range, but successive industrial development, combined with current northwestward expansion of the herd's range, may impose some constraints. But this again is a minor impact, and in marked contrast to the impact that the pipeline and energy corridor would have on the Porcupine caribou herd on its calving grounds in the Northern Yukon.

I think that these few examples indicate that the mammals of the Delta-Beaufort region will respond differently to industrial development. Some, like the white whales, will be very vulnerable at certain times and places. Others, like the muskrats, reindeer and caribou, may be affected but not threatened. This distinction is important because it dictates how impacts should be controlled. In some cases, a species can be protected effectively only by prohibiting industrial activity in critical areas, but in other cases regulation of industrial development may be adequate. The critical consideration in each case is the degree of biological sensitivity.

Biological Sensitivity

THE FOOD CHAIN

Although arctic ecosystems have been described as sensitive, or even fragile, I think it is more accurate to say that they are vulnerable. At the beginning of this report, I quote Dr. Max Dunbar to explain this idea of vulnerability and how it relates to the small

number of species in the Arctic and to simple food chains.

The sensitivity of wildlife in the Delta-Beaufort region is not determined simply by assessing the direct effect of industrial impact on large and conspicuous species like the white whales. Dr. Norman Snow of the Department of Indian Affairs and Northern Development reminded the Inquiry that the highly visible components of the ecosystem — the birds, mammals and fish — represent only about five percent of the animal kingdom. The other 95 percent is composed of invertebrates, some of them microscopic in size but exceedingly numerous. These populations are the crucial links in many food chains, and on them the whole ecosystem, therefore, depends.

Biologists who testified before the Inquiry were careful to explain that, despite the relative simplicity of arctic food chains, their nature is not well understood. We have only begun to study them, but we have learned enough to understand their vulnerability. The native people understand this problem very well, and it is, in fact, their concern for the vulnerability of the food chain that underlies many of their fears about the impact of oil and gas exploration and development. At Holman, Simon Kataoyak told the Inquiry:

You know, we talk about oil spills and so forth. I'd like to say a little bit about it because, if there's an oil spill, it's going to involve Holman Island and all this part of the area because of the currents. . . .

You see, if an oil spill occurs, it's going to spread. That's for sure, you know that. Well, seals are not going to die right away, we know it. It takes a long time to get rid of [them]. The thing we're going to get rid of first is the shrimps [and] what they eat. . . . Seals are going to live for a little longer time but what the fish and whales eat are the things that are

Mackenzie Delta. (Native Press)

Polar bear rumaging through garbage dump. (CWS)

Ringed seal. (ITC)

Simon Kataoyak, Holman. (P. Scott)

going to be first to be killed. Then the seals are going to be killed....

So you see, they have to study hard to prevent these things first before they ever go ahead because there's little — they call them *amogoak*, you know those shrimps, there's a lot of them in the water. That's what the seals [eat], you find them in their stomach, *amogoaks*, and even whales....

But when you [are] travelling in the ocean, something like that — it's nice, it's calm weather. What happens when you look in the water? You could see those little creatures that are this long, they're just like jelly and they've got a red head and they're moving like this all the time. Well, that's what whales and seals eat. So if an oil spill occurs, if that thing slows up or if it's drifting around, that's the first thing that's going to be killed. So they got to know how to prevent those things....

They tell us they know how to drill. Sure, we agree because they're experts. But do they know how to do the safeties? They haven't tried it. [C3943ff.]

Marine biologists from Environment Canada described the Beaufort Sea marine ecosystem. Although complex by arctic standards, it is nevertheless a simple food chain compared to food chains found farther south where the diversity of species is greater and none of them is dominant. The relation between what eats what in the Beaufort Sea is easily illustrated. A typical sequence is diatom–shrimp–fish–seal; another is flagellate–krill–whale. There are, of course, alternative linkages in arctic marine food chains, such as a bird preying on fish or man killing a whale. Nevertheless, as Kataoyak told the Inquiry, a group of shrimp-like creatures underpins most of the food chains in that cold sea.

These shrimp-like creatures depend on the marine equivalent of pastures. Part of this marine pasture, one that is unique to the arctic seas, is an under-ice flora that appears

to be an important component of the diatom–shrimp–fish–seal food chain. In late spring, before the ice is thin enough for the light to penetrate to stimulate the growth of the microscopic plants that float in open water, dense concentrations of diatoms grow under the ice. They flourish briefly on the limited nutrients that are available in the ice and with far lower light intensity than other forms of phytoplankton require. They provide a "pasture" for crustaceans on the bottom of the floating ice, and they form the base of the food chains that include arctic cod, seals and whales. It will be seen at once that these under-ice colonies of diatoms peculiar to the Arctic would be highly vulnerable to oil trapped under the ice. Our present scant knowledge of these food chains makes it difficult to assess the extent of the damage that would occur to them, but it is clear that they are highly vulnerable to pollution or disturbance.

CRITICAL LIFE STAGES

The second concept basic to understanding the sensitivity of arctic species is that of critical stages in the life of a species. This is a fundamental aspect of wildlife sensitivity everywhere, but the highly developed winter-summer seasonality of the arctic environment and the relatively simple nature of the arctic food chains combine to make certain life stages critical to the survival of whole populations of certain species.

I have described how the calving grounds of the Porcupine caribou herd and the staging areas of the snow geese in the Northern Yukon are critical to the survival of those two populations because almost all the animals are concentrated in small areas at a time when their vulnerability to disturbance is high, and because there are no

suitable alternative areas for calving and staging.

In the Delta-Beaufort region there are critical life stage areas that are essential to the survival of other populations. The nesting, staging and moulting areas of the outer Delta are vital to very large populations of various species of birds. The offshore leads are critical for birds, seals and polar bears. The spawning and overwintering waters and migration routes in the Delta region are critical for various fish populations. The calving grounds in the shallow waters of the Delta are critical for the white whales of the Beaufort Sea. Similarly, other mammals of the region have den sites, calving areas, migration routes and wintering areas that are critical.

The most sensitive species are those that concentrate a major portion of the population on very limited habitat during a critical life stage. If industrial development impinges on that habitat, the species will be very vulnerable to impact, either directly through disturbance or indirectly through alteration of habitat or disruption of the food chain.

The State of Environmental Knowledge

Any attempt to assess the environmental effects of industrial development in the Delta-Beaufort region is hampered by the gaps in our knowledge, despite the extensive studies made by industry, by ongoing government programs as well as by the Beaufort Sea Project and the Environmental-Social Program. Both physical scientists and biologists have spoken to the Inquiry of our lack of knowledge about various natural

Map labels:

BEAUFORT SEA

BANKS ISLAND

Sachs Harbour

Approximate southern boundary of permanent pack ice and northern boundary of seasonally open water

Northeastern limit of petroleum leases

Prudhoe Bay

Kaktovik

Approximate boundary between winter stationary land-fast ice and moving winter pack ice

Approximate outer limit of continental shelf (generally less than 600 feet deep)

○ Dome 1976 drill sites

▲ Artificial Islands

AMUNDSEN GULF

ALASKA

Arctic Gas route

Tuktoyaktuk

0   Kilometres   200

0   Miles   100

YUKON

Aklavik

Inuvik

N.W.T

Paulatuk

THE BEAUFORT SEA: A POTENTIAL OFFSHORE PETROLEUM DEVELOPMENT AREA

processes, about reactions to changes induced by man, and about the effectiveness of mitigative measures.

Before assessing change, it is absolutely essential to understand first what is an undisturbed or normal condition. Only then can we adequately appreciate many of the effects of impact. A great deal of work over a period of years and at all seasons of those years is required to demonstrate the range of normal annual and seasonal variations and to define the major factors that make the ecosystem function. Complementary to this work, there should be studies of specific anticipated impacts.

Dr. Art Martell, of the Canadian Wildlife Service, listed some of the important gaps in our knowledge of the biology of species that inhabit the coastal areas and the Delta. He included freshwater fish, birds (particularly waterfowl), certain furbearers, caribou, moose, Dall sheep, bears and whales.

There are even greater gaps in our knowledge of the Beaufort Sea. Dr. Allen Milne, head of the Beaufort Sea Project, and James Shearer, who had conducted research under this program described how little we know of aspects of the physical environment, such as sea-bed scour and sea-bed permafrost. Dr. Douglas Pimlott of the Canadian Arctic Resources Committee told the Inquiry that there is a pronounced imbalance between our knowledge of arctic marine ecosystems and the proposed industrial developments. In his view, our present knowledge approximates to a time base of 1890 as compared to other areas that are experiencing similar development. Dr. Jonathon Percy of the Fisheries and Marine Service, Environment Canada, said our knowledge of the effect of oil on the arctic marine environment is meagre and fragmented and that we have little knowledge of

even the most basic ecology and physiology of most of the arctic marine species. Percy testified that our ecological ignorance makes it difficult to sustain or to refute predictions of widespread environmental disaster. Although attempts have been made to determine the impact of oil upon marine mammals and waterfowl, little attention has been paid to smaller organisms on which the larger forms of life depend. Where oil spills have occurred in the Arctic, we have learned very little because there was a complete absence of pre-spill baseline data.

We must learn more about the rates of degradation of oil by bacteria under varying circumstances. Assessment of the degradation rates will require greater knowledge of the populations of bacteria and of their natural variations. In laboratory tests, crude oils inhibit productivity and growth of phytoplankton under many, but not all, circumstances. We need to understand these interactions. We must also learn about effects of oil on the algal bloom that forms on and within the lower surface of ice in spring. This ice flora is an important fraction of the total biological production in the Arctic Ocean.

The gaps in environmental knowledge that I have listed here for the Delta-Beaufort region are complemented by a similar need for environmental information in the other areas that are of concern to this Inquiry: the Mackenzie Valley and the Northern Yukon. Together they underline the fact that present scientific knowledge is inadequate to serve the needs of government in assessing the impact of proposed oil and gas developments in the North. If government is to conduct such assessments effectively, it must undertake the scientific research that is required to provide this information.

Dr. Max Dunbar wrote *Environment and*

Common Sense in 1971. What he said then about our knowledge of the North is still applicable today:

> We have been caught in a state of scientific near-nudity in the particular respect in which we now so urgently need protective covering: namely, knowledge of what the proposed developments will do to the environment, in precise terms, and knowledge of what should be done to conserve and to protect [it]. [p. 53]

Industry's Plans

Although the oil reserves at Norman Wells have been known to the industry since 1919, it is only within the last two decades that we have seen oil and gas exploration expand into the Northern Yukon, the Mackenzie Delta and the Beaufort Sea. In 1968, the discovery of gas at Prudhoe Bay in Alaska stimulated activity in the Western Arctic and focused national attention on the Delta-Beaufort region as a potential petroleum-producing area.

Drilling in the Delta region began in the mid-1960s, and Imperial made the first discovery of oil at Atkinson Point in 1970. Other discoveries of oil and gas have followed, and more than 100 holes have been drilled in the Delta region. About three-quarters of the region that is of most interest to the industry lies offshore under the Beaufort Sea. The permits granted so far in the Delta-Beaufort region cover the whole continental shelf out to and even beyond the 600-foot water-depth line.

In 1973 exploratory work began in the shallow waters adjacent to the coast. Artificial islands, built as drilling bases, have all been located within the zone of land-fast ice and in water less than 60 feet deep. Imperial and Sun Oil have already built about 15

Gulf Mobil rig near the Caribou Hills. (L. Bliss)

Oil rig in the Mackenzie Delta. (NFB—McNeill)

Fuel storage bladder. (J. Inglis)

islands, and they expect to build several more.

In the summer of 1976, exploratory drilling began in the deeper water of the Beaufort Sea, when Canadian Marine Drilling Limited (CANMAR), a wholly-owned subsidiary of Dome Petroleum, moved two drill ships into the Beaufort Sea. They began by drilling two holes and made preparations for a further five. The first two holes are in water depths of 85 and 190 feet, and both are in the shear zone between the land-fast ice and the permanent polar pack ice. Moving ice may threaten drilling operations here even in summer.

But exploratory drilling, whether on land or offshore, is only part of the total activity that leads to the delineation of reserves and their eventual production. The Delta-Beaufort region has witnessed more than a decade of all phases of exploratory work. The forested portion of the Delta is a grid of arrow-straight paths bulldozed by seismic crews in their mapping of subsurface geological formations. There is already a major infrastructure of camps, wharves, stockpile sites, airstrips and winter roads to support this exploration. For example, the Gulf base at Swimming Point in the Delta is a self-sufficient distribution centre for men and material. It has a winter airstrip for jet aircraft and crews are rotated in and out directly from Calgary. Imperial and Shell have extensive facilities at Tununuk and Camp Farewell, respectively, and Imperial has a base camp and other facilities at Tuktoyaktuk.

Over the years, the exploration program has produced results; oil and gas have been found. There is a great deal of controversy about the extent of reserves in the Mackenzie Delta and the Beaufort Sea, but they are believed to be large enough to justify the expenditure of millions of dollars.

Now there are two proposals for multi-billion dollar natural gas pipelines before us. Three gas-processing plants are proposed. Exploration has expanded to offshore areas, and discoveries have been made there. Offshore production facilities would involve the creation of islands, and sea-bed pipelines would be needed for production. If a gas pipeline is built, it will probably be looped, and an oil pipeline may follow. Airports, roads, docks, stockpile sites — a whole industrial infrastructure would be needed for production. Tanker terminals and tanker transportation may follow.

These prospects indicate that the Delta-Beaufort region may become one of Canada's major oil and gas producing regions. With this in mind, let me turn to the proposals for a gas pipeline and gas production facilities.

Pipeline Proposals

When Arctic Gas first sought a right-of-way in March 1974, they proposed to build a pipeline from Prudhoe Bay, along the north slope of the Yukon, then southwesterly around the head of the Delta, crossing the Peel River near Fort McPherson and the main channel of Mackenzie River at Point Separation. West of Travaillant Lake, it would join the line from the Taglu gas plant on Richards Island, and from there, the main line would run southeasterly, along the east side of the Mackenzie River.

In January 1976, Arctic Gas announced that they would seek a right-of-way to transport Alaskan gas across the northern part of the Delta (the Cross-Delta Route) to join the main line from Richards Island near Tununuk Point. This proposal caused changes in about 150 miles of the route between Taglu and Thunder River. The main reason why Arctic Gas prefer the Cross-Delta Route is that it is about 100 miles shorter, and would thus cost about $180-$190 million less.

The Cross-Delta Route involves about 52 miles of right-of-way across the northern part of the Mackenzie Delta. Of this, 16 miles would be 48-inch-diameter single pipe, and 36 miles would be 36-inch-diameter twinned pipes. The two pipes would normally be laid 50 feet apart on land, 200 feet apart under Shallow Bay and as much as 4,000 feet apart under some of the main channels of the Delta. In crossing the Mackenzie Delta, some 12 miles of the right-of-way would be under water. This includes the 4.5 miles across Shallow Bay and the major crossings of West Channel, Middle (or Reindeer) Channel and Langley Channel. The four major water crossings would be built in summer, but the rest of the construction, including some 35 separate crossings of small channels and lakes, would be done in winter.

Because Arctic Gas want to carry Alaskan gas to the main north-south line by either the Cross-Delta or the Circum-Delta Route, their activities in the region would be much more extensive than what Foothills propose. The Foothills route south from the Delta gas plants would not differ substantially from that proposed by Arctic Gas. But their construction plan for the northernmost 50 miles is different in that the pipe would be laid in fall from a gravel work pad instead of during winter from a snow road.

Both pipeline proposals include permanent compressor stations and the construction and maintenance of support facilities. The Arctic Gas Cross-Delta Route would involve a compressor station on the eastern edge of the Delta at Tununuk Junction and

REMOTE WELL CLUSTER

400'
Sump
180'
Helipad
Control room and living quarters
500'
Tank farm
Process, utility compressor units
Flare
Gathering lines
Block valve building

Flare

Sewage plant and incinerator
500'
Water treatment
Power plant
500'
Utilidor
Utility bldg.
200 MAN CAMP AREA
Raw water storage
Pad

Utilidor
Roadway

Pump house
Staging area
400'
Dock
400'
Channel

WHARF

WELL CLUSTER
Well head
400'
Service rig access
180'
Sump
Gravel pad
Heater

Process bldg.
Office
Warehouse, shop, garage
Gravel pad
700'
GAS PROCESSING PLANT

850'
Compressor bldg.
Diked tank storage
Injection liquid building

Sales gas (buried)

SCHEMATIC DRAWING OF A GAS WELL AND GAS PLANT COMPLEX

LANDING STRIP

Not to scale

seven construction work pads, three wharf and stockpile sites and one helipad on the Delta. The gravel for the Cross-Delta Route would have to be hauled from west of the Delta or from the Richards Island area to the east.

The Circum-Delta Route, on the other hand, would involve facilities on the west and south sides of the Delta, including three compressor stations, four wharf and stock-pile sites, two airstrips and nine helipads. Gravel for this route would be hauled from about 13 borrow pits along it.

Gas Plant Proposals

There are three proposals before the Government of Canada to build facilities in the Delta area to process natural gas for pipeline transmission. These facilities, like the pipeline, tell us something about the broader picture of future industrial development in the Beaufort-Delta region.

The combined output of the three plants would be about 1.25 billion cubic feet per day (bcfd) of gas, yet the sizes of the trunk and lateral pipelines in both the Arctic Gas and Foothills proposals imply much higher throughputs — in the three to four bcfd range. The Taglu and Parsons Lake gas plants have been designed with excess capacity in anticipation of future discoveries. Clearly the industry has great expectations for the future in the Delta and offshore areas.

Two of the proposed gas plants, those of Imperial at Taglu and Shell at Niglintgak, will be in the Delta. Gulf propose to build the third plant at Parsons Lake, east of the Delta proper. Gas gathering systems will bring the gas from the fields to each of the plants. The capital cost of these three gas plants and gathering systems will exceed $1 billion.

To illustrate the way in which these plants will be constructed and operated I will describe the plant that Imperial propose to build at Taglu. The Shell and Gulf proposals differ only in detail.

THE IMPERIAL PLANT AT TAGLU

The Taglu gas field covers about 10 square miles. The plant to tap and process the gas would be built south of Big Lake, west of Harry Channel and would lie within the Kendall Island Bird Sanctuary. It would cover approximately 1,000 acres, including the well clusters, plant site, dock, access roads, airstrip and flow lines. The well heads will be clustered on elevated gravel pads, approximately 500 feet by 1,600 feet, and the pads will have the drilling sump beside them. The wells will radiate outward from each pad, and each well will be drilled to approximately 10,000 feet.

Flow lines from the well heads to the plant will run above ground. They will be supported on piles, frozen into the permafrost, for protection against flooding and to prevent thermal disturbance to the ground. For construction, 1.5 million cubic yards of granular material will be required for the gravel pads. Much of this material will be brought from the Ya Ya Lake esker, 20 miles away, which is accessible by barge in summer and by truck over the frozen river channels in winter. There will be a 2,500-foot STOL airstrip, a dock, and an adjacent staging site reached by barge from the East Channel. Fuel will be delivered to the site in conventional bulk fuel barges.

The gas plant will be of modular construction. Ocean-going barges will carry the larger, heavier modules (some of them weighing up to 1,000 tons) from the Pacific coast around Point Barrow to the Mackenzie Delta plant site. At the mouth of the East

Channel of the Mackenzie River, in Kugmallit Bay, the barges will be lightened, with cargo transferred to river barges, to reduce draft and enable them to be towed to Taglu. On arrival, the modules will be transferred onto special heavy-load crawler transporters, moved along specially built roads and set on piles at the plant site.

Imperial say that, with maximum use of these modules, site construction will require about 400 specialized tradesmen. Non-modular construction would require about 700 skilled tradesmen working in less shelter and under very difficult physical and climatic conditions. Permanent operating and maintenance staff will number about 65, and they will live in a self-sufficient housing and recreation complex accommodating up to 100 people on the site.

Future Prospects

So here is a large-scale construction program, employing 1,200 men or more to build three gas plants, and these men are in addition to the substantial labour force working on the pipeline in the area. The construction of the three plants and the pipeline will greatly increase barge traffic down the Mackenzie River, along the Arctic coast, and in Kugmallit Bay. When the plants and systems are in place, there will be gas plants, pipelines, compressor stations, flow lines, camps, on-site housing, all-weather roads, airfields, docks and regular passage of aircraft and vehicles across the Delta.

The extent of these operations is apparent, but they may well be only a beginning, for we can expect additional developments in the Delta and the Delta region. If there are pipelines running along an energy corridor from the Arctic to the mid-continent, there

Construction of a drill site pad. (L. Bliss)

Drilling at Taglu. (DIAND)

Recreation room on the Unark offshore island rig. (DIAND)

will be an extension of exploration and development into the Beaufort Sea. Roland Horsfield of Imperial suggested that most of the remaining potential of the Mackenzie Basin lies offshore in the Beaufort Sea. Dan Motyka of Gulf told the Inquiry that the hydrocarbon potential of the area increases farther offshore. What does all this mean for the future of the Beaufort-Delta region?

Industry was unwilling to forecast for the Inquiry its own view of the scope and extent of future oil and gas exploration and production activity in the Beaufort Sea. I suppose that is understandable; their estimates of reserves may be subject to change, and they seek to limit any consideration of impact to the proposals that they have advanced. But even though industry was unwilling to forecast future developments, the Inquiry must attempt to do so. There is a good deal of information to go on. We know, for instance, that over 100 holes have been drilled in the Delta. We know that the larger part of the basin lies under the Beaufort Sea. It seems likely that, in time, as many or more holes will be drilled offshore as have been drilled in the Delta. To bring oil and gas finds into production and to markets in the south would require a network of sea-bottom flow lines, a series of tank farms and processing plants onshore, a system of gathering lines to feed the products into one or more gas pipelines, and possibly an oil pipeline, along the Mackenzie Valley. Such developments would result in a high level of year-round human activity spread over the whole region for a generation or more. There will be areas of concentrated activity in Inuvik, around Tuktoyaktuk and along the coast at gas plants and tank farms.

E.R. Walker in *Oil, Ice and Climate in the Beaufort Sea*, the final report of the Beaufort Delta Project, offered this scenario:

The sub-sea formations extending under the Beaufort Sea to the edge of the continental shelf are estimated to contain from 3×10^9 (EMR 1973) to as much as 4×10^{10} barrels of recoverable oils according to some oil industry estimates. Industry sources estimate this oil may be accompanied by as much as 50 trillion cubic feet of gas.

Exploration has already commenced and will continue at least through 1980. In the exploration until 1980, approximately 20 wells will be drilled from 20 artificial islands in water depths less than 15 to 20 m. Another 20 wells may be drilled from floating platforms or ships in water depths up to 150 m. If significant quantities of gas and particularly oil are found, the level of exploratory activity may double or triple. If no significant finds are made by 1980, the activity may well taper off. The total number of exploratory wells might range from 40 to 50 by 1980 to as many as 120 to 150 by 1990.... The production phase may begin before 1985 and continue at least until 2010. The removal of oil may be as much as 300,000 barrels per day in 1985 and 600,000 barrels per day by 1990. To bring this oil to the surface, from 50 to 200 wells may be producing by 1985 and perhaps 100 to 300 wells may be producing by 1990. The oil will most likely be gathered by sea-bed pipelines. [p. 15ff.]

James Shearer, appearing for the Canadian Arctic Resources Committee, estimated that if total production offshore came to 20 to 30 trillion cubic feet of gas and two to three billion barrels of oil, there might be 300 to 400 exploratory holes offshore. They could be spread over an area 200 miles long, from Cape Bathurst in the northeast to Ellice Island in the southwest, and 80 miles wide from the coast of the Mackenzie Delta and Tuktoyaktuk Peninsula out to the edge of the continental shelf at about the 600-foot water-depth line.

Granted, no one can say for sure what will happen. The whole future of hydrocarbon activity in the region obviously depends on the discovery, and the rate of discovery, of oil

and gas. However, it is plain from statements made by both industry and government, and from the extent of the present permits, that there is the potential for a major petroleum producing province in the Beaufort-Delta region.

Delta Region Impacts

If we deal with each project piecemeal, we run the risk of missing the point. We are considering the establishment of a major petroleum province in the Delta-Beaufort region, and our predictions of impact will be sound only if we consider them comprehensively. The Delta supports a unique ecosystem and has been aptly compared to the Everglades. The ecosystem must be protected as a unit. However, to illustrate the impact that the pipeline and related activities will have on the Delta region, I shall concentrate on the principal biological concerns, the fish, birds and white whales. I intend to discuss the whales separately in the next section because of the direct threat that oil and gas developments pose to that population as a whole. Impacts on other species such as muskrat, beaver, reindeer, caribou and bear will be limited in extent and can be ameliorated by the kind of measures that I shall advance in Volume Two of this report. Little is said here about oil spills and their impact, because this subject is dealt with in some detail in a subsequent section.

FISH

Arctic Gas say in Section 14d. of their Application:

The Mackenzie Delta is probably the most important fisheries area along the entire

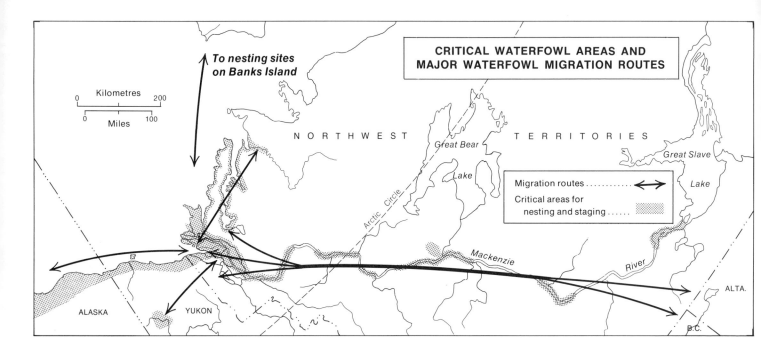

pipeline route. Fish utilization of the area is extensive. The Delta serves as a spawning, rearing and overwintering area and also as a migratory pathway for many fish species. [*Supplement ... Relative to Alternative Routing for the Alaska Supply Lateral Across the Mackenzie Delta, p. 27*]

Impacts on fish could result from changes in the smaller food organisms and exclusion from important habitats. There may also be changes in the habitats themselves, such as oxygen depletion, and sedimentation of spawning and overwintering areas. As industrial development proceeds, fuel and other toxic substances may be spilled, and, of course, there will be more people in the area to increase sport, domestic and commercial fishing.

I think that it is only realistic to assume that successive developments will progressively alter and perhaps diminish the productivity of the aquatic ecosystem in the Delta. The fish populations will feel this impact directly and indirectly throughout the food chain. The extent of these impacts cannot be calculated, but much will depend on the pace and scope of industrial development, its regulation and, of course, the progress of aquatic research. Concern for this latter aspect is all the greater because of the recent truncation of some government research programs in the area.

Granted, a properly regulated, scheduled and routed gas pipeline project, in itself, will probably have only local and short-term impact on fish, and little or no long-term impact — assuming there are no large spills of toxic materials. But it is not reasonable to consider the pipeline by itself; there will be other projects, and they will pose risks to the fish. The effects will be evident in decreased populations of the most economically important fish species, such as humpback whitefish, broad whitefish, inconnu, arctic char,

and arctic and least cisco. Development will also disrupt fishing activities in the area.

The pipeline proposals offer a choice of two routes. The Arctic Gas Cross-Delta Route will cross the outer part of the Delta, and the alternative route circumscribes the Delta. Which is better in terms of impact on fish and fisheries? Dr. Peter McCart, fisheries consultant for Arctic Gas, told the Inquiry:

> It's not possible to distinguish between them. There are advantages to one and disadvantages which are balanced as far as we can see by the advantages and disadvantages of the other. [F20487ff.]

When asked about the possibility of establishing an oil pipeline and an energy corridor along the route (in keeping with the government's 1972 Pipeline Guidelines), McCart said that he would be very reticent about a proposal to put an oil pipeline across the Delta. Jeff Stein of Environment Canada told the Inquiry that the Mackenzie Delta has been designated by the federal Fisheries and Marine Service as an area likely to be sensitive to pipeline construction. He concluded:

> ... the Mackenzie River Delta provides essential habitat for the maintenance of the freshwater, coastal marine and anadromous fish resources in much of the southern Beaufort Sea area and lower Mackenzie River. The inshore zone is an important nursery, feeding and overwintering site for both nearshore and offshore organisms. It is especially important to those anadromous species which form the basis of the domestic and commercial fishery in the Delta; that is, broad whitefish, arctic char, arctic cisco and inconnu. Standing stocks of fish are greatest nearshore, since the anadromous species tend to frequent shallow coastal waters during the summer months rather than moving far offshore. Proposed developments in the Delta region can be expected to adversely affect aquatic resources. [F18436ff.]

Of course, pipelines are not the only kind of development that can adversely affect fish populations in the Delta. The construction and operation of gas plants, drilling and other exploration activities, and dredging or gravel-pit operations could all have impacts. For example, the plan that Imperial Oil described to the Inquiry for dredging sand at Big Horn Point could cause risks to important fish populations, but insufficient information was then available about the site to predict the magnitude of this concern.

BIRDS

Dr. William Gunn, ornithological consultant to Arctic Gas, told the Inquiry that the whole of the Delta is important for waterfowl. In June, July and August 1975, he made four aerial surveys along the Arctic Gas Cross-Delta Route and found that the greatest number of nesting waterfowl occurred along the outer Mackenzie Delta section of the route in June. The Cross-Delta Route crosses some prime waterfowl habitats, especially on Ellice Island, where staging geese concentrate and there are important nesting grounds for swans, cranes and ducks. Originally a compressor station was planned for the middle of that area, but Arctic Gas have agreed, on the advice of Gunn, to move the compressor station to the eastern fringe of the Delta. Gunn also found that the Delta habitat may, in a given year, be as vital as the north slope of the Yukon to the snow geese. Normally, the majority of the snow geese stage on the north slope, but in 1975, it was snow-covered in early September when the geese arrived, and most of the geese moved into the Shallow Bay area of the Delta. The peak number of geese there was an estimated 325,000 out of a total of 375,000 in the entire region. These birds are extremely vulnerable to aircraft overflights

Canada geese. (C. & M. Hampson)

Seismic lines across the Delta. (M. Jackson)

White-fronted goose, a common breeding bird of the Delta. (C. & M. Hampson)

and to the kind of disturbance that would be associated with the summer construction of the Shallow Bay crossing as well as the ongoing activity associated with an operating pipeline.

That is why Gunn and Dr. Tom Barry of the Canadian Wildlife Service would prefer a crossing farther upstream than that now proposed by Arctic Gas. They are concerned that the route chosen by Arctic Gas will cross vital nesting and staging areas in the Delta.

The Arctic Gas Circum-Delta Route, although it impinges upon habitat used by a wide variety of birds, avoids the areas of high concentration characteristic of the Delta proper. Granted, it does approach a number of raptor nest sites, and if the pipeline is built, they would have to be protected by rigorous terms and conditions.

Gunn told the Inquiry that from the point of view of impact on birds, the Circum-Delta Route is clearly preferable to the Cross-Delta Route. The possibility of an oil pipeline along the Cross-Delta Route raises extremely important concerns for birds. Both Gunn and Barry spoke at length about the devastating impact of oil spills on birds. Both emphasized the lack of any suitable means of rehabilitating birds that come into contact with oil, even in temperate climates. Oil mats the feathers together so they are no longer able to function for flight, to repel water or for insulation. Once this happens, the birds generally die by drowning or exposure; they are also harmed by the direct toxic effects of oil when ingested through preening their feathers in an attempt to rid themselves of contaminants. When cross-examined about an oil pipeline following a gas pipeline across the Delta, Gunn said:

My concern is with the possibility of oil leaks or spills along the line, in areas that are of

particular importance to birds, since there are numbers of these in the Delta. I feel that it might be difficult to find a suitable route across the Delta on that basis. [F20213]

In his report, *The Need to Preserve the Integrity of the Mackenzie Delta,* Gunn went beyond the pipeline proposals and considered the impact of a broad range of hydrocarbon developments in the Delta. He noted that the pipeline, in itself, and a reasonable number of oil and gas wells would not, in themselves, compromise the integrity of the environment. But he added:

The problem, however, comes with the establishment of processing plants at or near the wellhead for the purpose of modifying the composition of the gas (or oil) to a form suitable for extended transmission.

If full development of such processing plants were permitted on the Delta, it would entail intensive on-site and support activity during construction, and a fairly high level of human presence, aircraft and vehicular (and perhaps barge) activity during the lifetime of the project. There is also the problem that such plants are much more difficult to maintain as an environmentally "clean" operation than a well site. Of the companies presently known to be planning production in or near the Delta, the Gulf site at Parsons Lake presents no direct threat to the Delta since it is well clear of the Delta. Imperial's site at Taglu and Shell's site at Niglintgak, however, are not only well within the outer Delta but are actually within the confines of the Kendall Island Bird Sanctuary, which is of great importance to geese, swans, and other waterfowl. If Sun Oil were to develop their gas find on or near Garry Island, they would probably wish to have their own processing plant, and the Sanctuary would then be effectively ringed by plants. The proliferation of other plants and sites on the Delta would be difficult to prevent. Although the environmental effects of any one of these plants might individually be acceptable, we are particularly concerned with the combined and cumulative effects. Because we believe that they would

unquestionably result in deterioration of the Delta as a viable ecological unit, we are therefore strongly opposed to processing plants on the Delta. In our view, these plants should be located on the "mainland" to the southeast, where they could be connected to Inuvik by a permanent road. [p. 9ff.]

Amelioration of Impacts in the Delta Region

The first condition for the amelioration of impact in the Delta is a requirement that no pipeline be allowed to cross the Mackenzie Delta; that is, if a pipeline is built from Alaska, the Circum-Delta rather than the Cross-Delta Route should be followed. This conclusion is based on the pipeline's impact on birds and fish that I have outlined, the impact on white whales that I will discuss in the next section, and on the overall importance and sensitivity of the outer Delta ecosystem in general.

To protect the fish resources of the Delta, research must keep pace with development activity. It is only by filling in the gaps in our knowledge that effective measures can be instituted to limit impacts to an acceptable level. This can be done on a project-by-project basis.

Such measures will not, however, suffice to protect the birds of the Delta. The migratory birds that use the region are an important international wildlife resource; the whole Delta, and particularly the outer Delta, is critical for them. Gunn has said that the whole Arctic coast from Prudhoe Bay to the Delta is ornithologically sensitive. I have already discussed the importance of the north slope of the Yukon for birds, particularly snow geese. The wilderness park in the Northern Yukon that I have proposed would protect them.

Various witnesses before the Inquiry said

that the boundaries of the Kendall Island Bird Sanctuary are being redrawn. On the basis of the evidence placed before me, I consider it important to extend the sanctuary westward to cover the entire outer Delta across to the wilderness park that I have recommended for the Northern Yukon.

The establishment of such a bird sanctuary, unlike the wilderness park, will not prohibit oil and gas exploration and development. In fact, there already are proposals for two gas plants within the Kendall Island Bird Sanctuary. But a sanctuary does provide protection to the birds by placing regulatory powers in the hands of the Canadian Wildlife Service, which has a statutory mandate to protect migratory birds. I urge that when the sanctuary is established, the means should be provided at the same time to protect the habitat on which the birds depend.

Gunn's report concludes on a note that I endorse:

We realize that the acceptance of these environmental requirements will require a great deal of additional effort on the part of design engineers representing the producing and transporting companies. We can only say that we think these requirements would receive strong support from biologists who have given serious study to the proposed development. Because the developmental companies have spent an extraordinary amount of time and money in carrying out environmental base-line impact studies, we have the unprecedented opportunity of planning industrial development within one of the world's great deltas before it takes place, and of doing it in such a way that will ensure the preservation of the environmental integrity of the Delta at the end of the process. It would be a pity to throw away our chances for success when we have come so close with such effort. The Delta should be allowed to exist as an example of what can be accomplished if we put our heads together. [op. cit., p. 10ff.]

Whales and A Whale Sanctuary

In summer the white whales of the Beaufort Sea converge on the Mackenzie Delta to calve. The herd — some 5,000 animals — remains in the vicinity of the Delta throughout the summer, then leaves for the open sea. For these animals, the warm waters around the Mackenzie Delta, especially Mackenzie Bay, are critical habitat, for here they have their young. Nowhere else, so far as we know, can they go for this essential part of their life cycle. We must preserve these waters from any disturbance that would drive the whales from them.

Construction of the gas pipeline across Shallow Bay, as proposed by Arctic Gas, and construction of an oil pipeline along the same corridor, together with associated barge and aircraft activity, would have a definite impact on the whale population; but the long-term threat comprises the whole complex of petroleum activities in the coastal waters bordering the Mackenzie Delta, Richards Island and adjacent areas. These activities would include construction of artificial islands or other drilling platforms, associated dredging and barge movements, drilling of wells, construction of flow lines, and blasting. The cumulative and long-term impact would be great.

It is imperative, if we are to protect the whales, to establish a whale sanctuary in Mackenzie Bay and to forbid oil and gas exploration and development and pipeline construction within it.

Our knowledge of the white whales of the Beaufort Sea is limited. We do not even know whether they winter in the Pacific Ocean or remain in the Arctic Ocean. In spring, they migrate along leads in the pack ice into the Beaufort Sea from the west, arriving in May or June. The whales move into the warm, shallow water around the Delta in late June or early July as soon as there are open leads through the ice, and stay around the channel mouths until mid-August. They are there in large numbers: the population was estimated at 3,500 to 4,000 in 1973, 1974 and 1975. Whales have been sighted throughout the Delta, and even as far south as Point Separation.

The Inuit who spoke to the Inquiry at Tuktoyaktuk testified that whales come from Mackenzie Bay into Kugmallit Bay as soon as the ice north of Kendall Island allows them to get around it, in late June or July. Even though they may go back into Mackenzie Bay, they return to Kugmallit Bay and stay there well into September. If summer is late, the whales may not reach Mackenzie Bay until mid-August, and they will then stay in Kugmallit Bay until late September. By the end of September, they can be seen offshore near the pack ice.

Many Inuit and some Indians regularly go out to hunt whales from camps in the Delta, and the people of Tuktoyaktuk go out from the village daily. Archaeological finds indicate that the Inuit have hunted white whales from Kittigazuit and Radio Creek for at least 500 years. Today, they take about 150 whales a year. It is estimated that they kill about 300, but they are able to recover only about half of that number. This level of hunting does not diminish the herd.

Robert Webb of Slaney and Company conducted a study of white whales for Imperial Oil in the area between Kugmallit Bay and the west side of Mackenzie Bay, and south into Shallow Bay, beyond the proposed pipeline crossing. The purpose of the study was to determine the effect that the

White whales. (R. McClung)

White whale ready for butchering. (W. Hoek)

Preparing "muktuk" for storage. (W. Hunt)

Whale camp at Whitefish Station. (M. Jackson)

construction of offshore islands would have on the distribution of whales in the Delta and on the taking of whales by native people. The study, which began in 1972, continued through the summer of 1975. In two of these four years, apparently few whales entered Shallow Bay; but in the other two years they were observed as far south as the mouth of Reindeer Channel. However, Webb feels that the infrequency of the observations and the turbidity of the Delta water may limit the reliability of these observations. Perhaps whales did enter Shallow Bay in larger numbers, but were simply not observed. It is not known exactly where the whales drop their calves. New-born calves have been sighted in Shallow Bay and Kugmallit Bay, but their dark colour makes them difficult to see in the turbid water. Probably most calves are born in the main whale concentration area in west Mackenzie Bay-Shallow Bay. The warm river water is essential habitat for the newborn young until they develop enough blubber to survive in the colder oceanic water. If they had to move out earlier, the calves would lose body heat and die in the cold water.

The Long-term Threat

The construction of a pipeline across the Delta may bar the whales' access to Shallow Bay. If it does keep them from Shallow Bay, the herd probably will be diminished only slightly, if we can assume that the crossing would be built in just one summer, and that the only calves lost would be those that would have been dropped in Shallow Bay. Even if the whales were kept right out of Mackenzie Bay by barge traffic and related activity during the period of pipeline construction, and even if the construction took

two or three years, the worst that might happen would be the loss of two or three years' calves. These losses could reduce the size of the herd but would not threaten its survival. But a pipeline across Shallow Bay cannot be considered in isolation. It is only a beginning.

If the pipeline is built, there will be increased oil and gas exploration and development in the Beaufort Sea. This development, both nearshore and offshore, will have a large impact on the whale population, greater in the long run than that of a pipeline crossing the Mackenzie Delta.

Although the whales concentrate in west Mackenzie Bay-Shallow Bay, east Mackenzie Bay and Kugmallit Bay, it is the west Mackenzie Bay-Shallow Bay area that is critical. Dr. David Sergeant of the Department of the Environment, who is Canada's leading authority on white whales, says that if calving were seriously disrupted annually, the population could ultimately die out. He is supported by Dr. Paul Brodie, who is also an authority on the subject. Sergeant's view is that the cumulative impact of oil and gas exploration and development may lead to the gradual expulsion of the calving whales from Mackenzie Bay. Sergeant called our attention to the experience at the mouth of Churchill River, at Churchill, Manitoba, which was once a calving ground for white whales. The port facilities there have driven the whales away to calve elsewhere, and their major calving area now is at the mouth of Seal River, about 20 miles to the north which, fortunately, can accommodate them.

Sergeant cannot see any other river mouths in the neighbourhood of the Mackenzie Delta that could receive a large number of whales for calving. None receive them now. A few whales move into Liverpool Bay and around the mouth of the

Anderson River in late July, after they have left the Delta. But these waters become free of ice later than those around the Delta, and to reach them the whales would have to postpone calving. That may or may not be possible. In any event, the warm water available at the mouth of the Anderson River could not support the herd that now calves around the Mackenzie Delta, and the seasonal variation of ice conditions might well close off that estuary in some years. Sergeant, summarizing his evidence, stated:

> ... the population of white whales which calves in the Mackenzie is virtually the whole of the population in the Beaufort Sea. I postulate that simultaneous oil and gas activities throughout the whole Delta in July each year could so disturb the whale herd that they would be unable to reproduce successfully. In time, the herd would die out. If we wish to maintain the herd, we must initiate measures now [for example, establish a special reserve for calving whales] which we can be certain will allow its successful reproduction annually. [F18496ff.]

A Whale Sanctuary

I think a whale sanctuary should be established in west Mackenzie Bay, where the main mass of white whales gather in July, and where the main calving area is located. No oil and gas exploration should be allowed there, no artificial islands built there, no wells drilled there, and no pipelines allowed to cross it.

Sergeant and Webb agree that, of the three areas where the whales are found in concentrations between June 20 and August 15, west Mackenzie Bay is the most important area because it is the main calving area. The sanctuary should be the same size or greater than the area used by the main herd of whales in west Mackenzie Bay in most years.

PROPOSED WHITE WHALE SANCTUARY IN RELATION TO PETROLEUM EXPLORATION ACTIVITY

Artificial islands .... ▲

Gas or oil wells .... O

Gas fields .... (stippled)

Principal areas used by
   whales in July ....

West Mackenzie Bay
   concentration area ....

Area of concentration used
   each year, 1972-1975 ....

Proposed whale sanctuary ....

Note: The sanctuary as originally
   proposed by Dr. Sergeant
   extended further to the
   northeast

MACKENZIE BAY

Tuktoyaktuk

Richards Island

Parsons Lake

Arctic Gas route

YUKON

N.W.T.

Kilometres   0   50

Miles   0   30

In recommending a whale sanctuary, I have relied upon the evidence of Sergeant and Brodie. Their views on the long-term threat that oil and gas exploration and development in the Mackenzie Delta hold for the white whales were not challenged by Arctic Gas or Foothills. Neither were they challenged by Imperial, Gulf and Shell, all of whom were represented by counsel when the evidence was heard. I have relied also on the evidence given by Inuit hunters at the hearings held in the Delta communities.

Is there any alternative to a whale sanctuary? It could be argued that, if oil and gas exploration and development were suspended in the summer, to be resumed again in winter when the whales are out at sea, the sanctuary would not be necessary. I think this idea is impractical. Once you permitted exploration of the waters of the sanctuary, even if you began by restricting such activity to the winter, you would inevitably find that certain activities must go on in summer. If industry is permitted to explore in these waters, there may be a need for summer seismic exploration, artificial islands for drilling platforms, and barge traffic during the short ice-free season. If oil or gas is discovered, then flow lines will be built. There are, in fact, a multitude of activities that can be carried out efficiently and economically only in summer.

Sergeant has proposed a sanctuary in which not only oil and gas exploration and development but also whale hunting by native people would be prohibited. There is an irony here. Many native people in Aklavik, Tuktoyaktuk, Sachs Harbour, Holman, Paulatuk and Inuvik told the Inquiry that they oppose oil and gas exploration and development in the Mackenzie Delta and the Beaufort Sea because of the impact they fear it will have on whales. A sanctuary would offer a measure of protection to the herd, and it would coincide with the wish of the native people to protect the herd. But if, at the same time, they are denied the right to hunt whales, what I regard as one of the main purposes of the sanctuary would be undermined.

I do not advocate a sanctuary in which native people are forbidden to hunt: I think their claim on these animals is fundamental. I think native hunting can be permitted without endangering the herd. Hunting is heaviest in Kugmallit Bay, and east Mackenzie Bay, which are remote from the proposed sanctuary. If hunting pressure appeared to threaten the herd, it could be reduced or even prohibited. But no such check could be imposed upon oil and gas exploration and development in the sanctuary, once a pipeline is built and the corridor established.

Is a whale sanctuary in west Mackenzie Bay a practical proposition? What will its effect be on future oil and gas exploration? Will it impose an unacceptable check on oil and gas exploration and development in the Mackenzie Delta and the Beaufort Sea? These are very difficult questions to answer. However, I note that the areas of intense petroleum exploration, to date, lie east of the proposed whale sanctuary, both offshore and onshore. Moreover, there has been substantially less seismic work in the sanctuary area than in adjoining areas to the east. If this trend continues, and if it reflects a difference in petroleum potential, then a whale sanctuary can be set aside, and oil and gas activity can be forbidden there without impairing industry's ability to tap the principal sources of petroleum beneath the Beaufort Sea.

Let it be understood that the proposed sanctuary is itself a compromise. The evidence shows that in past years there have been whale concentrations northeast of the proposed sanctuary, in an area where a number of artificial islands have recently been established. I am not proposing that the sanctuary extend that far: that area has already, in a sense, been given over to industrial use. I should draw the northern boundary of the sanctuary south of the Adgo field, where gas and oil have been found. This seems to me a reasonable compromise between the competing uses. The sanctuary would not then deny industry access to any waters where discoveries have been made, and yet it would retain within its waters the areas where most calving occurs.

The trend of exploration appears to offer us an opportunity to set aside certain offshore waters as a whale sanctuary, but this trend is by no means a certainty. In the final analysis, the Government of Canada will have to decide whether or not to protect this herd of whales. If we decide to protect them, we must establish a sanctuary that will be inviolate regardless of the prospects for oil and gas discoveries. Once a discovery has been made within the sanctuary, it would be difficult to resist the urge to look for other reserves near it. We must decide whether we are going to protect these animals or not. If we are going to protect them, we must establish a whale sanctuary now.

Offshore Concerns

The Move Offshore

Exploration has now moved offshore. Permits granted cover the whole continental shelf of the Beaufort Sea. Spokesmen for the industry told the Inquiry that the greatest potential reserves are thought to be there. Ten wells have already been drilled offshore.

CANMAR drillship Explorer. (DIAND)

Vince Steen, of Tuktoyaktuk. (M. Jackson)

Reporter and crew member aboard drill ship.
(Native Press)

from man-made islands. Dome Petroleum, through its subsidiary CANMAR, has begun a 16-hole deep-water exploratory program from drill ships. Two wells were drilled in the summer of 1976.

Offshore petroleum development in the Beaufort Sea is in its infancy. But if the pipeline were approved and industry were assured of a transportation system for gas and a corridor for oil, both onshore and offshore exploration would be intensified. Flow lines, pipelines, oil and gas processing facilities, delineation drilling and related logistics and support activities would expand beyond the Delta and the man-made islands already built.

The Beaufort Sea offers one of the world's most hostile marine environments to oil and gas exploration. Much of it is covered by the permanent polar pack ice, which circulates slowly around the Polar Basin. The area between the polar pack and land is seasonally covered by ice. Land-fast ice forms during the fall along the shoreline and shallow water areas, and drilling from man-made islands has taken place in this zone. Between the land-fast ice and the polar pack is the shear zone, where currents and other forces cause the ice to move, forming huge pressure ridges with intermittent leads of open water. It is in this shear zone that Dome Petroleum's wells are located. In summer, when CANMAR drills these wells, ice flows moving across this area are a hazard to the ships and drilling operations.

The industry's ability to do this work under these formidable conditions represents a major achievement, and it has taken us across a technological and geographic frontier that no other nation has yet crossed. It is, nevertheless, a pioneering venture that entails serious short-term and long-term environmental risk. Vince Steen, in speaking to the Inquiry, voiced the concern of many Inuit people:

Now they want to drill out there. Now they want to build [a] pipeline, and they say they're not going to hurt the country while they do it....

If they drill out there, if they finish off what little whales are left, what little seals are left, what little polar bears are left, with one oil spill of any size big enough to hurt those animals, we're finished. The Eskimo population and culture is finished, because you [will] have to live as a white man and you [will] have nothing left. You have no more seals to feed the foxes. You've got no more fish to feed the seals, and you've got no more seals to feed the polar bears, and the polar bears are going to go looking for some white men then, because they've got nothing left to eat.

Already in the Eastern Arctic there are Eskimos getting seals covered with oil, and there's no oil work there yet, just from ships spilling their used oil; and seals, because they're covered with oil, they've got no more hair on their heads, no more hair on their body, and they're starving. That's on record in Yellowknife the last two weeks or so.

If they get ... an oil spill out there in that moving ice where they can't control it, that's the end of the seals. I think that not only will this part of the world suffer if the ocean is finished, I think every [Eskimo, from Alaska] all the way to the Eastern Arctic is going to suffer because that oil is going to finish the seals. It's going to finish the fish, and those fish don't just stay here, they go all over. Same with the seals, same with the polar bears, they go all over the place, and if they come here and get soaked with oil, they're finished.

For the Eskimo to believe now that the white man is not going to do any damage out there with his oil drilling and his oil wells is just about impossible, because he hasn't proven himself, as far as I'm concerned he hasn't proven himself worthy of being believed any more. That includes the federal government because I know I've worked with them, and I've done seismic work for them where they just blew up fish, and they had to be shut down by the federal Fisheries, there were so many fish killed. But he was not going to shut himself down, not as long as there was nobody seeing him doing it. ... So how can you just blame the oil company or the average white man? It's the government. The government is not running things — they're not even controlling themselves, how can they control anybody else? [C4201ff.]

The move to drill offshore began in 1971, when Imperial Oil applied for permission to build an island to use as a drilling platform in the Beaufort Sea. The Government of Canada granted that permission in 1973, and the artificial island, called Immerk, was built in shallow coastal waters with material dredged from the sea floor.

In the winter of 1973-1974, Panarctic drilled their first well in the high Arctic from reinforced ice in Hecla and Griper Bay, near Melville Island. This and subsequent offshore wells in the high Arctic have been drilled from ice-thickened pads on sea ice. The drilling is done in late winter and early spring, but it must stop while there is still enough time in the season to drill a relief well, should one be required to control a blowout.

The drilling in Hecla and Griper Bay and from Immerk set a precedent of great importance; it marked the transition from land to marine operations in the Arctic and the first move toward a new frontier of exploration. This frontier was extended when, on July 31, 1973, the Cabinet gave approval in principle to Dome's drilling program in the Beaufort Sea.

Because Dome's program is in the shear zone, drilling from the ice is impossible; it must, therefore, take place during the short summer season from ships. Special safety precautions and quick evacuation measures have been developed in case ice threatens the drill sites. But the summer season of open water is very short, and, if there were a blowout, the time available to drill a relief well would be severely limited. If a blowout occurred late in the season, it might not be possible to control it with a relief well until the following summer.

Although drilling from artificial islands poses similar problems, the risks are not of the same order of magnitude. If another island had to be built to control a blowout, that could be done in summer and winter, although break-up and freeze-up might prolong the construction period. Artificial islands in deep water may create further problems because of the long time required to build the island needed for the relief well.

After the Cabinet's approval in principle of offshore drilling, the government initiated the Beaufort Sea Project. This joint government-industry venture was planned as a two-year program, and much of the work took place during the season of open water, which usually lasts about two and one-half months.

I have examined the reports of the Beaufort Sea Project and have heard evidence from many of the scientists that took part in it. Indeed, that evidence has been the basis of my analysis of the impacts of offshore drilling. The government established the project to assess the impact of a limited program of drilling from drill ships in the Beaufort Sea. On the basis of that work, the government decided that Dome's drilling program could proceed. It is not for me to express an opinion on that decision. The government obviously weighed all the issues carefully. But it is the Inquiry's task to consider the long-term consequences of an expanded program of exploratory drilling and gas and oil field development in the Beaufort Sea. If a pipeline is built, the industry will be eager to proceed with a drilling program going far beyond Dome's 16 wells. It is the risks of this expanded program that concern me.

Sea-bed Permafrost and Ice Scour

To illustrate the novel technological challenges that lie ahead in petroleum development in the Beaufort Sea and the risks that may lead to oil spills, let me describe briefly some problems created by sea-bed permafrost and ice scour. According to James Shearer, floating ice in the Beaufort Sea scours the sea floor out to about the 100-foot contour, although most recent scouring is thought to be within water depths of up to 60 feet. The depth of scour penetration into the sea floor varies: most are less than 10 feet, but some scours 25 feet deep have been noted. This ice action obviously poses real threats for platforms and sea-bed installations, such as pipelines or flow lines connecting wells to offshore and onshore production facilities.

The native people who live in the Beaufort region are well aware of this problem and are therefore quite anxious about offshore development. Here is what Sandy Wolki told the Inquiry when we visited North Star Harbour:

> I am concerned about the drilling offshore ... it may be disaster for sure.... At one time ... I was chasing a polar bear along the ridges and I had to jump from one ridge to another because they were like huge mountains ... I got among those pressure ridges, it's way out and it's very deep, but in the gouges from that pressure it was bringing some mud up and [I] saw some earth on top of the pressure ridge that was almost unbelievable because it was in the deep water....
>
> If they build a pipeline from the Beaufort Sea to the mainland, if that type of pressure starts to build up [it doesn't matter how] much

protection or no matter how well you put it in, it will have some effect on the pipeline because of the ice and the gouges that it worked with. Taking mud from the bottom is something that we haven't studied yet.

> ... even the scientists or whoever is studying that area ... haven't done enough studies or don't know enough about it because when [I] was out there ... the pressure ice was so heavy that it was just like mountains...that's just the surface part. What about the bottom part? ... [I] know the large percentage of ice is in the bottom and when [I saw] this mud coming up from the deep water [I am] really concerned because nobody really has studied it or made any true look at it.... [I've] seen it with [my] own eyes and if they can do that gouging way out down deep, there must be some ... heavy or strong pressure ... somewhere in order to develop this type of mud. Because of the rolling, I guess it starts to build up pressure, the ice starts to build up pressure. [I] saw some thickness of the ice ... it's not just thin ice, it's all heavy ice.
>
> [I am] concerned about it because nobody really knows anything about that pressure ridge. It's really strange to see it, and if they build a pipeline anywhere in the Beaufort Sea and this type of thing should happen to occur there's bound to be some damage or disaster within that time. [C4151ff.]

There is permafrost in the ground below the Beaufort Sea. In some places the frozen soils seem to be very close to the surface, but we do not know how much ice they contain. If, as appears likely, the offshore flow lines must pass through frozen ground, it will be important not to melt the permafrost, in order to prevent subsidence and damage to the flow lines. The same kinds of problems that we discussed earlier in connection with a buried refrigerated gas pipeline are present here: the melting of permafrost and the possibility of creating frost heave.

When I discussed frost heave, I said that

Sun Oil rig on artificial island, Beaufort Sea. (W. Hoek)

Workers on arctic drill rig. (NFB–McNeill)

Sea ice and tanker Manhattan. (GNWT)

Mackenzie Delta. (NFB–McNeill)

the Government of Canada has a fundamental responsibility to undertake independent research into the problems that face oil and gas exploration and development projects in Northern Canada. Questions relating to offshore permafrost, ice scour and offshore production and transportation of hydrocarbons cannot be left for industry alone to solve. I therefore urge again that the Government of Canada establish a northern research program into these basic problems to provide the knowledge it will require concerning industrial development in the North.

Spills and Blowouts

One of the major risks in an expanded program of offshore exploration and development is an oil spill. I am talking here about a major oil spill, such as from a blowout beneath the sea or the sinking of an oil tanker. The chances of such a spill are difficult to calculate and different estimates of the probability have been quoted. But this much is clear: increased activity increases the possibility of such a spill. The consequences of a major oil spill would be catastrophic.

How much oil might be released from a blowout on the sea bottom? Dr. Allen Milne said that, if an undersea blowout ran wild for a year, the volume of oil discharged under the ice would be comparable to that carried by a supertanker. E.R. Walker, in his report *Oil, Ice and Climate in the Beaufort Sea*, offered these estimates:

The oil industry believes the possibility of a subsea well blowout with a significant escape of oil is very small. If we postulate one blowout which runs wild for one year, then if the release rate is 2,500 barrels per day at the start, and 1,000 barrels per day after the first month, the blowout will release 382,500 barrels of oil. ... Each barrel of oil will be accompanied by 800 cubic feet of free gas. This blowout could occur anytime during the exploration phase. We may expect additional small releases of fuel oil throughout the exploration phase because of minor spills. We may roughly estimate those as being less than 1,000 barrels per year. We might expect losses of oil from artificial islands to occur all around the year. Most releases from ships will probably occur in summer....

Although the terms of reference of these Beaufort Sea studies cover only the exploration phase, it is interesting to speculate upon the amounts of crude oil likely to be released if exploration proves reserves of the size estimated above [up to 40 billion (4×10^{10}) barrels of oil and 50 trillion cubic feet of gas]. ... To estimate the releases of oil during the production phase in a crude way, we may assume a loss factor (for all causes) of the total oil likely to be produced. There is considerable dispute about the appropriate loss factor [ranging from] 0.1 percent [to] 0.001 percent [the latter figure being supplied by the oil industry]....

If we use the (perhaps high) figure of 1×10^{10} barrels of oil in the Beaufort Sea, then for the loss factors of 0.1 percent and 0.001 percent, the total loss of oil would be 10^7 and 10^5 barrels respectively, or 4×10^5 barrels per year and 4×10^3 barrels per year if the oil release is spread evenly over a production phase of 25 years. The assumption of uniform release rate seems reasonable since the losses during the production phase will probably be small spills with a remote chance of a larger accident....

We assume that a blowout on man-made islands is equally likely at any time of year. In summer, oil will presumably escape into open water. In winter, it will probably run out on the top of ice, probably land-fast first-year ice. With some luck and forethought, oil escaping in the winter could be collected or burned.

Blowouts of wells drilled from floating platforms or ships are most likely to occur over the period August to October. The probabilities of stopping the flow of oil from blowouts in this situation (if natural bridging-over does not occur) are hard to gauge. They are probably less in incidents occurring toward the end of the season, and presumably a blowout could continue to emit oil and gas from one autumn to the next summer.

Oil from such a blowout will initially be released into open water or loose pack ice. Heavier pack ice could move over the site. Depending on the location of the blowout, the winter situation could include ice cover ranging from land-fast annual ice to polar pack ice. [p. 15ff.]

There have been blowouts in the Arctic, but fortunately, none has involved oil. Of the two gas wells that have blown out in the high Arctic, one ran wild for nine months, discharging gas into the air. Dome Petroleum had trouble with the two wells drilled in the Beaufort Sea in 1976: one well had a blowout involving fresh water, the other had an underground blowout in which gas escaped from the well into a porous rock formation before it reached the surface. Both were said to be under control by the end of the 1976 drilling season.

When you consider the industry's high hopes and, indeed, their oft-stated expectations of substantial oil and gas reserves under the Beaufort Sea, you see that the chances of an oil blowout in these hazardous waters cannot be discounted. There is much to be said for a very conservative approach in these matters.

Dome's drilling program has made us all aware that blowouts are one source of an oil spill, but there are other possibilities, too. Once offshore discoveries are made, production, storage and transportation facilities will be required, and they offer a variety of risks for spills of their own. But the origin of the spill is of little consequence once it has happened. At that point our concern will be the magnitude of the spill and its impact.

We should not forget that the people who are most concerned are the native people. Here is what Sam Raddi, President of the Committee for Original Peoples Entitlement, told me in Inuvik:

> For the people that want to drill on Beaufort Sea, Mr. Berger, I want you to take note of this. I spent a lot of time with my father – he is 74 years old – and his cousin, Phillip Nuviak, who is 84 years old. . . . They tell me in their stories that the old-timers, their great-grand-fathers, would tell them that one day, if the ocean, the Beaufort Sea ever loses its fish and wildlife, the whales, the fishes, the seals, the polar bears, if the Beaufort Sea will lose that, the natives – the Eskimos – will have very little chance to survive. They said the main source of food comes from the ocean and they always tell us to respect the whole Beaufort Sea.
>
> So we have been trying all these years to protect the whole Beaufort Sea, and also the animals on the land, respect the land and the animals, not to overkill them. Now, Mr. Berger, it seems like this is the end of a lot of food for us. If they ever drill in the Beaufort Sea, if they ever have an accident, nobody really knows how much damage it will make on the Beaufort Sea. Nobody really knows how many fish it will kill, or whales, polar bears, the little whales and the bowheads.
>
> These people that did research on the Beaufort Sea will never be able to answer these things. When will the fish and the whales come back? They got no answer, and yet they want to go ahead and drill on the Beaufort Sea. It's the Eskimos that will pay for any damage, any oil spills, any damage to wildlife, it will be us that will be paying for it the rest of our lives. God knows if the fish and the whales will ever come back. We don't know.
>
> Mr. Berger, I hope you take note of this and it's unfair to us because there's very little research done on the Beaufort Sea. Two years of research and they feel they have enough information to give a permit to go out and drill. That's not true because we lived here millions of years, and we know in two years

they cannot get all the answers to what they are trying to achieve. [C3458ff.]

Spill Clean-up

Throughout this report I have stressed the need to examine the proposals before us in the context of the Pipeline Guidelines. They specify that effective plans be developed to deal with oil leaks, oil spills and pipeline rupture. In my opinion, the long term, principal concern is for oil spilled in the course of drilling, and from production and transportation of hydrocarbons originating in the area. Blowout spills are of this kind and such spills can occur onshore as well as in the sea. On a more limited scale, I am also concerned over spills of fuel brought into the area for use in connection with one or other of the large projects involved in petroleum development. The importance of fuel spills should not be underestimated, particularly if the fuel gets into water. There is a tendency to understate concerns over spills connected with a gas pipeline or gas producing facilities when compared with an oil pipeline and oil wells. But, nonetheless, there are real and major concerns over fuel spills connected with construction of the gas facilities because of the very large quantities of fuel that are involved. Arctic Gas say that 2.6 million gallons of fuel will be stored at a typical wharf and stockpile site during construction. Foothills' requirements are somewhat less, but they are of the same order of magnitude. Foothills are considering using a 35,000-ton tanker to carry fuel through the Bering Strait and into the Beaufort Sea to supply their construction sites in the Delta. Imperial, Gulf and Shell will also require large quantities of fuel

during the construction of their gas plants: Taglu, located in the heart of the Delta and subject to seasonal flooding, will require 12 million gallons; construction of Niglintgak will require about 4 million gallons; Gulf's plant at Parsons Lake will require about 9 million gallons. Volume Two of this report will offer specific recommendations that are designed to reduce risk of fuel spills from the pipeline. But no matter what design and inspection measures are taken, the risk of spills will always be present. Commission Counsel submitted that industrial development on the scale proposed will render spills inevitable. I concur with that view.

Delta Spills and Clean-up

A spill within the Delta would quickly spread through its myriad channels, sub-channels, swamps, bogs, lakes and mud flats. Although the degree of pollution would vary with the site of the spill and the river level at the time, it is physical conditions such as these that led Dr. Norman Snow, a biologist with the Department of Indian Affairs and Northern Development, to conclude:

> . . . the Mackenzie Delta and its immediate adjacent offshore area represents a set of conditions which would tend to maximize the adverse effects of an oil spill if one were to occur there. [F19125ff.]

Spills on land are relatively easy to manage. The main concerns and problems arise when a spill reaches water. If there is a major spill in the Delta, it is highly probable that it will get into the water, because of the myriad channels and lakes that make up the Delta and because of the extent of seasonal flooding.

But it is not just a spill within the Delta that would threaten it. A spill anywhere along the lower Mackenzie River could be

Dredging to construct an artificial island. (J. Inglis)

CANMAR testing oil spill cleanup techniques. (GNWT)

Sam Raddi. (DIAND)

Oil spill containment boom. (GNWT)

carried into the Delta. Oil spilled in the Beaufort Sea could be carried along the coast into the waters bordering the Delta and, through the action of storm surges and reversing currents, onto the Delta itself. If an oil spill did spread through the Delta, the possibilities of cleaning it up are minimal. The oil would remain for a long time.

An oil spill in the Delta could seriously impair the productivity of its wildlife resources. Chemical pollutants in the water could alter the food chain. Valuable habitat could be lost. Salt marsh grasses, seaweeds and other aquatic vegetation could be destroyed. If such damage is extensive, sediments normally held stationary by the roots of these plants could be eroded. Vegetation so polluted generally takes two or three years to recover. We know from an oil-spill experiment in Caribou Bar Creek that a small quantity of crude oil reduced the zoobenthic organisms to one-third of their previous abundance. Snow said that successive spills or heavier contamination would produce an even greater decrease, thereby impairing a stream's capacity to sustain fish. He summarized the effects of an oil spill on birds in these words:

> Seabirds are probably the most obvious casualties of oil spills. Mortality usually results from the destruction of the water-proofing and heat-insulation ability of their feathers and also from oil ingestion during preening. The Delta and offshore areas are utilized extensively by many bird species ... [and] apart from the direct mortality from oil spills, [there is] the additional long-term component which may result from the loss of nestlings, the nest sites themselves being rendered useless for future generations, by oil contamination, and the threat of degrading feeding, brood-rearing and staging areas. [F19127ff.]

What response could be made to an oil spill in the Delta? If it were a major spill, there is very little that could be done. If a major spill cannot be efficiently cleaned up — and we know it cannot be — in the more favourable conditions of the temperate latitudes, one certainly could not be cleaned up in the harsher and remoter northern environment.

Arctic Gas, Foothills and the three gas producers, Imperial, Gulf and Shell, have developed plans to prevent and control spills. In the Delta, the Arctic Petroleum Operators Association have stockpiled petrochemical spill contingency equipment and have undertaken the training of manpower to develop what they call the Delta Environmental Protection Unit (DEPU). But DEPU and the contingency plans that the pipeline companies brought before the Inquiry will be of limited effectiveness if a major spill occurs. From the evidence brought before me, it is apparent that we do not have the technical ability to clean up a major spill in the Delta, especially if it is spread through the maze of channels and mud flats.

Beaufort Sea Spills and Clean-up

In discussing oil spills in the Beaufort Sea, I want it to be understood that I am not in any way suggesting the Government of Canada ought to reconsider its decision to allow Dome to drill 16 exploratory wells in the deep water of the Beaufort Sea. I simply believe that it is essential for the government to consider the risks entailed in proceeding with a full-scale program of oil and gas exploration and development there subsequent to the Dome program.

Spills of oil in the Beaufort Sea, whether from a blowout or from another source, may be caught up in the sea ice, dispersed in the water column, absorbed into bottom sediments and spread along the coast. The oil and ice interaction may take many forms. Oil could be encased in growing seasonal ice and could move long distances in that form before being released in the spring melt. Or it might be incorporated into the polar ice pack, where it would be retained for many years. Oil could accumulate under the floating ice or spread along open water leads.

The spread of oil in the vicinity of the Delta would be enhanced by the movement of the river water in rapidly changing patterns over the denser and colder sea water. Our knowledge of these water movements is limited.

In the spring, the higher forms of marine life, such as seal, polar bear and white whale, migrate along the open leads in the ice. Oil would also move along these leads as they open up in the spring. As the band of open water in the shear zone expands, oil will move closer to shore and, finally, when the land-fast ice melts, oil will move freely about and reach the shoreline.

Birds that migrate to the Arctic in spring seek out these areas of open water. Landing on oiled water is likely to be fatal for them. According to Dr. Tom Barry of the Canadian Wildlife Service, a lead of open water in the ice off Cape Dalhousie, at the tip of Tuktoyaktuk Peninsula, may be occupied by 50,000 birds at any one time in the late spring. These birds are replaced in a few days by 50,000 others, who need the open water to feed and rest, and so on through the migration period. The possibilities for enormous losses of bird life are obvious.

A spill of oil could work right through the food chain. I have described the under-ice biota in the Beaufort Sea. If oil reduces the food supply of benthic invertebrates and fish, the seals will be affected, and through them the polar bear is threatened. Even though the polar bears might not be threatened directly by an oil spill, they might well be threatened indirectly.

Dr. Allen Milne, head of the Beaufort Sea Project, testified that the consequences would be very serious if a major oil spill occurred in the Beaufort Sea. The Project's environmental assessment indicates that recovery of the Beaufort Sea marine ecosystem from even a single major spill could take as long as a decade.

Given the scale of hydrocarbon development that is envisaged for the Delta-Beaufort region, a major spill is not only likely, it is inevitable over time. That must be our assumption, and it is based on the experience of spills elsewhere during exploration, and during production, transportation, handling and storage. We have not yet developed clean-up techniques adequate for major spills in temperate or tropical waters. We simply are not prepared for a major spill in the Beaufort-Delta region. The equipment we do have will not be effective; our present knowledge of the marine ecosystem, of ice conditions and of the behaviour of oil in arctic waters is quite insufficient to provide the information that is needed. What we do know simply reinforces this conclusion: we could not clean up a major oil spill in the Beaufort Sea.

There has been no experience with the problem of cleaning up a large oil spill in arctic waters. We can, however, look elsewhere to get some idea of the general sort of problems we might face if we did have a major spill.

In late December 1974, a storage tank at the Mizushima Refinery in Japan containing 11 million gallons of bunker C oil broke and the escaping oil breached a dike, and spread into the adjacent harbour. Clive Nichol of Environment Canada's Environmental Emergencies Branch told the Inquiry that the spill could not be contained, despite the immediate availability of men and equipment and a relatively benign climate. The deployment of 30,000 metres of boom, 738 boats, 153 aircraft and 8,189 workers had little success. Within a week, between 1.6 and 2.1 million gallons of oil had spread through the Inland Sea of Japan. Over 290 miles of coastline were polluted. The spill is estimated to have cost over $160 million. This all happened despite the existence of contingency plans, a well-drilled spill-contingency team and almost unlimited manpower and equipment. The process of clean-up eventually had to rely on thousands of people using long-handled bailers and empty 45-gallon drums. The handling and disposal of the spilled oil and polluted material, once it was picked up, posed an additional problem. For each gallon of crude oil spilled, about five gallons of oil-sludge-water debris was recovered.

The Mizushima incident is a dramatic but not unusual example. We are reminded almost every month of our complete inability to cope with spills even under favourable circumstances. The barge Nepco 140, which grounded in the St. Lawrence River in June 1976, spilled about 240,000 gallons of oil, and attempts to clean it up cost $8 million. Other recent disasters include the 108,000-barrel Arrow spill in Chedubucto Bay and the Argo Merchant spill off New England. Major spills have resulted from drilling activity in the Mississippi Delta and the Gulf of Mexico. In the Santa Barbara spill off the California coast, 100,000 or more barrels were lost in a well blowout.

These experiences amply demonstrate that, despite our advanced exploration and development technology, we cannot handle large oil spills in areas of winds, waves and currents. These conditions are characteristic of the Delta-Beaufort region, and they are further complicated by isolation, low temperatures and moving ice. The deployment of the men and equipment necessary to deal with a major oil spill in the Beaufort Sea would be an awesome task and extremely costly. We might be tempted — or even forced — to follow the example of Chile when oil spilled from the tanker Metula near the Strait of Magellan. The Chileans decided the area was too remote and difficult to warrant clean-up of any kind.

The Pipeline Guidelines require the pipeline companies:

> . . . to provide documented evidence that they possess not only the necessary knowledge, but also the capability to carry out specific proposals. [p. 13]

Environmental Guideline 8 requires:

> . . . that effective plans be developed to deal with the oil leaks, oil spills, pipeline rupture, fire and other hazards to terrestrial, lake and marine habitats, that such plans be designed to minimize environmental disturbances caused by containment, clean-up, or other operations and to bring about adequate restoration of the environment, that they be designed to deal with minor and major incidents, whether they are single-event or occur over a period of time and that they include contingency plans to cope with major hazards or critical situations. [p. 15-16]

Although these requirements are clearly the obligations of the pipeline companies, they also have some bearing on the industry as a whole. Is clean-up technology adequate? Is the equipment available? Are the deployment plans sufficient? In the final analysis we must determine whether or not the industry — or the government for that matter — has the capacity to control and

Polar bears of the Beaufort Sea. (GNWT)

Biologists collecting fish in an arctic river. (Arctic Gas)

Diver carrying out underwater tests on Cornwallis Island, NWT. (NFB–McNeill)

CANMAR base near Tuktoyaktuk. (GNWT)

clean up a major spill. Today neither of them has.

Albedo, Climate and Research

On April 15, 1970, Parliament passed the Arctic Waters Pollution Prevention Act, a landmark in the development of legislation to protect the ecology of arctic waters. On that occasion, Prime Minister Trudeau used these words:

> The Arctic ice pack has been described as the most significant surface area of the globe, for it controls the temperature of much of the Northern Hemisphere. Its continued existence in unspoiled form is vital to all mankind. The single most imminent threat to the Arctic at this time is the threat of a large oil spill ... [which] ... would destroy effectively the primary source of food for Eskimos and carnivorous wildlife throughout an area of thousands of square miles. ... Because of the minute rate of hydrocarbon decomposition in frigid areas, the presence of any such oil must be regarded as permanent. The disastrous consequences which its presence would have on marine plankton, upon the process of oxygenation in Arctic North America, and upon other natural and vital processes of the biosphere, are incalculable in their extent. [p. 5ff.]

What did the Prime Minister mean when he said that the arctic ice pack controls the temperature of much of the northern hemisphere? What did he mean when he said its continued existence in unspoiled form is vital to all mankind?

He was referring to albedo, that is, to the reflective capacity of ice. The presence of oil would darken the ice, and lower its capacity to reflect light. More solar energy would be absorbed, which could lead to the ice melting earlier than usual. This change would enlarge the area of open water in the Arctic

Ocean and lengthen the open water season to some degree, which in turn could bring about changes in climate. Whether a reduction of the ice pack by this means would ultimately have an effect on the climate that would exceed the effect from natural fluctuations in ice cover is something we do not know.

The Beaufort Sea Project considered this very question when it examined the risks of the Dome drilling program. E.R. Walker wrote:

> The effects of oil on the large-scale heat budget of the Beaufort Sea and Arctic Ocean are dependent on the scale of oil release. For the scenario for exploratory drilling, of one blowout, or even for a much larger release of oil, the area covered by oil would be too small to affect the large-scale heat budget of the Beaufort Sea, let alone of the Arctic Ocean as a whole. [*Oil, Ice and Climate in the Beaufort Sea*, p. 35]

However, the Beaufort Sea Project's terms of reference were limited to only the exploratory phase of Dome's drilling program. Walker was not prepared to say that he was certain there would be no impact on climate in the production phase. He put it this way:

> ... it is certain that during the exploration phase of Beaufort Sea operations not enough oil is likely to be released to affect even local climate.
>
> The effect of oil release upon climate during a possible production phase is less certain. The writer's opinion is that while sizeable volumes of oil may be released, this oil will probably not spread over a sufficient area to affect anything but local climate. However as noted above several uncertainties remain. [p. 34]

These uncertainties relate to behaviour of oil in the ice, the migration of oil to the surface of the ice, the rate at which it evaporates, the rate at which it degrades, the circulation of the ice, the impact of open water on the weather and so on.

Milne felt that one major spill would not have any effect on the climate:

> ... it is unlikely that oil discharged into the Beaufort Sea from a single oil well blowout running for several years would have any effect whatever on global or even local climate. [F18988]

But he entered a caveat:

> This is not to discount the possible climatic effects which might occur from a continuation of oil spills which might result from more wells being drilled and offshore production, and production spills and pipeline breaks. Now we're getting into a different order of magnitude there. [F19011]

Arctic oil and gas exploration and production would not be limited to the Beaufort Sea. Drilling is also going on in the high Arctic, and there are plans for offshore drilling in the Eastern Arctic. The Americans are planning to drill offshore from Alaska's north slope. The Soviet Union may soon be drilling off its immensely long arctic coastline. Drilling may also take place off the Arctic coast of Norway and off the coast of Greenland. Do we have any idea of the impact of several major spills in arctic waters around the globe? These events may be only five, 10 or 15 years away.

Through the Beaufort Sea Project we now have assessed the risks faced by an initial exploration of Canadian waters in the Beaufort Sea. We are uncertain about the extent of the risks that production would cause in those waters, and we have not yet attempted to appraise the risks of simultaneous oil and gas exploration and development in arctic waters by all the circumpolar countries.

To what extent might the climate be affected by a series of major spills in arctic waters? No one can say. And no one is investigating the matter. The Beaufort Sea Project has been terminated. There is no

KILOMETRES

MILES

Sattelite photo mosaic showing lower Mackenzie River, Mackenzie Delta and adjacent parts of the Northern Yukon and Beaufort Sea.

Dogs and sleigh on arctic ice. (ITC)

international program underway to investigate this phenomenon. Canada, as the pioneer of arctic offshore drilling, ought to take the initiative.

A study must be made of the interaction of ice and oil, of the biological degradation of oil in icy waters, and of the possible influence of the loss of the polar pack on climate. Who should carry out this research? I say it should be fully funded by government, and carried out under government auspices. The Beaufort Sea Project will not do as a model. That project was jointly sponsored by government and industry. That kind of arrangement mixes up the functions of government and the goals of industry.

The Prime Minister referred in 1970 to the critical role of the polar ice pack in the world's weather system. Canada, having been the first to warn of the risks that are involved in spilling oil in arctic waters, and having been the first to drill in these ice-infested waters, should now lead the way in calling for an international program of research. Canada should propose that research should be undertaken jointly by the circumpolar nations into the risks and the consequences of oil and gas exploration, development and transportation activities around and under the Arctic Ocean.

The question of what effect oil spills in arctic waters will have on albedo and climate is one that is surrounded by controversy. I have cited the views of two Canadian scientists who take a conservative approach in the matter. It illustrates once again my general concern over the adequacy of scientific knowledge relating to oil and gas development in the North. It demonstrates the need for fundamental and applied research.

The albedo question is only one of a number of gaps in our knowledge that have hampered this Inquiry in conducting its assessment and in making the judgment that it has been called upon to make. Undoubtedly similar gaps in our knowledge will hamper the government's assessment of future petroleum development in Northern Canada for years to come.

I take as a basic principle that government ought to be in a position to make independent and enlightened judgments about engineering and environmental aspects of proposals advanced by industry for northern development. To be able to make such judgments, government must be capable of assessing the scientific and engineering research that industry has carried out. When fundamental questions of environmental impact are involved, government cannot leave it to industry to judge that impact. That is government's job and, to do this job, it must have advice of its own and competence of its own in the field concerned. Government must undertake whatever research is required to attain this competence.

It is my opinion, therefore, that government should initiate, plan and finance a continuing program of research to provide the knowledge that it requires and will require about northern development. Instant or crash programs will not adequately serve this need. Rather, such a program will require a continuity of support adequate to yield answers when they are needed. Although this research will necessarily deal with questions raised by individual projects, it should have the breadth and depth to deal also with the cumulative effects of successive developments and with questions of national or international importance.

Summary

In this chapter I have dealt with the implications and impacts of petroleum exploration, production, transportation and other activities that would accompany major oil and gas development in the Delta-Beaufort region, onshore and offshore. The Mackenzie Valley gas pipeline is viewed by many as the trigger that would bring about an abrupt transition in this spectrum of development.

As I see it, large-scale oil and gas development in this area is inevitable, whether a gas pipeline is built now or is postponed. Notwithstanding the disappointing level of discoveries in the Delta so far, the area has been rated by the federal Department of Energy, Mines and Resources as one of three frontier areas in Canada that potentially contain major undeveloped reserves of oil and gas.

Assuming then that large-scale petroleum development does go ahead, I urge the Government of Canada to adjust the pace of development and the conditions under which it is permitted so as to protect the environment and the renewable resources upon which the native people depend.

The Mackenzie Delta is environmentally sensitive and highly important for the native people. I urge, therefore, that no pipeline — either gas or oil — should be routed across the Delta, and that strict limitations be placed on locating other major oil or gas facilities on the Delta, particularly on its outer part. I recommend that special measures be taken to avoid disturbance of fish populations within the channels and lakes of the Delta and that sanctuaries be extended across the outer part of the Delta to protect migratory waterfowl. In order to preserve the white

Caribou Hills, Mackenzie Delta. (D. Mackay)

whale population of the Beaufort Sea from declining in the face of cumulative stresses imposed by ongoing petroleum exploration and production, I also urge the establishment of a whale sanctuary excluded from all industrial development, covering the principal whale calving area in the shallow water bordering the Delta.

Much of the oil and gas potential of the area is believed to lie offshore beneath the Beaufort Sea. The prospect of major exploration programs and production activities in the Beaufort Sea over a period of many years raises serious concerns for the environment and the native people. In permitting drilling in the Beaufort Sea from man-made islands and drill ships and in the high Arctic from ice platforms, Canada has become the first country in the world to embark upon petroleum exploration in arctic and ice-covered waters. We should proceed only with due care and caution.

The greatest concern in the Beaufort Sea is the threat of oil spills. In the long term, such spills could emanate from blowouts in exploration or production wells, production accidents, tankers, offshore pipelines or coastal facilities. Spills could pose a threat to mammals, birds, fish and the small organisms upon which they depend, in the Beaufort Sea, in leads in the ice, and along the coast. There is a possibility, too, that accumulation of oil in the Arctic Ocean from offshore petroleum development by all the circum-polar countries could decrease the ice cover on the ocean and bring about climatic change. In my opinion the techniques presently available are not likely to be successful in controlling or cleaning up a major spill in this remote area, particularly under conditions involving floating ice or rough water. Therefore, I urge the Government of Canada to ensure that improvements in technology for prevention of spills and development of effective technology for containment and clean-up of spills precede further advance of industry (beyond the current Dome exploratory program) in the Beaufort Sea. I further urge that advances in knowledge of the environmental consequences of oil spills should likewise keep ahead of offshore development. To meet this and other needs for new scientific information relating to petroleum development and its impact, and to ensure that government is equipped to assess the development proposals of industry, I recommend that government should undertake an ongoing program of northern research.

The Mackenzie Valley

The Pipeline Guidelines envisage two energy corridors in Canada's Northwest: one would cross the Northern Yukon, and the other would run the length of the Mackenzie Valley. I have recommended that no pipeline be built and no corridor be established across the Northern Yukon. In this chapter, I will address the Mackenzie Valley corridor.

The Mackenzie Valley is a transportation route that has seen several decades of industrial development. No major wildlife population is threatened by a pipeline along the Mackenzie Valley, and no major wilderness areas would be violated by it — but that is not to say that a pipeline would have no impact. Clearly there will be impacts, but they will be superimposed on those that have already occurred in the region, and in many respects they can be ameliorated. So, setting aside the very important social and economic issues and the overarching question of native claims, all of which I shall treat in subsequent chapters, there is no compelling environmental reason why a corridor to bring oil and gas from the Mackenzie Delta and Beaufort Sea could not be established along the Valley. However, to keep the environmental impact of a pipeline to an acceptable level, its construction and operation should proceed only under careful planning and strict regulation. The corridor should be developed only on the basis of a sensible and comprehensive plan that accounts for and resolves the many land use conflicts that are apparent in the region even today.

The Region

The Mackenzie River not only defines the Mackenzie Valley, it dominates the entire Canadian Northwest. The Dene called the river *Deh-cho*, the Big River. Alexander Mackenzie called it the Great River, by which name it was known until John Franklin descended this river during his first overland expedition, 1819-1822. Since then, we have known it as the Mackenzie River. It is the longest river system in Canada, one of the ten longest rivers in the world, and one of the last great rivers that is not polluted. The Mackenzie drainage basin encompasses nearly one-fifth of our country, taking in northwest Saskatchewan, the northern half of Alberta, most of northern British Columbia, the eastern Yukon and, of course, all of the western part of the Northwest Territories. Included within this great drainage system are the Peace, Athabasca and Liard Rivers, as well as the Finlay, Parsnip, Nahanni, Great Bear, Arctic Red and Peel Rivers. It drains the great lakes of the North: Great Slave Lake and Great Bear Lake, both of which are bigger than Lake Ontario. Within the Northwest Territories alone, the Mackenzie River and its tributaries drain an area of some one-half million square miles — an area larger than the Province of Ontario.

Historically, the Valley has provided a home and subsistence for the native people. It provided the main transportation route and resources upon which the northern fur trade was built, and today it is a vital link between the people and the communities of the region. The river is also the route over which machinery and equipment are sent to the base camps and the drilling rigs of the oil companies active in the Mackenzie Delta and Beaufort Sea. Along this river Arctic Gas and Foothills propose to move pipe, material, equipment and supplies to their stockpile and construction sites. And along this Valley it is proposed to establish an energy corridor.

The Mackenzie Valley region that would be affected by the pipeline and oil and gas activities includes not only the Valley itself but also the basins of Great Slave Lake and Great Bear Lake. Despite the diversity of this large region, the continuity and definition given the region by the river make it a logical entity to deal with as a whole. Because it is a natural travel corridor, it now sees many competing uses by wildlife, traditional activities of native peoples, and the advance of industrial development.

When you fly along the Mackenzie Valley, you have the impression of immense distances and great isolation, but in some senses this impression is misleading. It leads to the assumption that the land is virtually empty and that its capacity to absorb impact is limitless. As each activity advances — seismic exploration, drilling, roads, highways, mines and pipelines — we tend to overlook their cumulative effects on the land, the wildlife and the native people.

The People and the Land

Native land use within the Mackenzie Valley focuses on its renewable resources: moose, caribou, furbearers, fish and birds. Environmental impacts will, therefore, bear especially on them. It is only within comparatively recent years that the incremental changes to the environment caused by successive stages of industrial development have built up to a level that is obvious to the people who live in the Mackenzie Valley.

The land has changed. A cut-line here and there, a drilling site, a road or highway where none existed before, airstrips, and more and more aircraft flying overhead. These things together are effecting a cumulative environmental transformation.

The initial incursions of white people into the Mackenzie Valley were limited both in number and extent. Engaged in the fur trade, they lived close to the major river routes and were dependent for their living on the native people's annual harvest of furs. The pattern of that relationship has survived for more than a century. But it began to change in the early 1900s when geological parties began to explore the Valley and surrounding area. Oil was found at Norman Wells in 1920; uranium and gold deposits were discovered in the region in the 1930s. Slowly the activities of industrial man moved farther from the main river transportation routes, away from the trading posts, into lands that had been the exclusive domain of the native people.

In recent years, many hitherto remote areas have come under intensive use. Consider what is happening in an area that is still regarded as relatively untouched, the Fort Norman–Fort Franklin region. The native people have always used the lands and waters of this area to hunt, trap and fish. The main area of long-term use by the people of Fort Norman extends inland past Brackett (Willow) Lake at least 250 miles from Fort Norman, and occasionally travel takes the people another 150 miles. The people of Fort Franklin still use all of the lands around Great Bear Lake.

There has been a fur trading post at or near Fort Norman for more than 150 years. Half a century ago, industrial development began in a limited way with the discovery of oil at Norman Wells, and a refinery has been there since the 1920s. But, more recently,

there has been extensive industrial activity: now all of the lands around the communities at Fort Norman and Brackett Lake are held under petroleum exploration permit. The major permit holders include Aquitaine, Texaco, Decalta Group, Shell and Imperial Oil; some 25 wildcat wells have been drilled within 60 miles of Fort Norman, the nearest one only eight miles east of the settlement.

The oil companies have carried out widespread seismic exploration in the area for many years, and there are seismic trails everywhere. For example, Aquitaine has carried out 350 miles of seismic exploration on a block of land covering about 1,000 square miles.

There has been exploration for other minerals, too. Manalta Coal Limited of Calgary have exploration licenses on land covering some 240 square miles east and southeast of Fort Norman. They have put down about 30 shallow drill holes and found coal seams 20 feet thick at shallow depths. The same block of land is also held under a petroleum exploration permit.

There is barge traffic on the river in summer. The Mackenzie Highway alignment will pass along the north side of the village of Fort Norman, and its right-of-way is already partly cleared. The CN telephone land-line and a winter road run the length of the Valley. The feasibility of a hydro-electric development on the Great Bear River has been studied. There is extensive air traffic in the area, which rises and falls with exploration and development. A rash of activity by government and industry has anticipated construction of the pipeline.

The government regards the proposed pipeline as the key element of a transportation and energy corridor along the Mackenzie Valley. The pipeline issue has focused attention on the cumulative effects of other

forms of development on the environment and peoples of the region. The consequences of these varied developments and changes on the way of life of the native people in the region was described by Chief Daniel Sonfrere of Hay River:

> ... after the white man came, well things look different, everything's changing now. I'm going to tell you a few things about that....
>
> Look at it today. If we try to go in the bush and kill something, it's pretty hard for us to find [anything] because there are too many roads going different directions. There's too many people around. It's pretty hard for us to kill anything. We have to go quite a ways to get what we want off our land. Yes, even some people [are] complaining about the fish they're catching in this river because everytime they go and pull their net, when they want to have a feed of fish it always taste of fuel.... [We] have to go in the bush and do the hunting, [we] got to go quite a ways and got to get out quite a distance before [we] can get anything [we] want. [C588ff.]

Environmental Concerns

Many parts of the Mackenzie Valley terrain are sensitive to disturbance. The region is distinguished by its silty, clayey permafrost soils that are vulnerable to dramatic thermal degradation, particularly along the many river valleys and slopes of the region. These concerns are of major importance because the north-south direction of the corridor cuts across the many east-west valleys and slopes that converge on the Mackenzie River.

Although the valleys crossed by the corridor may constitute only a small proportion of the total landscape, they are the locations of disproportionately high land use and are of particular environmental, aesthetic and recreational values. They define essentia

Bear Rock behind Fort Norman. (L. Smith)

Stockpile site for petroleum exploration, Mackenzie River. (GSC—A. Heginbottom)

Peregrine falcon. (C. & M. Hampson)

Islands of the Mackenzie River near Norman Wells. (GSC—A. Heginbottom)

fish and mammal habitat and the vegetation along them is more varied and abundant than elsewhere. Valleys have always been and still are the preferred areas for many native people.

These factors give the location of pipeline compressor stations unusual importance, because many of the compressor station complexes would be located adjacent to the valleys that are the foci of the regional ecosystem. A gas pipeline would be a dynamic linear element across the northern landscape, with nodes of great activity at compressor stations at 50-mile intervals. These nodes would extend to include wharf sites, helipads, airfields and borrow pits. They generally lie at right angles to the pipeline right-of-way and corridor.

The immediate impact of industrial development would not necessarily be dramatic in a region like the Mackenzie Valley, where the influence of the white man has been evident for many decades. Wildlife populations are affected by the cumulative influence of such factors as weather, disease, predators and habitat conditions. But wildlife populations inevitably decrease as industrial activity takes over larger and larger portions of the landscape. This process is now well underway in the Mackenzie Valley, and it will accelerate as industrial development proceeds. Let me illustrate this point by referring briefly to some of the major wildlife species in the region.

Birds

Important areas for birds in the Mackenzie Valley are chiefly of two types: those that provide staging and nesting sites for waterfowl and those that are suitable sites for raptors, such as falcons, eagles and hawks.

The Mackenzie Valley is one of North America's great migratory bird flyways. Mills Lake near the head of the river, the islands and sandbars from Camsell Bend to Arctic Red River, and particularly the islands near Norman Wells and Little Chicago are heavily used by migrating waterfowl and shorebirds. These islands are an important link in waterfowl life cycles. River bars and flood plains, with their dynamic nature and early succession stage vegetation, are heavily used by migrating snow geese and swans in spring, because this is the first habitat available to them. The birds arrive immediately after break-up, landing on the exposed portions of the islands to feed and rest. Pair-bonding takes place during this part of their migration, and the pairs continue north to their nesting grounds in the Delta and beyond. With so short a season, they have no time to waste. Disturbance must be kept to a minimum.

Large numbers of ducks and some Canada geese, loons and shorebirds nest in the Mackenzie Valley. The most important nesting, moulting and staging areas for waterfowl along the Mackenzie Valley north of Great Slave Lake are the Ramparts River, Mackay Creek, Brackett Lake, Mills Lake and Beaver Lake. As in the Delta and the Northern Yukon, the birds are susceptible to disturbance during these critical stages in their life, but the consequences probably would not be as great because the populations are not as concentrated.

The raptors that nest in the Mackenzie Valley, Mackenzie Delta and Northern Yukon are significant portions of the surviving North American populations of these birds, especially of the peregrine falcon and the gyrfalcon. There are nesting sites for the peregrine falcon, an endangered species, and other raptors all along the proposed corridor and, in particular, in the Campbell Hills and

the Franklin Mountains. In recent decades, a number of factors, especially the widespread use of pesticides, have combined to reduce greatly the abundance of the peregrine falcon in most areas of North America. The plight of this bird is described by George Finney and Virginia Lang in the *Biological Field Program Report: 1975* prepared for Foothills:

> The population is at a dangerously low level and there is no indication that recovery is imminent. Due to the sensitivity of the peregrine population, developers have to face the fact that the destruction of a single nest site or interference with nesting in a single year is a serious and unacceptable impact. These constraints apply to no other birds species regularly nesting along the proposed pipeline corridor. [Vol. IV of IV, Section 4, p. 32]

I am of the opinion that we can avoid disturbance to the raptors by establishing suitable buffer zones between their nesting sites and industrial activities. I shall deal with this subject in Volume Two.

Mammals

No populations of caribou in the Mackenzie Valley are directly threatened by a pipeline. The Bathurst herd, which ranges from the north and east shores of Great Slave Lake to the south shore of Great Bear Lake, is used by hunters from Yellowknife, Detah, Rae, Lac la Martre and Rae Lakes. The people of Fort Good Hope, Fort Franklin and Colville Lake rely mainly on the Bluenose herd, which ranges from Great Bear Lake north to the tree line. Some woodland caribou are taken throughout the Valley.

The calving grounds of the Bluenose and the Bathurst herds are far away from the impact area, and their main populations lie outside the corridor. Nevertheless, even though industrial activity in the Mackenzie

Valley does not threaten the caribou populations, such activity will drive them farther from the Valley itself. Father Jean Amourous told us, when the Inquiry visited Rae Lakes, that this has already occurred to some extent:

> ... it's a fact that development means, in this country, the stop of development by traditional ways. For instance, when development took place with the mining, building of roads, cat roads, cat trains, on the lakes, at about that time the caribou stopped migrating right through the Pre-Cambrian Shield and stopped going ... across to the sedimentary grounds, limestone country, like Lac la Martre, and all the way down to the other end of Lac la Martre, in 1956. No caribou there for the last 20 years. And that was about the time that the uranium mines grew up in the country, right on the caribou migrating roads.
>
> ... it was about that time that on an expedition to the barren land hunting caribou, we couldn't find any caribou that had fallen, but we found plenty of moose that had run away from this part of the country in between the Pre-Cambrian Shield and the limestone country, because of the industrial activity. And those moose have been pushed back by the noise to more isolated parts of the country.
>
> And people here are witness to the fact that when the winter road is open, caribou don't come across it. And many times, certainly three or four times since the winter road is open to haul out to the South the minerals from around Great Bear Lake shores, it has spread the caribou pasturing in the country in between here and Great Bear Lake, and after the operation is going on of hauling that mineral ore outside, then you don't see the caribou alongside that road, or very few. [C8301ff.]

Moose, like caribou, are a heavily used resource in the Mackenzie Valley. They range widely over most types of habitat in summer and early spring. Hunting was the main cause for the decline in the moose

populations. Such a decline occurred following World War I, when there was an influx of trappers, traders and prospectors into the Mackenzie Valley. While not immediately sensitive to encroachment on its habitat, successive disturbances will cause moose to move away. The effect is subtle and gradual.

The furbearers of the Mackenzie Valley region, like the other mammals, are threatened by successive developments that affect their habitat and tend to push them farther and farther away from the corridor. Localized depletions of beaver, lynx, marten and muskrat have been felt directly by many of the trappers who spoke to the Inquiry. Joe Martin told the Inquiry about conditions near Colville Lake:

> There's parts around here, some areas where it used to be really good for trapping marten and stuff like that. Since explorations, all the seismic trails ... it's not so easy to go trapping and catch fur anymore. You have to really work for it, because it's really changed. Not so many furs like there used to be before.
>
> [Horseshoe Lake] where [I] was trapping last winter, there's a lot of seismic cut lines around there. It used to be real good trapping area around there ... [but] just even cut lines like that can disturb the land, and the fur is not the same, and the wildlife is not the same. [C8338ff.]

Fish

The Mackenzie River is more productive and has more fish species than either the Porcupine River or the north slope drainage of the Yukon. Most fish in the Mackenzie Valley have specific migration routes and limited spawning, overwintering, nursery and feeding areas. Suitable water quality and food sources are obviously necessary. These habitats and conditions are particularly important because of the generally limited ability of northern fish populations to recover after

a severe environmental disruption has reduced their numbers.

Of the many species of fish in the region, some are spring spawners, others are fall spawners and one species, the burbot, is a winter spawner. These species — grayling, yellow walleye, northern pike, longnose sucker, flathead chub, whitefish, cisco, inconnu, trout, goldeye, stickleback and others — have different sensitivities to disturbance depending on their life cycles and biological traits. The arctic grayling, for example, have a complex seasonal migration. Usually they spawn over gravel in small, relatively clear tributaries during spring break-up; then, it seems, the mature fish migrate to other feeding areas in the Mackenzie system, and they overwinter in lakes or in the mainstream channels. Nursery areas for fry and immature fish are generally in clear, swiftly flowing smaller tributaries. Changes in habitat, water quality (particularly by siltation of the clear streams), toxic spills and obstruction of channels could adversely affect species like the grayling.

We have limited knowledge of the population distribution and dynamics of fish in the Mackenzie drainage system. Jeff Stein of the Department of Fisheries told the Inquiry:

> Certainly we can identify the more significant populations and in some cases provide very specific measures for their protection. But for the vast majority of streams, especially small drainages, data are generally limited, thus requiring extrapolation from more intensively studied and hopefully similar watersheds. [F15723]

It is essential, therefore, that inventories and research on fisheries keep pace with industrial development in the Valley. Even so, we know that certain measures will have to be employed to protect fish habitat. These measures should include requirements for

Beaver. (NFB—Cesar)

Bundling dry fish near Fort Good Hope. (R. Fumoleau)

Moose. (A. Carmichael)

the design and construction of culverts, dykes, coffer dams, ice bridges, handling of toxic substances, siltation, water withdrawal and waste disposal. Measures such as these will be dealt with in Volume Two.

Development of an energy corridor could interfere with the Mackenzie Valley fisheries by disturbance of the fishing sites or by direct disruption of fishing. The domestic fishery has traditionally been very important throughout the area as a source of protein. If the fisheries are to be retained, both the fish and the fishing sites must be protected.

Recreation

In this report, I have said little about outdoor recreation. It may seem to have little relevance to a pipeline or an energy corridor, but recreation and tourism are increasing in the Valley, and in future they will be of greater importance. Therefore, industrial development should be designed to limit adverse impacts on areas of recreational value. Such areas should be identified now, before further development reduces the options that are available.

Studies by Parks Canada have demonstrated that the Mackenzie River, one of the few major rivers still free of dams, may be considered as an Historic Waterway. Some of its tributaries could qualify as Wild Rivers and sites such as Bear Rock and the Upper Ramparts have been identified for consideration as National Landmarks. There are many other areas of archaeological and historical interest in the Valley. Collectively such areas constitute a rich natural and cultural heritage worthy of protection.

Corridor Development

The Pipeline Project

As the map of the front of this report shows, the routes proposed by both Arctic Gas and Foothills along the Mackenzie Valley are very similar. Both routes run south from the Delta along the east side of the Mackenzie River. Starting from the Delta, they pass close to Inuvik, east of Travaillant Lake and then approach the Mackenzie River near Thunder River. From here to Fort Simpson, the Mackenzie River and the routes are generally parallel, except south of Fort Good Hope, where the pipeline routes cut through a gap in the Norman Range, and north of Fort Simpson, where the Arctic Gas route crosses the Ebbutt Hills and the Foothills route skirts west of the Ebbutt Hills. Both routes cross the Mackenzie east of its confluence with the Liard (east of Fort Simpson), and then continue southeast overland, to the Northwest Territories-Alberta border, just east of the Alberta-British Columbia boundary.

The pipeline will stretch 800 miles from the Delta to the Alberta border. But the project will not be just a line of pipe buried in a clearing through the bush; its effects will be felt in distance well beyond the right-of-way and in time far longer than the two winter seasons of pipelaying. All the material, supplies and equipment will have to be shipped down the river to the construction sites during the summer. The capacity of the fleet of tugs and barges on the Mackenzie River will have to be doubled. The Great Slave Lake railway and the Mackenzie Highway will be heavily used. Hay River, as

a railhead, a road terminus, and with extensive trans-shipment facilities, and Fort Simpson, which is on the Mackenzie Highway, will both experience a boom.

There will be compressor stations at about 50-mile intervals along the pipeline. Arctic Gas propose to have 18 in the Valley, and Foothills will have 17; with each station there will be a host of other developments. Let me describe briefly what is planned for just one of the 18 compressor station sites that Arctic Gas propose, the one at Thunder River.

The permanent facilities will comprise the compressor station itself, an airstrip (one of ten airstrips that Arctic Gas propose to build in the Valley) seven miles of all-weather gravel road, and a wharf. Temporary facilities will include a construction camp to house an 800-man pipeline construction crew and, once the pipe is laid, the 200-man compressor station construction crew, a material stockpile site, two or three gravel pits and many miles of snow roads. The construction of this complex will require over two million cubic yards of gravel and other borrow material. The permanent compressor station will have between six and ten large steel buildings, which will house 30,000-horsepower turbine compressors, 17,-000-horsepower refrigeration equipment, propane condensers to dispose of the waste heat from the refrigeration units, a workshop, garage, storage, control room, communications equipment, office area and living quarters for operation and maintenance staff. In addition, there will be outside storage areas for repair and maintenance material and vehicles, extra pipe, fuel and propane, a flare stack and an incinerator, a sewage lagoon and a communications dish to hook into the Anik Satellite. All this will require a fenced, gravelled pad about 1,000

SCHEMATIC DRAWING OF A COMPRESSOR STATION COMPLEX WITH WHARF AND STAGING AREA

Not to scale

Note: The main construction camp may be situated on the compressor station pad or at the wharf/staging area site

feet square. According to Carl Koskimaki, an engineer who gave evidence for Arctic Gas, the operating noise of the station turbines and at the fence line of the station would be equivalent to the noise level within 100 feet of an urban freeway in mid-morning. The material stockpile site at Thunder River will be at the compressor station site and, together with the wharf, it will be able to handle tens of thousands of tons of supplies, including 88 miles of pipe, which alone will weigh about 85,000 tons. All this, including both the permanent and temporary facilities, will require the clearing of nearly 350 acres of land.

The pipeline companies told the Inquiry that the choice of the east side of the Mackenzie River for their pipeline and their selection of a route through this area were based on financial and engineering considerations. The shortest distance, with due regard to major terrain features, such as mountain passes, river crossing sites and soil properties, defined the route in the general sense. They took the proximity of transportation facilities into account and as site-specific engineering, environmental and, to some degree, socio-economic information became available, they progressively refined the routing and made some minor adjustments. Compressor stations were located at hydraulically optimum points that were chosen for pipe and station size and design gas volumes, then adjusted slightly as required by geotechnical considerations. For engineering reasons that involve the maintenance of hydraulic balance and throughput efficiency, the degree of flexibility in choosing compressor station sites was said to be limited.

People in all the communities along the proposed route expressed to the Inquiry concern over the location of the pipeline and its associated facilities. Their concerns were related to the location of the pipeline near the communities themselves and in or near traditional land use areas. Both routes come within two to five miles of Fort Good Hope, Fort Norman, Norman Wells and Wrigley. In addition, both companies will locate regional headquarters at Fort Simpson, Norman Wells and Inuvik. Both companies have responded to some of these concerns by changing or suggesting changes in location. For instance, Arctic Gas have proposed to relocate wharves, stockpile sites, access roads and airfields. To expedite the shipment of material, they have also made plans to carry out a large part of their trans-shipment activities at a new facility at Axe Point, downstream from Fort Providence. To date, such changes appear to have been introduced unilaterally; there has been no apparent progress towards a review process to resolve differences regarding the route of the pipeline and the location of its facilities.

Other Developments

The proposed gas pipeline is neither the first major venture, nor the final stage of corridor development in the Valley. But in many respects it is a threshold. The pipeline will stimulate oil and gas exploration throughout the Mackenzie Valley, and further gas discoveries may well be made. Robert Blair, President of Foothills, spoke at Colville Lake of the likelihood that a pipeline would connect the Tedji Lake discoveries northwest of Colville Lake with the main pipeline. The Pipeline Guidelines, which envisage an oil pipeline and other transporation systems, refer to:

... a transportation corridor that might include in the long run not only trunk pipelines, but also a highway, a railroad, electric power transmission lines, telecommunication facilities, etc. [p. 3]

Most of these developments would be confined to a narrow strip of land on the east side of the Mackenzie River along the same general route as the proposed pipeline. The Pipeline Guidelines do not foresee a number of projects spread over a vast landscape. In many parts of the Valley, topography alone would constrict these developments into quite limited areas because restrictions on the route of one project are often similar to those of another. For example, the proposed Mackenzie Highway alignment, the CN land-line right-of-way, and the winter road between Inuvik and Fort Simpson as well as the pipeline commonly lie within a zone only a mile or two wide, and they pass through Gibson Gap, which is only one-half mile wide.

Unlike the Northern Yukon, some of these developments are already underway along the Mackenzie Valley corridor. Others are pending, and there may be others that we do not yet foresee. The gas pipeline will accelerate these activities and accentuate environmental change. It will begin a new round of impacts that may seriously affect the landscape and its wildlife.

Balancing Development with the Environment

The pipeline project has focused public attention on the need to resolve conflicts created by different demands on the environment. Dr. Ian McTaggart-Cowan of the Environment Protection Board summed this up:

... there is the oft experienced human tendency to argue that, now that some tolerable

The Ramparts along the Mackenzie River.
(D. Gamble)

Snow geese. (C. & M. Hampson)

Great Bear River looking west towards Bear Rock.
(GSC—A. Heginbottom)

impact has been permitted, it becomes easier to argue for each successive small increment — small change — each one on its own perhaps minor, but in the aggregate inducing serious impact. I have called this "destruction by insignificant increment." This process requires that proposals for initial incursions be viewed most thoroughly to determine particularly that the route designated for this project is the one least likely to be subjected to these incremental phenomena resulting from looping, from roads, from railways, from oil pipelines, etc.

[The Environment Protection Board] urges very strongly the preparation of a comprehensive land use plan for the Yukon Territory and the Mackenzie Valley area, taking into account the environmental and social components. The corridor concept makes this particularly important. [F6267]

Comprehensive land use planning can emerge only from a settlement of native claims. However, on purely environmental grounds, there are several areas of land that warrant immediate protection. I recommend that sanctuaries be designated to protect migratory waterfowl and falcons, and the sites that I recommend have already been identified under the International Biological Programme. They are the Campbell Hills-Dolomite Lake site, which is important to falcons, and the Willow Lake (Brackett Lake) and Mills Lake sites, which are of great importance to migratory waterfowl. Many islands in the Mackenzie River are also important to migratory waterfowl, and, in time, some of them should be designated as bird sanctuaries.

Many tributaries that feed into the Mackenzie River also warrant some degree of special protection from industrial impacts. These valleys, where the permafrost terrain and slopes are most sensitive, are the focal points for terrestrial and aquatic ecosystems that are important for traditional pursuits of the native people. These areas should be avoided by industrial development wherever possible, and any incursions that are permitted should be subjected to stringent assessments of impact and to the special ameliorative measures that I shall specify for the gas pipeline in Volume Two.

We must recognize that land will become a scarce resource in the Mackenzie Valley. It will not be long before competition for land (and competition for access to the resources that land contains) will become much more intense than it is now. The wildlife species of the region have definite requirements, and the native people will continue to need extensive lands for their purposes. Industrial developers will need land for their purposes, and yet other areas may be designated in time for such purposes as conservation and recreation. All of these uses will increasingly press against each other, and there will be conflict.

In the Mackenzie Valley, a large number of events that affect the pattern and character of land use have already occurred, and more such events may occur before a comprehensive plan of land use has been formulated and implemented. Some things are now fixed. For example, many of the communities and most industrial developments are located on the east side of the river. But we are still at a relatively early stage of development. There is still time to consider a variety of options. It is not good enough simply to promise ourselves that we can serve a variety of divergent uses equally and simultaneously.

Measures must be instituted to limit the impact of industrial development on the land and wildlife resources of the Mackenzie Valley. This step is, after all, only good housekeeping, as the urgency of large-scale frontier development threatens to overwhelm the sustaining natural values of one of Canada's greatest river valleys.

This step cannot be taken unilaterally: there are too many interests involved — all of them legitimate. Industry, government and the local people all acknowledge the need for a comprehensive plan. As a start, the location of the proposed pipeline route and the ancillary facilities must be refined to avoid destruction of areas important to the native people and wildlife and areas important for conservation and recreation.

A settlement of native claims is the point of departure from which all other land uses, including major industrial uses, must be determined. A just settlement with the native people will not only give them the kind of protection they need to plan their own future, it will also involve them fully in planning the future of the Mackenzie Valley. If the valley environment is injured, they will be most affected.

If we take a long view of corridor development in the Mackenzie Valley and plan accordingly, the various demands on land use in the region can be successfully reconciled. There will have to be some environmental impact and some environmental change — it is unavoidable. But the existence of major wildlife populations would not be threatened, and no unique wilderness areas would be violated. The challenge we all face in the Mackenzie Valley is to maintain its environmental values with the same resolve that we plan the development of energy and transportation systems. I think, so far as environmental considerations are concerned, this challenge can be met.

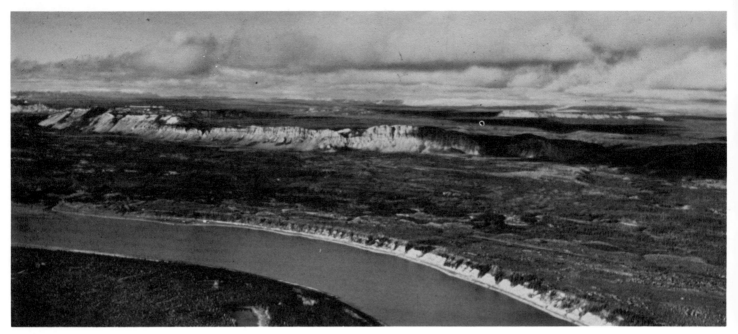

Mackenzie River and Norman Range. (Arctic Gas)

Hide being stretched and dried. (R. Fumoleau)

Cultural Impact

Cultural Impact: A Retrospect

Early Views of the North

Before considering the economic and social impact that the pipeline and the energy corridor will have, we should examine the history of the cultural impact of white civilization upon the native people of the North. The relations between the dominant society and the native society, and the history of that relationship from the earliest times to the present, should be borne in mind: they condition our attitudes to native people, and theirs towards us.

When the first Europeans came to North America, they brought with them a set of attitudes and values that were quite different from those of the original peoples of the continent. At the heart of the difference was land. To white Europeans, the land was a resource waiting to be settled and cultivated. They believed that it was a form of private property, and that private property was linked to political responsibility. This political theory about land was coupled with religious and economic assumptions. Europeans believed that the conditions for civilized existence could be satisfied only through the practice of the Christian religion and cultivation of the land. As an early missionary phrased it, "Those who come to Christ turn to agriculture."

To the Europeans, the native people's use of the land, based upon hunting and gathering, was extravagant in extent and irreligious in nature. But to the native people, the land was sacred, the source of life and sustenance, not a commodity to be bought and sold.

Chief Justice John Marshall of the Supreme Court of the United States, writing in 1823, described the attitudes of the Europeans in this way:

> On the discovery of this immense continent, the great nations of Europe were eager to appropriate to themselves so much of it as they could respectively acquire. Its vast extent offered an ample field to the ambition and enterprise of all; and the character and religion of its inhabitants afforded an apology for considering them as a people over whom the superior genius of Europe might claim an ascendency. The potentates of the old world found no difficulty in convincing themselves that they made ample compensation to the inhabitants of the new, by bestowing on them civilization and Christianity, in exchange for unlimited independence. [Johnson v. McIntosh (1823) 21 U.S. 543, 572]

It was to be the white man's mission not only to tame the land and bring it under cultivation, but also to tame the native people and bring them within the pale of civilization. This sense of mission has remained the dominant theme in the history of white-native relations.

In Northern Canada, even though the possibilities for agriculture were virtually non-existent in comparison with the prairie lands, the white man's purpose was the same: to subdue the North and its people. In the old days that meant bringing furs to market; nowadays it means bringing minerals, oil and gas to market. At all times it has meant bringing the northern native people within white religious, educational and economic institutions. We sought to detach the native population from cultural habits and beliefs that were thought to be inimical to the priorities of white civilization. This process of cultural transformation has proceeded so far that in the North today many white people — and some native people, too — believe that native culture is dying. Yet the preponderance of evidence presented to this Inquiry indicates beyond any doubt that the culture of the native people is still a vital force in their lives. It informs their view of themselves, of the world about them and of the dominant white society.

Euro-Canadian society has refused to take native culture seriously. European institutions, values and use of land were seen as the basis of culture. Native institutions, values and language were rejected, ignored or misunderstood and — given the native people's use of the land — the Europeans had no difficulty in supposing that native people possessed no real culture at all. Education was perceived as the most effective instrument of cultural change; so, educational systems were introduced that were intended to provide the native people with a useful and meaningful cultural inheritance, since their own ancestors had left them none.

The assumptions implicit in all of this are several. Native religion had to be replaced; native customs had to be rejected; native uses of the land could not, once the fur trade had been superseded by the search for minerals, oil and gas, be regarded as socially important or economically significant.

This moral onslaught has had profound consequences throughout Canada. Yet, since the coming of the white man, the native people of the North have clung to their own beliefs, their own ideas of themselves, of who they are and where they came from, and have revealed a self-consciousness that is much more than retrospective. They have shown a determination to have something to say about their lives and their future. This determination has been repeatedly expressed to the Inquiry.

The Fur and Mission Era

The penetration of European values in the North has been felt for nearly two centuries. In the early days of the fur and mission era, the native people were able to participate in the fur trade with comparatively little disruption to many of their patterns of social and economic organization, and with little change to their basic cultural values. For most of the year they still lived off the land, travelling in small groups of families in the semi-nomadic tradition of hunting and gathering peoples. Their aboriginal cycle of seasonal activity was modified to include visits to the trading post and mission to sell their furs, to buy tea, sugar, flour and guns, and to go to church.

Father Felicien Labat, the priest at Fort Good Hope, tracing a century of history through the diary of the mission, told the Inquiry about life during the fur and mission era:

> [The trading post] of Good Hope was deserted during the winter months. Christmas and Easter would see a good many of [the Dene] back in the Fort for a few days, but soon after New Year they would again go back to their winter camps. Then it would be the spring hunt, when beavers would start to come out of their houses and travel down the many rivers. Summer would bring nearly everyone back into Fort Good Hope.... The people lived close to nature, and their life pattern followed the pattern of nature. Winter and spring were times for working, when transportation into the heart of the land was easier. Summer, on the other hand, was a bit of a holiday, with drums echoing for days and days. That life pattern remained unchallenged until recently, when white people started to come down this way in greater numbers. [C1873ff.]

Even though contact with white civilization, the Hudson's Bay Company, the Church and, in later years, the RCMP was intermittent, its impact was pervasive. White society dictated the places and terms of exchange, took care to ensure that its rituals (social as well as religious and political) took precedence in any contact between native and white, and provided a system of incentives that was irresistible. Political, religious and commercial power over the lives of the native people came to reside in the triumvirate of policeman, priest and Hudson's Bay store manager.

Behind these agents at the frontier lay the power of the metropolis as a whole, a power that was glimpsed occasionally when a ship arrived, a plane flew overhead, or a law court with judge and jury came to hold court. White people in the North were powerful because of what they did, the goods they dispensed, and all that they represented. Their power became entrenched during the fur and mission era in the Mackenzie Valley and the Western Arctic.

Although the fur and mission era ended 20 years ago, the RCMP, Church and Hudson's Bay Company still possess considerable authority in the North, but their authority is no longer exclusive. Government has proliferated. The mining industry and the oil and gas industry have arrived. And these new authorities — governmental and industrial — possess a power that transcends the old order: a power to alter the northern landscape and to extinguish the culture of its people.

But make no mistake: the process of transformation has in a sense been continuous. With the fur trade, many native northerners became dependent on the technology and on some of the staples of the South, and this dependence gave outsiders a power quite out of proportion to their number. Although at that time many white people in the North needed the help of native people and had to learn local skills, they nonetheless controlled northern society — or were seen to do so. The authority of traditional leadership was greatly weakened. The power and influence of traders, missionaries and policemen were noticed by many early observers of the northern scene. No less an authority than Diamond Jenness believed that, "The new barter economy — furs in exchange for the goods of civilization" had caused great harm to the Inuit, and indeed had made them "economically its slaves."

But the native people did not always see it that way. They felt — and still feel — that they gained materially from the fur trade, even if at the same time they became dependent upon and subordinate to outsiders. The material culture of the fur trade did, in fact, become the basis of what is now regarded as the traditional life of the native people — and this is so throughout the Canadian North. It is not surprising that the fur trade era, dependent as it was on traditional skills and a blending of technology with aboriginal ways, often seems to have been a better time, for it was a time when life still had a coherence and purpose consistent with native values and life on the land. Today, when Indian and Eskimo people speak of the traditional way of life, they are not referring to an unremembered aboriginal past, but to the fur and mission era. Most of today's adults in the Mackenzie Valley and the Western Arctic were raised in it and remember it vividly.

The Government Presence

The traditional way of life, based on the fur trade, lasted until about 20 years ago. As native people became increasingly dependent on trade goods and staples, so their economic well-being became increasingly

Influences — fur traders, the Church, the Bay and the RCMP.

Furs baled at trading post in Fort Resolution. (Alberta Archives)

Old mission at Fort Resolution. (Native Press)

Hudson's Bay Company store, Fort Liard. (GNWT– M. White)

Treaty payment party paying treaty in Nahanni Butte, 1975. (GNWT)

tied to the fortunes of the fur market. It was the long depression in the price of fur in the years after the Second World War that led to the collapse of the northern fur economy in the 1950s. When the fur market failed, the federal government had to come to the aid of the native people.

It was at this time that the welfare state made its appearance in the North. Family allowances and old age pensions were paid to native northerners. Nursing stations and schools were built; then housing was supplied. All these things were provided by the federal government, which soon had a pervasive influence on the life of every native person. It offered what few parents anywhere would ever refuse — food, medicine and education for their children. Northern natives entered a system whose object — wholly benign in intent — was to reorder their daily lives.

In 1953 there were between 250 and 300 federal employees in the Northwest Territories. Today the Government of Canada (including its crown corporations) and the Government of the Northwest Territories have almost 5,000 employees there. What we are now observing in the North is a determination by native people to wrest from the government control of their daily lives.

The Growth of Settlements

Federal policy in the North since the late 1950s has proceeded on the assumption that the traditional way of life was dying, and that native people had no alternative but the adoption of the white man's way. The short-run solution to the northern crisis was the provision of health and welfare measures. The long-run solution was the education of native people to enable them to enter the wage economy.

The native people who were still living in the bush and on the barrens had to live in the settlements if they were to receive the benefits of the new dispensation, and if their children were to attend school. Doubtless, the promise of greater comfort and ease made the move to settlements seem more attractive; but evidence given at the Inquiry reveals that many people do not remember the move as entirely voluntary. Many were given to understand that they would not receive family allowances if their children were not attending school. At the same time, the children in school were being taught a curriculum that bore no relation to their parents' way of life or to the traditions of their people.

What occurred on the Nahanni River exemplifies much of what happened as settlements grew. In the past the Dene did not live at Nahanni Butte but in camps along the Nahanni River. The government brought them all into Nahanni Butte so that their children could be taught at the school the government had established there. Nahanni Butte, though a beautiful place with an awesome view, is not a particularly good location for hunting, fishing or trapping. Neither the establishment of the school nor the arrangement of the school year and the curriculum — much less the location of the settlement itself — was planned in consultation with the native people.

The establishment of new government facilities in the settlements made available a few permanent and some casual jobs, especially in summer. Typically, these jobs were at the lowest level, such as janitor and labourer. Thus a hunter of repute, a man who might be highly esteemed in the traditional order, joined the new order on the lowest rung. Yet so depressed was the traditional economy that even the lowest

paid native wage-earner lived with more security and comfort than most hunters and trappers. For those who wanted to continue living off the land, welfare was sometimes the only means of financing the purchase of ammunition and equipment. Whereas traders had previously extended credit to make sure families stayed on the land, now some administrators preferred the hunters to stay around the settlement to look for casual work rather than to give them welfare so they could go out hunting. Hence wage labour often came to be seen as antithetical to traditional life.

The building of the DEW Line accelerated this process in the Western Arctic. The DEW Line offered stores and medical facilities where there had been none. Many Inuit, such as those from Paulatuk, came to live in the shadow of the DEW Line stations. These sites had been chosen for strategic and military purposes, but they were often in areas without sufficient fish and game to sustain the native people.

When the people first moved into the settlements, they lived in tents or log cabins. The government, at the urging of those in the South who were disturbed by the plight of native northerners, decided that settlements should be modernized and new housing provided. These new communities were laid out to be convenient for services, such as sewage disposal systems, that were often never installed.

Along with the introduction of health, welfare, education and housing programs came new political models. Municipal government, derived from Southern Canada, was chosen as the institution for local government in the native communities. We ignored the traditional decision-making process of the native people, whereby community consensus is the index of approved action. Today in the Northwest Territories many native people sit on municipal councils, but the councils deal with matters such as water supply and garbage disposal, which the native people do not consider as vital to their future as the management of game, fish and fur, the education of their children, and their land claims. This is not to gainsay the usefulness of local government in the Northwest Territories. It is merely to remark that native people regard these local institutions as secondary to the achievement of their main goals. Their existence has not diminished in any way the growing native desire for self-determination.

Northern needs were defined by the government, or by Canadians concerned about northern natives. Programs were conceived and implemented in response to the sensibilities of southern public servants. And because few were able to find out how native people really lived or what they wanted, much less to heed what they said, many government programs were conceived and implemented in error.

This is not to depreciate the benefits that government has brought to the native people in the North. It is easy to discount these benefits now, but the attraction they held for the native people, and the need the people quickly felt for them, soon became apparent. Today housing, health services, schools and welfare are all made available by the government, and the native people have been continually and forcefully reminded of the advantages to themselves and their children of accepting these things.

As northern settlements have grown, white compounds have become established within them. In many places it is no exaggeration to speak of southern enclaves, occupied by whites who have no links with the native population, but are there to administer the programs of the Government of Canada and the Government of the Northwest Territories. Many native witnesses expressed the resentment they feel toward the white people within their communities who have large houses, clean running water and flush toilets, while they have none of these amenities.

It is important to recognize the speed with which these changes have come about: some of the children who were born in tents or log cabins and were raised in the bush or on the barrens, have gone to school; they now live in settlements and have entered the wage economy — all in just a few years.

The Wage Economy

Wage employment and the greater availability of cash have had an impact on native culture. Much of the income earned by native people is, of course, used to buy provisions and equipment, such as snowmobiles, guns and traps. In this way, wage employment serves to reinforce the native economy and the native culture. But much of the cash that is earned is not so used, and this has had consequences that have been destructive and divisive.

Wage employment has, within the past decade or so, been important chiefly in the larger centres — Inuvik, Hay River, Fort Simpson, Yellowknife. Even in these places wage employment has created possibilities for men who wish to improve their hunting gear, and has encouraged the flow of consumer durables and processed foods into many families. But this has also meant that many native people have taken — at least temporarily — a place on the lowest rungs of the pay and status ladder. Because the number of such participants has grown considerably in recent years, and because there are persistent and increasing pressures on virtually everyone to participate in the wage economy, the cultural and social ramifications have been very wide.

The Importance of the Land

There have always been indigenous peoples on the frontier of western civilization. The process of encroachment upon their lands and their way of life is inseparable from the process of pushing back the frontier. In the North, the process of detaching the native people from their traditional lands and their traditional ways has been abetted by the fact that fur trappers are at the mercy of the marketplace. There is no organized marketing system for their furs, no minimum price, no guaranteed return. Thus the fur economy is denied the support we accord to primary producers in the South. Nor is it comparable in any way to the network of capital subsidies, tax incentives and depreciation allowances that we offer to the non-renewable resource extraction industry in the North.

To most white Canadians, hunting and trapping are not regarded as either economically viable or desirable. The image that these activities bring to mind includes the attributes of ruggedness, skill and endurance; but they are essentially regarded as irrelevant to the important pursuits that distinguish the industrial way of life. This is an attitude that many white northerners hold in common with southerners. But the relationship of the northern native to the land is still the foundation of his own sense of identity. It is on the land that he recovers a sense of who he is. Again and again I have been told of the sense of achievement that comes with hunting, trapping and fishing — with making a living from the land.

Much has been written about the capacity

Government-built housing dominates Fort
Franklin landscape. (M. Jackson)

The Watade home, Rae Lakes. (GNWT)

Workers reporting for duty with Work Arctic in
Hay River. (GNWT)

Detah Indian village. (R. Fumoleau)

of the native people to wrest a living from
the country in which they live. Only to the
southerner does their land seem inhospitable; to the native people it offers a living. In
every village of the Mackenzie Valley and
the Western Arctic there are people who use,
and feel they depend on, the land.

The North is vast, and life in Sachs
Harbour is altogether different from life in
Yellowknife. In Sachs Harbour and in the
villages that lie beyond the advance of
industry — in Old Crow, Paulatuk, Holman,
Colville Lake, Lac la Martre, Rae Lakes,
Trout Lake and Kakisa Lake — the people
still live off the land and take pride in their
way of life. In these places, industrial development and the lure of the wage economy do
not each day offer an immediate and continuing challenge to the legitimacy of native
culture and native identity.

The Inuit of Paulatuk still live off the land.
They store their caribou and fish on the roofs
of their houses, away from the dogs. These
people had earlier left Paulatuk to live near
the DEW Line station at Cape Parry, where
they eventually found themselves in decline.
Now they have returned to the land they
used to occupy, where caribou and arctic
char are plentiful.

At Sachs Harbour the Inuit live off the
land, and they live well. Some 23 trappers
there cover a total hunting range as large as
Nova Scotia to harvest white fox. They also
live off caribou, seals, polar bear, muskoxen
and geese.

At Kakisa Lake the Dene still make their
living from the land. The people there have
consistently resisted the idea that they
should move from their tiny village to the
larger Dene community of Fort Providence.
They have built their own log cabins and
have insisted on the establishment of their
own school.

At Colville Lake, too, the Dene have
maintained their annual cycle of activity,
which sees them out in the bush for much of
the year, supporting themselves and their
families in the manner of their ancestors.
They, too, have built their own log cabins
and still burn wood in their stoves. They
resist incorporation into the metropolis by
continuing their traditional way of life.

Other people in Canada who live in rural
and isolated settlements are having their
lives changed by the impact of industrial
development. White people who lived to
some extent off the land by hunting, fishing
and trapping, and whose wants were few,
have been drawn into the path of industrial
development. Their own rural way of life
has been discarded under pressure from the
metropolis. But we should remember that
white people in rural Canada have generally
shared the economic and political traditions
that have led to the growth of the metropolis.
The challenge the metropolis represents to
their self-esteem is not as great as it is for the
native peoples. Although the impact of rapid
change on their communities and on family
ties is often quite severe, there are possibilities for translating some of these traditions
and values into an urban and metropolitan
context. Few such possibilities exist for the
native people of the North.

Some Implications of the Pipeline

In the days of the fur trade, the native people
were essential. In the North today, the native
people are not essential to the oil and gas
industry, and they know it. The outside
world may need the North's oil and gas
resources, but it does not need the native
people to obtain those resources. Outsiders
know exactly what they want and exactly
how to get it, and they need no local help.

Now they can travel anywhere with tractors, trucks, airplanes and helicopters. They
can keep themselves warm, sheltered,
clothed and fed by bringing in everything
they need from outside. They have, or claim
to have, all the knowledge, techniques and
equipment necessary to explore and drill for
gas and oil, and to take them out of the
country. They can bring all the labour they
need from outside. The native people are not
necessary to any of this work.

The attitude of many white people toward
the North and native northerners is a thinly
veiled evolutionary determinism: there will
be greater industrial development in which
the fittest will survive; the native people
should not protest, but should rather prepare
themselves for the challenge that this development will present. It is inevitable that
their villages should cease to be native
villages, for in this scheme, native villages
are synonymous with regressive holdouts.
"Progress" will create white towns, and the
native people will have to become like
whites if they are to survive. But this kind of
determinism is a continuation of the worst
features of northern history: southerners are
once again insisting that a particular mode of
life is the one and only way to social,
economic and even moral well-being.

We must put ourselves in the shoes of a
native person to understand the frustration
and fury that such an attitude engenders in
him. If the history of the native people of the
North teaches us anything, it is that these
people, who have been subjected to a massive assault on their culture and identity, are
still determined to be themselves. In my
consideration of the impact of the pipeline,
insofar as it bears on the predicament of
northern native people, I will return often to
the historical influences on the present
situation.

Schools and Native Culture

I have traced in a general way the impingement of the white man and his institutions upon the native people of the North. The changes that occurred were changes in the native way of life: the world of the native people was altered, whereas the world of the white man — his religion, his economy, his own idea of who he was — remained the same. We sought to make native people like ourselves, and native society like our own; we pursued a policy of cultural replacement. Perhaps nothing offers a better illustration of this policy than the schools we established in the North.

When we consider what culture is, we can see the importance of schools and education. Man puts his unique stamp on the world around him. His values, ideas, language and institutions exhibit his understanding of himself and his world. The schools, and what was taught within them, offered a challenge to the culture of the Dene and the Inuit, to their very identity as a people.

Of course, even before there were schools, the right of the Dene and the Inuit to name themselves and the world around them had been challenged. The Church established the use of English and French Christian names in preference to native names. Native place-names were gradually displaced in favour of a nomenclature that paid tribute to the white explorers of the North. *Deh-cho,* the Big River, now bears Alexander Mackenzie's name — an affirmation of one people's history and the theft of another's. In this and myriad other ways the native people suffered a denigration of their past; they were given to understand that the future was not theirs to announce.

Introduction of Formal Education

Prior to the arrival of the white man in the North and for a substantial period thereafter, the only school the native people knew was life in the bush and on the barrens. Children acquired their language, their cultural traditions and the skills for survival through observing and participating in the life of their parents and grandparents.

Formal education began in the Mackenzie District when the Grey Nuns established a residential school at Fort Providence in 1867, and for almost a century, education remained primarily the responsibility of the churches. Children were taken from their families as early as seven years of age, and kept at distant boarding schools for up to 10 months out of 12. The curriculum taught in the schools consisted of the catechism, and of reading, writing and arithmetic. The average period of school attendance was three or four years. Fort Providence, Hay River, Fort Resolution, Shingle Point and Aklavik were centres for schools and hostels. The few day schools that were established were largely in response to the needs of the southern whites who had come to the North.

There was no doubt about the purpose of the boarding schools; it was the same throughout Canada. It was expressed plainly by Hayter Reed, Superintendent of Indian Affairs, in the *Annual Report of the Department of Indian Affairs* in 1893:

Experience has proved that the industrial and boarding schools are productive of the best results in Indian education. At the ordinary day school the children are under the influence of their teacher for only a short time each day and after school hours they merge again with the life of the reserve. ... But in the boarding or industrial schools the pupils are removed for a long period from the leadings of this uncivilized life and receive constant care and attention. It is therefore in the interest of the Indians that those institutions should be kept in an efficient state as it is in their success that the solution of the Indian problem lies. [p. xviii]

The policy was rooted in the belief, held by laymen and churchmen alike, that the aboriginal population must be reconstituted, preferably painlessly, in the image of the new race that had come to live on this continent. Certainly very few southern whites questioned the wisdom of what was being done.

This policy, evolved in the South, was carried into the North. At residential schools the religious observances of the native people were banned and the use of their languages forbidden. When the children who attended mission schools returned to their homes, they had often become uncertain about the use of their own language, and they were almost persuaded that the beliefs of their own people were suspect.

Dolphus Shae told the Inquiry at Fort Franklin of the Dene experience at the Aklavik Residential School:

Before I went to school the only English I knew was "hello," and when we got there we were told that if we spoke Indian they would whip us until our hands were blue on both sides. And also we were told that the Indian religion was superstitious and pagan. It made you feel inferior to the whites.... The first day we got to school all our clothes were taken away ... and everybody was given a haircut which was a bald haircut. We all felt lost and wanted to go home, and some cried for weeks and weeks, and I remember one Eskimo boy every night crying inside his blanket because he was afraid that the sister might come and spank him. ... Today, I think back on the hostel life and I feel ferocious. [C689ff.]

École St. Joseph, Fort Resolution, 1916. (Native Press)

The Roman Catholic residential school once used in *Aklavik.* (Public Archives)

First Eskimo students to come to the Hay River *Mission School.* (Public Archives)

Alfred McKay and his brother ice fishing for the old mission school in Fort Resolution.
(Public Archives)

Rosemary Kirby, an Eskimo teacher who spoke to the Inquiry at Paulatuk, told of the Inuit experience in residential schools:

> There was a time after being raised in residential schools when an Eskimo person felt that they were useless. They were worthless, that what they were was something to be ashamed of, and so we grew up to feel ashamed of being Eskimos, being ashamed of being Indian. [C4465]

Yet by 1950 less than 15 percent of the young people of the North had had any formal schooling. The experience of those children who had attended the mission schools, despite the personal scars, had made only minor inroads into the social and economic patterns of hunters and trappers who continued to live in the bush and on the barrens. Most native people still spoke only their own languages, and the culture of northern communities remained rooted in native values and the native economy.

A *New Education Programme in the Northwest Territories* was announced in 1955 by Jean Lesage, then Minister of Northern Affairs. This program, designed to increase the rate of school and hostel construction, was based on compulsory school attendance, certification of teachers, construction of composite high schools (containing academic and vocational training), and the centralization of control in the hands of a single government agency. It was to be free, universal, compulsory and closely aligned to education programs in Southern Canada.

Facilities (schools and hostels), equipment (books and related materials), teachers (certified to meet the standards of the dominant society), curricula (developed for the Alberta school population), and laws (compulsory attendance and length of school year) were imposed on the traditional way of life of the native peoples. Little consideration was given to such basic matters as the function of language within native society, the effect of language loss on children, or its effect on the relationship between generations. Nor was consultation with the native people considered to be of primary importance. The education system developed for the dominant society was assumed to be adequate for the North as well. Indeed, there was an expectation that native northerners would, in due course, adopt the goals, preferences and aspirations of the people of the South.

Formal Education and the Native People

One of a society's purposes in requiring formal education for its children is to preserve and transmit to the next generation its history, language, religion and philosophy — to ensure a continuity of the beliefs and knowledge that a people holds in common. But the purpose of the education provided to northern native people was to erase their collective memory — their history, language, religion and philosophy — and to replace it with that of the white man.

The native people have an acute understanding of what we have been trying to do. In every native community, young men and women told of their experience in the schools. At Fort McPherson, Richard Nerysoo, 24, told the Inquiry:

> When I went to school in Fort McPherson I can remember being taught that the Indians were savages. We were violent, cruel and uncivilized. I remember reading history books that glorified the white man who slaughtered whole nations of Indian people. No one called the white man savages, they were heroes who explored new horizons or conquered new frontiers. ... That kind of thinking is still going on today. ... The federal government has told the McPherson people that they want to create a national historic site here. They propose to put up a plaque telling some of the important history of this area. As you know, my people have lived here in this area for thousands of years and there are many events that are worthy of recognition. There are many Indian heroes and many examples of courage and dedication to the people. We have a rich and proud history.

> But what events does the federal government consider history? Let me read you the text that they propose for the plaque. It is in both English and French, but I will read the English....

> *In 1840 John Bell of the Hudson's Bay Company built the first Fort McPherson ... it was for over fifty years the principal trading post in the Mackenzie Delta region and, after 1860, a centre of missionary activity. In 1903 Inspector Charles Constantine established the first R.N.W.M.P. post in the Western Arctic here. In the winter of 1898-99 a number of overlanders tried to use Fort McPherson as a base to reach the Klondike.*

> Where are we mentioned on this plaque? Where is there mention of any of our history? The history of the Peel River people did not begin in 1840. We have been here for a long, long time before that, yet we get no mention. Does the federal government not consider us to be human too? Do they think we don't make history?...

> The date on this proposed text ... is July 3, 1975 — not 1875, but 1975, today. Our history and culture has been ignored and shoved aside. [C1184ff.]

By the end of the sixties, between 95 and 98 percent of children of school age in the North were in school, a vocational program was well established, and adult education — though still only rudimentary — had begun. However, levels of achievement have remained low.

It is not to be denied that the new education brought advantages. Without it, native people would have been even less able to understand and cope with the changes taking place in the North and with the new institutional and administrative forms that were being imposed on them. My primary concern, however, is with the way in which formal education programs have been conceived and applied.

In the North, as in the South, the schools were agencies of cultural replacement and assimilation. Like dominant societies throughout the world, we believed that it is possible to direct, even command, other people to "improve" — that is to say, to become more like ourselves. If they will but don the trappings of our culture, then time and motivation will do the rest.

By the seventies, the native people had seen the negative results of the school system. Alienated from their own culture and rejected by the new, many of the young people who had gone through the northern school system were disillusioned, apathetic or — in many cases — angry. To many children the conflicting values of the home and school could not be integrated: not knowing whom to believe, they resisted both sets of values. Many native children became so bewildered that they dropped out of school. Their parents, to whom the formal education system was largely alien, concluded that once again the white man had not honoured his promises.

Many native witnesses described the confusion engendered by the northern education policy. Roy Fabian of Hay River addressed the Inquiry:

> I'm a young native Indian. I've got an education.... I went to school until I was about 16, then I quit ... then about three years later I went back to Fort Smith for the Adult Education Program, and I got my grade 11.... Since I was about 16-17 years old I have been travelling around trying to figure out where I'm at, what I can do for my people ... I thought if I

got this education, then I would be able to do something for them....

> So I come back and I find that people don't accept me as I am.... They really can't accept me as I am because they either can't accept the changes I went through or it's something else. I can't understand what it is. So I'm not really accepted back into the culture, mainly because I lost the knowledge of it ... and I can't really get into the white society because I'm the wrong colour. Like, there's very, very few white people that will be friends with native people. Any of these white people that are friends with native people, it's like a pearl in a pile of gravel.

> For myself, I find it very hard to identify with anybody because I have nobody to turn to. My people don't accept me any more because I got an education, and the white people won't accept me because I'm not the right colour. So like, a lot of people keep saying, "O.K. we've got to educate these young native people, so that they can become something." But what good is it if the person has no identity? ... I can't really identify with anybody and I'm lost. I'm just sort of a person hanging in the middle of two cultures and doesn't know which way to go. [C557ff.]

Abe Ruben, a young Eskimo from Paulatuk, told the Inquiry:

> This thing of shutting a person off, shutting an Inuit off from any expression that was related to his own culture ... didn't only stay in hostels. It went into schools. It went into just everything that you tried to do in living in a town. You were more or less told that you couldn't express yourself as an Inuit and you had to adopt a totally different life-style. What the hostels [and schools] were put there for was to make stereotype images of native people, setting them up or educating them where they would be able to fit into the mainstream of Canadian society.... A lot of these students couldn't cope with being this southern image of a second-class white person and going home in the summertime and trying to cope with going back to their parents or their villages and trying to live as Inuit....

They would get home and couldn't relate to their parents. They couldn't speak the language anymore and when they got back to the larger town, say in Inuvik, they couldn't fare any better there. They couldn't cope just being half people. [C4476ff.]

Native Languages

It is particularly important to understand the impact of the present education system on the native languages. When young men and women cannot understand their parents and grandparents, they learn little about their own people and their own past; nor do they acquire the confidence that comes with adult understanding. They tend to feel inadequate, and the elders themselves feel that much of what they represent and have to offer has been discarded. For grandparents it is a life without the consolations of old age. Anny Zoe, an old woman at Fort Rae, put it this way: the white man, she said, has spoiled everything for the native people, "even our own children." [C7978]

According to Robert Worl, a witness from Alaska, the same phenomenon has been observed in Alaska: in many villages, parents speak their native language, but their children tend to speak English. Consequently, a large number of children are unable to share important knowledge and feelings with their elders in either language, and, because their English is poor, they cannot communicate easily with their peers either.

The Situation Today

On April 1, 1969, responsibility for education in the Mackenzie District was transferred from the federal Department of Indian and Northern Affairs, Ottawa, to the territorial Department of Education, Yellowknife. Two men appeared before the Inquiry to argue

Indian residential school — early days, Fort Resolution. (Public Archives)

Inuit boys in typing class, Churchill, Man., 1960s. (NFB—Pearce)

At boarding school in Churchill, Man. (NFB—Pearce)

Inuit children at school. (NFB)

that nothing has changed with this transfer of responsibility. Bernard Gillie, Director of Education for the Northwest Territories from 1968 to 1972, said:

> The plan developed in detail in the *Survey of Education, Northwest Territories, 1972* is sound only for [a] program having its base in a belief that gradually the Dene people will be absorbed into the dominant Canadian culture and their identity as a distinct segment of the nation will disappear. [F23924ff.]

Paul Robinson, Director of Curriculum for the Northwest Territories from 1969 to 1974, indicated that, notwithstanding the efforts that have been made by the Government of the Northwest Territories, the educational process is still administered by whites and is still geared to southern values. The Government of the Northwest Territories says that Gillie and Robinson are wrong and that the Department of Education is not pursuing a program of cultural assimilation.

The native people are not in doubt on this issue. They say that, as long as the system is run by white people, it will reflect white views of what the northern curriculum ought to be. The native people argue that since its inception, the purpose of the government's education program in the North has been to assimilate them. They say it cannot be otherwise because the system was devised and is run by representatives of the dominant society. Steve Kakfwi of Fort Good Hope told the Inquiry about the Dene view of formal education in the North:

> The Dene allowed the government to educate their young when schools were first built in the North. The Dene believed the government could take care of their interests and that they knew what was best for them. Then a few years ago, people started to realize that something was wrong. There developed a gap between the young and the old. The elders had much difficulty in relating to the young.

Many of the young lost their language, their values and views, which they had learned from their elders. What the elders realized was that what was happening to their young in school was not exactly what they wanted. The government was literally stealing young people from their families. They saw that if the situation remained unchanged, they as a people, would be destroyed in a relatively short time. . . .

All people have a desire for continuity of themselves in the future. That is why people have families, so they can pass on to their children their values and their own way of relating to the world, so that their children can continue as they had before them. No human being would allow anyone to suggest that they are worthless, that they have no right to insist on the continuity of themselves in the future, no values worth passing on to others for the future. No people would knowingly give away their right to educate their children to someone else of whom they have no understanding, except where people have been led to believe they do not have such rights. [F23945ff.]

The Dene and the Inuit today are seeking to reclaim what they say is rightfully theirs. At the core of this claim, and basic to their idea of self-determination, is their right to educate their children — the right to pass on to them their values, their languages, their knowledge and their history.

The Persistence of Native Values

The native peoples of the North have values that are in many respects quite different from our own. These values are related to the struggle for survival waged by their ancestors, and they persist in their struggle today to survive as distinct peoples.

There is a tendency for us to depreciate native culture. Many white northerners have argued that the native way of life is dying, that what we observe today is a pathetic and diminishing remnant of what existed in the past. The argument arises as much from our attitudes toward native people as from any process of reasoning. We find it hard to believe that anyone would wish to live as native people do in their homes and villages. We show indifference, even contempt, for the native people's defence of their way of life. We tend to idealize those aspects of native culture that we can most easily understand, or that we can appropriate to wear or to place on a shelf in our own homes. We simply do not see native culture as defensible. Many of us do not even see it as a culture at all, but only as a problem to be solved. But we must learn what values the native people still regard as vital today. Only then can we understand how they see their society developing in the future, and what they fear the impact of a pipeline and an energy corridor on that future will be.

The Native Concept of Land

The native people of Canada, and indeed indigenous people throughout the world, have what they regard as a special relationship with their environment. Native people of the North have told the Inquiry that they regard themselves as inseparable from the land, the waters and the animals with which they share the world. They regard themselves as custodians of the land, which is for their use during their lifetime, and which they must pass on to their children and their children's children after them. In their languages, there are no words for wilderness.

The native people's relationship to the land is so different from that of the dominant culture that only through their own words can we comprehend it. The native people, whose testimony appears throughout this chapter — and indeed throughout this report — are people of all ages, from teenagers to the very old.

Richard Nerysoo of Fort McPherson:

It is very clear to me that it is an important and special thing to be an Indian. Being an Indian means being able to understand and live with this world in a very special way. It means living with the land, with the animals, with the birds and fish, as though they were your sisters and brothers. It means saying the land is an old friend and an old friend your father knew, your grandfather knew, indeeed your people always have known ... we see our land as much, much more than the white man sees it. To the Indian people our land really is our life. Without our land we cannot — we could no longer exist as people. If our land is destroyed, we too are destroyed. If your people ever take our land you will be taking our life. [C1183ff.]

Louis Caesar of Fort Good Hope:

This land it is just like our blood because we live off the animals that feed off the land. That's why we are brown. We are not like the white people. We worry about our land because we make our living off our land. The white people they live on money. That's why they worry about money. [C1790]

Georgina Tobac of Fort Good Hope:

Every time the white people come to the North or come to our land and start tearing up the land, I feel as if they are cutting our own flesh because that is the way we feel about our land. It is our flesh. [C1952]

Susie Tutcho of Fort Franklin:

My father really loved this land, and we love our land. The grass and the trees are our flesh, the animals are our flesh. [C684]

Joe Betsidea of Fort Franklin:

This land is our blood. We were born and raised on it. We live and survive by it. Though I am young this is the way I feel about my land ... we the people of the North know our land and could find minerals and be a millionaire one day. But the creator did not make us that way. [C761ff.]

Ray Sonfrere of Hay River:

I need and love the land I was born and raised on. Many people find meaning in different things in life. Native people find meaning in the land and they need it and they love it. ... Sometimes you stand on the shore of the lake, you see high waves rolling onto shore, and it's pushed by winds you can't see. Soon it's all calm again. In the winter you see flowers, trees, rivers and streams covered with snow and frozen. In the spring it all comes back to life. This has a strong meaning for my people and me and we need it. [C552]

Norah Ruben of Paulatuk:

As the sea is laying there, we look at it, we feed from it and we are really part of it. [C4456]

Marie Moosenose of Lac la Martre:

We love our land because we survive with it. It gives us life, the land gives us life. [C8227]

Charlie Gully of Fort Good Hope:

We talk so strongly about our land because we depend so much on it. Our parents are gone now. Our grandparents [are gone] but we still live on the same land that they did, so it is just like they are still living with us. I was born in 1926 and my father died in the year 1947, but the land is still here and I still could use it the way my father taught me to, so to me it is like my father is still alive with me. [C1918ff.]

Isadore Kochon of Colville Lake:

This is the land that we make our living on.... We make our living the simple way, to fish on it, to hunt on it and to trap on it, just live off the land.... This land fed us all even before the time the white people ever came to the North. To us it is just like a mother that brought her children up. That's how we feel about this country. It is just like a mother to us. That's how serious it is that we think about the land around here. [C8309ff.]

Joachim Bonnetrouge of Fort Providence:

We love the Mackenzie River, that's our life. It shelters us when it storms and it feeds us when there is hunger. It takes care of its chidren, the native people. [C7839]

Eddie Cook of Fort Good Hope:

Why do I go back to my land? Because I love and respect my land. My land was my supplier of food. It was my teacher, my land taught me. It taught me education which I could not learn in the white man's books. [C2037]

The Land as Security

The native people in every village made it quite clear to me that the land is the source of their well-being today and for generations to come. This is how Bertram Pokiak of Tuktoyaktuk talked about the land in the best years of the fur trade, 40 years ago:

In Aklavik a lot of fur them days, just like you white people working for wages and you have money in the bank, well my bank was here, all around with the fur. Whatever kind of food I wanted, if I wanted caribou I'd go up in the mountains; if I wanted coloured fox, I went up in the mountain; in the Delta I get mink, muskrat; but I never make a big trapper. I just get enough for my own use the coming year. Next year the animals are going to be there anyway, that's my bank. The same way all over where I travelled. Some people said to me, "Why you don't put the money in the bank and save it for future?" I should have told him that time, "The North is my bank." But I never did. I just thought of it lately. [C4234]

Pierre Tlokka told the Inquiry at Fort Rae:

I don't think that I will end up being like a white man or act like one. The white people they always have some money in the bank. I will never have any money in the bank. The only banking I could do is something that is stored in the bush and live off it. That's my bank. That's my saving account right there. [C8030]

Dogs pull Dogrib couple over spring ice back home to Detah, near Yellowknife. (NFB—Pearce)

Boiling sap in the open. (Public Archives)

Trapper Jean Rabiska, Fort Good Hope. (Native Press)

Moise Bezha and family, Fort Franklin. (R. Fumoleau)

The deep and abiding value of the land as the basis for the native people's long-term security is still central to native society. At Tuktoyaktuk, Inuit witnesses told the Inquiry of the proposal they had made to the federal government for a land freeze in the Cape Bathurst and Eskimo Lakes region to protect this land pending settlement of the Inuit claims. Jimmy Jacobson explained the thinking behind it:

> Lots of us Eskimos, they talk about Cape Bathurst and Eskimo Lakes. We thought that Eskimo Lakes and Cape Bathurst should be just like a reserve, kept free, not just keep it free for two or three years, [but] completely, have it for a reserve in case the pipeline come up; [then] we got something to go back on to keep our good hunting grounds, because if that pipeline ever come up, the people will be only rich for one or two years. They won't have money for years and years because most of the people after they work on the pipeline they bound to go and have a heck of a good time, most of them, and come back broke. They got to fall back on something. It's something that will be good to keep for the young people because they got to go back to hunting and fishing for sure. [C4255]

The Land as the Basis of Identity, Pride and Self-respect

The native people's identity, pride, self-respect and independence are inseparably linked to the land and a way of life that has land at its centre.

Jean Marie Rabiska, a trapper in his twenties, addressed the Inquiry at Fort Good Hope:

> I am strictly a trapper. I was born and raised in the bush. When I was seven years old, that is when I first started learning about bush life. I used to watch my brothers come back from the trap line. They would bring back marten and when they would go hunting, they would always bring back a moose or caribou. They

are good hunters and trappers. They seldom failed when hunting, and I used to envy them because they were good in the bush life. Ever since that time I had one thing in my mind: I wanted to be a trapper. From then on, I tried hard to learn the ways of bush life. I learned most everything from my mother. She is a tough woman when it comes to bush life. Through hardships and good times, we always stuck it out. We seldom complained for complaining is not the way of a true trapper.

> My Mum, she did a good job. She made a good trapper out of me. She taught me to follow in the footsteps of my ancestors. Today I stand out among trappers and I am proud of it. [C2013]

Paul Pagotak addressed the Inquiry at Holman, through an interpreter:

> He wants to see the Eskimos live the way they are for quite some time. He wants to see the children of the children on the land supporting themselves from the land. We don't have money among ourselves but our pride in living off the land is one thing we don't want taken away. [C3937ff.]

Even native people, who are not themselves hunters and trappers but who make their contribution to native society in other ways, see their identity and pride as people as linked to the land. Mary Rose Drybones, the social worker at Fort Good Hope, made this point quite clear:

> I am proud at this moment to say that my father was a real Dene because he made his living off the land for us. There was no welfare at that time. He died in 1953 and left a memory for me and my brother to be true Dene and we are still, and we would like to keep it that way. [C1940]

There is one other important characteristic of the native people's relationship to land. Traditionally there was no private or individual ownership of land among the Dene and the Inuit. They have always believed that all the members of a community have

the right to use it. That is why indigenous people do not believe they have the right to sell the land. It is not so much a limitation upon their rights over the land; it is rather something to which the land is not susceptible. Gabe Bluecoat of Arctic Red River addressed the Inquiry on this subject:

> The land, who made it? I really want to find out who made it. Me? You? The government? Who made it? I know [of] only one man made it — God. But on this land who besides Him made the land? What is given is not sold to anyone. We're that kind of people. What is given to us, we are not going to give away. [C4587]

Social and Political Values

Dene and Inuit societies have also developed important values that centre on the welfare of the group or community. They are values that have survived many changes and are still strong today.

The value of egalitarianism has important implications for the way decisions are made within native society. George Barnaby of Fort Good Hope, Vice-President of the Indian Brotherhood of the Northwest Territories, explained this tradition:

> No one can decide for another person. Everyone is involved in the discussion and ... the decision [is] made by everyone. Our way is to try and give freedom to a person as he knows what he wants. [F22003]

At the community hearings of the Inquiry, I discovered what Barnaby meant. In the native villages there was an implicit assumption that everyone shared in forming the community's judgment on the pipeline.

Those who wonder why the feelings of the native people have not previously appeared as strongly as they do now may find their answer in the fact that the native people themselves had substantial control over the timing, the setting, the procedure and the conduct of the Inquiry's community hearings. The Inquiry did not seek to impose any preconceived notion of how the hearings should be conducted. Its proceedings were not based upon a model or an agenda with which we, as white people, would feel comfortable. All members of each community were invited to speak. All were free to question the representatives of the pipeline companies. And the Inquiry stayed in a community until everyone there who wished to say something had been heard. The native people had an opportunity to express themselves in their own languages and in their own way.

Egalitarianism in northern native communities is closely linked with the people's respect for individual autonomy and freedom. Peter Gardiner, an anthropologist who spent a year among the Dene of Fort Liard, spoke to the Inquiry of his experience:

> Living with the people, you can see that they try to act with respect, even toward people who are young, or people who are confused, or people who are different; they are tolerant beyond anything white Canadians ever experience. When the people here give freedom to one another, they give equality. Then, many of us have a lot to learn from the people. . . . These are values that other Canadians can appreciate. They are ancient values though, and we should not see them as a result of our better teachings. [C1705ff.]

The Sharing Ethic

The tradition of sharing is seen by native people as an essential part of their cultural inheritance. Joachim Bonnetrouge told the Inquiry at Fort Liard:

> We do not conquer, we are not like that. We are sharers, we are welcomers. [C1718]

Joe Naedzo at Fort Franklin:

We native people, we help each other. We have good words for each other. And we share the things that we have with each other. I am not talking just for Fort Franklin. This happens throughout all of the North. . . .

When we visit another community, you never buy food. You don't have to buy the food. I went to visit Fort Good Hope with a dog team for five days. My dogs were fed and I was fed, I had a place to stay. And on the return trip, they gave me food for the dogs. They gave me enough food to make sure that I [could] come home. . . .

In this community, if one hunter went out hunting and got five to ten caribou, that person feeds everybody. They share that whole meat until it is all gone with everybody. That is the way the native people live among each other. They share.

It is the same thing for fishing. If a person went out fishing and got some fish, that person shares it with the community. We help each other. That is how our life continues. We share all the time.

Our ancestors have taught us a lot of things. They have taught us how to make life continue. They teach you that for your neighbours, when they are in need and when you are in need, the neighbours will feed you. Take care of each other and share with each other. [C810ff.]

Louis Norwegian at Jean Marie River:

If a person kills one moose, he shares and shares alike, and everybody have some amount, no matter how big the people around here. This is still carried out. If they kill one moose, everybody get a share of it. . . . If they go to fish, a few of them go to the lake and get some fish, everybody gets the same amount of fish. That's just the way we live here, at Jean Marie. [C2855ff.]

It is not only among the Dene that sharing is highly valued. In the Inuit communities the people told me the same thing.

Alexandria Elias at Sachs Harbour:

Long ago people helped one another all the time. They used to go down to Kendall Island

every summer, and they go there for whaling, and lots of people go there. Once they got a whale everybody got together and ate. Nobody ever looked down on one another, everybody helped one another, the poor, and who had some and who didn't have. They never try to beat one another or try to go against one another. They were all just like one big family. . . .

The Delta used to be as full of people then, and [I] never ever remember government ever helping them. They never ever asked for government help. Everything they got was what they got themselves and what they shared with one another ... [I] never ever remember being poor. [I] didn't know what poor meant. [C4066ff.]

The observations of anthropologists provide additional support for the persistence of the sharing ethic in present-day native society. Joel Savishinsky, in *Kinship and the Expression of Values in an Athabascan Bush Community,* a study of the people of Colville Lake, writes:

> In addition to generosity in terms of food, the people's concept of interdependence and reciprocity extends into matters of hospitality, cooperation, and mutual aid. People adopt and care for one another's children, help each other in moving to and from bush camps, get one another firewood in cases of immediate need, do sewing for each other, camp with one another for varying periods in the bush, and also offer each other assistance for mending and operating boats, motors, chain saws and other equipment. Generosity, therefore, covers both goods and services, and these two aspects often are interchangeable in terms of reciprocity involved in the people's behaviour. [p. 47]

Although the tradition of sharing is still regarded as vital, it has of course undergone some adaptation, particularly over the last 20 years with the movement of the native people into permanent settlements. Thus, in the larger communities, a single moose may

Inquiry witnesses were all ages. (D. Crosbie)

Louis Norwegian and Jim Sangris in Jean Marie River. (N. Cooper)

Cecile Modeste gathering firewood, near Fort Franklin. (R. Fumoleau)

Taping the old legends, Fort McPherson. (L. Smith)

not be distributed among every single household, but it will be shared within the extended family group. Even in the larger communities, however, wherever circumstances and the magnitude of the kill allow, communal distribution is still practised.

The native people have described not only how sharing and generosity characterize relations among themselves, but also how they have characterized their relations with whites. They told the Inquiry how, during the days of the fur trade, they shared with the traders their knowledge and their food, both of which were indispensable to the traders' survival in the North. This is how Philip Simba of Kakisa Lake remembers those days:

> When the first snow comes, they come into camp and the Hudson's Bay [manager] has at least 12 men working for him. Each man had a team of six dogs. These people went and got the moose. This was provided to the Hudson's Bay for his food. In the winter time they provided him with rabbits and all that. This is how they helped the Hudson's Bay. That's how he grew rich on the misery of the people, I guess. That's how come he's got a beautiful store today. [C7930]

Joe Naedzo at Fort Franklin told how native people extended the same generosity to some of the white trappers that came into the North:

> The native people don't only share among themselves. There was one white man who lived among us. His name was Jack Raymond. He went to Johnny Hoe River with us. He had no money. He had five pounds of flour and that is supposed to last him for the whole year that they spent at Johnny Hoe River.... Before the end of November there was no flour....
>
> At the time ... there was a lot of people living in Johnny Hoe. And Jack Raymond and his family had no more food. And they had only six dogs left. And for five months we shared our food with him. From January to April we

fed them, we fed their dogs. And then at the end of April, with their six dogs, they went to Port Radium to find a job.

> They have a job and they make money. But we never asked them to pay us back for all the five months that we took care of them. This is what our ancestors taught us. You know the kind of sharing we had with Jack Raymond. ... The white man and the native people, no difference, we share our food. [C814ff.]

Many native people expressed the view that, although they have extended to white strangers the same generosity with which they have traditionally treated each other, the white man has not reciprocated.

Gabe Bluecoat of Arctic Red River told the Inquiry:

> Us people, Arctic Red River people, if a white man came and asked to stay with us, sure, right away we'd say, "Yes, yes, my friend." The white people, why can't they be like that? Everything they do is money, money, money. Why don't they be our friends and use everything, share everything, just the same as the other? Why don't they do that? It's always money. It really makes me feel bad. [C4588ff.]

Native people have also commented with some bitterness on the lack of reciprocity which they say has characterized our dealings with the mineral resources of the North. Cecile Modeste of Fort Franklin expressed the sentiments of many native people in the North:

> In Port Radium, radium was discovered. In Norman Wells oil was discovered. In Yellowknife gold was discovered. All of these discoveries were [made] by Indian people. But all of the people who have discovered those minerals and stuff like that, the ways of making money, have died poor. They have died really poor. And those, the white people who have come in — we just go ahead and let them have all of these things, we never say anything about getting money back....
>
> But now it has come to a point where they are

deciding to take the whole land. Then we have to say something about it. [C633ff.]

The Role of the Elders

There exists among the native people a special respect for the old. The elders are their historians, the keepers of their customs and traditions. They are respected for what they are, for the experience and the knowledge that their age has given them, and for all that they can in turn give to others. George Barnaby put it this way:

> Respect for the old people is another law, since all the laws come from the teaching by our elders, from stories that give us pride in our culture, from training since we are young; we learn what is expected of us. Without this learning from the elders our culture will be destroyed. [F22003]

The role of the elders and the respect they receive are important in the native people's attempts to deal with the problems that face them today. René Lamothe told the Inquiry at Fort Simpson about the activities of the Koe Go Cho Society, a community resource centre that serves the educational, cultural and social needs of the native people of Simpson. He explained the central role of the elders in the society's activities:

> We don't look at senior citizens' homes as they are looked at in the South or by the industrial economy.... The reason for having senior citizens here is a service to them of course. If they choose to come here there would be no charge to them. We would ask them to come as leaders of the people, as people who have the knowledge of the ways of life of the people to teach to the young here. They would come, not as people who have no further productive reality in the existence of the people, but as the crucial element, the age which passes on the life to the young. One of the perspectives of life that is lacking in the industrial economy, which is a very real thing ... in the Indian world, is the fact that we are

Kilometres
0   400
0   200
Miles

Sachs Harbour
North Star Harbour
Holman
Tuktoyaktuk
Paulatuk
Aklavik
Old Crow
Inuvik
Arctic Red River
Fort McPherson
Colville Lake
Arctic Circle
Fort Good Hope
Willow Lake
Fort Franklin
NORTHWEST TERRITORIES
Norman Wells
Fort Norman
Rae Lakes
ALASKA
YUKON
Wrigley
Rae/Edzo
Latham Island
Yellowknife
Lac la Martre
Detah
Fort Simpson
Fort Providence
Fort Resolution
Whitehorse
Nahanni Butte
Jean-Marie River
Kakisa Lake
Pine Point
Fort Smith
Trout Lake
Hay River
Fort Liard

born every day, and that every little bit of information that we learn is a birth. As we learn the way of life from the old, as we get older, we understand different things, we hear a legend, we hear it again, we hear it again, we hear it again, and every time at a given age this legend takes on new meaning.

So the senior citizens by their presence, their knowledge of the past, of language, of songs and dances, of the legends, the material aspects of their culture, such as the building of canoes, snowshoes, this kind of thing, will be very instrumental in creating the spirit, the atmosphere in which the culture thrives. The senior citizens will be present to give moral support to the adults in alcohol rehabilitation. They will be present to assist the research and information crews to build a library of native folklore. Their presence in the education system as it is developing will make it possible for them to take up their rightful and ancestral role as teachers of their people. [C2698ff.]

Native Leadership

Until the signing of the treaties and the establishment under the Indian Act of the chief and band council model of Indian government, the Dene had no institutionalized political system as we understand it. However, as they made clear to the Inquiry, they did have their own ways of governing themselves. Chief Jim Antoine of Fort Simpson told the Inquiry:

Before 1921 people used to live off the land along the rivers ... my people at that time were a nation. They had their own leaders, they had elders who gave direction, they had learned men who knew how to cure people and give good directions to the people, so that they could continue living off the land. [C2619]

Joe Naedzo, of the Fort Franklin Band, told the Inquiry:

In those days, too, the government wasn't there to tell them how to do this and that, to

survive. So the Indian people chose leaders and these leaders were the government for the people. They decided in what way the people should go this year, what to do before the winter comes. ... These chosen leaders were the government. [C640]

When the Dene were still living in semi-nomadic extended-family groups, their leaders were the most respected hunters. The acceptance of their leadership rested on the deference of others to their wisdom and judgment and on their ability to provide for the group. Guidance was also provided by the shamans, men knowledgeable in spiritual and psychological matters. Leadership, however, was not usually autocratic; it respected the basic egalitarian structure of the group. Dr. June Helm, an anthropologist who has specialized for many years in Northern Athabascan society, described its nature in a paper written in 1976:

The traditional Dene leader ... is, on the basis of his superior abilities, consensually recognized by the group to serve as organizer, pace-setter and spokesman for the group. He is not the "boss" or independent decision-maker in group matters, as the Euro-Canadian might surmise. [*Traditional Dene Community Structure and Socioterritorial Organization*, p. 20, unpub.]

The Dene told the Inquiry about some leaders of the past. The Dogrib people of Fort Rae spoke of their great Chiefs Edzo and Monfwi, and the Loucheux people of Fort McPherson talked of the guidance given by Chief Julius. Both Chief Monfwi and Chief Julius were respected leaders when Treaty 11 was signed in 1921, and they became the first chiefs of their respective peoples under the system of elected chiefs instituted by the Indian Act.

Because no treaties were ever made with the Inuit, and because they were not brought within the framework of the Indian Act,

they have not developed an institutionalized system for electing leaders. However, Inuit witnesses told the Inquiry that they, too, had their traditional leaders. Frank Cockney at Tuktoyaktuk described through an interpreter how, as a young man, he came to be aware of these leaders:

At one time Eskimos used to get together in Aklavik after ratting and just before it was whaling season time. ... He said he was big enough to understand, and that was the first time he saw the Indians there. And the Indians and the Inuit used to mix together, and that was the first time he also found out that there were chiefs. And he said the Eskimo Chief was Mangilaluk and there was other people there that got together with the Indians, Muligak and Kaglik, that was the Eskimo leaders. He said the other Indian people he found out only later were Paul Koe and Jim Greenland and Chief Julius. He said he used to wonder how they always got together, but later he found out they were making plans about their land. ... He found out only later, even though he didn't see them very often, that the older people always used to get together. They always planned how they would look after their land, so he said now, after he grew up, he knew it's nothing new that people plan about their land and how they look after it. It was done a long time ago also. [C42512ff.]

Charlie Gruben also told the Inquiry at Tuktoyaktuk about Inuit leadership:

When we were young we had a Chief Mangilaluk. He tell us not to kill this and that. We don't do that because we want to listen to our chief, so good, we don't overkill. It was better than game wardens we got today, I think. That's the way the people used to handle their game that time. We don't kill game just for the sport, we just kill what we need and that's it. [C4254ff.]

Mark Noksana, one of the men who took part in the five-year reindeer drive from Alaska to the Mackenzie Delta in the 1930s told the Inquiry how the wise judgment o

Transportation in the old days, Great Slave Lake.
(Alberta Archives)

William Mangilaluk had continued to serve the Mackenzie Delta Eskimos. He explained that Mangilaluk had been asked by government representatives whether the Eskimos wanted to take and receive treaty money like the Indians:

> [Mangilaluk] heard of some reindeer in Alaska. There was no caribou at all here in Tuktoyaktuk. You have to go far down to Baillie Island to get your caribou. No caribou at all at that time.... So the chief asked the government if he could get the reindeer from Alaska for the Eskimos. See, they don't want no money. He says money is no good to him. That's what he told me. He said he'd rather get reindeer so that he can have meat all the time for the new generation coming.... That's what happened.... I'm glad about it because the reindeer this year has been a real help to the Delta people at Tuk, McPherson, Arctic Red, Aklavik. There is no caribou on the west side this year. The reindeer have been real helpful for the people in the North. If it wasn't for the reindeer brought here, a lot of them would have been hungry for meat at Tuk, all these places, this year. [C4273ff.]

In the last few years the structure of native leadership seems, at first glance, to have changed. In many villages the Dene have elected young men to be their chiefs, and young people now play an essential role in the development of native political organizations. On closer analysis, however, the structure of leadership today can be seen to be continuous with traditional ways. In the old days, native leaders were chosen for their ability as hunters and as spokesmen in dealings with the white man. Today, the young and educated Dene and Inuit, who have learned to speak English and to articulate their aspirations to the outside world, have been chosen as leaders in the contemporary struggle for survival.

As leaders, however, the young people look to the elders for guidance. They seek to blend the knowledge they have acquired through education with the knowledge of the elders. Isidore Zoe, Chairman of the Settlement Council of Lac la Martre, a man in his early twenties, explained to the Inquiry the role of the new leadership:

> My position is to go between the young and the old. It is the sort of thing like you compare from the old to the young generation to see what is suitable for both....
>
> We young people are the ear of the old people, to listen to what has been said. We hear what the politicians say — to pass it on to old people, in order for them to support and to make decisions.
>
> We young people are the eyes of the old people, to see what is happening down South, what we read, and to compare what is the best for the Dene people.
>
> We young people are the tongue of the old people ... to say what they have to say. [C8197ff.]

Conclusions

There have been great changes in the life of the native people, particularly in the last 20 years, but they have tried to hold fast to the values that lie at the core of their cultures. They are striving to maintain these values in the modern world. These values are ancient and enduring, although the expression of them may change — indeed has changed — from generation to generation. George Erasmus, President of the Indian Brotherhood of the Northwest Territories, told the Inquiry at Fort Rae:

> We want to be our own boss. We want to decide on our land what is going to happen. It's not as some people keep referring to as looking back. We are not looking back. We do not want to remain static. We do not want to stop the clock of time. Our old people, when they talk about how the Dene ways should be kept by young people, when they talk about stopping the pipeline until we settle our land claims, they are not looking back, they are looking forward. They are looking as far ahead into the future as they possibly can. So are we all. [C8068]

One of the greatest fears of young native people is that the impact of the pipeline will reduce to little more than a memory the values by which their parents and grandparents have lived. Bella T'Seleie spoke to the Inquiry at Colville Lake:

> I was born in Fort Good Hope in 1953. When I was three years old my mother caught T.B. and was taken away. I was taken care of by the people of Good Hope. The people there are like that. If a kid doesn't have a mother, it is everybody's responsibility to make sure this kid doesn't starve ... the kid is not taken off to some home, you know, to strangers either. I was kept by many families until my foster parents ... learned about my situation. They weren't young and they had three children alive and they already had three younger girls who died. But they are kind people and they knew that I needed help, so they adopted me.
>
> For the rest of my childhood I was raised in Colville Lake. In the summer we lived in fish camps, always working together making dry fish, cutting wood, and I look back on those days as really happy. I was happy....
>
> I look at Colville Lake today ... [the people] still have their own lives; they still have their pride. I don't want my people to have nothing but memories of what their life used to be....
>
> There's a lot of young people, like myself, that want to have something other than memories. That's why we want control of what's going to happen to us and our lives in the future. I think about all that and I know that we are one of the last people to have our own land and still have our own kind of life in the world. I think the government and oil companies should consider that, after all they've done to the native people in the South, they should know that it doesn't work. It didn't work for them. They are not happy people;

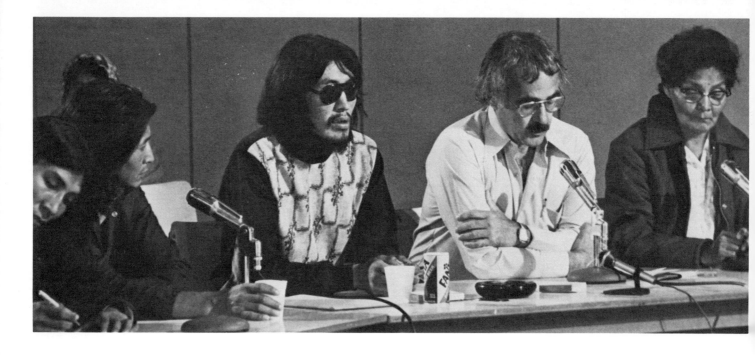

they are not proud people. All they have is memories. [C8329ff.]

The native people of the North insist that they have the right to transmit to future generations a way of life and a set of values that give coherence and distinctiveness to their existence as Dene, Inuit and Metis. Frank T'Seleie, then Chief of the Fort Good Hope Band, expressed his hope for the future of his people:

> Our Dene nation is like this great river. It has been flowing before any of us can remember. We take our strength, our wisdom and our ways from the flow and direction which has been established for us by ancestors we never knew, ancestors of a thousand years ago. Their wisdom flows through us to our children and our grandchildren, to generations we will never know. We will live out our lives as we must, and we will die in peace because we will know that our people and this river will flow on after us.
>
> We know that our grandchildren will speak a language that is their heritage, that has been passed on from before time. We know they will share their wealth and not hoard it, or keep it to themselves. We know they will look after our old people and respect them for their wisdom. We know they will look after this land and protect it, and that 500 years from now, someone with skin my colour and moccasins on his feet will climb up the Ramparts and rest, and look over the river, and feel that he, too, has a place in the universe, and he will thank the same spirits that I thank, that his ancestors have looked after his land well, and he will be proud to be a Dene. [C1778]

It may be asked why I have devoted so much space to these statements of native values. It may be said that the task that is at hand is the development of the North. But I have given this space to the native people's own words because they felt it was essential to say these things. By these statements the native people have affirmed their belief in themselves, their past and their future, and the ideals by which they seek to live. These are the values and the principles that must underlie the development of the North.

The Native Economy

Assessing the Native Economy

The native people of the North have lived for generations in a world of their own, a world that has been obscured from the eyes of the rest of the world by the many myths our society has woven around it. Now they are emerging from the shadows, and they appear as themselves, not as imitations of us. And we can see that their world and their economy have a reality as tangible as our own.

Charlie Chocolate of Rae Lakes made this point quite explicit:

> This land is our industry, providing us with shelter, food, income, similar to the industries down South supporting the white peoples. [C8289]

We have always undervalued northern native culture, and we have tended to underestimate the vitality of the native economy. We have, at times, even doubted its existence. I can perhaps illustrate how white people typically understand the native economy by referring to a report by Gemini North, prepared for Arctic Gas, on the number of persons who are still engaged in trapping in the Mackenzie Valley. The report says:

> A survey made in 1972 revealed that only 96 persons, out of a study region population of 23,600 and a male working age population of 7,830 were engaged in full-time and regular part-time trapping. [Arctic Gas application, Section 14.c, p. 17]

Yet the evidence of the native people was altogether to the contrary. The Land Use and Occupancy Study, carried out by the Indian Brotherhood of the Northwest Territories, sets forth conclusions that are quite different from those of Gemini North. The Brotherhood claims there are 1,075 persons actively engaged in trapping in the Mackenzie District. Although not all of them are totally or equally dependent on the land, the evidence given in the communities by hundreds of native witnesses and the Land Use and Occupancy Study maps, all indicate the extent to which the native people are still engaged in hunting, fishing and trapping. These maps were presented and discussed at each community; the composite map, prepared by the Brotherhood, was introduced at the Inquiry's formal hearings in Yellowknife. The evidence I heard in the Inuit villages was similar. Like the Brotherhood the Committee for Original Peoples Entitlement introduced a series of land use and occupancy maps to substantiate their claim of continued intensive native use of and dependence on the land. In the Yukon, the people of Old Crow presented similar evidence.

The discrepancy between the evidence of Gemini North and that of the native people arises from different assumptions about the nature of trapping. To Gemini North, and to most white people, trapping is a job, much the same as any other job. So, determining the number of trappers is simply a matter of counting how many people during the period of the survey ran a trap line and sold furs. The native people, however, do not see trapping as a job; it is, rather, a way of life based on the use of the land and its resources, running a trap line is but one of a number of seasonal activities. A trapper is, therefore, someone who sees himself as following that

Frank T'Seleie, Chief of Fort Good Hope, at Inquiry hearing with Foothills' president, Robert Blair and interpreter, Mary Wilson. (Native Press)

Country foods: muktuk boiling at Inuit whaling camp. (W. Hunt)

Mary Jane Sangris of Detah eating caribou. (R. Fumoleau)

Fish — an important resource. (R. Fumoleau)

---

way of life. A man who is working for wages with a seismic exploration crew (and who would, therefore, enter Gemini North's figures as a wage employee) might still regard himself as a trapper (or hunter) because he intends to use part of his wages to buy a new snowmobile, a new boat, new traps or a new rifle. In his own eyes, therefore, he is working at "a job" to support "his way of life" as a trapper.

Charlie Neyele of Fort Franklin explained this attitude to the Inquiry:

> This winter I have been working for the Co-op. I get two days off on the Saturday and Sunday. In those days I usually go out trapping and I go out hunting.... Right now I have no boat and no canoe, no kicker, so I plan to work for some kind of company, like I am working for Imperial Oil right now. I didn't work for the money, but I work for a canoe and a kicker, and after I get this canoe and kicker I will use that for travelling around Bear Lake.... If I really want a gun ... I work for a gun only, not for money. [C715]

I do not think that statistics on the number of "trappers," however they are defined, are the best evidence of the extent to which the native people still live off the land. It makes more sense to look at the evidence of their actual use of the land today: whether they are engaged in hunting and fishing for subsistence, or trapping for fur, or both. We can understand the native people's vehement rejection of the contention advanced by Arctic Gas that very few of them are trappers only if we appreciate the persistence of their way of life on the land and the persistence of their values associated with the land.

At every community hearing, the native people told me about their dependence upon the land. Such dependence is not just a question of what people say; it is founded on realities that we often have not seen or have

not recognized. You can walk through any native village in summer, and at every home see fish drying on racks or being smoke-cured in teepees. Anyone who, like myself, has been to the native villages of the Mackenzie Valley and the Western Arctic is struck by the extent to which people still rely on the bush and the barrens: the "reefer" chock full of game at Fort McPherson, thousands of muskrat pelts at Old Crow, caribou carcasses butchered at Holman, hunting and fishing camps of the native people throughout the Valley and the Delta. In every community you find people eating country food: caribou, moose, arctic char, whitefish, trout, muktuk and sometimes muskox.

Our tendency to underestimate the vitality of native culture and the native economy is exemplified in the value that Gemini North said should be attributed to country food. They found that it accounted for less than five percent of native income in the Mackenzie Valley and the Mackenzie Delta. How could they reach such a conclusion, when everywhere in the North there is evidence that people still rely heavily on country food? I think the main reason is that, long ago, we concluded that the native economy was dying, that the land could not sustain its native population, that the people had lost the skills they needed to live off the land, and even that they had lost the desire to do so.

The fact is, the native economy exists out of the sight of white people: out of sight, out of mind. Furthermore, the true extent of the native economy is difficult to measure; it cannot easily be reduced to statistical form. Gemini North attributed to country food only a "local exchange" value, that is, the price that one person would charge another for a commodity, say caribou, within a

native community. This method of calculation ignores the fact that the distribution and exchange of country food takes place within the context of kinship obligations and family ties; it is nothing like an ordinary market transaction. So, if we are to understand the real economic value of country food, a standard other than "local exchange" must be used. It is clear from the evidence that the standard that should be applied is the "replacement" value, that is, the amount it would cost a native person to buy from the local store the imported equivalent of the country food he now obtains from the bush and the barrens. It must be plain to anyone that if native people did not or could not obtain country food, they would have to buy meat and fish from the store to replace the food they get now from the land.

Evidence from the Community Hearings

What then is the actual extent of the use by native people of the game, fish and fur of the land for subsistence and for cash? The Inquiry visited 35 communities in the Mackenzie Valley and the Western Arctic. At each hearing, native people spoke of their reliance upon the land, and what they said has been strongly supported by the evidence of social scientists. I will review this evidence in some detail because, as I have said, for more than a generation we have undervalued the native economy.

FORT FRANKLIN

For three days in June 1975, the Inquiry held hearings at Fort Franklin, a Dene village of approximately 400 people on the shore of Great Bear Lake. The evidence of the Dene there, together with the evidence of Scott Rushforth, an anthropologist who lived in

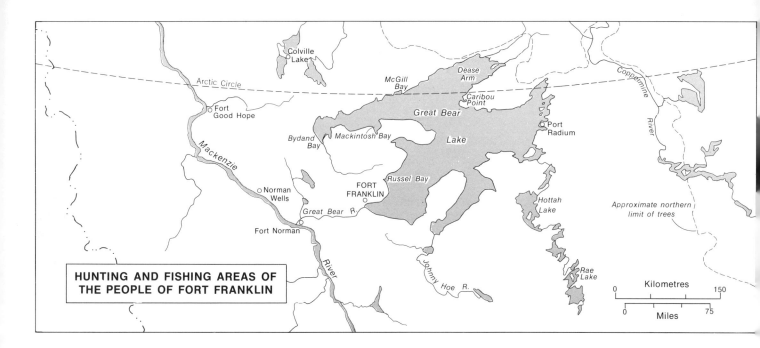

HUNTING AND FISHING AREAS OF THE PEOPLE OF FORT FRANKLIN

Fort Franklin in 1974 and 1975, provides a detailed insight into the nature and extent of the native economy and of the native reliance on the land.

These people traditionally lived in small kinship and family groups in camps around Bear Lake wherever fish and meat were abundant. If a group of Bear Lake people living at a fish camp received word that a large herd of caribou had been seen on the north shore, they might immediately pack up their essential belongings and move there to hunt. Abundant fish and game, and a strategic knowledge of these resources, gave the Bear Lake people security in a land that can be harsh and inhospitable. Following the changes the fur trade brought, their seasonal activity came to focus on trips to the trading posts at Fort Franklin or Fort Norman, at the mouth of Great Bear River, to sell furs for essential supplies. This way of life continued until the 1950s, when the people moved into the settlement of Fort Franklin. Liza Blondin, who was born in 1911, speaking through an interpreter, told the Inquiry at Fort Franklin about the traditional life of the native people during the fur trade era:

[She] and her husband used to travel by boat with paddles.... When they get to the area where they want to go trapping, her husband gets their fishing net in the lake ... and then he goes hunting. And after he gets some meat for his wife to live off, he is away. Then he finally goes trapping ... he sets his traps [and usually] they trap right up until Christmas.... When she is alone after her husband goes trapping, she has to go out and visit the nets, she has to go hunting to feed her children, and ... sometimes her husband also gives her a few traps so that she can trap around the area that they are living in. When they are out trapping, she makes all of the dried fish and dried meat. And she prepares it for the long journey back to [Fort] Franklin. They usually come back to Franklin around Christmas ...

all this time she has been preparing the food to come back to Franklin. She also makes all of the clothing for the children because coming back across the lake it is really cold.

After spending Christmas in Franklin they go back in January. It is a very cold month. Nearly 60 to 70 [Fahrenheit] below in Franklin but ... they still have to set the net. They set four nets at a time and they still have to fish and they still have to hunt.... When you set four nets like that ... if the ice freezes over with that temperature, [it] freezes ... to at least a foot. And you have to dig a hole right [through it. And when her husband comes back from trapping,] he takes the fish for his dogs so that he can feed them while he is on the trap line. And then while he is gone she has to go fishing ... [and] hunting and she sets snares for rabbits. She has to go hunting for ptarmigan. ... And it includes maintaining the home too. Like getting brushes [spruce boughs] and putting the brushes on the floor [of the tent], getting wood and sewing.

When her husband brings back a moose, she has to cut off ... the meat from the inside, and then they have to scrape the skin while it is still damp. And then they have to tan it....

When they go spring hunting they usually leave about May 7 ... to fish, hunt and get some wood ... feed the children, make dry fish, paint the boat and get the boat all ready. ... When [the men] come back they bring back beaver and muskrats. So you have to clean the beaver [skins] off and the muskrats ... until it is all smooth on the inside and then [you have to nail it to a stretching board].... While you are doing that, you teach your children all of these things, how it is done. [C625ff.]

In the early 1950s the Bear Lake people moved into Fort Franklin. As a result, they have faced many changes in their way of life, but, despite these changes, they have retained much of their traditional culture and many of their traditional values. In organizing their way of living, they rely, for the most part, upon their own cultural knowledge and their own values — not on

those of white society. Rushforth, in his study *Recent Land-use by the Great Bear Lake Indians,* concluded that the number of people engaged in traditional land use activities has remained constant in recent years and that the people have not abandoned their traditional means of making a living despite changes in their life. Although many aspects of social organization have changed since the days described by Liza Blondin, the economic life of Fort Franklin still centres on hunting, fishing and trapping.

Rushforth described the seasonal cycle of land use in Fort Franklin. Nowadays, men leave the community in mid-October to go trapping. With a few exceptions, their families no longer accompany them; instead a trapper travels with a male relative or friend. Trappers who still use dogs leave somewhat earlier than those who use snowmobiles. They pitch camp near a fish lake then set the nets to take advantage of the late-October run of whitefish. They keep their nets in the water until they have enough fish for themselves and their dogs and perhaps some to send back to Fort Franklin. For example, the men who trapped at Johnny Hoe River in November and December 1974 fished long enough to feed themselves and at least 12 dogs and to send back approximately 1,000 whitefish, that is over 3,000 pounds of fish, to Fort Franklin.

In addition to fishing while on their trap lines, the men also spend some time hunting for moose and caribou. If the hunt is successful, the trappers keep some of the meat for themselves and send the rest back to Fort Franklin to feed their families. During the 1974-1975 trapping season, at least ten caribou and four moose were divided in this way. The men go back to Fort Franklin in mid-December to trade their furs and to spend Christmas with their families. After

Dog-team on the ice in April. (R. Fumoleau)

Trapped muskrat. (R. Fumoleau)

Theodore Tobac of the Hare tribe. (R. Fumoleau)

the New Year, some, although not all, of the men go back out to their trap lines and stay until February. In addition to full-time trappers at Fort Franklin there are a number of men who trap part-time. By trapping every weekend, these part-time trappers can supplement their wage income by selling some furs, catching a few rabbits, shooting a few ptarmigan or grouse, and bagging an occasional caribou or moose; and — what is most important to many of them — they can maintain contact with life in the bush.

In the last few years, hunters at Fort Franklin have organized community hunts in February and March for barren ground caribou. In 1975 they made two such trips to the east end of Great Bear Lake. On the first, five men spent ten days at Caribou Point; on the second, 27 men spent three weeks in the Port Radium region. Altogether, these hunters killed at least 165 barren ground caribou and three moose. Approximately 90 of the caribou were stored in the community freezer for distribution among all of the people of Fort Franklin; the others were distributed among the individual hunters' families.

In fall and winter the Fort Franklin people sometimes go out to hunt moose; during 1974-1975, they took 17 moose.

During May, the men of Fort Franklin hunt beaver and muskrat on the rivers and lakes around Great Bear Lake. From the spring hunt, they get both fur to sell and plenty of meat to eat. Meat that is not consumed in the bush is dried and brought back to Fort Franklin. Like trapping in winter, the spring beaver hunt is undertaken almost exclusively by men because school is still in session and the women normally stay in Fort Franklin with the children.

During August, there is usually another community caribou hunt from Fort Franklin

and, because school is out, the men take their families with them into the bush. In August 1974, about 25 hunters, many of them with their wives and children, making in all a party of about 120, went on a summer hunt to McGill Bay on the north shore of Great Bear Lake. While the men went hunting each day, the women remained in camp to scrape and tan hides, dry the meat, and mind the children. I visited that camp at McGill Bay, arriving while the men were out hunting. Everywhere caribou and fish were drying on racks and in teepees. After a meal of dried meat and fish, I flew in a small plane along the north shore of the lake, landing near "Nanook," the big schooner the Franklin people use to travel around the lake. As the plane landed, the men sighted caribou, turned back to shore and made a kill.

Fish are a major source of food for the Bear Lake people. In the vicinity of Fort Franklin itself, people fish throughout the year except during the two or three months of freeze-up and break-up. From December to May, they set nets under the ice for trout and herring, and they set hooks for trout. The nets are removed before break-up, then reset after the ice is gone. From July to September, they net hundreds of large trout. In July, a fisherman can catch between 50 and 100 grayling during a canoe trip to Great Bear River. The people make fishing trips throughout the year to many places around Great Bear Lake, during which they may catch hundreds of fish in a short time. For example, in June 1974, some fishermen went by snowmobile to Russell Bay; they set three or four nets under the ice for three days, and returned to Fort Franklin with approximately one thousand trout and whitefish.

Although the Fort Franklin people do not rely upon birds as much as, for example, do the people in the Mackenzie Delta, they do

take many ptarmigan, grouse and ducks, and when they are at their spring camps, they can hunt the ducks and geese flying north to their breeding grounds on the shores of Beaufort Sea.

It has been assumed that, with the change to permanent settlement living, native people no longer use much of their traditional land base. The evidence challenges this assumption. Rushforth stated that, although the Bear Lake people no longer live in small dispersed groups at places like Johnny Hoe River, Hottah Lake, Caribou Point, Dease Bay, Bydand Bay and Mackintosh Bay, they continue to use all of these places, as well as others, to hunt, trap and fish. For example, at Johnny Hoe River there are six cabins that are used every year during the winter trapping season, during the spring beaver hunt, and during the seasonal fish runs. The Bear Lake people continue to use the entire area that their ancestors used and that they themselves used as recently as 25 years ago. At the hearing in Fort Franklin, Chief George Kodakin's 15-year-old son Paul showed me on a land use map where he and his father had travelled on hunting trips — the places were the same as those the older people of the village had identified as important traditional territory. New technology, such as snowmobiles, larger boats and chartered aircraft, and differently organized work units, such as community hunting groups, permit the Bear Lake people to reach quickly areas far from Fort Franklin, and to spend a shorter time at areas in which, in the old days, they would have camped for a whole season.

Chief Kodakin told the Inquiry:

The whole lake is like a deep freeze for Fort Franklin. Our ancestors have used it as a deep freeze and we will use it as a deep freeze for the future children. [C751]

Gemini North estimated the value of this "deep freeze," that is, the value of country food to the people of Fort Franklin, for the year 1972, at approximately $42,000. Rushforth, on the other hand, found that the Fort Franklin people derive an important, even a critically important, proportion of their food from the land. By calculating the *replacement* value of food, he concluded that the Bear Lake people derived between $223,000 and $261,000 in income from their land during 1974-1975. These figures, when broken down, reveal that the Dene households of Fort Franklin derived an average income from land use activities during 1974-1975 of between $3,500 and $4,100 and, on a per capita basis, between $630 and $750. Rushforth concluded that the Bear Lake people still derive 25 to 40 percent of their food from the land. I think Rushforth's standard of measurement — replacement value — is the right one.

Although it is important to adopt an appropriate standard to measure the native economy and the value to be imputed to country food, quantification by itself is not enough. We should not allow the figures of measurement to obscure the qualitative importance of country food and of the way of life that is associated with it. The figures do not show how much native people prefer country food to store-bought food. Not only does country food taste better to them, but virtually all country food has far greater nutritional value than processed and packaged foods bought in stores. Still more important, these figures do not and cannot indicate the intrinsic importance of hunting, fishing and trapping as social and cultural activities. Neither do they nor can they indicate the value to the native hunter of the environment that provides these resources.

WRIGLEY AND FORT SIMPSON

You may say: it is all very well to talk about Fort Franklin, but is it a representative community? Can we apply Rushforth's findings to the Mackenzie Valley and the Western Arctic as a whole? After all, Fort Franklin is located on Great Bear Lake, not on the Mackenzie River itself, and is generally regarded as a traditional community.

Dr. Michael Asch, an anthropologist, tried to deal with this question. He compared Wrigley, a village of 200 people, with Fort Simpson, a town of 1,200. Both settlements are on the Mackenzie River, and are about 110 miles apart. Gemini North found that in Wrigley, a relatively isolated community, the native people still live off the land, whereas at Fort Simpson, a more urban community accessible from the Mackenzie Highway, the native people no longer rely significantly on the land. Asch argued that, even accepting Gemini North's figures regarding the quantities of game taken at Wrigley and Fort Simpson, the results, upon analysis, do not bear out the conclusion reached by Gemini North.

Gemini North tried to calculate the proportion of country food in the economy of every community in the Mackenzie Valley. These values range from a low of zero at Norman Wells (essentially a white community), to a high of 50 percent at Fort Good Hope. Even at Wrigley, which Gemini North considered to be a traditional community, the value of country food came to only 19 percent, whereas at Fort Simpson it was a mere five percent. The claim that the native economy is dying is based on these figures.

Of course, Gemini North's calculations were based on local exchange value. I have already indicated that this method of calculating the value of country food should be rejected. But Asch argued that a further

mistake was made. Gemini North compared the imputed income, based on the value of the country food consumed, with the "total estimated income," in each settlement. This latter figure includes the income of both white and native people, and it is, thus, the total estimated income for the whole community. Therefore, communities that have large white populations — with governmental, business and industrial infrastructures — have very high estimated total incomes (such as $7.4 million for Inuvik and $2.3 million for Yellowknife). Native communities with small white populations, such as Nahanni Butte and Trout Lake, have very low total estimated incomes ($56,000 and $14,000, respectively). In this way, Gemini North compared the income imputed to country food (which they had undervalued) with the incomes of all residents in a community, both native and white. This is not a meaningful comparison. White people in the North do not hunt and fish for a living — therefore they do not contribute to the native economy. At the same time, virtually all whites in the North have highly paid jobs — therefore their salaries greatly inflate the figure for total income.

In 1972, Gemini North imputed a value of $92,364 to the country food used by the people of Fort Simpson; the equivalent figure for the people of Wrigley was $24,130. Whether or not these figures represent true value, the same errors were made in both cases. Consider only the relationship between them and you will see that the figure for Fort Simpson is roughly four times that for Wrigley. Then, if you compare the native populations of both communities, you will see that Fort Simpson, at the time, had approximately 650 native people — or about four times as many as Wrigley. Hence, the figures appear to show that the native people

Joe Blondin on the Great Bear River. (R. Fumoleau)

Leo Norwegian. (Native Press)

Trapper Philippe Codzi, Colville Lake. (R. Fumoleau)

Young people at Paul and Mary Rose Wright's lodge, to learn bush skills. (Native Press)

in both communities depend to about the same extent on country food. In other words, the native people of Fort Simpson — a group that had supposedly abandoned the land — were just as dependent on the land as the people of Wrigley.

However, some words of caution are necessary. The figures upon which Gemini North's conclusions were based relate to 1971-1972, only a year or two after the Mackenzie Highway reached Fort Simpson. The native people at Fort Simpson told me that in the five years since its completion as far as the town, the highway has brought many changes, and the social and economic fabric of the native residents has been weakened. At the present time, therefore, the native people themselves see significant differences between the native economy of Fort Simpson and of Wrigley. In the time that has passed since Gemini North's survey, dependence on the land has, I think, diminished in Fort Simpson. This is not to say that the land is no longer important to the native residents of Fort Simpson, nor that they have abandoned the native economy. Links with the land are important to many of the native people there. Leo Norwegian and Jimmy Sanguez, two of the older men, told the Inquiry how they are taking school children into the bush to teach them how to live off the land.

At Fort Providence a similar program is underway. Chief Albert Canadien described how:

> This summer we have established a small camp down the river ... for the native students from ages of eight to 16 try to get their interest in everyday life or routine ... of the native people living in the bush. We have three couples down there looking after the students, and of the three we have two of them who speak English quite well. The other two couples don't speak it at all. And this is

primarily to encourage the students, the children, to talk in their native language again.

> This is in a sense land use on the part of native people. We are not trying to forget our ways of life. We are trying to encourage the students to remember the old ways, not necessarily live them. It's their choice to do and live the way they want. We cannot dictate to our young people and say, "This is the way it is." Every individual has his own mind and they can choose what they want. But to encourage them we have this camp ... we have nets in the water and some of the young girls make dry fish, and they take the older boys out hunting and I think everybody goes out and snares....

> What I am trying to say is that we are far from forgetting who we are and how we live. [C7894ff.]

COLVILLE LAKE

Hyacinthe Kochon, the Chief at Colville Lake, told the Inquiry that his people continue to depend upon the land for their livelihood:

> Around here we make our living by hunting for our meat, fish on the lakes and trapping.... We depend on the land. [C8309]

Joel Savishinsky, an anthropologist, has written that at Colville Lake the people still rely heavily upon caribou, moose, hare, waterfowl and fish for human and dog food; their diet consists primarily of country food. The people still use dog teams, and fish is the most economical food for maintaining their animals.

Martin Codzi of Colville Lake told the Inquiry:

> Even now today we are still living the way our old people used to live. Right now my brother has put his camp on the shore of the lake here and he is getting a lot of fish and he is putting up dry fish for the winter. That's the way that we've always been making our living. [C8333]

Virtually all of the fuel used for heating

and cooking is wood obtained from the local forest, and spruce wood is the primary building material in the village. There is only one pre-fabricated structure in the community; the RCMP use it on their infrequent overnight stays at the settlement.

OLD CROW

The evidence heard at Old Crow left me in no doubt that life on the land is still of vital importance to all the people there. Dr. John Stager, who made a study in 1974 for the Environmental-Social Committee, concluded that a very large proportion of the total food consumed in Old Crow came from the land. Caribou is the most important food resource and Stager's report states that, in 1973, the Old Crow hunters killed a total of 751 animals. Almost every male over 11 years of age goes on the spring hunt, when the caribou migrate past Old Crow to their calving grounds on the Arctic coast, and on the fall hunt, when the caribou return to their wintering grounds. In 1973, the people of Old Crow secured more than 90,000 pounds of caribou meat. Although the trapping of fine furs — marten, mink and lynx — has gradually declined, the number of families involved in the spring hunt for muskrat and beaver has recently increased. During spring 1975, almost everybody in the village was out hunting on Old Crow Flats; not only did the muskrat harvest provide an income, which in 1973 averaged $900 per trapper, but it also provided an important source of meat for the people and their dogs.

In the summer and fall, when salmon are running up the Porcupine River, fishing is an important activity in Old Crow. Stager estimated that in 1973 the total salmon catch was in the neighbourhood of 30,000 pounds.

Robert Sharpe, the school principal at Old Crow, helped the community to prepare a land use map that was presented at the community hearing. He testified that, in preparing the map, he found that the younger people were able to identify almost all of the places that were regarded as important by the older people. This testimony is consistent with the evidence given by the young people at Old Crow: they have not given up interest in the land.

MACKENZIE DELTA AND BEAUFORT SEA COMMUNITIES

Dr. Peter Usher, a geographer who has had a long association with the region, reviewed the season of 1973-1974 (the last for which he had comprehensive data) in the Western Arctic communities of Aklavik, Inuvik, Tuktoyaktuk, Paulatuk and Sachs Harbour (but excluding Holman). He estimated that the native people harvested over $800,000 worth of fur and nearly $1.6 million worth of food in the region. For a population of about 2,000 Eskimos, comprising some 300 families, these figures represent an average income of about $8,000 per family from the land. Although Usher properly used replacement value as the standard of measurement, the values he imputed were somewhat high. At the same time it should be remembered that 1973-1974 was a very good year for trapping. Notwithstanding these qualifications, Usher's evidence established that the value to be imputed to the native economy in the Western Arctic is greater than has generally been thought. Continued and widespread use of country food is confirmed in a general way by survey of the diets of northern households carried out by the federal Department of National Health and Welfare.

In three of the Western Arctic communities, Sachs Harbour, Holman and Paulatuk, virtually all families make their living from the land. Roy Goose, who is an Eskimo and the local Wildlife Officer at Holman, described to the Inquiry the extent of the people's use of the land:

> There [have] been approximately 200 to 225 caribou killed in Holman Island since October of this year. That's an average of six per family.... Most of the people ... are professional hunters and trappers. They are the people that know the land, that know the ocean, that know everything relating to the environment. And up to date, the white fox catch is approximately 900 by approximately 25 serious trappers. ... Their seal catch ... would be approximately 1,700 ringed seals.... Their income from the seals would be approximately $60,000 and their income from the white foxes ... $39,000. As you can see from these figures ... they're very wealthy people, they're well off, they're happy. The full use from the land and from the ocean that these people have can be shown from their income and from the way they live.
>
> Now to go over to the fishing, the people do all of their fishing in the fall of the year, in October when the snow comes over and the ice freezes over on the lakes enough for them to travel to the Fish Lakes. ... It's a three-chain lake and these chain lakes empty into the Minto Inlet. ... The approximate pounds per hunter that are harvested from the Fish Lakes would be approximately 300 to 350 pounds of arctic char. ... So that's 5,000 to 6,000 pounds harvested per year....
>
> The settlement of Holman Island has a quota of 16 polar bear per year ... and 99 percent of the polar bear taken this year was taken within a 25- to 30-mile radius of Holman.... The income from these polar bear would be $700 to $800 per hide this year.... A few years ago [the Japanese] raised the price right up to $2,000 or $3,000 in some cases for a hide and that was only for one year....
>
> A long time ago the Eskimo utilized the muskox quite a bit for food and for clothing ... the early explorers started killing muskox because of the similarity to beef in taste, and since then the numbers have gone down to

very little, and this made the Canadian Wildlife [Service] and other government agencies involved close off the hunting of it as an endangered species. For the past few years there have been sightings of these animals. The sightings continue to be more frequent ... and the people here have been continually asking for a quota.

> Generalizing now, the total of all the income from the land and from the ocean would be in the near figure of $100,000 for the settlement of Holman Island, and that's the income only from fur-bearing animals. That's not counting the other monies that they make from handicrafts and/or carvings. [C3963ff.]

This figure relates only to cash receipts. It does not include the replacement value of all of the country food upon which the Holman people depend.

I have been to Holman in winter. I have seen the meat and furs that are everywhere in the village. I understand what Roy Goose means when he says the people of Holman are "well off."

At Sachs Harbour, in addition to the food obtained from the harvesting of caribou, muskox, fish, geese and polar bear, the income derived from the trading of white fox and polar bear skins is normally higher than that which the villagers could earn if they were employed as wage labourers.

Even in Tuktoyaktuk and Aklavik — communities where urban and industrial influences are considerable — people do some trapping as well as wage employment. But even those who work for wages full-time often spend weekends and holidays hunting. Moreover, this is not mere recreation, but an attempt to secure both the foodstuffs and the sense of identity that are so important to native people throughout the Western Arctic.

In Inuvik, virtually no one lives exclusively by hunting and trapping, partly

Salmon hanging to dry, Old Crow. (G. Calef)

Caribou kill near Old Crow. (G. Calef)

Caribou carcasses in natural freezer, Holman. (DIAND)

Muskoxen. (GNWT)

because the native people who chose to move there did so in response to wage opportunities, and partly because Inuvik is essentially an urban community. Nonetheless, native men in Inuvik go out hunting and trapping. Many of them told the Inquiry of their continued commitment to the land.

Colin Allen said:

[We] are not like ... the people that come from South and have government jobs; they go down South and have a rest on their holiday, whereas the Eskimos — they use a holiday to hunt as much food as they can so that they don't have to buy from the store, and that will help them to live through the winter. Even though they have a job, they need to get their food in order to keep up with themselves. [C3455]

Ishmael Alunik, President of the Inuvik Hunters and Trappers Association, added:

We do not think of our jobs as a substitute for living off the land. Jobs are another way to help us live. We still want to trap and eat the food from our land. [C3448]

Usher, on the basis of his work on the Inuit Land Use and Occupancy Project, concluded that, although there had been a reduction in trapping by the Inuit of Inuvik, Tuktoyaktuk and Aklavik, their dependence on fish and game for subsistence was still considerable. He pointed out that even the shift toward limited wage employment had not reduced the use of land. Key hunting areas still include the Richardson Mountains for caribou and sheep, the whaling areas in Shallow Bay and near Whitefish Station, the goose-hunting areas along the main channel of the Mackenzie River, and the Delta itself for trapping.

Colin Allen described for the Inquiry his land use patterns before moving to Inuvik, and he explained how, although he has taken up permanent residence in town, he

still uses many of his old hunting and trapping areas on a part-time basis:

Today I work in Inuvik for about 15 years altogether, but still all these hunting grounds, goose-hunting area, caribou-hunting area, whale-hunting area, I still use them even though I worked that long. The hunting has never changed for me from the time I was driving dog team and paddling canoe. Now today I've got no dog team, [so I] use skidoo, and today I use the outboard motor ... and still I go to them places today that I used to go to when I was walking and dog team. [C3768]

Usher also pointed out that, in the Tuktoyaktuk region, after construction of the DEW Line and the movement of the people into the village, there had been a contraction of the general hunting and trapping areas for a few years, but since the introduction of the snowmobile the people once again hunt and trap areas they had temporarily abandoned. The Tuktoyaktuk people now cover their traditional hunting areas as effectively from the one settlement as they did many years ago from the various camps along the Arctic coast between Kittigazuit and Cape Bathurst.

There was evidence of this increase in hunting effectiveness in the other villages on the Beaufort Sea, as we saw when the Inquiry visited Paulatuk. On the very day of the hearing there, two young trappers returned to the village, and pointed out to me on a map where they had been trapping. They included an area that was not marked on the maps that indicate the most recent areas of land use, but which did appear on the maps that indicate land use 20 years ago, when the people were still living in camps. These men, both in their twenties, are now using again, with the help of modern technology, trapping areas used by their fathers and grandfathers.

The Persistence of the Native Economy

Throughout the Western Arctic there exists an elaborate network for the exchange of country produce. Arctic char from Paulatuk and caribou from Banks Island are eaten in Inuvik, and muktuk from Tuktoyaktuk adds to the diet of the Bankslanders. Those unable to provide country food for themselves receive it from their neighbours or relatives; the native people in Inuvik, the most urban of the Mackenzie Delta communities, receive food from relatives in other settlements. Hence none of the Inuit are divorced from the land or the sustenance it provides.

Sam Raddi, President of the Committee for Original Peoples Entitlement, now lives in Inuvik. He told the Inquiry:

I still rely on the country for food ... I still rely on the other settlements for my food. I get my caribou meat from Sachs Harbour, Tuk and Aklavik, and sometimes from Komakuk. I get my muktuk from the Co-op of the Hunters and Trappers Association in Inuvik. I get my fish from the Delta here and also from Tuk. [C3456]

We observed this mutual exchange of country food ourselves. Wherever we went in the Western Arctic, caribou carcasses, dried meat or fish would be loaded onto our aircraft to be taken back to Inuit friends and relatives in Inuvik. I observed a similar pattern of exchange among the native people and communities throughout the Mackenzie Valley as well.

Native northerners are well aware of their good fortune in having plenty of fish and game. As Usher put it, "The North may well be the only place where a poor man's table is laden with meat." [F25818] The Inuit regard as imprudent the risk of impairing the

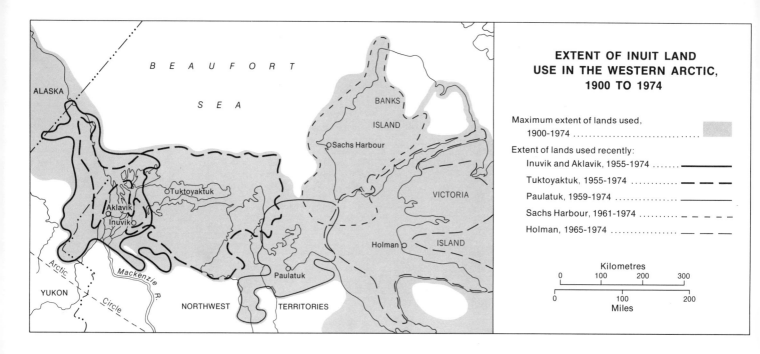

productivity of lands and waters that supply their meat and fish, especially at a time when the world may be entering a period of food shortages.

Usher has taken issue with Gemini North's conclusions on the value and importance of the traditional economy to the native population of the Western Arctic. Gemini North say that, in 1972, income from furs in Aklavik, Tuktoyaktuk and Inuvik amounted to about $188,000 and that income in kind (country food) amounted to about $97,000. The latter figure is less than 20 percent of what Usher calculated it to be for 1973-1974. In 1973, according to Gemini North, the total income for the three communities was just over $9 million, of which almost $8 million accrued to Inuvik alone. If you make a generous calculation of the native component in the total income for Inuvik and assume that virtually all income in the smaller settlements accrues to the native people, it would seem reasonable to estimate that native income in the three communities is about $2 million altogether — almost all of which comes, according to Gemini North's calculations, in the form of wages.

Hobart provided figures on income the native people have received from employment connected with oil and gas exploration, which, between the years 1971 and 1975, averaged about $1.15 million. In 1973-1974, the year in which Usher calculated income from food and fur in the Western Arctic to be about $2.4 million, exploration activity provided them with less than $1.1 million in wages. Usher maintained that, in recent years, native income from hunting and trapping is about equal to income from wages — about $2 million in each case. Thus, hunting and trapping produce, not five percent, but more like 50 percent of native

income. I think that both the degree of poverty in the Western Arctic and the need for wage income have often been overstated.

Usher's evaluation of the importance of the native economy is supported by the work of Dr. Derek Smith in his study, *Natives and Outsiders: Pluralism in the Mackenzie River Delta, Northwest Territories.* Smith states that, in the Delta:

> More people are engaged in casual labour and are living in the settlements in improved housing. But this does not mean that the land and its resources have become less significant for Native people. There is less fishing, since there are fewer dogs to feed, but there is more hunting (and more effective hunting) for meat for human consumption. [p. xiii]

The survival of the native economy has depended primarily on the native people's special relationship with the land. To native people, the land is more than just a source of food or cash: it is the permanent source not only of their physical, but also of their psychological well-being and of their identity as a people.

Rushforth, in his evidence on Fort Franklin, offered these observations:

> The Bear Lake people work in the bush not only because they derive income from their land, but also because that work represents a link in their cultural tradition to a way of life characterized by industrious activity and the acquisition of knowledge through bush experience, independence and self-reliance, and generosity and mutual support. These values help explain why Bear Lake people maintain strong ties to the bush in spite of increasing pressures from outside of their socio-cultural system which undermine their continued economic use of the land. [F22668]

The independence and self-reliance characteristic of life in the bush are highly prized by the native people. Dr. Peter Gardiner, an anthropologist who spent 15 months with the people of Fort Liard, told the Inquiry that

the transformation in them as they left the settlement for the bush could be clearly observed:

> ... going with them, I have seen them change as they leave town and the pressures of town life behind them. Faces are simply more relaxed ... they're more open ... when you get out of town, there's no boss. And this is a tremendous relief. In the world of towns, you have people asserting themselves in authoritarian ways constantly. That's just the white world. [C1705ff.]

Jim Pierrot of Fort Good Hope told the Inquiry:

> That is the way how we live our life on our land. We like to be free. [C1814]

Leslie Carpenter, a 19-year-old Eskimo from Sachs Harbour, reflecting on the increased urbanization and industrialization he foresaw with the pipeline, told the Inquiry:

> Then that won't be our native life, because we won't be free. Once you take our freedom you take most of our life. [C4128]

The Reality of the Native Economy

Some white people are inclined to romanticize the bush and the barrens. But make no mistake, it is a hard life — the native people have no illusions about this. Abe Okpik told the Inquiry in Aklavik about hardships and bad times in the Mackenzie Delta:

> ... when we have severe cold winters ... and there is hardly any snow, the lakes freeze to the bottom, and all the muskrats ... will disappear.... In the springtime, when we are out hunting muskrat with the canoe ... and when the weather turns cold, especially around Shallow Bay, the ice gets about two inches thick and you can't walk out on it ... you can't paddle on it, so sometimes we will be stuck for a whole week trying to live off what may be around.... [In the summer] we

CBC broadcaster, Abe Okpik explains whaling techniques, Whitefish Station. (W. Fraser)

Skinning a beaver. (R. Fumoleau)

Fort Good Hope trappers Jean Rabiska (left) and Leon Turo on the trapline near the Arctic Circle. (Native Press)

Cultural Impact   109

used to go down to Fish Station, and we hunted gulls ... and you got nothing to eat for about three days. And maybe the dogs screaming for life [from the mosquitoes], and you tried to build smudges to keep them alive. ... In the fall sometimes ... when it is heavy rain ... you go knee deep or lower in the mud ... and we didn't have the rubber boots like we have now....

Some years, when there is a big west wind before freeze-up, the water flows back around Shallow Bay ... and all the fish that are supposed to go up the creeks hardly come up, and you have a hard time getting any good load of fish, and you really have to work to get that....

Although all these things that we strive and struggle with, we like this land. [C140ff.]

Life in the bush and on the barrens is hard; it also demands industriousness. There is always something that must be done. Food must be obtained, fires must be kept, clothing and shelter must be looked after, dogs must be fed, and boats, snowmobiles and toboggans must be repaired. Trapping is not a mechanical activity in which a trapper simply sets his traps and hopes the animals will walk into them; the trapper must be able to predict where the animals are likely to go and to set his traps accordingly.

The native people told the Inquiry that life in the bush requires constant learning. Randy Pokiak, the young President of the Hunters and Trappers Association of Tuktoyaktuk, explained that point:

One thing I learned about trapping, one thing I learned about hunting, is that we never know everything all at one time. No matter how old you get, I believe you keep learning — you find out something new, and this is what I like about it. Because sometimes you figure you know everything, and then again there's times you find out that it's not true, and you are sort of happy that there are other things to learn. [C4227]

Among the northern native people, there is a powerful commitment to the land that is their home. Native people of the Western Arctic and the Mackenzie Valley regard their environment as rich and productive.

Native Preferences and Aspirations

A decade ago we felt we knew where the native people stood. They appeared to be turning away from the native economy and to have expressed a preference for entry into the wage economy. Dr. Charles Hobart, a sociologist who testified for Arctic Gas, believes that research carried out by anthropologists in the early sixties under government auspices showed a clear preference among the native people for wage employment over trapping at that time. There is other evidence to support this view: there is no doubt that the native people moved away from trapping in the fifties and sixties.

There were a number of reasons behind the movement away from the traditional economy: the low prices of fur during the fifties and sixties; the availability of welfare, family allowances and old age pensions; and the denigration of native values in the new government schools. The curriculum of the schools was calculated to diminish native pride and confidence in their own history, customs, and ways of making a living. It is not surprising that many Dene and Inuit appeared, for a time, to prefer white ways over their own ways. Hobart feels that, more than anything else, the attraction of the metropolis and the comforts it offered, as opposed to the hardships of life in the bush and on the barrens, accounted for the tendency to turn away from trapping that was

observed in the sixties. In his opinion, the preferences the native people expressed in the sixties are still their preferences in the seventies, and he considers that trapping as a means of making a living is passing into desuetude, because it has failed to satisfy native needs for a cash income. He regards the experience of Sachs Harbour, for instance, where a whole village earns a very good income from trapping, as an exception that merely proves the rule. He would ask, how many other such villages can you point to? And there are no others where the income from trapping equals that of Sachs Harbour, although there are many villages where potential for trapping is considerable, and a large proportion of the food that the people eat comes from the land.

Hobart and others who share his views — and his views have been urged upon the Inquiry by Arctic Gas and by Imperial, Gulf and Shell — feel that the native people now have no effective alternative to wage employment. They feel that the schools, the Mackenzie and Dempster Highways, and television are irresistible forces altering the fabric of the native people's lives. In Hobart's view, it is unrealistic to talk as though the native people have any real choice, except the one that the oil and gas industry offers them, because they are dependent upon white governments and institutions.

The Evidence of the Community Hearings

Yet Hobart's view is at variance with what native people said at the community hearings. I heard close to one thousand native witnesses in 35 northern communities. They insisted upon their desire to continue trapping. But Hobart holds that, notwithstanding what the native people may say, they have been voting with their feet. He cites the interest shown by young men throughout the Northwest Territories in working for Hire North, and the interest shown in the Delta and throughout the Valley in working on oil and gas exploration crews.

However, this discrepancy in the evidence may not be as great as it at first appears. The people in the villages often spoke through interpreters. There is a tendency for them (as there is for us) to use the word "trapping" as a generic term to comprehend hunting, fishing and trapping; that is, to cover all activities in the bush and on the barrens, whether for food, fur or cash. The people in the villages insisted, time and again, upon the very great extent to which they still depend upon the bush and the barrens for food, and upon their attachment to the land as an affirmation of identity. They often described life in the bush and on the barrens as "trapping," and they were determined to discredit studies and reports that seemed to them to depreciate the extent to which they still use the bush and the barrens today. At the same time, I do not think that the native people were rejecting wage employment altogether. They are alive to the consideration that dominates Hobart's thinking: how can they secure a meaningful and productive way of life for the young and rapidly expanding population of the North?

As far as the native people's expression of preferences is concerned, it seems plain enough that their perception of the world of wage employment has changed since the sixties. They now have had the experience of a decade or more of an alien school system and wage employment that has largely consisted of unskilled work. Their willingness to renounce native ways for white ways, which sociologists and anthropologists observed in the sixties, no longer exists.

I think that Hobart is right to this extent: income from wage employment, especially in the Delta communities of Inuvik and Tuktoyaktuk, has become an essential source of cash to many native families. But this does not mean that they wish to pursue such employment exclusively. Many white northerners, whose experience and knowledge of native people are often limited, tend to discount expressions of native preferences. You could spend two years in Yellowknife and never get to know or talk to a native person, let alone establish a friendship with one. You might see native people on the street, sometimes drunk or hanging around the bars, but you would not necessarily know anything of their culture and their lives. Virtually all you might discover about the North from a city like Yellowknife is that it is colder than the city you came from in the South.

I think we must regard the decline in the native people's use of the land in the sixties as a result of the economic crisis in the fur trade, the first impact of schooling-for-all, and as the people's initial — although temporary — reaction to living in settlements. It was an involuntary, unforeseen and demoralized retreat, and there is abundant evidence now of a renewed determination to maintain the native economy.

The Place of Wage Employment

At the same time, the Dene, Inuit and Metis are proud of their history, traditions and identity. They are now trying to adapt to the modern world in ways that will not destroy their culture and that will not lead only to their assimilation into white society — or to relegation to the fringes of that society. They are seeking means of earning a living from the land and participating in the wage economy without becoming entirely dependent on wage income. They want to achieve a measure of control over their own lives and their land to ensure that their communities remain essentially native communities.

Hobart feels that, if we build a pipeline, the native people's movement away from trapping to a wage economy will likely reach its ordained result. Hunting, fishing and trapping as a way of life will receive their quietus. If we do not build the pipeline, the Dene and the Inuit will be condemned to a life of idleness and dependence. Given the events of the last two decades, there is, according to this argument, no choice for us or for the native people; the die has already been cast.

The question comes down to this: are traditional customs and values essential to the native people's sense of identity and well-being today? Or have they fallen into desuetude?

Dr. Michael Asch and Scott Rushforth, anthropologists called as witnesses by the Indian Brotherhood of the Northwest Territories, criticized Hobart for relying too heavily on changes in technology as an indication of acculturation. They said that, merely because native people have adopted certain items of western technology, they do not necessarily adopt western values with them to replace their traditional values. Dr. Derek Smith, in *Natives and Outsiders: Pluralism in the Mackenzie River Delta, Northwest Territories,* has also cautioned against equating technological adaptations with a change in values:

> Technological change, which is very visible, should not be allowed to obscure the less visible, but very important, continuities in reliance upon traditional resources. [p. iii]

The fact is that, without modern equipment including rifles and snowmobiles, the native

Holman Islanders describe arctic hunting life through interpreter. (M. Jackson)

Ski-doo outside log cabin near Great Slave Lake. (Native Press)

Hunting bison with rifles near Fort Resolution. (Native Press)

Caribou meat being loaded into plane after community hunt. (Native Press)

people would find it virtually impossible to continue their traditional land-based subsistence activities in the contemporary situation because, in some cases, they live in villages far removed from traditional hunting grounds and, in others, the concentration of population has led to a depletion of game nearby.

The evidence heard at the Inquiry has led me to conclude that the selective adoption of items of western technology by the Dene and the Inuit is, in fact, one of the most important means by which they continue to maintain their traditional way of life. These items, like other modern or southern elements in the native society, have become part of the life that native people value.

The Native People's Own Voice

English has not been wholly an instrument of acculturation: rather, Dene groups have used it as a lingua franca to achieve a measure of unity among themselves that was never possible when they spoke only the five Athabascan languages. They have used English, not to become like us, but to tell us that they wish to be themselves. English has become one of their principal means of expressing their desire for self-determination. It is English that has, paradoxically, helped the Dene to insist upon their identity as a distinct people.

Some recent studies have thrown a good deal of light on native preferences. Between 1971 and 1973, for example, Hugh Brody carried out, under the auspices of the federal government's Northern Science Research Group, more than 150 interviews in communities of the Canadian Eastern Arctic to see how the white and native populations regarded each other. Having interviewed members of each generation, Brody found

that Inuit of all ages identified themselves with their land, and they regarded continued use of the land as central to their identity. He found that most of the men wanted to spend an important part of their time hunting, fishing and trapping; and this included those who had only recently returned from training schools in Churchill and elsewhere and who, on the evidence of appearance and material culture, would be regarded as highly acculturated. Brody found, too, that all of them, old and young alike, regarded land use activities in quite modern terms: they consider that good hunters are men who can use snowmobiles, high-quality rifles and other recent technological developments that might be useful in hunting.

The Inquiry's hearings revealed the same attitudes among Dene and Inuit in the Mackenzie Valley and the Western Arctic. Expressions of native pride and identity returned many times to the importance, and therefore to the defence, of the land.

I do not want anyone to think that I regard the evidence of these social scientists as decisive by itself. They, like other white people in the North, have been willing to tell me what they think the native people want. But if we are truly to understand what the native people want and what kind of life they seek, we must let them speak for themselves. They must describe their own preferences. Their testimony, heard in community after community, is the best evidence of what really are the native goals, the native preferences and the native aspirations. In village after village, the witnesses made one point clear: they do not want to become white men with brown skins.

Here is how some of them expressed their deeply-felt conviction on this subject. Richard Nerysoo at Fort McPherson:

We do not have to become brown white-men

to survive. We are Indians and we are proud to be Indians. All the education, all the schooling that you have given us cannot destroy that in us.

We are Indian people. We will survive as Indian people, and we will develop our own ways based on the strengths and traditions of the old ways. We will always see ourselves as part of nature. Whether we use outboard motors or plywood for our cabins does not make us any less Indian.... The young people from Fort McPherson hunt and fish and get out into the bush whenever they can. We are Indians just like our fathers and grandfathers, and just like our children and grandchildren will be. [C1187ff.]

Peter Green at Paulatuk:

I have sat down many times and thought over the differences or the distinction between my people's way of life and your way of life. It's pretty hard for me to say that your way of life is superior.... I would prefer the Inuit way of life, our way of life.... Your way of life, down South as white people, is a way of life I myself would not want to live. We are people who are free to go hunting every day. [C4444ff.]

Paul Andrew, Chief of the Fort Norman Band:

We do not want any other way of life. We do not know enough of any other way of life. We cannot go into the white man's world and expect to live like him. ... We wish for the upcoming generation ... to carry on our identity, our language and our culture. [C878]

Alexis Arrowmaker, former Chief of the Dogrib people:

It seems that the government's intention is ... to persuade native people to become like or act like white people. And there is no way that we native people want to lose our culture.... There is no way they are going to change native people or have them like white man. [C8081ff.]

George Erasmus, President of the Indian Brotherhood of the Northwest Territories:

The decision that is before the Dene people

today, as it has been now since Confederation, since the beginning of Canada as a nation, for the original people, for the native people, is: do we assimilate? Do we remain distinct people?

For us in the valley here, it's a decision: do we want to continue on as Dene people? Or do we want to forget that and become like everybody else? The decision before us, I think, has been made already, and people are acting on it. Clearly we want to remain as Dene people. We do not want to assimilate. [C8067]

The programs of the Government of Canada and the Government of the Northwest Territories have conferred some real benefits on the native people. But the critical result of these programs has been to create a dependence on them. And this dependence, in turn, creates in the native people a frustration that is almost palpable.

Native people have expressed this frustration to the Inquiry. Mary Elias at Sach's Harbour:

> Long ago [our] parents they didn't have nobody, [no] Government to tell them what to do or ask them anything. They used to have a real good life because they lived only the way they wanted to. Nobody told them how to live, and they knew how to make a good living, and they were good people then. But now [it is] just like they are having government substitute the way of life, everything is government. [C4063]

Robert Clement at Fort Norman:

> I remember a few years ago, the people lived in their homes. They cut their own wood and hauled their own water. People were happier then, when they didn't have to depend on the government all of the time. We were happier then and we could do it again.
>
> But look what has happened. Now the government gives the people everything, pays for the water and the fuel and the houses, the education. It gives the people everything, everything but one thing — the right to live their own lives. And that is the only thing

that we really want, to control our lives, our own land. [C897]

This time native people say they want to decide their future for themselves. And they want to be allowed to choose a life that is still connected to the land and their own tradition. So many hundreds of people came forward at the hearings and said these things that I must regard them as an expression of the people's deepest convictions.

Many white people in the North ask how the native people, after all that has been done for them, can now be dissatisfied or ungrateful. The native people reply: "These are things you chose for us. We did not choose them for ourselves."

The old and the young alike are of one mind on this issue. Mary Kendi, an elderly woman from Fort McPherson, told the Inquiry:

> We would like to see our children and theirs carry on the ways of our ancestors and ourselves. We don't want to be changed into something we don't understand. If we must make some changes, we don't want it through someone pushing us into it. We must be given time to think and do it our own way. [C1135]

These thoughts were echoed by Isaac Aleekuk, a young trapper at Holman:

> I want you people to understand [that] the way of life I am leading is very important to me, and I would like to keep it and use it to the best of my knowledge. I don't want it to be taken away from me or from anyone else here living at Holman. I am 24 years old now. I got married at an early age, and I do feel strongly about this, my way of life, and the way I am living it. I want my children to live that way if they want to. I'll teach them what I know. I still want them to keep this land long after we have gone. [C3948ff.]

If the native people are given the right to make their own choices, the future will be hard and difficult — both for them and us.

The question is, ought we to give them that right? And the next question must be, is it possible to give them that right? Here the moral, political and economic questions intersect. Here the industrial system impinges directly upon the native people, and the values of the two ways of life are in opposition. Here we are faced with the fundamental problem of the future of the North: whose preferences should determine the future of the North? Those who think of it as our last frontier? Or those who think of it as their homeland?

Harry Deneron, Chief of the Fort Liard Indian Band, told the Inquiry:

> This is not a virgin land, it is not a pioneer land, it is the Indian [and Inuit] land. [C1664]

Two Different Views

The industrial system is now impinging on the northern native people. History and perceived economic necessity have brought the white and the native societies into contact on our northern frontier, a frontier occupied from time out of mind by the native people.

White people, in general, are driven by economic and social values that are very different from those that motivate native society. White people have always regarded the North as a land rich in desirable commodities: first furs, then gold and uranium and now oil and gas. The white man, therefore, has progressively encroached upon the land and life of the Dene and the Inuit to secure for himself those commodities that he believes the native people leave unused or underused.

In all the years of contact between the two societies, the white man still sees the North from his own point of view, and he still wishes to conquer the frozen and waste

Inuit children. (ITC)

Drum dance, Fort McPherson. (L. Smith)

Richard Nerysoo. (Native Press)

Cemetery, Fort Norman. (L. Smith)

spaces that he sees, with roads, mines, drilling rigs, gas wells and pipelines. He dreams of the technological conquest of the northern frontier.

The Dene and Inuit see their land as unbounded in its ability to fulfil their deepest needs. They see moose, herds of caribou and rivers and lakes teeming with fish. To them the frozen sea does not cover riches, nor is it an obstacle to shipping, but it is a storehouse from which they can take what they need: fish, seals, walrus and whales. The native's preferences and aspirations are formed by his way of looking at the North. Even though many Dene and Inuit have adopted southern dress and speak English, they retain their own ways of thinking about the land and the environment and their own idea of man's destiny in the North.

It has been difficult for the native people to convince us that their preferences and aspirations are real and worthy of our respect. Deeply rooted conceptions underlie the responses that have revealed themselves in the dealings of Europeans with aboriginal groups throughout the world. Hugh Brody, in his evidence, described this devaluation of native people in the European's terms of nature and culture:

> [We regard] the native person [as] at the very edge of, or just beyond, the world of culture. Insofar as he is beyond the frontier and stays outside the economy and society that the frontier is seeking to advance, he remains a part of nature. . . . Peoples in that condition do not know what is best for them (they cannot understand progress) and can only learn by acquiring religion, schooling, housing, money, modern conveniences, jobs. This picture of the native beyond culture, beyond the frontier, suggests that he has no real religion, no effective schooling, no proper houses, still less conveniences, money or jobs. As these are supposed to be the very hallmarks of culture, of civilization, and as they are the indices by which we measure progress, then if people do not have them, and do not get them, they cannot progress. [F25873ff.]

Hence many southerners — including policy-makers and administrators — arrive at a moral imperative to bring industrial development to the frontier.

It is for reasons of this nature that the oil and gas companies and the pipeline companies are convinced that their activities will greatly benefit the people of the North. The representatives of the companies regard their presence in the North as benign. They are, therefore, shocked and disbelieving when native people suggest the contrary: they attribute any negative response to their proposals to ignorance or sometimes to the influence of white advisers on the native organizations.

Those who represent the industrial system have a complete and entire commitment to it, as a way of life and as a source of income. This is so whether we are public servants, representing a government whose goals are based on ideas of growth and expansion, or executives and workers in the oil and gas industry.

Seasonal employment that oil and gas exploration offers in the Mackenzie Delta has become an important source of income to many Inuit. Yet that does not mean that they — any more than the Dene — are prepared to give up their claim to the land. If our specialized vision of progress prevails, it is likely to prevail with indifference to — or even in defiance of — native aspirations as they have been expressed to this Inquiry.

Oil derrick, Mackenzie Delta. (DIAND)

Economic Impact

Discussion of the northern economy is always bedevilled by two related problems. In the first place, the relationships between social, cultural and economic problems of the native people are so intimate and intricate that it is not possible to separate the narrowly economic from the more broadly social. It is impossible, for example, to assess the problems of employment and unemployment in the North in isolation from the kinds of lives that the native people want to lead, or without regard to the present condition of their culture. The discussion in this chapter must, therefore, draw on that of the last and must anticipate some of the discussion in the next.

The second and more serious problem is the quality of the statistical information that is available. Louis St-Laurent once remarked that, for a long time, Canada had seemed to govern its North in a state of absence of mind. Although he was referring to the 1930s and 1940s, his judgment may cast some light on the situation today. Despite the expenditure of millions of dollars and the efforts of thousands of public servants, data on some crucial aspects of northern economic life are either simplistic or are not to be found at all. I shall in this chapter have occasion to use employment figures, but I am bound to conclude that those made available to the Inquiry by the Government of the Northwest Territories are so flawed by conceptual error that they are almost useless. I shall also, both here and in a later discussion of renewable resources, need precise information on the present and potential productivity of the land. But such information, despite the enduring importance of hunting, fishing and trapping, is inadequate.

The absence of data is, of course, an indirect consequence of policy. We have

been committed to the view that the economic future of the North lay in large-scale industrial development. We have at times even persuaded the native people of this. We have generated, especially in northern business, an atmosphere of expectancy about industrial development. Although there has always been a native economy in the North, instead of trying to strengthen it, we have, for a decade or more, followed policies by which it could only be weakened or even destroyed. We have believed in industrial development and depreciated the indigenous economic base. Indeed, people who have tried to earn a living by depending on that base have often been regarded as unemployed.

The consequences of federal policy priorities in the past go beyond the problem of inadequate statistics. The development of the non-renewable resources of a region can bring serious pressures to bear on its population: people who try to continue to live on the renewable resources experience relative poverty, and may be faced with the loss of a productive way of life. Gradually more and more people give up one kind of work, and therefore relinquish the way of life associated with it, in favour of another kind of work and life. Where this has happened, they often feel they had very little choice in the matter. If the neglected sector of the economy represents a preferred or culturally important way of life, if it is a means of self-identification and a source of self-respect, then the devaluation of that way of life can have widespread and dismaying consequences. These consequences are exacerbated if the industrialized economy offers rewards that are only short-term.

Long ago, the native people of the North developed an economy based on the seasonal harvesting of renewable resources, which

was for centuries the sole basis of their livelihood. That economy is still a vital part of their livelihood today, but the growth of industries based on non-renewable resources has created an imbalance in the northern economy as a whole. The traditional or native economy has come to be associated with relative poverty and deprivation. To the extent that a person tries to live off the land, he must often accept a low income and, in relation to the values of the white world, a lower social status than those who do not. Because success in hunting, fishing and trapping are the hallmarks of traditional native values, this imbalance may all too easily undermine the native people's whole way of life.

In this chapter, I shall refer to the total intrusive effect of the industrial economy on native society. By this process, the native people are pushed and pulled into the industrial system. The process, which is caused by several economic and social factors that will be spelled out, begins with the depreciation of a way of life and ends with the demoralization of a whole people. If a pipeline is built and an energy corridor established before the present severe imbalance in the northern economy is redressed, its intrusive effects will be total.

I do not mean to suggest that native people will not want to participate in the opportunities for employment that industrial development will create. Some native people already work alongside workers from the South. Many native people have taken advantage of opportunities for wage employment on a limited or seasonal basis to obtain the cash they need to equip or re-equip themselves for traditional pursuits. But when the native people are made to feel they have no choice other than the industrial system, when they have no control over entering it or leaving it, when wage labour becomes the strongest, the most compelling, and finally the only option, then the disruptive effects of large-scale, rapid development can only proliferate. Eventually the intrusion of the industrial system is complete, and the consequences for the native people disastrous.

Southern views of "development" and "progress" have resulted in distorted data on unemployment; consequently, many non-renewable resource projects have been at least partially justified on the grounds that they would create jobs for the native people. Government subsidies have been sought and obtained because it seemed appropriate for government to help solve the unemployment problem. But the fact is that large-scale projects based on non-renewable resources have rarely provided permanent employment for any significant number of native people. Even in its own terms, therefore, the policy of the past two decades has not been a success, and there is abundant reason to doubt that a pipeline would or could provide meaningful and on-going employment to many native people of the Mackenzie Valley and the Western Arctic.

It is important to understand the main point of this chapter. The failure so far of large-scale industrial projects to provide permanent wage employment for large numbers of native people has led to expressions of indignation by government spokesmen and by native people. But the real danger of such developments will not be their continued failure to provide employment to the native people, but the highly intrusive effects they may have on native society and the native economy. The real failure of the past lies in a persistent refusal to recognize, and therefore to strengthen, the native economy and native skills. This

failure is evidenced by our tendency, perhaps our compulsion, to adopt solutions that are technologically complex. We, as members of an industrial society, find it difficult, perhaps impossible, to resist technological challenge. Technology and development have become virtually synonymous to us. In the North new technology or technology-for-its-own-sake may sometimes inhibit solutions. It seems easier to ship prefabricated housing units from the South than to build log cabins from local materials. When that kind of thing happens, local skills rust or remain undeveloped.

The real economic problems in the North will be solved only when we accept the view that the Dene, Inuit and Metis themselves expressed so often to the Inquiry. We must look at forms of economic development that really do accord with native values and preferences. If the kinds of things that native people now want are taken seriously, we shall cease to regard large-scale frontier industrial development as a panacea for the economic ills of the North.

This consideration of economic impact leads inexorably to the conclusion that the interests of native people are in conflict with those of large-scale industrial developers. In the short run, the strengthening of the native economy in the Mackenzie Valley and Western Arctic should take first priority; otherwise its very foundations will be undermined by the intrusive effects of pipeline construction. But, once the native economy has been strengthened, the Mackenzie Valley corridor could be developed as a pipeline right-of-way. Only by this means can we ensure that these interests will not be in conflict in the long run as well as in the short run.

In the end, it is the native people who will have to live with the economy that is

developed in the North; their interests must therefore, be kept very clearly in mind. I do not mean by this that the white business community, or any economic interest in the Mackenzie Valley or the Western Arctic should simply be ignored. In this chapter, shall try to assess the impact of a pipeline on these other interests; both in estimating the consequences of a decision to proceed with the pipeline now and in estimating the consequences of a decision to postpone its construction. But we must face the fact that where interests conflict, and only one choice can be made, priorities must be set.

If we build the pipeline now, the native people's own land-based economy will be further weakened or even destroyed, and many of them will be drawn into the industrial system against their will. They strongly oppose this prospect. We must recognize now that if we remain indifferent to their opposition, that indifference will bring yet more severe deformation of the native economy, serious social disarray, and a cluster of pathologies that will, taken together, constitute the final assault on the original peoples of the North.

The Development of the Northern Economy

By North American standards the regional economy of the North is not large, complex or mature. Both its demographic base and the number of industrial sites are small. Viewed from the perspective of the hydrocarbon potential upon which hopes for its growth and elaboration are so often pinned, it is not only an economy with a brief history, it is also an area of production remote from the main markets of Canada and from the home

Freight handling, Fort Resolution in the old days.
(Public Archives)

Northern traders and trappers:

William Firth of Fort McPherson.
(NWT Metis Assoc.)

"Slim" Semmler, trader and merchant in Inuvik.
(NFB—McNeill)

Napoleon Lafferty of Fort Resolution.
(NWT Metis Assoc.)

of those who own and invest in its resources. In all these respects it is a frontier economy — but its frontier aspect is not quite as new as many in the South believe.

Much of Canada's history is related to the export of staples from successive geographic frontiers to serve the needs of advanced industrial centres. The great Canadian export commodities have been fish, fur, lumber, wheat, pulp and paper, minerals, and oil and gas. All of these staple industries have been created to serve the needs of the metropolis — once France, then Britain, and now the great industrial centres of Canada and the United States. H.A. Innis, in his work *Empire and Communications,* wrote:

> Concentration on the production of staples for export to more highly industrialized areas in Europe and later in the United States had broad implications for the Canadian economic, political, and social structure. Each staple in its turn left its stamp, and the shift to new staples invariably produced periods of crises in which adjustments in the old structure were painfully made and a new pattern created in relation to a new staple. [p. 5ff.]

The first great staple industries in the North were the fur trade and whaling; then followed mining; now there is oil and gas. But the impact of exploration for oil and gas has not been the same as the impact of the fur trade, which depended on the Indian, the Eskimo and the Metis. The fur trade did not sever the age-old relationship between man and the land, nor did it call into question the ownership of land.

Dr. Melville Watkins, a witness for the Indian Brotherhood of the Northwest Territories, described some aspects of the fur-trade economy:

> The prosecution of the fur trade depended, at least initially in each region into which the trade expanded, on the Indian as fur-gatherer.

As such the Indian was a commodity producer, not a wage-earner, and the fur trade was literally a trade, or a commercial activity, not an industrial activity. The Indian became dependent to the extent that he became vulnerable to the exigencies of the trade, but he did not have to make two critical and traumatic adjustments. ... Firstly, he did not have to become a wage-earner, and secondly, which is really the opposite side of the coin, he did not have to yield up his ownership of the land. To put the matter differently, neither his labour-time nor his land had to become themselves marketable commodities. [F23582ff.]

Dr. Peter Usher's evidence also dwelt on the characteristics of the early staple economies of the North. He pointed out that although whaling, which was extremely profitable in the Western Arctic between 1890 and 1906, brought disease to the Inuit of the area, from the strictly economic point of view,

> ... had the whalers simply left the country and not been replaced by outsiders ... the Eskimos could have reverted to their traditional means of livelihood and survival. [F25894]

The whalers were quickly followed into the Western Arctic by fur traders. Usher, like Watkins, emphasized that the fur trade brought relative economic stability, cultural continuity, and some real prosperity, at least to the Inuit of the Delta:

> At the best of times, good trappers had far higher incomes than the average southern Canadian. The fur trade economy permitted a significant increase in regional output and wealth, although the dramatic increase in both the production of surplus and the return on it, far higher than elsewhere in the Arctic, must be balanced against the shortage of some country foods, which was the legacy of over-hunting during the whaling era. [F25895]

The fur trade economy lasted, in effect, until the 1950s. It was the fur traders who

explored and established the lines of communication and transportation in the North. And it was the fur trade that brought the northern peoples within the purview of the western world's economy and into the metropolitan sphere of influence.

Even during the fur trade, however, the non-renewable resource potential of the North was important. The Klondike gold rush led to an interest in the base metals of the region. When the first great flush of enthusiasm for gold had subsided, prospecting and mining became a recognized part of northern economic life in certain areas, although they employed comparatively few people.

In the Mackenzie Valley, however, oil has, for some time, seemed to offer the prospect of economic development. In 1912, oil was found near Fort Norman and, in 1914, the geologist T.O. Bosworth staked three claims to seepages that Alexander Mackenzie had seen in 1789. In 1920, Imperial Oil drilled a well there, a year after acquiring Bosworth's claims, but according to Imperial Oil, the well did not become economic until 1932.

In the 1930s, economic activity also centered on rich mineral deposits at Yellowknife and Port Radium, and mines in the Great Slave Lake and Great Bear Lake areas have had continuing importance. In the 1960s, base metals became the focus of renewed and, at times, fervent economic interest in the Northwest Territories. Before 1964, no more than 6,000 claims were staked North of 60 in any one year. Between 1964 and 1969, approximately 90,000 claims were staked in the Pine Point and Coppermine areas alone. In 1970, the value of mineral output for both the Yukon Territory and the Northwest Territories was in the region of $200 million.

Other activities that preceded the oil and

gas industry in the North included the construction of highways, the Pine Point railway, and the DEW Line stations. Each of these projects required the transportation of large volumes of material and supplies and large numbers of men, and each of them, as we have already seen, had some influence on the native people's cultural and economic situation. Each of them represented an advance of metropolitan and industrial interests into the hinterland.

In their historical development, the fur trade, mining, and the oil and gas industry have overlapped one another. Some capital-intensive projects, based on the exploitation of non-renewable resources, were taking place while furs were still being harvested and exported from the Northwest Territories. From the native people's point of view, however, whenever an area or a community became involved in a new staple such as mining, that staple left its mark upon their economic and social lives. The mining and petroleum industries, in particular, have raised the issues of land ownership and of wage employment, and these questions obviously bear directly on the interests of the native people.

If we return to Innis' historical view of the Canadian economy, we can see the succession of economic ventures in the North in a clearer perspective. The impact of each of the staple industries is, of course, what Innis referred to as its "stamp." And, as Watkins said in applying Innis' theory to the economic development of the North:

> The impact of the proposed pipeline is simply the "stamp" of the oil and gas industry on Canada in general and the North in particular. The North is experiencing "the shift to a new staple," the result is a "period of crisis" and of "painful adjustments." [F23579]

In fact the real impact of the oil and gas industry on the North takes us back only to the late 1960s and early 1970s. Although an exploratory well was drilled on Melville Island in 1961, only after 1968 did attention focus on exploratory drilling wherever oil reserves might be found. This surge of interest has been reflected in increased expenditure on exploration — from $34 million in 1970 to $230 million in 1973 — and by the fact that, by the beginning of 1973, petroleum leases covered almost 500 million acres of the Northwest Territories.

Oil exploration does not need local labour: it is the land, not the people who live on it, that has now become important. Of course this was also true of mining, but the difference between mining and the hydrocarbon industry is one of scale. The impact of mining is limited to a comparatively restricted area; the hydrocarbon industry, because of the nature of both exploration and its delivery systems, is likely to have a much greater impact.

The establishment of an economy based on mining or, more particularly, on the oil and gas industry could deprive the people who live on the frontier of their rights to their lands, and it could offer them employment for reasons that have nothing to do with their real needs. Because the oil and gas industry does not depend upon them, the native people cannot depend upon it. And if they can no longer rely upon the land for their living, they will cease to have any essential relation to any form of economic activity. The native people's assertion of their claims must, in this historical perspective, be seen as an attempt to negotiate an alternative course of economic development.

The history of the North illustrates the relation that often exists between the metropolis and the hinterland: large-scale frontier projects tend to enrich the metropolis, not the communities on the frontier.

The pipeline project is of a piece with this pattern, but we must remember that the pipeline project is of extraordinary proportions. For example, Stelco's plant at Hamilton is the only steel plant in Canada where the pipe itself can be manufactured. Northern businessmen cannot participate in manufacturing the pipe, nor can they supply any of the machinery or equipment essential to the project. The construction of the pipeline will demand the most advanced technology, machinery and transportation systems. The project will be so huge that only companies that function on a national or international scale will be able to participate in many aspects of the work.

The development of the northern economy is sometimes viewed as a model of the political and economic formation that has taken place in other parts of the country. In this view, frontier development leads to secondary economic growth. The theory that underpins this has to do with spin-offs and multipliers, which affirm the connection between investment, investment returns, and a spreading through reinvestment of these returns into other economic activities. In this way, an economy expands, diversifies and eventually becomes the base for towns, cities and large political entities. It was in this way that the western provinces were carved out of the old Northwest.

The necessary condition for secondary economic growth, however, is the retention of earnings and of returns on capital within the frontier region. This condition has not been met in the Northwest Territories. The profits from the fur trade and from whaling were earned in the markets of Europe and America and they generated secondary

Gold mine — Yellowknife. (DIAND)

Work crew, Norman Wells in the early days.
(Public Archives)

Oil well gusher, Norman Wells, 1921.
(Public Archives)

Drill crew, Norman Wells, 1921. (Public Archives)

activity only in France, England and Southern Canada. Only a fraction of the profits were returned to the Indians and Eskimos. The mining industry has also taken its profits out of the Northwest Territories, and the oil and gas industry will do the same.

The present state of the northern economy shows two continuities. On the one hand, the native people are being drawn into the dominant economic modes that originate in the metropolis, and they are now faced with the possibility of large-scale industrial development that will disturb the land on which the native economy is based. On the other hand, primary economic activity in the North has been and continues to be frontier in character. Local economic formation has persistently been isolated; the returns have been taken south. The local impact of frontier development has been great, but it has not resulted in a shift towards a broadly based, self-sufficient regional economy.

In the rest of this chapter, I shall consider whether or not a Mackenzie Valley pipeline would alter or consolidate these trends.

Objectives of Economic Development

When the Honourable Jean Chrétien addressed the House of Commons Standing Committee on Indian Affairs and Northern Development in March 1972 to introduce the *Statement of the Government of Canada on Northern Development in the 70s,* he said:

Fundamental to the Government's statement is our belief that native northerners should derive early, visible, and lasting benefits from economic development. Our efforts must not only be turned to developing the natural resources of the North for the benefit of Canada as a whole. The development of northern resources must first improve the standard of living and the well-being of northern residents. All too often the economic activity of the past was at their expense. [*Introductory Remarks,* p. 8]

Like Mr. Chrétien, I have found that native northerners have not in the past realized "early, visible, and lasting benefits from economic development." Will the construction of a Mackenzie Valley pipeline provide such benefits?

I can recommend some terms and conditions that would provide early and visible benefits from the construction of a pipeline to native northerners, but I do not think any terms and conditions could be imposed on any pipeline built today to ensure that native northerners would derive *lasting* benefits from it. Indeed, it is my judgment that the social costs of the pipeline to native northerners would outweigh any economic benefits they may derive from it.

I am speaking, as the Minister was, of native northerners and of wage employment for native northerners. I can recommend terms and conditions that would enable northern business to achieve real and substantial growth during the construction of a pipeline. But these benefits would not accrue to native northerners, except to those few — and they are very few — who possess the capital, the knowledge and the inclination to take advantage of the business opportunities that pipeline construction would offer.

We have always assumed that large-scale industrial projects, in the North as elsewhere, are good in and of themselves. Our whole economic history, which is one of earning and spending, saving and investing, encourages this belief. If a project achieves a measurable surplus or gain, such as increased profits, additional tax revenues or higher employment, that is thought to be sufficient justification for it; no other test need be met.

This assumption should be looked at more closely. Can the pipeline project and its aftermath be subjected to any realistic cost-benefit analysis? What is the purpose of the project? In whose interest is it being undertaken? What economic gains will be made? How should the gains be shared? Is anyone likely to be hurt by it? Can the negative impacts be ameliorated?

We have already begun to ask these questions. Sometimes we asked them in the past, but we did so diffidently because of the complexity and imprecision of the concerns we were addressing. Moreover, merely by raising such questions, we implicitly suggested that curbs or limitations might have to be placed on large-scale industrial development, a suggestion that is regarded as inimical wherever the industrial system is seen as the great engine of progress.

We must take a hard look at what our objectives in the North really are. For example, it may be important to build the pipeline as quickly and as cheaply as possible. Certainly the pipeline companies would regard this as vital: rapid construction and an early flow of gas would generate income sooner. Once the capital has been borrowed, every month and year that passes before the gas begins to flow will increase the interest to be paid.

But suppose we consider the project from the point of view of its external economics — from the point of view of society's profits and losses. We might then urge that the project be delayed, that its construction phase be spread over a longer period to maximize employment and income for northerners. We might urge the building of a

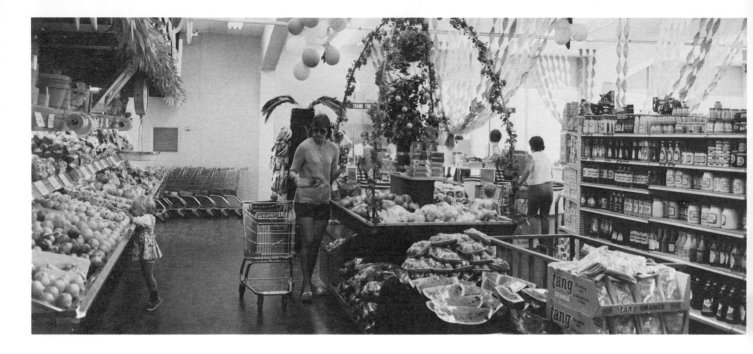

smaller diameter pipeline in order to conserve gas and extend the operating phase. These measures might well reduce social costs and result in a net saving to the Government of Canada. Federal welfare and other programs for northerners and northern business could be curtailed if they did not have to respond to the boom-and-bust cycle that the market, unaided or undeterred, would set in motion.

But if one of our objectives is to provide gainful employment for native northerners, is a pipeline the best way to do it? Native people have insisted that, because the resources of the land and sea have always provided a living — and still do for many of them — ways should be sought to make that living more productive. These ways can be tried only if construction of the pipeline is postponed.

Economic Development and Self-sufficiency

Many white northerners have asserted that the northern economy could become self-sufficient if the pipeline were built. But the northern economy is the product of its history. It is paradoxical to suggest that a large-scale frontier project designed to supply energy, the modern staple, to the metropolis will result in regional self-sufficiency. The pipeline will not serve regional objectives; it will serve national and international demands for energy.

Federal policies and programs have not resulted in a regional economy in the North that will capture and regionally contain a significant proportion of the income that is generated by major private and public investment there. Most capital and consumer goods are still imported into the region, and most of the industrial labour needed is also brought in from the South. By and large, the persons making up this imported labour force have little or no commitment to the North. They do not, generally, bank their money there or invest surplus earnings in any way that would expand employment within the region; nor do royalties, profits, or taxes stay in the North.

But federal policies have brought industrial development to the North. Mining and the oil and gas industry have responded to government initiatives by undertaking some large investment programs. Some of them, such as Pine Point, have been highly profitable. With others, investment still awaits a major return, but a large part of the cost of these ventures has been publicly absorbed. Mining companies and the oil and gas industry have found the North an attractive place in which to invest. But such federally supported investment, which has no long-term multiplier effects, will not secure the economic self-sufficiency of the Northwest Territories.

The northern economy is not going to become self-sufficient, no matter what support systems are devised for it. Indeed, there is no reason why the Northwest Territories, any more than any other region, should have a self-sufficient economy. Regional interdependence is part and parcel of Canadian economic life. Mr. Chrétien's goal, of encouraging economic development that would provide real and lasting benefits to the people of the North is one that can be rationally pursued. It is a goal that we can reach if we are prepared to diversify the northern economy by strengthening the renewable resource sector.

Perceptions of Development Priorities

Economic impact is perceived in different ways. The pipeline companies believe that a pipeline will produce great benefits to the North, although they concede that there will be some social costs. Northern businessmen see the pipeline as their long-awaited opportunity to expand. Social scientists, in general, fear that the project will greatly aggravate the region's existing social and economic problems, although some of them argue that the project is nevertheless necessary if the northern economy is not to stagnate. The native people see the pipeline as a project that will certainly impede and may finally frustrate the attainment of their goals.

In the same way, there are differing views on what the objectives of economic development ought to be. It should be evident that the present economic problems in the North are, to a considerable extent, the consequences of federal policies, which have usually been moulded by southern, metropolitan interests: development has been conceived as the transformation of the northern economy from a traditional to an industrial economy. From the native people's point of view, it is questionable whether or not this can be said to be real development.

In the end, we must accept that anyone's view of the objectives of economic development in the North is value-laden. But there are, and there must be, priorities; and these priorities, if they are real, must decide between interests that are fundamentally irreconcilable. It is my judgment that the interests of the native people, as they themselves perceive them, should take priority now.

Supermarket in Yellowknife. (NFB—McNeill)

Peter Usher, advisor to Committee for Original Peoples Entitlement. (Native Press)

Mel Watkins, right, and Gerry Sutton, advisors to the NWT Indian Brotherhood. (Native Press)

Hugh Brody. (N. Cooper)

The Mixed Economy

The development of the northern economy has successively given rise to mixtures of economic activity, to overlapping modes of production, consumption and exchange. The fur trade added a new layer of activity to the original subsistence economy. The governmental presence provided some opportunities for wage employment and transfer payments. Mining and the oil and gas industry have added industrial wage employment to the mixture of economic elements in the North.

The northern economy is often thought of as dual, consisting of a native sector and a white sector. This duality emphasizes the differences between the native way of life, with its long roots in the region's aboriginal past, and the white way of life, which represents the extension of the southern metropolis into the northern hinterland. The first is the traditional economy, based on renewable resources; the second is the industrial economy, based on the exploitation of the non-renewable resources of the frontier.

The differences between the two sectors today are accentuated by the scale and technological complexity of the industrial sector of the economy. Extractive industries located in a harsh environment and far from their markets can be economic only if they are large. This has given rise to the sharp contrast that is now coming to exist between the ways of the life preferred by most native people and the scale of industrial development. In his evidence, Hugh Brody referred to the striking contrast:

… when industry does come to the North, we find the smallest, most isolated societies alongside some of the most costly and technically complex development projects in the world. Hence the paradox: the smallest alongside the largest, the most traditional alongside the most modern, and the most remote becoming involved with national or even international economic interests. [F25780]

This concept of a dual economy in the North may, however, be misleading. Dr. Charles Hobart and Dr. Peter Usher both pointed to changes and adaptations in traditional life; it has absorbed and now even depends upon some elements of the economy of the newcomers. Usher pointed out that this dependence upon outsiders, especially when it is reinforced by great (if at times unseen) political authority, has inevitably given rise to some flexibility in the native society. This does not mean, of course, that there are no limits to this flexibility, but this ability to accommodate to change reveals the danger in oversimplification: looked at in one way the northern economy is a dual economy, yet looked in another way, it is rather more complicated.

In fact, the native people's own idea of traditional economic activity does not correspond to the idea of an economy that is dual in nature. Neither Dene nor Inuit regard the aboriginal past, when they were isolated from and independent of southerners, as their traditional life. Ever since the first days of the fur trade, they have willingly adopted new techniques and equipment, and some of the social practices that the white man brought to the North. These elements were amalgamated into the native economy, and have to some extent become integral to the way of life that the native people are now trying to maintain and defend. At every stage there have been the dual aspects to the northern economy: the native society, with its emphasis on hunting, fishing and trapping, has stood apart from the white society that has gradually established itself in the North. This duality has never become fixed, and it continues to evolve.

At the present time, the clash between the interests of the oil and gas industry on the one hand, and the native (though not the aboriginal) economy on the other, does invite us to see two distinct economic modes. But Dr. Melville Watkins argued that the whole idea of a dual economy erroneously emphasized a separation between the "traditional" and the "modern":

According to this view, the North is a two-sector economy, consisting of a "modern" sector and a "traditional" sector, and these two sectors are substantially separate. The "modern" sector is seen as essentially an "enclave," where "development" takes place, while the "traditional" sector is stagnant and full of problems, and is not experiencing the benefits of "development." The logic of this position is that the solution lies in moving people out of the "traditional" sector and into the "modern" sector. The transition, though painful, is necessary. At the end of the road — or in this case, at the end of the pipeline — what will be created is a one-sector "modern" economy with everybody experiencing the benefits of "development." [F23604]

There are, in reality, four sectors in the northern economy: subsistence, trading of renewable resource produce, local wage employment, and industrial wage employment. We can trace the history of the native economy along a spectrum that has subsistence activities at one end and industrial wage labour at the other. But we must bear in mind that overlapping or mixed economic forms are now integral to the native economy.

The question with which we are faced here can then be stated as, how will the mix look as a result of the pipeline?

The native economy includes a large

subsistence-harvesting component. In general, the native people harvest the renewable resources without fundamentally affecting their populations or the land that produces them. How much a man can produce and consume (and, in the case of furs and other trade items, exchange) depends upon the productivity of the land, local knowledge of the land gained through long experience of it, and the technology used. The bush and the barrens do not at present produce surpluses, but they still provide a living — or the greatest part of a living — for many families.

Many native witnesses told me how they make a living from the land. At Fort Norman, Stella Mendo said:

My dad taught me how to put nets in, to hunt and to trap, he [taught me] all those ways of life in the bush ... it was a hard life, but yet it was good in a way because we were brought up living on wild meat, fish. We get moose hide; the hide we tan it, we use it for a lot of things, for mitts. ... After I got married I still do the same. I go out in the bush every year. Sometimes it is hard for me, and yet I still do it because I just love being out in the bush and making our living, because that is the way that I was brought up. [C913ff.]

The native economy today also includes the production of fur for the market. The Dene, Inuit and Metis view of traditional life includes all of the economic activities upon which the fur trade is based.

In some ways, wage employment has been useful to the native economy. The jobs made available by settlement growth and the government presence, along with some transfer payments, have substantially increased the flow of cash into native hands, and hunters and trappers have used this cash to improve their equipment. But in other ways wage labour has had adverse effects on the traditional life: a regular schedule of work conflicts with a hunter's

need to respond quickly to weather and to animal movements; cash tends to flow to the men who are least committed to a life of hunting, fishing and trapping; and employment in a settlement may put a man at a great distance from his hunting and trapping areas. But it seems fair to say that local and limited wage labour was included in an economic mix that was compatible with the realization of many native values and aspirations.

In the native economy, the individual or the family combines production, exchange and consumption activities, at least during certain parts of the year. But in the cash economy, which is based on production for the market, these activities tend to be divided. An individual does not consume what he produces, nor does he sell his product directly to the ultimate consumer. Specialization of activity has enabled the industrial economy to become extremely productive; surpluses are produced that, when re-invested, promote the growth of further productive and consumptive capacity. An ever higher degree of specialization is one of the basic principles on which the industrial economy operates.

In the North today, the lives of many native families are based on an intricate economic mix. At certain times of the year they hunt and fish; at other times they work for wages, sometimes for the government, sometimes on highway construction, sometimes for the oil and gas industry. But if opportunities for wage employment expand and the pressures to take such work increase, the native economy may be completely transformed. Men will then leave the small communities to work at locations from which they cannot possibly maintain a mixed economic life. Many people have expressed the fear that, if the industrial

economy comes to every settlement, if wage employment becomes the only way to make a living, then the native economy will be debased and overwhelmed.

Native people have learned to depend upon some wage labour because of the inability of the traditional economy to resist changes imposed upon it by the external economy — especially in the form of unstable fur prices. This is to some extent the result of decades of indifference on the part of authorities in the South. The first opportunities for wage labour were seized upon, but, in time, and with the persistence of southern ideas of progress, there has seemed to be no alternative to ever more wage labour. In terms of the four-fold model I have outlined, the native people have been drawn into a dependence on local wage employment, and have been prepared for absorption into industrial wage employment. Absorption into the industrial economy will tend to undermine the mixed economic life that the native people have evolved during their contact with white society. Absorption into the industrial economy can only mean displacement of the native economy: migrant workers cannot also be hunters and trappers.

The native economy should not be preserved merely as a curiosity. The northern peoples have demonstrated before this Inquiry that their economy is not only a link with their past, but it is also the basis of their plans for the future. The continued viability of the native economy should be an objective of northern development, not its price.

Open pit mine, Pine Point. (Canadian National)

Gold miners washing up after shift. (NFB–Pearce)

Guy Dagenais at Yellowknife gold mine. (NFB–Pearce)

Lead-zinc concentrate southbound from Pine Point. (Canadian National)

The Local Experience of Economic Development

It is self-deception to believe that large-scale industrial development would end unemployment and underemployment of native people in the North. In the first place, we have always overestimated the extent to which native people are unemployed and underemployed by understating their continued reliance on the land. Secondly, we have never fully recognized that industrial development has, in itself, contributed to social, economic and geographic dislocations among native people.

Fort Resolution and Pine Point

Fort Resolution, at the mouth of the Slave River, is one of the oldest communities in the Northwest Territories. Its population is largely Indian, but there are a substantial number of Metis. Pine Point, about 40 miles to the east, is one of the newest communities in the Territories, and it is predominantly white. The development of each of these two communities is, to a considerable extent, representative of economic development in the North.

The lead-zinc mine at Pine Point began operation in 1964, pursuant to an agreement between Cominco and the federal and territorial governments. The nature and size of the federal investment in this project gives some idea of the priorities for economic development during the sixties. In 1961, under the Roads to Resources Program, the federal government, Pine Point Mines Limited, and Canadian National Railway made an agreement whereby the government undertook to construct a railway to Pine Point, and Cominco undertook to bring the mine into production. Total investment, including the railway, mill and hydroelectric plant, came to $130 million. In 1962 railroad construction began; in 1963 the townsite was laid out, and in 1964 the railway reached Pine Point. In 1965 Cominco began to ship ore to British Columbia. The largest part of the government's investment was in the construction of the Great Slave Lake Railway. This investment, together with CNR's purchase of special railway cars to carry the lead-zinc concentrates, amounted to almost $90 million. The government spent another $9 million on the Taltson River Hydro Project to provide Pine Point and Fort Smith with hydro-electricity, and close to $3 million to extend the Mackenzie Highway from Hay River to Pine Point. Taking into consideration the government's financial contribution to the establishment and maintenance of the town site at Pine Point, the total federal investment amounted to approximately $100 million.

The participation by the people of Fort Resolution in the mining venture at Pine Point has been very limited. Professor Paul Deprez, in his study *The Pine Point Mine and the Development of the Area South of Great Slave Lake,* attributed their limited involvement mainly to the fact that between 1964, when the mine was opened, and 1972, there was no all-weather road between the mine and Fort Resolution, a distance of some 42 miles. Men from Fort Resolution who wanted to work in the mine had to live at Pine Point; they could not commute. The limited housing available to native people at Pine Point, combined with their own preference for living at home, kept the level of native employment low.

Deprez found it "most disturbing" that, although the federal and territorial governments were prepared to spend approximately $100 million to permit Cominco to develop the mine, they were not prepared to give any priority to the development of a link road between the mine and Fort Resolution.

In 1976, the population of Pine Point numbered about 1,800. Yet, out of a work force of 500 or more, there is a negligible number of native workers. Although Cominco supplied figures showing the number of northerners it employs, these do not reveal the number of northern natives employed. Estimates from all sources agree the number is very small. Once the complement of white workers was installed in the town, not only was there no incentive to employ native people, there was a disincentive. The presence of native employees would have altered the character of the town.

In the eyes of the people of Fort Resolution, the Pine Point mine is not simply a development in which they have not participated. It is a development that they feel threatens their land and their livelihood. At the community hearing in Fort Resolution Mike Beaulieu said:

> We, the Dene people, do a lot of hunting and trapping and fishing. Our hunting has decreased a lot due to the construction of the highway, the building of the mine, and the increase of the people from the South. . . . Our traditional grounds are slowly being overtaken by these [mine] employees. There is virtually no benefit to be spoken of from the mine. [C2994ff.]

It is important to compare the Pine Point mine development with the Slave River sawmill operation in Fort Resolution. The sawmill provides employment for 30 to 35 men on a labour-pool basis. This means that a man can take time off to go out hunting or fishing, provided someone else can take his place in the mill. In addition, during part of the spring, the mill closes down completely, because most of the men choose to hunt beaver and muskrat at that time. The operation, therefore, provides wage employment, but in a manner consistent with the maintenance of traditional economic activity; indeed it complements that activity by providing the means to buy equipment and supplies. Being community-based, the men are able to work without being separated from their families, and to participate in an endeavour that encourages community cooperation.

Father Louis Menez, the priest at Fort Resolution, pointed out, however, that the demand for the sawmill's lumber is small. The modern school building at Fort Resolution, for example, is built entirely of imported lumber. Nothing was supplied by or sought from the Fort Resolution sawmill — although the imported lumber was stored for a time in the local lumber yard. Ray Orbell, the manager of the sawmill, explained that its production capacity is three million board feet per year, but that they are unable to sell it in the Northwest Territories. He added:

> It is hard for the people of Fort Resolution to understand why, when we produce only three million foot board measure, and there is 17 million foot board measure used, that we cannot sell our lumber. [C3039]

Fort Liard and the Pointed Mountain Pipeline

In 1972 a gas pipeline was built from Pointed Mountain in the Northwest Territories to Fort Nelson, British Columbia. Pointed Mountain is approximately 15 miles from Fort Liard, an Indian community of about 300. The construction phase of the Pointed Mountain project extended from late spring 1971 to August 1972, with most of the work

being carried out early in 1972. Amoco built a gas dehydration plant and an associated gas gathering system in the Pointed Mountain field; Westcoast Transmission built a pipeline from Pointed Mountain to Beaver River in northern British Columbia, which feeds Pointed Mountain gas into the main Westcoast system.

It is the only operational pipeline in the Canadian North. Its construction and current operation exemplify the pattern of economic development in the non-renewable resource sector in the North, and indicates the extent to which native people have profited, in employment and in income, from non-renewable resource projects in the past.

The direct impact of the construction phase of the project on the native economy may be summarized quite simply. Because all of the materials and equipment were purchased in the South, there were no multiplier effects associated with these expenditures in the Northwest Territories.

What about employment? Michel Scott, in his report *The Socio-Economic Impact of the Pointed Mountain Gas Field,* prepared for the Department of Indian Affairs and Northern Development in 1973, estimated that a total of between 65 and 70 native workers were employed on the project at one time or another during the construction period. Peak native employment on the project coincided with peak total employment. Towards the end of February 1972, the work force comprised 465 men, of which 60 or 12.9 percent were native persons. In general, native employment was intermittent and of relatively short duration. Native workers from the settlement of Fort Liard worked an average of 12.4 weeks during the construction period, and native workers from Fort Simpson, an average of 4.6 weeks.

Using sample data, Scott estimated that

total native income from the project was between $50,000 and $75,000 for Fort Liard, approximately $40,000 for Fort Simpson, and between $6,000 and $10,000 for Nahanni Butte. These totals may be compared with total construction costs of approximately $15 million.

Over 90 percent of the jobs held by native people were in the unskilled category, with their main employment being clearing and grading. Now that the gas plant is in operation, there are only eight permanent positions available, of which half are categorized as skilled and half as unskilled. All eight positions are held by personnel from the South.

The cost of constructing a gas supply system to the community at Fort Liard was estimated to be about $500,000, but the expense could not be justified on the basis of expected field life and market size.

Gains to the native people of Fort Liard from the project were not large, but they strongly feel that their losses, because of the project, were considerable. Harry Deneron, Chief of the Fort Liard Band, explained the feeling of his people:

> Somewhere the people are getting richer and richer and the people down below, the Indian people from the lake shoreline, are getting poorer and poorer every day. When I say that the Indian people are getting poorer, I don't mean money in the pocket is going out, I mean they are losing game. When you have this sort of activity in your area, the moose, fur animals, they sort of disappear. They start going away from this area. [C1662]

Native witnesses told the Inquiry at Fort Liard that the area around Fisherman Lake, near which the gas plant and gas-gathering facilities are located, has been adversely affected by the development. Johnny Klondike, a trapper, said:

> Before the pipeline came into our country I

Sawmill at Fort Resolution. (A. Steen)

Interior—Fort Resolution sawmill. (DIAND)

At Fort Liard hearing. (Native Press)

Chief Harry Deneron, second from left, with Judge Berger at Pointed Mountain gas field. (P. Scott)

lived there and raised my family, and I used to hunt fish, meat, fur, marten, lynx and moose. . . . I was hoping to raise my family until they get of age, and then they could make a good living out of that country, because there was lots of game. But now, since the pipeline came in, I am scared to go any place. I don't know where to go, because wherever I want to go, there is a seismic line, with trucks rolling back and forth on it, and planes are flying overhead and it scares the moose and the game away. Ever since they came in I couldn't make a living out of the country. This is my trouble now. There is all kinds of money made around me with the oil, and they don't give me anything. They don't think that I am a person living there. I was living there before them but they don't take that into consideration. It seems they don't care about how the kids are or how I feel. There is only one pass through the mountains where I used to trap — they are occupying that, so that doesn't give me much chance to make a living. [C1667ff.]

Impact and Returns

Let us now consider the economic impact the pipeline would have in the North. I think it should be plain enough that the principal beneficiaries of either of the proposed pipelines would be southerners, not the people who live in the North. This should surprise no one. The huge sums that are to be invested in the pipeline and in gas field development are for the express purpose of transporting this northern resource to the markets of the South. Even so, Arctic Gas and, to a lesser extent, Foothills have insisted that northerners will benefit from the project: the native people will find jobs, local businessmen will get contracts, and the territorial government will receive tax revenues from the pipeline and associated economic development. I want now to consider the probable extent of

such benefits to the people of the North and to indicate what the short-run and long-run economic impacts of the pipeline are likely to be.

Short-run impacts are individual events or trends that occur while a major change is taking place. During the construction phase, the people of the Mackenzie Valley would not be aware of the full range of all the pipeline's effects, but they would be well aware of its immediate effects. If wages go up, they will receive them; if prices go up, they will pay them. The long-run impact may be thought of as the cumulative result of the short-run impacts, and it will determine what the economy of the North will be like in the future. Long-run impacts cannot usually be reversed. If we opt now for a northern economy that is dominated by the oil and gas industry, that is the economy we shall have for many years to come.

In trying to predict the impact of large-scale frontier projects, we should be realistic about the cost estimates that the companies present. Large-scale frontier projects usually cost very much more than was initially estimated. We have seen the estimated cost of the James Bay project increase three-fold, from $6 billion in 1971 to $18 billion in 1976. In 1970, the estimated cost of the trans-Alaska pipeline was $900 million; today, with the project near completion, it is apparent that its cost will be approximately $8 billion. The Alyeska Pipeline Service Company originally advised the State of Alaska that it would require some 6,000 to 8,000 workers to build the pipeline. In fact, during both the 1975 and 1976 construction seasons, 24,000 workers were employed on it.

We have seen the estimated cost of the Arctic Gas project rise from 5.6 billion in March 1974 to approximately $8 billion today. This estimate is not, of course, the cost

of the whole pipeline, but only of the part of it that will run through Canada. The Foothills pipeline north of 60 has undergone a similar increase, from an estimated $1.71 billion, when it was first proposed in 1974, to over $3 billion in 1977. Arctic Gas will be asking the Government of Canada and the Government of the United States to guarantee repayment of their borrowings, for cost overruns, and Foothills will seek a similar guarantee.

The complexity and the scale of the pipeline project will probably mean that our predictions understate the costs, the changes, and the impact of the pipeline. Its economic impact will probably be very much greater than anyone today predicts: it is likely that more materials, more workers, more money and more time will be required than present estimates suggest.

Economic Problems: Short-run

The Mackenzie Valley pipeline will be one of the largest construction projects ever undertaken. Thousands of workers will be required to build the pipeline, and yet more thousands will go North to look for work. Huge volumes of material and large numbers of machines will be moved into the North.

The majority of people who come to the North to work on the pipeline will dispose of most of their earnings in Southern Canada. But they will spend at least some of their wages in the North. Because the northern economy has limited capacity to accommodate additional demand, an increase above present spending levels will force up prices. The supply of goods and services is likely to be interrupted because existing supply lines do not easily or cheaply permit northern merchants to replace depleted stocks. The seasonal river-based transportation system requires major stocks of commodities to be laid in each summer for the coming year. Capacity in housing, retailing, community services and local public works cannot be expanded quickly, particularly during periods of high demand.

The short-run impact of the pipeline will depend on the degree to which such matters as population flow and the surges of local demand are controllable and controlled, and on the degree to which the activities related to, and induced by, pipeline construction are able to bypass businesses and transportation capacity related to community supply in the Northwest Territories. Both Arctic Gas and Foothills have claimed that the movements of the workers and supplies they will need are controllable and that they will, in fact, be controlled. They have argued that the pipeline project will be carried out in an orderly way, and that it will entail no more than minimal pressure on communities and local suppliers. The companies recognize that there may be some problems related to the pipeline, for example, the influx of transients, but they do not think these problems will be serious, and they maintain that government should be able to manage them.

THE ALASKAN EXPERIENCE

In trying to predict the impact of pipeline construction in the Canadian North, can we learn anything from the experience of the Alyeska pipeline?

David Boorkman, an urban sociologist who gave evidence for Arctic Gas, described some of the problems the Alyeska pipeline has brought to Alaska. The principal problem has been the wave of in-migrants attracted from the Lower 48 by the prospect of high wages. In 1974 and 1975, an estimated 70,000 to 80,000 people (no one knows

exactly how many) arrived in Alaska, increasing by 20 percent the total population of the state, which in 1970 had stood at 300,000. This in-migration spawned a whole range of other problems: it disoriented the local economy, increased the pressure on public services, and led to a high rate of inflation.

Boorkman told the Inquiry that Alaska has had successive waves of in-migrants in the past. They came with the gold rushes, with the military construction during and after the Second World War, with the building of the DEW Line stations in the 1950s, and with the discovery of oil and gas on the Kenai Peninsula in the 1960s. The present surge of people into Alaska is only the latest of a series of waves of migration. Americans have always regarded Alaska as a place to make a new start or a quick fortune.

Before pipeline construction began, Boorkman had predicted that the peak in-migration during 1974 and 1975 would be around 40,000 people. In the event, about twice that number came. In explaining his underestimate, Boorkman pointed out that Alyeska had predicted that they would employ 6,000 to 8,000 workers, but in fact they had employed about 24,000 workers during peak construction.

The high pay on pipeline construction attracted qualified workers away from lower-paying jobs in both the public and private sectors of the Alaskan economy. Because of the rapid population increase, the budgets for such cities as Fairbanks, Anchorage and Valdez, and the state budget have swelled. There is a severe shortage of housing, utilities are overloaded, crime has increased (although not at a greater rate than the population), and inflation is running at double the national average.

The State of Alaska, in Boorkman's opinion, unwittingly contributed to this high rate of in-migration by its local employment policy. The Local Hire Act, passed in 1972, required that Alaskan residents be given preference for jobs on the pipeline. Union hiring halls were established in Fairbanks, and thousands came from the Lower 48 looking for work. Because there was no precise definition of Alaskan residence, they qualified as residents and were eligible to work on the pipeline. Thus, although the statistics show that a large percentage of the workers on the pipeline are officially qualified as Alaskan residents (66.7 percent at December 31, 1975), many are residents only in the sense that they are living there while working on the pipeline.

A policy designed to limit employment to Alaskan residents, even if it had been enforced, would not necessarily have stopped people coming into Alaska from the Lower 48. Alaskans might perhaps have obtained more of the jobs on the pipeline, but there would still have been a large influx of people drawn there by the prospect of a chance to make big money on the frontier. Of course many highly skilled workers would have been required, who could not have been found in Alaska. Nevertheless, construction workers constitute no more than 15 percent of the total in-migrant population. The remaining 85 percent is made up of people who came to Alaska to look for work. The unemployment rate in Alaska is, therefore, higher now than it was before the project began. Attempts to dissuade workers from flocking to Alaska were not effective: they came anyway.

We can get some idea of what would happen to a town such as Hay River, Fort Simpson or Inuvik by examining the experience of Valdez, the southern terminus of the

Pumping station under construction, trans-Alaska pipeline. (Alyeska)

Pipeline worker at construction camp, Alaska. (E. Weick)
Attaching insulation, Alyeska pipeline. (Alyeska)
Archeological research on right-of-way, Alyeska pipeline. (Alyeska)

---

pipeline, a town of just over 1,000 in 1970. Dr. Michael Baring-Gould and Marsha Bennet, sociologists at the University of Alaska, told the Inquiry that the population of Valdez increased by 34 percent between 1970 and the end of 1973: it was then 1,350. By July 1975, the population of the town proper — not including construction camps and outlying communities — had increased to more than 3,500, roughly triple the population in 1973. The town and camp population together reached a peak of 6,500.

Local employment in Valdez changed from substantial dependence on jobs with the public service to dependence on pipeline construction and related activities. In 1975, for example, 135 new businesses opened in the Valdez area; they were predominantly Anchorage-based suppliers of equipment and services to the pipeline project, but there were also new stores to meet increased consumer demands. The labour market in Valdez has changed substantially in structure, almost wholly because of the influx of new residents and employers. Private sector activities such as fishing that were once significant in Valdez have become much less important. Incomes have risen: the per capita income of heads of households rose dramatically from a median of $11,940 in 1973 to $24,500 in 1975; the median family income rose from $16,430 in 1974 to $30,600 in 1975.

Several other factors in the Valdez situation warrant attention. The increases in income were not restricted to workers on the pipeline: they occurred in all occupations. Employers in general, including the city and state, were forced to raise salaries to meet local inflation and to prevent loss of personnel. Nevertheless, increases in income were greatest among the pipeline work force. Since most of the workers who moved into pipeline employment came from the less

skilled, lower paid and less permanent levels of employment within the community, the result was a levelling of incomes within Valdez between 1974 and 1975. But the disparities may return. When high-paying construction employment is no longer available, the people who now have this work will be forced back to their former level of employment and will be obliged to readjust to a lower level of income.

The state provided funds to communities such as Valdez to deal with problems created by the impact of pipeline construction. For the most part, these funds were insufficient and came too late to be of real assistance to communities to overcome their immediate problems. The funding programs were restrictive in their application, and often they did not address the problems the communities were facing in, for example, the fields of housing, health and pollution. Worse, the problems frequently could not be solved merely by the injection of cash. Sometimes there was little that a community could do with money because materials and skilled personnel were not available. Long delays between planning and implementation simply could not be avoided.

In Alaska, as a result of the pipeline boom, in-migration has caused serious shortages because of greatly increased demands for services, utilities, commodities and housing in such key cities as Fairbanks and Valdez. Prices, especially rents, have risen greatly. Alaskans who had not formerly been part of the labour force, such as married women, native people and high school students, have now entered it. Many municipal employees and people working in service jobs or for local contractors left to work on the pipeline, and they were either replaced by less qualified personnel or not replaced at all. There is a high turnover in all jobs as workers try to

make more money to meet the rising cost of living. Persons with relatively fixed incomes, for example, pensioners and state and municipal employees, sustained losses — sometimes severe — in real income.

APPLICATION TO THE NORTHWEST TERRITORIES

The impact of the Alyeska pipeline, which has included in-migration, inflation, shortages and an increase in unemployment, shows what might happen in the Canadian North.

Wayne Trusty, an economist who gave evidence for Arctic Gas, said that construction of a pipeline in the Canadian North would not have the same impact as it had in Alaska. In the past, construction workers coming to northern Canada have not remained, whereas the workers who come to Alaska have a greater tendency to take up residence. He said that southern cities such as Edmonton will perform the functions of logistics and supply that in Alaska are performed by Anchorage and Fairbanks. Edmonton's dominant role in supplying northern construction will tend to discourage the relocation of businesses in the North and will therefore limit in-migration. Trusty thought that, although Arctic Gas would no doubt procure some goods and services locally, the basic north-south system of supply would not change markedly.

Arctic Gas say their policy will be to limit in-migration. (An in-migrant, by their definition, is someone who intends to live in the North, not someone who goes there simply to work and who will leave when the job is over.) They will limit in-migration by hiring non-resident workers only in the South, then flying them back and forth from Edmonton. The workers will have no chance to stop in the communities. Furthermore, Arctic Gas intends to publicize information about the arduous nature and seasonality of pipeline work.

Trusty pointed out that, in the Northwest Territories, the federal government has always played the vital role in economic development. He argued that the area has always had a closed, planned economy. He meant that the federal government and its creature, the territorial government, are the principal employers and the principal source of wages, salaries and transfer payments. Because the government controls the disposition and use of land in the Northwest Territories, he felt that this tight control of the sale and use of crown land could be used to discourage in-migration.

In comparing impacts of pipeline construction in Alaska with those that may occur in the Northwest Territories, we should not overlook the fact that the Alyeska pipeline project, although it is very large, is smaller in relation to the Alaskan economy than either the Arctic Gas or the Foothills project would be in relation to the economy of the Northwest Territories. It has been suggested to me that the difference in size of the two economies would actually work to the advantage of the Northwest Territories. It is said that because its economy is rudimentary the preponderant impact of the pipeline project would necessarily have to occur outside the territorial boundaries.

The trans-Alaska pipeline project has been described as an $8 billion pipeline grafted onto a pre-pipeline economy of $2 billion. This disproportion between the project and the local economy would be even more pronounced in the Northwest Territories. The local economy of the Northwest Territories is very much smaller than the economy of Alaska and, therefore, less able

to absorb the kinds of impact that such large projects inevitably generate. It is probable that the kinds of economic impact that the Alyeska pipeline had in Alaska would also occur in Canada, but to an even greater degree.

The short-run economic effects of the pipeline would lead to a higher rate of local inflation than there would be if no pipeline were built. Migrants to the Mackenzie Valley and Western Arctic would compete for available accommodation: the market for private housing is small and poorly developed, and it could not easily expand to meet surges in demand. There would also be shortages of goods and services. In the communities most affected by the pipeline project, these shortages would be serious, and they would affect the daily lives of every resident in them.

There would be significant changes in the structure of the labour force. People who are not now part of the labour force would enter it to take work on the pipeline or to fill jobs left by others to work on the pipeline. As in Alaska, the distribution of income would change: workers with direct access to the main money streams associated with the pipeline would see their incomes rise much more rapidly than those without such access. People with relatively fixed incomes such as pensioners would certainly suffer because their incomes would not rise as fast as prices. The climate for local business would undoubtedly be good, but there is a real possibility that local business could not expand enough to meet demands. Sloughing off expanded capacity after completion of the pipeline project could be painful and disruptive.

I am mindful of the evidence that both pipeline companies presented on the controls they would impose on their activities and

their labour force, and I believe that the companies could exercise a measure of control over the movement of their own personnel, materials and equipment. Similarly, the pipeline contractors should be able to exercise a measure of control over their personnel, materials and equipment. But the activities of the pipeline companies and their contractors will give rise to a great number of secondary and tertiary activities, and the pipeline companies have understated the impact that these activities would have. The Alaskan experience enables us to understand a great deal about that kind of impact. It will simply not be possible to control all forms of activity. In Canada, citizens have the right to travel where they will; if any of them decide to travel North of 60, there is no legal way to stop them. Although we might wish to control the impact of the pipeline boom, it would in many ways be quite beyond direct control: we should have to accept serious short-run dislocations of the economy. I do not see any way that these effects could be prevented.

Economic Problems: Long-run

In considering the long-run impact of either the Arctic Gas or the Foothills pipeline, we must remember that, once an energy corridor is established, other pipelines would be built along it, too. New reserves of oil and gas would probably be developed, and communication and transportation systems would be further expanded. So the pipeline must be regarded as a threshold: once crossed, there is no turning back.

THE ALASKAN EXPERIENCE

Since the discovery in 1968 of oil at Prudhoe Bay, the structure of the Alaskan economy has changed. Before 1968, military spending provided a relatively firm income base along

Yellowknife gold miners. (NFB—Pearce)

Kakisa Lake store. (GNWT)

Echo Bay Mines, Great Bear Lake. (DIAND)

A Yellowknife bar. (News of the North)

he Fairbanks-Anchorage corridor. Many Alaskans depended on the fishing industry, which is regionally important all the way from Ketchikan in the Panhandle of southeast Alaska around to Kodiak Island and the Aleutians in the west. Forestry and pulp and paper were also important in the southeast, and there was some farming in the Matanuska Valley, near Anchorage. Government services tended to provide relatively stable employment in the urbanized centres.

The changes that have occurred in this pattern since 1968 all derive from the very large scale of industrial activity that has been associated with petroleum development: they are not the result only of the trans-Alaska pipeline. Many millions of dollars have been spent on exploration and development on the north slope. Many millions more will be spent on further exploration of Naval Petroleum Reserve No. and of Alaska's outer continental shelf.

Government services have proliferated throughout Alaska. In 1969 the state received almost $1 billion from the sale of oil leases on the north slope, and this money has now been spent to develop infrastructure that Alaskans saw as necessary to achieve parity with the Lower 48. New buildings, roads, ferries and improved social and health services have all been costly to establish and maintain. At the same time, the greatly expanded population of Alaska demands more and more of these things and, because it now earns higher incomes, it demands services of higher quality.

Oil was expected to flow long before it actually will; the government thought it would have early access to royalties and tax revenues, but building of the pipeline was delayed by environmental litigation and the negotiation of native claims, and the state's expectations of early revenues were frustrated.

The state government is now on a treadmill. It has created services and a bureaucracy that require very large sums of money to maintain. There is only one source from which enough money can be obtained, and that is the oil and gas industry. The government must, therefore, support further oil and gas exploration and development, and pipeline construction, even though it may have misgivings about them.

Alaska's native people have been drawn into the Alaskan economy. The nature of the Alaska Native Claims Settlement Act was such that, once it was signed, the future of the native people depended on acceptance of, not opposition to, industrial development. The value of the lands they obtained under the Act depends not on their production of game, fish and fur, but on the existence under them of minerals, oil and gas. Because the native corporations were created to be profit-making entities, the native people must now become workers or businessmen if they wish to have a share in the economic future of the state.

Petroleum development in Alaska has affected every major Alaskan interest: the government, the white people, the native people, the unions, the businessmen. All of them now focus on a single activity: the continued search for, and development of, oil and natural gas. There is now less room than before for economic diversity, although military spending, commercial fishing and forestry are still important elements in the state economy. The native person who wants to continue a life of hunting, trapping and fishing is not encouraged. The land that he uses for these purposes is sought by developers, including native developers.

APPLICATION TO THE NORTHWEST TERRITORIES

Is this the experience that awaits the Canadian North? Once embarked on a program of oil and gas development, the Northwest Territories will be committed to such a course for many years. There will be little control within the Territories over the rate or the direction of such development. A relatively autonomous political entity like Alberta can exercise some real control over the rate at which its oil and gas reserves are to be used, and the extent to which the province's economic growth will be determined by the oil and gas industry. But this degree of political autonomy is possible because the province's economy is not completely dependent on the oil and gas industry. Albertans can exercise a measure of control with respect to the development of oil and gas to the extent that they have developed other industries, especially agriculture.

If the Northwest Territories (or for that matter Alberta) were to permit the oil and gas industry to develop to the exclusion of all other sorts of economic development, government would face the long-term threat of eventual economic decline. Resources like oil and gas must give out: they cannot continue forever. Alberta is fortunate in having an agricultural, as well as a petroleum, base. And the Northwest Territories, like Alberta, could also develop a firmer economic future by strengthening its renewable resource sector.

Although in many respects dependence on large-scale petroleum development would be beneficial, the control of the northern economy would not lie with northerners nor, indeed, with the Government of Canada itself, for at least a generation. Annual expenditure on the Mackenzie Valley pipeline during construction would greatly exceed the value of the annual production of the Northwest Territories. The cumulative expenditure on all of the oil and gas projects that can be foreseen in the North would greatly overshadow every other form of economic activity in the region. Given the present state of the northern economy, a decision to build the pipeline now would severely limit the possibility of northern residents having any real control over the rate and extent of the economic growth of the region.

Returns to the Government of the Northwest Territories

In its budget for 1976-1977, the Government of the Northwest Territories, which has limited sources of revenue and is heavily subsidized by the Government of Canada, projected a total income of $215,790,900. Of this amount, $189,539,200, or better than 87 percent, was to come from the Government of Canada in the form of grants, loans and transfer payments.

The costs of providing increased health and social services necessitated by the pipeline will be high. Population growth and the expansion of key centres, such as Hay River, Fort Simpson and Inuvik will require substantial public funds. Normal territorial programs in the fields of health, education, welfare, recreation, game management and corrections will have to be expanded and diversified. As the Government of Alaska is discovering, the costs come first, the benefits — in the form of government revenues — come much later. What revenues, then, will accrue to the Government of the Northwest Territories over the long-term if a pipeline is built?

Potential returns to the territorial government can be estimated by applying existing territorial tax legislation to the proposed pipeline. Under the Northwest Territories Act, the territorial government has the power to impose a property tax on pipelines: such taxes are levied under the Taxation Ordinance. During the 1975-1976 fiscal year, the Government of the Northwest Territories collected $55,216.50 from levies on the Pointed Mountain pipeline and its ancillary facilities.

If Schedule A of Commissioner's Order 181-74 is applied to the proposed Mackenzie Valley pipeline, the annual tax revenue to the Northwest Territories for a 700-mile length of 48-inch pipeline, assessed at $10.65 per foot (that is, at 25 mills) would amount to $984,060. For a 42-inch pipeline over the same distance, assessed at $9.71 per foot, the annual tax revenue would be $897,204. These figures do not give the full picture; they do not include taxes on ancillary facilities such as compressor stations. They do, however, indicate that, if the present assessment rates are retained, the revenues that would accrue to the territorial government would be so low as to be insignificant. They would come nowhere near meeting the social costs of pipeline construction that the Government of the Northwest Territories would have to bear.

David Nickerson, a member of the Territorial Council, gave his view of the matter to the Inquiry:

> The solution to this problem is obvious — the rates must be made to approach fair actual value, and I would suggest that pipelines be taxed at 66⅔ percent of such fair actual value just as are many other improvements . . . as specified in Commissioner's Order 477-73.
>
> It would be my supposition that revenues to the Northwest Territories resulting from the operation of a pipeline system such as that proposed by Arctic Gas should on no account

be less than $50 million per annum and that, should the Territories be unable to extract that amount by way of property taxation, it would lead us to press vigorously for some other form of taxation such as throughput taxes.

Nickerson said the pipeline company might find a throughput tax to its advantage because taxes payable would decrease when the pipeline was not operating at full capacity. He went on to give specific figures:

> As an example of the type of revenues which might be collected using such a tax, I give the following illustration: if a levy of one day's throughput for each 100 miles of pipeline were made on a pipeline 700 miles long carrying four billion cubic feet of gas per day (the volume proposed by Arctic Gas within a few years of start-up), the total government take would amount to 28 billion cubic feet. Assuming a value at the Northwest Territories border of $1 per thousand cubic feet, in dollar terms this amounts to $28 million. Were a certain proportion of the government's gas to be taken in kind, it could be used for electricity generation or other purposes designed to keep the cost of living in the North comparable to that in Southern Canada. [F29273ff.]

But, of course, a throughput tax could not be applied to Alaskan gas being carried to the Lower 48; such a tax would be excluded by the treaty between Canada and the United States. And the territorial government has no power to impose a throughput tax on Canadian gas being transported in the pipeline.

What revenues would accrue to the Government of the Northwest Territories as the result of expanded economic activity associated with the pipeline? The largest single source of additional revenue attributable to general economic growth would be receipts

Inuvik in the 1960s. (GNWT)

Inuvik business establishment. (GNWT)

Inuvik mayor, Jim Robertson. (P. Scott)

Territorial councillor, Dave Nickerson.
(News of the North)

---

from the sale of liquor because the Government of the Northwest Territories has a monopoly of such sales.

There would, of course, be more cash in the hands of northerners, but the power to tax personal and corporate income lies exclusively with Ottawa.

It is clear that, unless there is a fundamental redistribution of revenues between the Government of Canada and the Government of the Northwest Territories, the deficit of the Government of the Northwest Territories, despite increased earnings from the sale of liquor, will be even greater after the pipeline is built than at present, and the territorial government will be even more dependent on the federal government than it is now.

Benefits to Northern Business

A considerable proportion of the whites resident in the North are there as representatives of large organizations that have headquarters outside the region. Public servants employed by the Government of Canada fall into that category and, given the dependence of the territorial government on the federal government, public servants employed by the Government of the Northwest Territories may also be said to fall into that category. So also do employees of the mine at Pine Point (Cominco) and of CN Telecommunications, Pacific Western Airlines, and the oil companies. Typically, such employees are in the North only temporarily.

The pipeline will probably not have a major effect on the lives of these temporary residents. They will, of course, be affected by higher prices, and they may have to wait longer for telephones and other utilities. Some of them, as in Alaska, may leave the jobs that brought them to the North for higher paying jobs on the pipeline. But, in the main, their lives will not be greatly affected if the pipeline is built.

However, there are some white people who have lived in the North for a long time and intend to remain. They are independent tradesmen or owners of small- to medium-sized businesses in the larger communities and in some of the native villages. They have created the commercial establishment that provides the communities with many everyday goods and services. These white people would find it difficult to withdraw from their commitment to the North and would not easily avoid the effects of the pipeline. But evidence presented to the Inquiry by the Northwest Territories Chamber of Commerce, the Association of Municipalities, and many private individuals, indicated that most of these people feel that the pipeline will benefit them. They think the pipeline is necessary to growth and development of the northern economy, although they recognize that it may not be wholly a blessing. Jim Robertson, the Mayor of Inuvik, put the matter this way:

> With respect to development, I could tell you what we'd like, which is no development and a standard of living twice what we have right now. I can tell you what we honestly expect is that, in order to maintain what we have, we're going to have to put up with a certain amount of development and inasmuch as we take that to be a cornerstone, you're not going to get a tax base until you get some activity. You're not going to get activity without certain adverse results. [C3703]

White people permanently resident in the North are clearly worried about some of the less desirable changes that would accompany the pipeline project. They recognize that they might find themselves torn between two sets of considerations. On the one hand, they are uneasy about many of the effects that the pipeline might have on their families and communities. Living through the construction phase of such a project will not be easy or peaceful, as Alaskans have learned. On the other hand, northern whites, and particularly those in business, recognize that the pipeline could lead to a significant increase in their material well-being. Many of them have lived for years in the hope and, in recent years, with the expectation that a pipeline would be built.

Businessmen who have invested their savings in ventures designed to serve the northern market operate under difficult circumstances. Don Tetrault, a prominent Hay River businessman, outlined some of the problems:

> Now, as far as the businessman is concerned, I am not the only one that has taken a long look at pipeline construction and how it would affect the businessmen. There are many businessmen in Hay River, Simpson, Inuvik and Yellowknife, who have taken a long look at plans, at the pipeline and how it would affect their businesses, and consequently they have expanded their businesses with larger fleets, if they're in the trucking business, larger hotel rooms or more accommodation, more camps if they're in the camp business. This has taken a considerable amount of funds, and these funds had to be generated outside the Territories to a large degree, particularly in light of the fact that ... until recently, [the territorial government's] small business loans were limited to approximately $15,000-$20,000. Now it has gone to $50,000, and as far as the businessman is concerned, today they are talking about millions of dollars and hundreds of millions in construction for camps, materials; the local businessman in the Northwest Territories is restricted for borrowing on the territorial level to $50,000, and [at] today's prices and costs, $50,000 is very little. Consequently we have to go outside to either banking firms or the Industrial Development Bank [IDB].

This has caused considerable hardship to

many of the small companies, and they have, in turn, turned to the larger existing companies outside the Territories for assistance, either direct financial involvement in their firm, or establishing other firms or other businesses relative to their industry, but on a joint-venture basis. A good example is our own commitment whereby we got involved with another major transportation company to purchase a second vessel to be used exclusively in the oil exploration, pipeline development. This was brought about by necessity, lack of funds available through the Territories or the IDB, ... and many companies are going to have to do this and have done [so] already ... they have involved themselves with large companies outside in a form, either partnerships or joint ventures, simply because we need their money; they need our expertise assistance. In other words, we have ability to move across the country, we're familiar enough ... with manpower problems that we can cope with them satisfactorily. Maybe not [to] the satisfaction of the bankers, but to our Board of Directors' satisfaction. [C240ff.]

Many of the minor and virtually all of the important decisions that affect the northern economy are made outside the Northwest Territories. This situation causes the northern businessman frustration and difficulty: it creates uncertainty and, of course, nothing underlines this situation more clearly than the fact that the decision whether or not to build the pipeline will be made in Ottawa and Washington, D.C. Georgia Moniuk, a hotel proprietor at Norman Wells, told the Inquiry:

The business community here would love to have the opportunity to partake in this great venture, but cannot prepare due to the uncertainty of the whole thing. The businesses here have the people with ability to be of great assistance in the early planning stages of the pipeline and in the overall working program, but unless decisions are made soon, the conditions are such that many of the old northerners will pull out and leave the chaos to the

money-grabbing southerners, as they have been called many times.

The town council here, as in Inuvik, Fort Simpson and other communities, is also at a dead end, for they cannot prepare without money, without planning and without decisions. The people likewise cannot prepare for the future, for a future of what? Unprecedented boom? Or irrevocable depression? The government cannot prepare, for although everyone and everything depends on their wisdom and money, neither can be seen under the smoke-screen of uncertainty, lack of money, lack of planning, lack of personnel, lack of power, lack of direction and lack of decision.

What will be the results of a decision in favour of the pipeline? Chaos. And what will be the results of a decision against the pipeline? A depression and more chaos. [C2090ff.]

Northern businessmen are not alone in finding that they exert little influence on the course of events: businessmen in the provinces face the same problem. Northern businessmen, however, face a variety of other problems that are not usually encountered in the provinces. Local markets are small, and the connections among them are not well-developed. The supply of a commodity or service may exist in one community, and there may be a demand for it in another community nearby, but there may be no means of bridging the gap between the supply and the prospective buyers. Northern businesses are distant from sources of supply, and not only is the cost of transportation extremely high, but water-borne transporation is seasonal. Inventory costs are therefore also high. Capital markets that are normally available to southern firms are virtually absent in the North.

Many small firms in the Mackenzie Delta have made substantial investments on the strength of the high level of hydrocarbon exploration that prevailed in the early 1970s.

The recent drop in such activity there has resulted in losses, some of them considerable. Thus businessmen in the Delta are, not surprisingly, eager to see the pipeline project proceed. Without an affirmative decision soon, they fear there will be a further decline in business activity in the area. I think it is fair to say that virtually all of the businessmen in the Mackenzie Valley and the Mackenzie Delta feel that the pipeline would enable them to profit from unprecedented growth and expansion.

It is unlikely that, in the ordinary course of events, the pipeline company and its contractors would rely at all strongly on local firms, for such firms would be unable to supply the goods and services in the volumes and with the regularity that a project as large as the pipeline would require. The pipeline company, if it is to keep its schedules, will have to rely extensively on firms from the South. Nor would it be desirable for northern firms to be drawn completely into activities closely related to the pipeline. Their services would be needed by the local market.

I have no doubt that terms and conditions could be imposed on the grant of a right-of-way that would enable northern businesses to expand during the construction of the pipeline. In Volume Two of this report, I shall lay out a scheme to give appropriate preferences to northern business, along the lines of the scheme already accepted in principle by the Department of Indian Affairs and Northern Development for public expenditures North of 60. Such a scheme is essential if northern business is to take full advantage of the pipeline boom.

But there are hazards for northern businessmen. Construction of the Mackenzie Valley pipeline could produce a serious distortion of the small-business sector of the

Norman Wells refinery. (GNWT)

Electric light station, Fort Simpson, 1898.
(Alberta Archives)

Oil well — Norman Wells, 1921. (Public Archives)

Mine machine shop, Yellowknife. (NFB–McNeill)

Northwest Territories. This would raise problems for orderly development of regional economic and commercial activity in the long run. Local businessmen might be drawn too heavily into ventures directly associated with the pipeline, and therefore be vulnerable to fluctuations in the fortunes of the oil and gas industry. Indirectly, this dependence could lead to uncertainty in the lives of those who work for or depend upon local businesses. The consequences of a bust are evident: persons and institutions that have become dependent upon a high level of economic activity may quite suddenly find, in the bust, that they have lost heavily. In the case of native people and of whites permanently resident in the North, these losses may be still more acute. Booms often mean that alternative sources of revenue or livelihood are curtailed or eliminated. In this way, the risks intrinsic to the effects of total intrusion are realized.

But the fear of a bust following the boom is likely to mean that every effort will be made to keep the boom going. This course would produce other, less obvious problems. Dependence upon a high level of economic activity, such as that generated by the petroleum industry, would result in the need, often acute, to keep that activity underway and expanding. Anyone who believes that his livelihood or the economy of the region can be maintained only by more exploration, followed by more development, will urge further exploration and development. This is the treadmill effect to which I referred earlier. It offers the possibility of cumulative impact of every kind, with any alternative form of economic development excluded.

Impact on the Native Economy

What is the place of the native people in the northern economy today? Many of them receive welfare, old-age pensions and family allowances, but most of them are at the edge of the capital and income flows that dominate the northern economy. Native people earning wages are engaged mainly in low paid, unskilled, casual or seasonal employment.

In 1972, Dr. Chun-Yan Kuo prepared *A Study of Income Distribution in the Mackenzie District of Northern Canada,* which revealed that in 1969-1970, the mean annual per capita cash income of whites living in the Mackenzie District was $3,545, of Metis $1,147, of Inuit $840, and of Indians $667. The study also indicated that 22 percent of the native people of the Mackenzie District received a cash income of less than $4,000; only one percent of the native population had an income in excess of $10,000. In contrast, 22 percent of the white families had an income above $10,000. Mean income for white families was $9,748; for Indian families $2,568. There is no reason to believe there has been any significant change in the proportional distribution of income in the Northwest Territories since Kuo's study was made.

These differences in income show the extent to which the developed money economy of the North is confined to urbanized enclaves. Kuo's figures did not, of course, take into account the extent to which the native people still live off the land: income in kind is still vital to native people. If they were to be totally absorbed into the industrial system, whether employed or unemployed, they would lose their income in kind.

Such wage employment as the native people have had has not suddenly put an end to their reliance upon country food, nor to their earnings from trapping and the sale of furs. Indeed, because wage-earners can afford to improve their equipment, a wage income can actually be beneficial to the traditional economy. But, in the longer run, the trend toward an industrial economy leads to a decline in the use of land and in the harvesting of country food.

This trend has its influence on income distribution within small communities. The native people have always shared the food they obtain from the land. Such produce is shared more readily than money, and the land is generally regarded as communal. The shift towards a money economy has created new possibilities for poverty: those in want are more likely to stay in want, and inequalities in native communities can become more marked. If income in whatever form it may take is not shared, it is possible for the average per capita income to rise at the same time the number of households experiencing poverty is also increasing. The number of poor people and a community's total cash income may rise concurrently. No assessment of the economic gains and losses of oil and gas development in the North can overlook a predictable decline in the native economy and the losses that decline will entail for virtually every native family in the North. Economic development will make native communities poorer in some ways as they become richer in others.

The impact of large-scale labour recruitment on the small communities will be felt by everyone in them: its intrusion into village social life will not be selective but total. With small-scale economic developments, persons who are particularly qualified for, or inclined towards, wage labour are selected or select themselves; with large-scale developments, all available manpower is recruited and moved to the place of work. Because the hunters and trappers who work only occasionally are usually regarded as partially or wholly unemployed, there will be pressures exerted on them to take wage employment, with results that will be felt throughout the traditional sector of the northern economy. These pressures are intensified by the fact that the men whose lives are most firmly committed to the harvesting of renewable resources also suffer from recurrent cash problems. So it is that the persons — or even whole communities — that have the strongest cultural and personal links with the land and its resources are the ones that are most firmly pushed towards participation in industrial activities. Hence the effect of total intrusion into community life.

Of course, if the pipeline is built, it will tend to justify itself in the statistical tables. The gross domestic product of the region will increase substantially. Per capita income will rise. Consultants who now recommend the construction of the pipeline on the grounds that it will benefit the native people of the North, will be succeeded by consultants willing to support whatever conclusions government and industry are then anxious to justify.

Statistics enable you to keep the problem at one remove. When using figures, you do not have to consider the reality of what is happening on the ground; with pages of text, flow charts and graphs, you can express ideas about cash income and gross domestic product and avoid all consideration of what is really occurring among the families of the native communities.

Any community, in the North or in the South, would bear certain social costs if it were associated in any way with a project of the magnitude of the proposed pipeline.

These costs, which include urban congestion, shortage of housing, separation of families, alcoholism, violence and crime, and problems of mental health, are magnified in the North. The social and health services that are provided to deal with these ills are a spin-off from the project, and they, too, are sometimes categorized as a form of economic growth. The federal and territorial governments will provide these services, but their cost should be regarded as a debit, not a credit, in any cost-benefit analysis.

You may question why I am pessimistic about the prospect of the pipeline as a means of bringing the native people more fully into the industrial system. Can they not participate in some way or other in such a project and reap the benefits that so many people firmly believe can be realized? If the native people cannot be painlessly transformed into industrial workers, is it not, nevertheless, inevitable that they must become industrial workers, albeit painfully?

The fact of the matter is, however, that if the North continues to be regarded solely as a frontier for industrial development, there will not be an assimilation that is either more or less painful. On the contrary, the North will become the home of a demoralized, confused and increasingly angry people who believe that they have been oppressed and weakened ever since white men came to their land.

The impact on the native economy of pipeline construction in the near future would be serious, perhaps irreparable. Pipeline construction now, and all that it would bring, would impel the northern economy during the next generation or more toward further industrial development. If that shift occurs now, before the native economy has been strengthened, the very possibility of strengthening it will have been undermined.

All northerners seek a diversified economy, but the possibility of diversification, which depends upon strengthening the renewable resource sector, will be lost if we build the pipeline now.

Employment and the Pipeline

The Question of Unemployment

Jack Witty, Chief of the Employment Division, Department of Economic Development, Government of the Northwest Territories, told the Inquiry that there is a labour force of 17,000 in the Northwest Territories. This figure represents all persons, male and female, between the ages of 14 and 65, in the Northwest Territories. According to Witty, there are between 10,000 and 12,000 jobs, and he concluded, therefore, that 5,000 or more people have no jobs. Most of those employed work for the Government of Canada, the Government of the Northwest Territories, local municipal bodies, the mining industry, and the oil and gas industry, a largely white work force. When, therefore, we talk about unemployed northerners, we are talking about 5,000 or more native people in the Northwest Territories whom the government regards as unemployed.

But these calculations have an unreal flavour. The labour force figure of 17,000 comprises all persons, male and female, between the ages of 14 and 65 — including housewives, many children in school, the disabled and ill, and even able-bodied adults engaged in hunting, fishing and trapping. can be seen at once that such a figure is an unsound basis for determining what the potential labour force really is. Calculation

A government-funded Local Initiatives Project, Jean Marie River. (Native Press)

Pipline welding, Alaska. (Alyeska)

Oil rig worker. (DIAND)

Pipeline research, Inuvik. (NFB—McNeill)

derived from it obscure, rather than reveal, how many able-bodied persons are working or might actively be seeking work.

The concept of endemic unemployment among the native people of the Northwest Territories has been one of the primary justifications for the pipeline project. Official willingness to justify construction of a pipeline on the basis of an inflated figure for unemployment complements the official tendency to discount the importance of the native economy. Witty's testimony is an example of this tendency:

> ... there is no equality of opportunity for employment — because the employment simply does not exist. Of 67 communities in the Northwest Territories, only 9 [Yellowknife, Hay River, Pine Point, Tungsten, Inuvik, Arctic Bay, Resolute Bay, Echo Bay and Norman Wells] ... could be considered to have a substantial economic base outside government support....

> The population of the 67 communities ... is estimated at 45,488 [May 1976]. The population of the 9 communities that I consider to have a reasonable degree of employment stability is 20,251 or slightly less than 50 percent of the total. [F31223ff.]

This analysis does not take into account the continuing strength of the native economy that sustains communities like Sachs Harbour, Holman, Paulatuk, Colville Lake and Trout Lake. Hunting, trapping and fishing for subsistence are simply ignored.

Of course, many native people do seek wage employment, and many of them find it. But what they seek is employment on a seasonal basis, as part of a wage-and-subsistence economic mix. Very few are seeking permanent employment in the industrial system.

Public servants who have perceived an overriding necessity to provide industrial wage employment for the unemployed native people have also tended to regard the native economy as moribund. This perception became fixed in the 1960s, when the native economy was at its nadir because of more than a decade of low fur prices, administrative neglect, and rapid social change.

Although it is a mistake to talk about a pool of 5,000 or more unemployed persons in the Northwest Territories today, it is nevertheless true that a significant number of native persons may properly be classified as unemployed or underemployed. I do not pretend to know how many such persons there are, and I venture to say that no one knows for sure.

Even were we to assume that the number of unemployed is large, and that it will be increased by the entry into the labour market of a large school-age population, certain questions would still remain. Without increased wage employment, will the native people have to choose between a life in the North on welfare or relocation to Southern Canada? Can pipeline construction offer them opportunities for meaningful and productive employment? Or, as the native people themselves have argued in the testimony quoted in these pages, does that opportunity lie in the strengthening of the native economy?

Pipeline Employment

Northern policy-makers have concluded that the only way to supply jobs to unemployed northern people is to build a pipeline. But would a pipeline supply these jobs? I think that we can ensure that, through a scheme of preferential hiring, native people who want to work on the pipeline will be given the opportunity to do so. But let there

be no doubt about this point: the work offered them will not solve the long-term problem of native employment as it is understood by government officials.

This extract from the brief submitted by the Pipeline Contractors Association of Canada offers an insight into this difficulty:

> Pipeline construction is a relatively new sector of the construction industry. It was not until the year 1947 that pipeline construction came into prospect as a major construction force in Canada. The construction of pipelines is unique by comparison to other types of construction. Work methods, techniques, specialized equipment and employee skills are peculiar to this type of construction.

> The pipeline construction spread is made up of several production units or crews which are interdependent. Welding standards, to ensure quality welds with structural integrity, require intensive training on the part of employees operating welding equipment in the down-hand, stick rod, semi-automatic and fully automatic welding techniques. The specialized equipment utilized in pipeline construction is rarely, if ever, used in other sectors of the construction industry. Such equipment ... requires specially trained operators.

> During the early to mid-1950s, the major pipeline construction projects in Canada were carried out by contractors of American origin. Because there were few, if any, Canadian workmen with the specialized skills for this work, it was necessary to import American personnel to the extent of approximately 90 percent of the skilled work force. [F27836ff.]

Today the highly skilled jobs in the Canadian pipeline construction industry are filled by Canadians. But this state of affairs has taken a generation to achieve.

Only now is it becoming apparent that no skilled jobs will be open to the native people. Skilled jobs on the pipeline will not be available to them because they have no training for these types of jobs and, even were they to qualify for these jobs, once the pipeline was finished, they would have to travel to other parts of the world to pursue their specialized trade. In fact, very few native northerners have ever left the North to pursue successfully a career in the South.

There will be severe limitations on the type of work native northerners can do. During clearing and grading, some native people would operate heavy equipment and drive trucks, but most of them would be employed in cutting brush. During pipelaying, some native workers would be employed in semi-skilled jobs, but most of them would be employed in various unskilled capacities.

It is all very well for Arctic Gas to say that there will be employment for everyone, but the pipeline contractors and the unions — not Arctic Gas — will be controlling the hiring. And the unions (the Plumbers and Pipefitters, Operating Engineers, Teamsters and Labourers), in a letter to the Inquiry, dated January 14, 1977, made their view of the matter plain enough:

> The Unions and the contractors have the ability to absorb new trainees into the pipeline construction industry with reasonable assurance of employment continuity depending upon the volume of pipeline work that follows the northern pipeline construction and provided that the trainees are willing to move to pipeline construction projects in various parts of Canada. Training in pipeline skills will not afford northern residents long-term employment opportunities within their own locale. Those who will wish to remain in the North must be satisfied to obtain a basic training and upgrading in pipeline skills for the term of the project. The greatest long-term employment opportunities in the territories will accrue to those residents who receive training and obtain tradesmen's qualifications in the building construction phase of the project.

> The Unions agree that the Government role

should be restricted to providing guidelines to be followed in evolving a plan for their commitment to northern participation in the pipeline project as an alternative to Government-imposed stipulations. However, the unions are not willing to make any commitments with respect to northern participation at the present time for the following reasons:

> a) Unions are expecting no change in their methods of operations insofar as entry requirements and apprenticeship programs are concerned.
> b) It is felt that the situation differs between skilled and unskilled trades people, and therefore the unions cannot entertain the acceptance of new members until an actual count is made of the various skills available.
> c) Persons trained by and skilled on industrial projects are often found to be poor workers on pipeline projects.
> d) The tenure of a worker on a pipeline project is seldom lengthy enough for proper training.
> e) The chances of continuing employment in the pipeline construction industry are very low unless the worker is willing to move extensively to the various and ever-changing locations of construction activity....

> The criteria for entry into the unions are based on skills possessed. The emphasis on northern manpower delivery should be directed toward plant construction, as opposed to pipeline construction, for the possibilities of longer employment and continued use of acquired skills....

> The consensus of the Advisory Council is that heavy emphasis in programming northern participation must be placed on the building and construction trades, where there is at least some assurance of a continuity of apprenticeship training that is not found with the pipeline construction trades. [p. 2ff.]

The unions say that northern manpower delivery should be directed toward plant construction, as opposed to pipeline construction, for the possibilities of longer

employment and continued use of acquired skills. What they mean is that native people, in order to obtain skills that will be of lasting use to themselves and the North, should seek employment, not on the pipeline, but on the construction of the gas plants in the Delta, and presumably on the construction of the compressor stations. This statement is altogether at variance with the position taken by counsel for Arctic Gas at the close of the hearings. At that time, Arctic Gas maintained, as they have from the beginning, that pipeline construction would offer the native people an opportunity to acquire skills that would be of continuing benefit to them in the North. In my judgment, this position is not tenable. And, moreover, no evidence has been advanced to show that there will be a significant number of opportunities for native people to acquire long-term skills on gas plant or compressor station construction.

The positions available to northern natives will be unskilled; so far as semi-skilled employment may be available to them, it will consist largely of employment as operators of trucks and heavy equipment. Except on the Mackenzie and Dempster Highways there will be no long-term requirement for any considerable number of these operators, once the pipeline is built. In fact, with the cutback in the Mackenzie Highway construction program, there is already a surplus of native heavy equipment operators.

David Boorkman gave us this picture of the employment of native people on the trans-Alaska pipeline project:

> On a statewide basis, a significant number of natives have been hired by Alyeska. It has been estimated that 5,100 individual natives have worked for Alyeska and that 8,000 total jobs have been filled by natives. These totals are the result of the four major native employment programs now in effect in Alaska. [F24325ff.]

Cookhouse at gold mine, Yellowknife. (NFB—Pearce)

Learning to operate heavy equipment, Fort Smith. (Native Press)

Work Arctic employee, Alex Tambour of Hay River. (GNWT)

Hire North camp. (GNWT)

But only a small percentage of the Alaskan native people employed have come from rural areas. No surveys of the pipeline's impact on the small villages in the state have been completed, but some statistics are available. We know that, in June 1975, the percentages of rural native people then or previously employed on the pipeline was low, ranging from over 20 percent of the total population for Allakaket to two or three percent for Nenana and Anderson. Many native people complained about the difficulty of obtaining work on the pipeline because most of the unions required them to register at the union hiring halls in Fairbanks and to be there when the call for employment was made. This requirement entailed the difficulty and expense of travelling to Fairbanks. Rural natives were also dissatisfied because they lacked information concerning pipeline employment, the union hiring hall procedures, and the relationship between the various federal, state and native organizations, including the Alaska Federation of Natives, the Bureau of Indian Affairs, and the State Department of Labor.

By learning from the Alaskan experience we can, I believe, overcome some of the problems that the native people in Alaska had in obtaining employment. But I do not want to pretend that any scheme for native preference in hiring would necessarily be wholly effective in placing native people on the job. Once construction is underway, the unions will have a measure of control over hiring that will make it likely that their own hiring rules will be enforced, rather than any procedure recommended by this Inquiry, even if it has the sanction of Parliament. But let us assume that we could ensure that thousands of native people were given work on the pipeline: What would have been achieved then?

In the past, the Adult Vocational Training Centre at Fort Smith emphasized the training of heavy-duty equipment operators. Today, many of these operators are unable to use the skills they have acquired. How much heavy equipment can there be in Sachs Harbour, Gjoa Haven or Arctic Bay? At least four or five men in Sachs Harbour know how to operate such equipment, but, at the latest report, there was only one such machine there. And, very likely, there is no need for more than one. In many villages we heard the same sort of story.

During the past two decades, northern native people have been drawn into large-scale construction projects, from the building of the DEW Line to the construction of the Mackenzie Highway. In every case, many of them acquired a range of experience and a variety of skills. But when each of these projects was completed or cut back, most of the jobs disappeared. The native people went back to their communities, possessing knowledge and skills many of them would never use again. More important still, while these major projects were underway, government administration and the industrial economy intruded with particular force into the daily lives of the native communities and greatly inhibited the normal functioning of the renewable resource economy. Following the completion of these major projects, the native people who had worked with them often found themselves left with reduced, rather than expanded, options.

Hire North

Hire North, a program established by the federal government in 1972, sought to find ways in which native people could work together as a unit and at the same time acquire the kinds of skills that are best learned on the job. In this way, the native people could learn skills and work habits that would assist them to enter the wage economy on a permanent basis.

Hire North was given a contract, without competitive bidding, to carry out the clearing and subgrading of approximately 17 miles of the Mackenzie Highway north of Fort Simpson. The usual shift was for 30 days, at the end of which time a worker could go home to rest or he could stay on the job for another shift. By this means, Hire North provided hundreds of jobs for native men. In this sense, it was a success. In another sense, however, it was a failure. One objective of the program was to train men for employment with contractors who were constructing other sections of the Mackenzie Highway. Although most of the men, while with Hire North, had learned to operate road-building equipment, most of them were still not prepared to work with the fully experienced equipment operators and shift-bosses that the contractors employed; few native workers lasted very long with any of the contractors.

Now the Mackenzie Highway construction program has ceased, except for some work on a small part of the route. What happened to all of those native people who had learned new skills while employed by the Hire North project? The Government of the Northwest Territories was unable to tell us how many, if any, are currently employed in work that makes use of whatever skills were acquired during employment on Hire North. It seems plain that their skills are not now marketable. Probably many of them are considered to be unemployed, but no doubt some of them returned to hunting, fishing and trapping and are not really unemployed.

NORTRAN

The petroleum industry's showpiece for the training of northern native people is the Northern Petroleum Industry Training Program (NORTRAN). Funded by both pipeline companies and by Imperial, Gulf and Shell, NORTRAN was begun in 1971 to provide training in the operational phases of the industry.

Trainees are chosen on the basis of academic qualifications and job-experience levels. After an orientation course, usually at the Adult Vocational Training Centre at Fort Smith, they are sent to Alberta, where they learn to operate and maintain gas pipelines and gas plants. Housing is provided for them and their families, and they are given various kinds of extra instruction as well as on-the-job training. The program is intended to prepare them to return to the North and, in due course, take employment in operations and maintenance jobs in the petroleum industry. If the trainees should not wish to return North, or if no pipelines or gas plants are built in the North, the companies have guaranteed them permanent jobs in the South. One of the principal differences between NORTRAN and other training schemes for native people over the years is that in NORTRAN all of the trainees are supposed to be enrolled and treated as employees.

However, like the other northern training programs, NORTRAN has met with mixed success. When the program began, there were 16 trainees; in April 1976, 117 trainee positions were available, of which 109 were occupied. Of these, 93 were held by northerners. Of 224 trainees who have entered the program since its inception, 115 have dropped out. The principal reasons given for dropping out were loneliness and homesickness, which in many cases led to excessive drinking, absenteeism and, eventually, to termination of training.

NORTRAN has nothing to do with training for employment on the pipeline itself; its training is for the 200-250 permanent jobs in operations and maintenance that will become available once the pipeline is built. The industry rightly maintains that only in operations and maintenance will there be long-term jobs or careers for northern native people in the industry. However, Barry Virtue of NORTRAN expressed his concern over whether or not NORTRAN will be able to retain its trainees, once pipeline construction, with its highly paid work, actually begins. NORTRAN is prepared to send any of its trainees to sites where they may obtain construction experience and continue their training for operations jobs, but it is recognized that many trainees may then desert the program in favour of unskilled but well paid work.

NORTRAN officials are still trying to recruit men from the Mackenzie Valley and the Mackenzie Delta, despite the fact that, out of a reported 400 applicants, they regarded only about 25 as suitable, by virtue of their academic backgrounds, for the program.

Is it going to be feasible to train northerners for skilled work in pipeline construction? The unions say it is not. They say (quite apart from their contention that their own members must come first) that such training should take place on the job. However, the last major pipeline built in Canada was the Sarnia-Montreal oil pipeline and no pipeline is at present under construction. It is, therefore, not possible at present to train any large number of northerners anywhere in Canada for the skilled work that pipeline construction will require.

Employment and Unemployment

Except during the construction phase of a project, the petroleum industry is capital- rather than labour-intensive. Those who argue that the employment of native people on a project like the pipeline will equip them with skills that will be of lasting use to them and to the North have not made their case. What is more, that case is based on an idea of native aspirations and needs that is at odds with what so many of the native people themselves have expressed to this Inquiry. The pipeline, even if it were to provide many long-term jobs, would not solve the problems of the northern economy.

It is, perhaps, worth considering at this point the employment of native people in the government sector. At present the Government of Canada, including crown corporations, employs about 1,900 in the Northwest Territories: only about 250 of these jobs are held by natives, and their work is mainly clerical or unskilled labour. It is now 10 years since the Government of the Northwest Territories transferred its headquarters from Fort Smith to Yellowknife. Yet, in 1976 out of 3,069 people on the payroll of the Government of the Northwest Territories only 603, or 20 percent, were native and of these 603, most worked at clerical or unskilled labour.

Both government and business have insisted on the importance of introducing the native people into wage employment. This has been one of the reasons for the subsidies provided to industrial development in the North. Quotas requiring a certain number of native employees have been imposed by

Native crew clearing brush on Mackenzie Highway. (GNWT)

NORTRAN trainee. (Arctic Gas)

Student at Adult Vocational Training Centre, Fort Smith. (GNWT)

Inuit touring Pine Point mine. (DIAND)

have not, however, been met, and all concerned have expressed dismay. No one yet has been ready to examine the false assumption that lay behind the quotas. If the creation of jobs for native northerners is really a primary objective, there must be better ways of achieving it, from the point of view of northern development, than the past and present emphasis on the extraction of non-renewable resources.

In the past few years, Imperial, Gulf and Shell together have been employing about 250 native people at any one time in the Mackenzie Delta at the peak of their winter drilling season. Although the average length of employment is only nine weeks per worker, these jobs have assumed a real importance for Delta people, especially for the Inuit. It should not be forgotten, however, that there are grave social problems in Inuvik and Tuktoyaktuk, and that many of these problems are closely associated with the intrusion of the oil and gas industry into them. The most serious problem of all may, in the end, turn out to be the dependence that the native people are coming to have on industrial employment. In the absence of an alternative source of income, people may become locked into a dependence on the oil and gas industry — whatever its relation to their environment or to their culture and aspirations. They may, therefore, quickly come to the point where they feel unable to oppose further industrial development. People who are locked into an economic condition because of their dependence on it can only acquiesce in the perpetuation of that condition.

When we consider the creation of employment for northern native people, we must be quite clear, however, about the unemployment that may also be created. Policymakers in Ottawa and Yellowknife have tended to underestimate the extent to which native northerners are gainfully employed. Men who support their families — and even have surplus to share among other families — can hardly be said to be idle. Yet, there has been a tendency — and it seems to be one that persists — to classify such persons as unemployed, the result, obviously, of equating the category "employed" with that of "wage-earner." But, in native economic life, there are persons who, at any given time, may not be wage-earners, but who are nonetheless productively employed. I suggest that such persons should be regarded as "self-employed."

If, however, communities in the Mackenzie Valley and Western Arctic are made to depend exclusively on industrial wage employment — if the production of country food for local consumption ceases to be an important component in the economy, then the self-employed will certainly become the unemployed. The point is simple enough: the extension of the industrial system creates unemployment as well as employment. In an industrial economy there is virtually no alternative to a livelihood based on wage employment. Those who are unable or unprepared to work for wages become unemployed and then dependent on welfare. To the extent that the development of the northern frontier undermines the possibilities of self-employment provided by hunting, fishing and trapping, employment and unemployment will go hand-in-hand.

So, employment on the pipeline for native people will be seasonal. Seasonal employment, offering native people an opportunity to acquire cash to supplement their income from hunting, fishing and trapping, can, of course, be extremely useful. In some respects the seasonal wage employment available in the Delta has been just that. The danger lies, however, in the way that the intrusion of the industrial system leads to undermining and abandonment of the native renewable resource economy. This process has already been observed in the Delta, despite the fact that the seasonal wage employment available there (with the exception of Inuvik and Tuktoyaktuk) has, even over the past six years, been comparatively limited. The pipeline would offer seasonal employment for only two or three years. But it would intrude throughout the Mackenzie Valley and the Western Arctic in a way that would threaten the native economy to an unprecedented extent. Seasonal employment will be of little use to those who wish to maintain their own economic life: the very possibility for that economic life will have been removed.

If the Pipeline is Not Built Now

I have indicated that the economic impact of the pipeline will not bring lasting benefits to native northerners. In the next chapter, I shall outline the social costs of the project. They will be very high. And I shall have to say that construction of the pipeline now would irremediably compromise the goals embodied in native claims. All of these considerations lead inexorably to the conclusion that the pipeline should not be built now.

I speak of a postponement of the pipeline, not of its cancellation. Although the oil and gas reserves discovered so far in the Mackenzie Delta have been disappointing, the Government of Canada is committed to an exploration program of the oil and gas potential of the Beaufort Sea. The drilling program undertaken there by Dome Petroleum will continue and, if sufficient reserves of gas are discovered, in due course a pipeline may be built along the Mackenzie Valley to deliver this resource to market.

In their final submission, Arctic Gas urged the Inquiry to address this question: What will be the impact of a decision not to build a Mackenzie Valley pipeline now? They offered their own answer: they said that without a pipeline there would be no development of business opportunities, of employment, of economic growth in the Mackenzie Valley and the Western Arctic. They were supported in this answer by the Northwest Territories Chamber of Commerce and the Northwest Territories Association of Municipalities.

Jim Robertson, the Mayor of Inuvik, on behalf of the latter Association said that at least 50 percent of the present labour force in the Mackenzie Delta is employed directly or indirectly in oil and gas exploration and development. He insisted that, rightly or wrongly, education over the past 15 years has prepared the native people to take their place in the wage economy, and that there would be no alternative to out-migration from the Mackenzie Delta, if the pipeline did not proceed.

Robertson maintained that the pipeline would provide an urgently needed tax base for the larger centres in the North. He argued that there would necessarily be a reduction in the level of local services if the pipeline were not built, because there are not sufficient funds to pay for them. He pointed out that Northern Canada Power Commission, Northern Transportation Company Limited and other crown corporations have invested money in preparation for anticipated growth. If such growth does not occur, these companies will have to recover their capital

and their operating and maintenance costs from a much smaller market than they had anticipated. Robertson said that this situation would lead to economic hardship in communities like Inuvik. He also argued that the erosion of the local tax base could have as great, if not greater, adverse impact than that predicted as a result of pipeline construction:

> Without prospects of growth, capable persons in all areas of expertise together with many dedicated civil servants would again invariably have no option but to pursue their careers in geographic areas where personal fulfilment and family advancement could be obtained.

> While many families, especially in the smaller communities, could continue to provide for themselves with an existence from the land, it is doubtful that many would freely elect to live off the land on a full-time basis for an indefinite period of time.

Robertson concluded:

> Mr. Commissioner, the foregoing ideas are placed before you not to assume a disaster if resource development is discontinued, but to illustrate what the Association perceives could be some serious problem areas arising as a result of an indefinite moratorium on resource development. [F29713]

However the case is put, it reflects the concept that, without a pipeline, there will be no economic development in the Northwest Territories. I find this point of view an oversimplification of what might happen. It reflects a decade of insistence by political figures and spokesmen for the oil and gas industry that there can be no form of northern development except a pipeline; ergo, without a pipeline there will be no development in the North.

If the pipeline is not built, the northern economy will not come to a sudden halt. To begin with, the native economy will not be

seriously affected. The program of modernizing and expanding the native economy, which the native people have called for, can be undertaken. The mining industry will not be affected. The oil refinery at Norman Wells will not shut down. The Mackenzie River transportation system will continue to supply and resupply the communities of the Mackenzie Valley and the Western Arctic. The government bureaucracy, which is the largest employer and main source of income for both white and native northerners in the Northwest Territories, is not likely to diminish significantly in size simply because a pipeline is not built now.

Finally, a decision to postpone pipeline construction would not necessarily mean that oil and gas exploration in the North would be ended. As I said earlier, Dome's exploration program in the Beaufort Sea will continue, and exploration by independents is not likely to stop. I do not think the majors will necessarily cease drilling altogether: they would run the risk of losing their leases. In any event, if the federal government were to decide that, in the national interest, exploration should continue, Petro Canada is the instrument by which such a policy could be carried out.

Nevertheless, there would be a serious setback to Inuvik and perhaps (although this is less certain) to other Delta communities. Many northern businessmen, encouraged by spokesmen for the Government of Canada, have proceeded with their investment programs on the assumption that the Minister of Indian Affairs and Northern Development would grant a right-of-way, and the National Energy Board would grant a Certificate of Public Convenience and Necessity, to enable either the Arctic Gas or the Foothills project to proceed. Both government and the oil and gas industry have encouraged businessmen in this belief. If the pipeline is postponed, the losses that northern businessmen would suffer would be as attributable to the raising of these expectations as to the postponement itself.

As I have said, I am proceeding on the assumption that the oil and gas in the Mackenzie Delta and the Beaufort Sea will, in due course, be delivered to the South by a pipeline. Given this assumption, the setback ought not to be as severe as many northern businessmen have predicted. Although a number of businesses may suffer from a postponement, the fact is, the decline in oil and gas activity in the Delta over the past two years has already resulted in a significant reduction in business activity.

According to John MacLeod, an economist from Inuvik, most of the businesses in Inuvik were established between 1970 and 1973. They have operated at a very high level of activity because of the high level of exploration work that went on in the early 1970s. It is not necessary to start construction on a pipeline tomorrow to keep these businesses alive. What is necessary, according to MacLeod, is to keep the prospects for pipeline construction positive enough to maintain drilling activity. He said that these businesses would be healthy if drilling activity were maintained at its 1974 level.

Nevertheless, if expectations of ever building a pipeline are dampened, there will be a decline in business activity in the Mackenzie Delta, and some businesses may be forced to liquidate. But I do not think the decline would be as severe as Arctic Gas predict, because the drilling program in the Beaufort Sea will continue. This program has already created an unprecedented level of economic activity in Tuktoyaktuk, a level well above that reached during the peak years of oil and gas exploration in the Mackenzie Delta in the early 1970s. We are not contemplating the end of oil and gas activity in the Western Arctic. Exploration and related activities may be more strictly controlled, and development may be spread over longer periods of time than some have recently anticipated, but investment in the North will undoubtedly continue at moderate levels. This investment will continue to generate a range of economic opportunities that may fall short of a boom, but will certainly not be anything like the recession that many white businessmen seem to fear. The business community's disappointment would be real, but many of its gloomy economic forecasts would not.

Clockwise from top left:

Holman woman and baby. (P. Scott)

Danny Smith of Inuvik working on Great Slave Lake Railway, 1968. (Canadian National)

Houses dot landscape in isolated settlement. (GNWT)

Noel Crookedhand and son, Yellowknife. (R. Fumoleau)

Judicial party at Fort Providence, 1921. William Norn, lower right, was interpreter. (Public Archives)

Newly-constructed office, apartment and church complex, Yellowknife. (News of the North)

Social Impact

There is a tendency, in examining the impact of a large-scale industrial project, to accept the prospect of negative social impacts and to make recommendations for remedial measures that could or should be taken. There is also a tendency to minimize the importance of conclusions that are unsupported by "hard data." Usually those in favour of the project are able to say approximately how much it will cost, although experience with some other large-scale frontier projects, such as the James Bay hydro-electric project and the trans-Alaska pipeline, has indicated that the early estimates of costs have been completely unreliable. But at least there is a set of figures to work with, and they offer the comforting illusion that you are dealing with hard data.

In considering the social impact of large-scale developments, very few figures are available. All that can safely be said is that the social costs will be borne by the local population and that the financial costs will be borne by industry and the government. There is a strong tendency to underestimate and to understate social impact and social costs, and there is a tendency to believe that, whatever the problems may be, they can be overcome. The approach here is curative rather than preventive. No one asks for proof that the problems anticipated really can be ameliorated in a significant way — the assumption is that they can be. This assumption has been made with respect to problems of the proposed pipeline, and I think this assumption is demonstrably false.

Let me emphasize one thing at the outset: changes occur in the lives of everyone, changes that we have come to look upon as either necessary or inevitable. Everyone agrees that life is not static: each individual and every society has to accept change. A home owner may find that he has to give up six feet of land because a street is being widened, or his home may even be expropriated to make way for a new road. The location of a new airport near an urban centre may mean that hundreds of people must give up their homes. A farmer may have to agree to an easement across his land for hydro-electric transmission lines — or for a pipeline.

But the proposal to build a pipeline and to establish an energy corridor from the Arctic to the mid-continent will bring changes to the native people far greater in magnitude than the examples just mentioned. The pipeline and the energy corridor would change the North, alter a way of life and inhibit — perhaps extinguish — the native people's choices for the future.

The social impact that I foresee in the Mackenzie Valley and the Western Arctic, if we build the pipeline now, will be devastating — I use the word advisedly — and quite beyond our capacity to ameliorate in any significant way.

The Northern Population

There are two populations in the North, a native population and a white population. Although the latter has increased dramatically since the early days of the fur trade, the native people are still in the majority in the Northwest Territories. Native people fear that the pipeline and the energy corridor will bring with them an influx of white people into their homeland, with consequences that will be irreversible. Richard Nerysoo made that point in Fort McPherson:

> The pipeline means more [white people] who will be followed by even more white people. White people bring their language, their political system, their economy, their schools, their culture. They push the Indian aside and take over everything. [C1190]

It is important to understand the composition of the northern population and how it has changed under the impact of industrial development and the proliferation of government. Only on the basis of such an understanding can we predict the social impact of the pipeline on the people of the North.

A Hudson's Bay Company trading post was established at Fort Resolution in 1786, three years before Mackenzie's journey to the Arctic Ocean. Other posts along the Mackenzie River followed in the early years of the 19th century. James Anderson, in his 1858 census of the Dene trading at Forts Liard, Rae, Simpson, Wrigley, Norman, Good Hope and McPherson, estimated their total number at 3,000.

In the Delta, in 1840, the Hudson's Bay Company erected a trading post on the fringes of Inuit territory at Fort McPherson. At that time, according to Diamond Jenness, there were 2,000 Inuit inhabiting the Arctic coast between Demarcation Point (at what is now the international boundary between Alaska and the Yukon) and Cape Bathurst.

During the 19th century, the Metis became established in the North. They trace their ancestry through two sources: as descendents of the Metis who moved into the Mackenzie Valley from Manitoba and Saskatchewan after the Northwest Rebellion; and as descendents of unions between the early fur traders and Dene women.

Until the middle of the 19th century, except for a few European explorers, the only whites in the Mackenzie Valley were Hudson's Bay Company traders and their clerks. In the 1860s the missionaries came. The native people adapted their traditional life of subsistence hunting and fishing to a trapping and hunting economy, which included seasonal visits to a trading post and, later, to a mission near it. Although the fur trade introduced many technological innovations to native life and some dependence on manufactured goods, the people still lived on and from the land.

The Gold Rush

Toward the end of the 19th century, large numbers of whites poured into the North in search of gold: in 1898 alone, some 30,000 prospectors and others joined the Klondike gold rush and headed for Dawson City. Two anthropologists, Dr. Catherine McClellan and Julie Cruikshank, described to the Inquiry the effect of this influx on the Indians of the Southern Yukon:

> Indians along the route to the gold fields became temporarily involved in packing, guiding and providing food for the white prospectors. Some became deck hands on the river boats. A few Indian women married white prospectors and left the country. The Tagish, who were themselves involved in the discovery of gold, and the Han, who lived at the mouth of the Klondike River, were the natives most affected. The latter were virtually destroyed. [F23094]

When the excitement died away, at the turn of the century, most whites left the area. In 1900 the population of the Yukon had climbed to 27,000 (of whom about 3,000 were Indians), but by 1912 it had shrunk to 6,000, and by 1921 to 4,000.

The gold rush of 1898 also affected the native people of the Northwest Territories. One of the routes to the Klondike was down the Athabasca and Mackenzie Rivers to the Mackenzie Delta and then overland via the Rat River to the Porcupine River, or via the Peel River to the Wind River and thence

across to the Yukon. By the end of 1898, some 860 prospectors had reached Fort Smith, and an estimated 600 of them camped that winter in or near Fort McPherson. Some turned aside from their rush to the Klondike when news spread of rich gold deposits at the eastern end of Great Slave Lake. The influx of prospectors into the Mackenzie Valley played a significant part in the government's decision to make a treaty with the Indians in 1899. Charles Mair, a member of the Halfbreed Commission, which was established to deal with those Metis who chose not to sign the treaty, described what happened:

> The gold-seekers plunged into the wilderness of Athabasca without hesitation and without as much as "by your leave" to the native. Some of these marauders, as was to be expected, exhibited on the way a congenital contempt for the Indian's rights. At various places his horses were killed, his dogs shot, his bear-traps broken. An outcry arose in consequence, which inevitably would have led to reprisals and bloodshed had not the Government stepped in and forestalled further trouble by a prompt recognition of the native's title. ... The gold seeker was viewed with great distrust by the Indians, the outrages referred to showing, like straws in the wind, the inevitable drift of things had the treaties been delayed. For, as a matter of fact, those now peaceable tribes, soured by lawless aggression, and sheltered by their vast forests, might easily have taken an Indian revenge, and hampered, if not hindered, the safe settlement of the country for years to come. [cited in R. Fumoleau, As Long As This Land Shall Last, p. 48ff.]

Anglican missionaries were appalled by the corruption that accompanied the invasion of prospectors. One wrote:

> The influence of the class of people now rushing into the country in search of gold is worse than I can describe.

And another added:

> I have always dreaded the incoming of the mining population, on account of the effect it would have upon the morals of our people, but did not think it would touch us so closely. [cited in Fumoleau, op. cit., p. 49]

The prospectors who reached the Klondike by the Rat River left their imprint on the minds of the native people of Fort McPherson. They still remember the location of Destruction City, the miners' winter camp on the Rat. Some of the native people from Fort McPherson, who guided miners over the mountains to the Klondike, stayed there for a few years, earning their living by supplying Dawson City with meat.

Whalers, Traders and Trappers

In the 1890s, the American whaling fleet from San Francisco entered the Beaufort Sea, and Herschel Island and Baillie Islands, off Cape Bathurst, became the focal points for the whaling industry in the Western Arctic. Native people were attracted to these harbours where the whaling ships wintered, and they were hired to gather driftwood to conserve the ships' stocks of coal, and to hunt caribou and muskox to supply the whalers with fresh meat. Some winters there were as many as 600 white people at Herschel Island. Whaling took a heavy toll not only of the bowhead whales but also of muskoxen and caribou. But it was not just the animals that were affected. Diamond Jenness, in Eskimo Administration: Canada, provides us with a graphic description of the effect of the whalers on the Inuit of the Delta:

> Whaling ships churned the waters of the Beaufort Sea until about 1906. ... By that date not only had the number of whales and caribou gravely diminished, but the number of Eskimos also. A little earlier influenza and other diseases introduced by the whalers had produced a similar diminution in the population of the Eastern Arctic; but there, for some

HMS Discovery *wintering in arctic waters, 1895.* (Public Archives)

Mrs. Gerhart, first white woman at Great Bear Lake, 1932. (Public Archives)

Oil strike, Norman Wells, 1921. (Public Archives)

White man with Slavey Indians, 1922. (Public Archives)

reason which is not yet clear, the whaling captains had carried only limited stocks of intoxicating liquor, and had restricted its consumption very largely to their own crews. In the Western Arctic, on the other hand, they not only distributed liquor to the Eskimos with full hands, but taught them how to make it by distilling molasses or potatoes from one five gallon coal-oil can to another.... Syphilis took root among them, increasing the death-rate, especially of infants, and causing apparently widespread sterility. Then in 1902 some Indians who had contracted measles in Dawson City conveyed it to Fort McPherson, whence it reached the Eskimos of the Delta, carrying off nearly 100 persons, about one-fifth, Stefansson estimated, of the surviving population. This population continued to decline after the whalers departed, though the decline was masked by a stream of immigration from Arctic Alaska, set in motion by the depletion of the caribou in that region. [p. 14]

Dr. John Stager of the University of British Columbia told the Inquiry that, when the whaling industry collapsed in 1908, out of an original population of 2,500, there were only about 250 Mackenzie Eskimos left in the region between Barter Island and Bathurst Peninsula.

Yet in 1901 the resident white population of what is now the Northwest Territories was still only 137. It included Hudson's Bay Company factors, free traders, white trappers, missionaries and some church and residential school personnel. The first Northwest Mounted Police detachment was established in 1903; then came Indian Agents, nursing sisters and game officers.

By 1919-1920, fur prices had achieved a very high level, and white trappers and traders entered the Mackenzie Valley and Western Arctic in large numbers. There were 110 trading stores in 1920 in the Northwest Territories; the number doubled by 1927. In Fort Rae alone, 41 trading

licences were issued in 1926. Statistics compiled by the RCMP in 1923 show that there were 118 white trappers in the area around Fort Smith and Fort Resolution.

During this period of intense competition, the Hudson's Bay Company's trade monopoly was broken, and the nature of the fur trade was altered. In particular, the old practice of outfitting the native hunters on credit was replaced by the cash system.

The Rise of Industry

The discovery of oil at Norman Wells in 1920 brought another surge of white people into the Mackenzie Valley. In the winter of 1921, some 24 parties travelled by dog team from Edmonton to Fort Norman to stake claims, and other parties came overland from Dawson City and Whitehorse. Before the first steamer reached Fort Providence that summer, boats of every description had passed the village on their way north. Most of these white people left as quickly as they had come. In 1921, after the signing of Treaty 11, the census for the Northwest Territories indicated there were nearly 4,000 Indians living in the Northwest Territories, but only 853 "others" — a category including Metis, non-status Indians and whites.

In the years after the signing of Treaty 11, the native population was increasingly ravaged by the diseases the white people had brought. Father René Fumoleau told the Inquiry:

A discouraged Doctor Bourget, Indian Agent at Fort Resolution, wrote in 1927, "We seem to be in a period of readjustment which will show seriously on the Indians." Deaths from tuberculosis alone outnumbered births in most places. Many infants died a few months after birth. Most families lost parents and children alike. Periodic outbursts of smallpox, measles and flu took a heavy toll over the years. In 1928, the influenza epidemic struck

the Mackenzie District. While all the whites recovered, the sickness killed 600 Indians, one-sixth of the Indian population. At Goulet's camp near Yellowknife, 26 Indians died and the seven survivors fled in panic. [F21835]

Prospecting and mining brought a significant increase in the white population. The richest uranium mine in the world opened at Port Radium in 1932. When gold was discovered at Yellowknife in 1933, prospectors and miners rushed to stake claims there. In 1937, there were 400 prospectors searching for minerals in the Mackenzie District. Census figures for the Northwest Territories have always been unreliable, but we know that during the 1930s the number of people classified as "other" stood at 1,007 in 1931, and swelled to 4,000 by 1941. In the same decade, the population classified as Indian and Eskimo rose by only 700.

Since the Second World War, the white population in the Northwest Territories has increased rapidly. Hay River, for example, which is now an important transportation centre, has changed from a small Indian community into a predominantly white town of 3,500, with the Indian village on its periphery. The Mayor of Hay River, Don Stewart, described the changes since the Second World War:

I came to the Territories in 1946, as a young married man and have remained, with the exception of two years since that date, in Hay River. Through this period of time we have noted many changes. ... When I first came to Hay River there was only the Indian village on the east bank of the river, one small Imperial Oil tank, a dirt runway with an American Quonset hut, a leftover of the Northwest Staging Route, an emergency landing field for aircraft going to Alaska during the last war. ... The Americans had come and gone. ... There were five white people in Hay River. We found a village that was self-sufficient, we found people with pride ... we found people living in the same type of housing ... everything was similar.... Everybody had the 45-gallon barrel in the corner that sufficed for [a] water supply, and this was, for the most part, ice that was cut during the winter time and used in the summer time. There were no vehicles to speak of. I think we had one truck in Hay River at that time. [C409ff.]

Mining, development of transportation facilities and oil and gas exploration have all contributed to the growth of the white population in the Mackenzie Valley and the Western Arctic.

The Government Era

The proliferation of government in the North has been the chief cause of the growth of the white population since the Second World War. An increasing number of white people administer the health, education and welfare services now provided to the native people in various regional centres. In 1953, there were between 250 and 300 federal employees in the Northwest Territories. In 1966, there were about 2,600. With the establishment of the territorial government in Yellowknife in 1967 came a further increase. By 1976, there were something like 3,000 employees on the payroll of the Government of the Northwest Territories alone, and in addition there were approximately 2,000 employees of the Government of Canada and of federal crown corporations in the Northwest Territories. Of these 5,000 government employees, 80 percent or more are white; they and their families account for the majority of the white population of the Mackenzie Valley and the Western Arctic, if not the Northwest Territories as a whole. And, unlike earlier waves of white in-migration into the North, this one has not receded.

Although the white population in the North has increased dramatically in the last 20 years, the majority of whites who go North still think of home as somewhere in the South. They soon leave, to be replaced by others. This is characteristic of the employees of the Government of Canada, the Government of the Northwest Territories, and of the mining and the oil and gas industries. Indeed, in the three years since the Inquiry was appointed, the Department of Indian Affairs and Northern Development has had three Regional Directors of Northern Operations and three Regional Representatives, Indian Affairs Program, in the Northwest Territories. Members of the RCMP and the Canadian Forces perform a tour of duty, then they too return south. At Fort Resolution, in a graveyard 85 years old, only two white adults and two white children are buried.

A large percentage of the white population in the North is on rotation: the numbers increase, but the faces constantly change. Some individuals do remain who have decided to make the North their permanent home. Their numbers are increasing slowly, but not in the dramatic way that the white population as a whole has increased.

Northern Population Today

What is the composition of the population of the Northwest Territories today? In 1974, the latest year for which figures from the Government of the Northwest Territories are available, there were 7,533 people classified as Indian, almost all of whom lived in the Mackenzie Valley and the Mackenzie Delta; 13,932 classified as Inuit, of whom some 2,300 resided in the Mackenzie Delta and Beaufort Sea communities; and 16,384 "others."

This ethnic breakdown into Indian, Inuit and "others" is not, however, as helpful as it

may appear. The people classified as India are only those whose names are on the ban lists. The number of Indians does not, there fore, include non-status Indians — persons of Indian ancestry who have become enfran chised under the Indian Act. An India might, in the past, have sought enfranchise ment for a number of reasons: to vote, to bu liquor — things that treaty Indians then ha no legal right to do. The most commo example of enfranchisement has been by th operation of law when a treaty India woman married a non-status Indian, a Met or a white man. Such marriages are n uncommon, and when they occur, th woman ceases to be an Indian under the law she and her children are henceforth enumer ated as "others." Virtually all of non-statu Indians still regard themselves as Dene, ju like their treaty relatives, and at the commu nity hearings their views were indistingu ishable from those of Dene who are sti treaty Indians. The distinction, therefor between treaty and non-status Indians, fc my purposes, is not significant. Virtually a of these people regard themselves as Den Nor does the category described as Indian i the census include people of combine white-and-Indian ancestry who regar themselves as Metis and distinct in the heritage from the Dene and the white popu lations. These people, too, are included in th census as "others."

Because the Indian Act was never applie to the Eskimos, the distinction betwee status and non-status categories has nev been legally relevant to them. The childre of non-Eskimo fathers married to Eskim women acquired "disc numbers" — th method of identifying the Eskimos until th 1960s — and they were counted as Eskimos.

To arrive at an accurate count of th native peoples, we must add to the figur

Yellowknife then and now:
Mining town, 1940. (Public Archives)

Modern housing. (NFB—Pearce)

Franklin Avenue. (GNWT)

"Rainbow Valley," native housing area.
(Native Press)

for Indian and Inuit a portion of the number designated "others," because these "others" include non-status Indians and Metis. The number of non-status Indians and Metis is a matter of dispute. In attempting to determine actual figures I have considered the evidence of the Government of the Northwest Territories, the Indian Brotherhood, the Metis Association, and Dr. Charles Hobart. I have also examined the 1976 Preliminary Counts of the Census Divisions of the Government of Canada. I do not think there are more than 4,500 non-status Indians and Metis altogether.

The number of Metis is a matter of some confusion. Following the signing of Treaty 11 in 1921, 172 Metis took scrip. This would suggest that the number of native people who saw themselves as distinctively Metis was comparatively small at that time. That this is still the case is indicated by the federal government's study entitled *Regional Impact of a Northern Gas Pipeline,* published in 1973, which says, "The Metis formed only an estimated 10.5 percent of the total native population of 17 [Mackenzie] Valley communities in 1970." [Vol. 1, p. 35] This statement is based on the number of persons who said that they were Metis when questioned about their ethnic affiliation for the purposes of a manpower survey. Applying it to the present native population of the Mackenzie Valley and Western Arctic suggests that the population that regards itself as distinctly Metis would lie currently somewhere between 1,000 and 1,500 people. This analysis of the figures would correspond with the evidence at the community hearings, where the vast majority of people of Indian ancestry who spoke identified themselves as Dene.

Taking natural increase since 1974 into account, there must be about 12,500 people of Indian ancestry in the Northwest Territories

today, virtually all of whom live in the Mackenzie Valley and Mackenzie Delta. Again taking natural increase since 1974 into account, there must be about 2,500 people of Inuit ancestry living in the Mackenzie Delta and Beaufort Sea communities.

I estimate the number of white people living in the Mackenzie Valley and the Western Arctic today to be about 15,000. Thus the native population and the white population are more or less equal. But the figure for the white population is in a sense misleading because it includes so many people — undoubtedly the majority — who do not regard the North as their home and who have every intention of returning to the South. These are heavily concentrated in Yellowknife and the larger centres.

The native population in the Northwest Territories is a young one. Statistics show that live births per 1,000 population rose from a low of about 20 in 1931, to about 40 in 1947, and peaked at almost 50 between 1960 and 1964. This figure may have been among the highest in the world at that time. The birthrate has declined since then to 40 in 1970 and to 27.8 in 1974. This figure can be compared to a rate of about 10 per 1,000 for Canada as a whole. It seems safe to say that 50 percent of the native population of the Northwest Territories is under 15 years of age today.

Population and the Pipeline

Gemini North have attempted to project population increases in the Northwest Territories that would result from pipeline construction. They say that, by 1983, there would be 3,000 or so more whites in the Northwest Territories, even if a pipeline were not built. With the construction of a gas pipeline, they forecast that another 6,000 people would move north. Gemini North's figures do not take into account increases in the white population that might result from expanded exploration in the oil and gas industry, completion of the Mackenzie and Dempster Highways, looping of the gas pipeline and construction of an oil pipeline. Nor do their figures include the increases that would result from expansion of government activity, such as the establishment of a Mackenzie Valley Pipeline Authority, that accelerated industrial development would bring. It is obvious that whites would soon easily outnumber native people in the Mackenzie Delta and in the Mackenzie Valley.

The transition from a native majority to a white majority — a transition that would be accelerated by construction of a pipeline and establishment of an energy corridor — clearly has implications for the future shape of political institutions in the North. The native people told the Inquiry that, although they have always been a majority, so far they have played only a secondary role in the political life of the North. It is important to understand what their experience has meant, because they fear a future in which their political strength will be even further diminished unless — as they repeatedly urged upon me — there is a settlement of native claims.

Social Impact and Industrial Development

The pipeline companies and the oil and gas industry maintain that a pipeline will have a beneficial social impact on the people and the communities of the North. In particular, they say a pipeline will reduce the unemployment, welfare dependence, crime, violence and alcoholism that are at present characteristic of many northern settlements.

Dr. Charles Hobart, analyzing social malaise in the North, attributed it to two main factors. First, massive government intervention in the people's lives over the past two decades has undermined their traditional independence and self-esteem, creating social and psychological dependence. Second is the frustration and anger that many young people, who have been brought up in the white man's educational system, experience on leaving school. They find that the promise of useful and dignified employment is an empty one. Hobart suggested that new employment opportunities associated with the pipeline and the oil and gas industry will offer a positive response to both causes of social malaise. He argued that stable employment will "facilitate native identification with new identities, which are prideful and relevant to the world in which native people must live today." Here is how he put it:

The lack of opportunities to experience employment demanding responsibility and commitment, to obtain the training that would lead directly to such employment, and to aspire towards such employment, tends to perpetuate anti-social patterns. Without more stable employment becoming available, there are no opportunities for the structural and motivational reasons for such anti-social

behaviours to change, nor are there generally effective mechanisms for reinforcing more socially constructive behaviour. However, increased stable employment opportunities, with opportunities for training, upgrading and advancement, would provide alternative motivations and reward alternative constructive behaviour. [F25109ff.]

I disagree with Hobart on this point. I have come to the conclusion that in this instance his analysis will not hold up. Our experience so far with industrial development in the North has been recited. That experience has revealed two things: first, that native people have not participated in the industrial economy on a permanent basis; and secondly, that the native people have paid a high price in terms of social impact wherever the industrial economy has penetrated into the North.

Stable employment and an ever-increasing disposable income are part and parcel of what we regard as progress and prosperity. We see wage employment as the answer to the problems of our urban poor. Why, then, do so many native people in the North view the pipeline in such negative terms, as something that will undermine their communities and destroy them as a people? For, as the following statements show, many native people do see the pipeline in this way.

Fred Rabiska at Fort Good Hope:

If the pipeline is built we will be very unhappy people. We will drift farther from each other as well as [from] our land. [C1787]

Mary Rose Drybones, a Dene social worker, at Fort Good Hope:

It will destroy their way of life, their soul and identity. We have enough to cope with without another big issue [such] as the pipeline. It will touch everybody at all levels. It will not leave [any] one alone. [C1947]

Edward Jumbo at Trout Lake:

Talking about the pipeline ... that is just like

somebody telling us they're going to destroy us. [C2398]

Bruno Apple at Rae Lakes:

If this pipeline should get through, there's going to be a lot of people here. When this pipeline gets through, it's going to be like the end of the world here. [C8255]

I think the basic reason for this gul between our belief in the benefits of indus trial employment and the native people' fear of it is that the native people of th North are not simply poor people wh happen to be of Indian, Inuit or Meti descent. They are people whose values an patterns of social organization are in man ways quite different from those that under lie the modern industrial world. Solution based on the industrial system may easil become problems when they are applied t native people.

The Fort Simpson Experience

We can get some idea of the impact c industrial development in the Northwes Territories by examining the experience c the native people at Fort Simpson. Th Mackenzie Highway was completed to Fo Simpson in 1970, and the Inquiry was told c the social consequences it has had in tha community. People in Fort Good Hope, Fo Norman and Wrigley told me that the deepest fear was that, if the pipeline wer through, their communities would becom like Fort Simpson. Native witnesses at Fo Simpson told me that their people's ir volvement in the construction of the Ma kenzie Highway, through the Hire Nort project, has resulted in major social problem such as high rates of alcohol abuse, crin and violence, and family breakdown.

Betty Menicoche gave the Inquiry her ow family's history as an example of what tl native people mean when they say, "We don't want to become another Fort Simpson." She explained how her parents, after leading a traditional life in the bush, had moved into Fort Simpson to earn wages to supplement the living they earned by hunting and fishing. She told of the hardships her parents endured while trying to cope with the two ways of life, and she described the social pressures brought about by the construction of the highway:

> By 1970, things in Simpson had reached a point of social disorder and ultimately of breakdown in [the] cultural value system. The scene in Simpson for natives was one of excitement, and one way they began enjoying this fun was through alcohol, [thus] beginning misuse through misunderstanding ... it was since 1970 that I found the breakdown of our family as a result of alcohol, stress and strain, created by this need to achieve an economic base, a wage economy. At this time my family experienced the biggest social disaster ... that was the ultimate breakdown of my mother. She had kept our family going despite the thin threads of the family. The strain of trying to tie two ways of life into one another was too much to bear. ... All the frustrations and the difficulty of coping with this transition are easily remedied by the bottle. That was the final breakdown of a once solid family....
>
> We have been accused of being young radical Indians, only repeating ideas of left-wing people. These are just a few examples of what has occurred in Simpson. Further social and economic injustices will be experienced if the pipeline goes through. Tell me, is it wrong to begin standing on two feet, [telling] what you yourself and your people have truly experienced? [C2667ff.]

Theresa Villeneuve was born in Nahanni Butte and spent her early years living with her parents in the bush. In those days her father came to Fort Simpson only to sell his furs and buy supplies. She has lived most of her married life in Fort Simpson and has seen the changes that have occurred:

> Since 1968, things have been happening too fast, and people cannot put up with them. The Dene people are not involved in what things are happening. They have never helped in planning for future development ... because Dene don't think like the white man. [C2656]

Seen through the eyes of the native people of Fort Simpson, their experience with wage employment during the construction of the Mackenzie Highway was debilitating. Jim Antoine, the young Chief of the Fort Simpson Indian Band, summed up the views of the Dene on the impact of the pipeline:

> I'm not worried about the money or jobs that this pipeline is going to give because, as Indian people, we don't think about the money. We think about the lives of the people here because, the way I see it, if this pipeline goes ahead, it's just going to destroy a lot of people. It's going to kill a lot of people indirectly. ... I don't want the pipeline to come in here because, with the highway coming in in the last five to six years, it has changed Simpson altogether. A lot of problems arose out of this highway. If this pipeline comes through, it's going to cause problems to be a hundredfold more. We're the people that live here, and we're the people who are going to suffer. [C2624]

Native Values and the Frontier

René Lamothe, a Metis, described to the Inquiry some of the deep-seated reasons for the confusion and frustration that have beset the native people of Fort Simpson. In his view, the assumption that native people will adapt to and benefit from industrial development is too easily made. He argued that, in the Northwest Territories, the philosophy of life, the values, and the social organization that have been developed by a hunting-and-gathering society, together with the modifications introduced by a trapping economy during the last century, go very deep.

As we have seen, the native values and the native economy persist. But the values and expectations of the industrial system push in a different direction. Hugh Brody described the process in his evidence:

> Inuit and Dene peoples are proud of the ways in which they share the produce of the land. The activity of hunting may be comparatively individualistic, but its produce tends to be communal — at least insofar as those in want are able to approach successful hunters and ask for food. Also, the basic means of production — land — is regarded as communal. Requests for food were never refused; the right to use land was rarely disputed. Money, however, is not so readily shared. It tends to be regarded as the earner's own private property, and spent on his or her immediate family's personal needs. Moreover, it tends to be spent on consumer durable goods, which cannot be divided among neighbours. [F25787ff.]

The result of this difference is not only that the sharing ethic is undermined, but the cohesion and homogeneity of the community are threatened when new inequalities begin to develop.

When those who live by hunting and trapping are seen to experience poverty, they tend to lose their status within the society. Once again, the native community's sense of cultural distinctiveness is eroded, and the traditional ways of according respect are undermined. Wage labour is not necessarily an adequate substitute for the traditional social system, once the values of the traditional system have been eroded by the industrial world. René Lamothe explained this danger to the Inquiry:

> ... the hunting economy permitted a man to support an extended family; whereas the

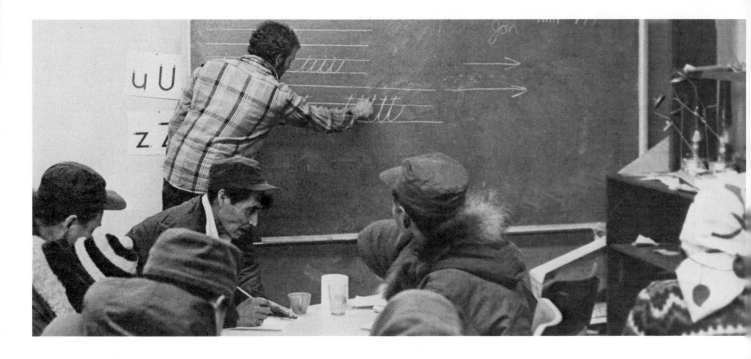

wage economy does not adequately support an immediate family within the expectations that the industrial economy raises. ... We have elders alive now who in their youth supported up to 40 people. Etoli, an old man living in the hospital right now, in his youth supported up to 40 people by hunting. Who of us with our salaries today can support 10? Etoli is living in the hospital here primarily because the expectations of ourselves, his relatives, have been changed by education, the churches, the industrial economy; and secondly because the wage economy ... does not generate enough cash to support more than one nuclear family ... young women are raised among the Dene people to expect specific benefits from a husband. However, these benefits are found in a hunting economy, not in a wage-earning economy. Young men are raised to believe that to be a man one must provide these benefits, and again these benefits are not found in a wage-earning economy....

We are a people caught in an industrial economy with a mind prepared for a hunting economy. The expectations women have of their men [and] the men of the women [are] not being realized in everyday life [which] results in frustrations, confusions, misunderstandings and anger that net broken homes. [C2687ff.]

Lamothe's views may seem, at first glance, out of keeping with modern notions of industrial motivation, but there is a hard practicality to what he said. His views are especially relevant in the North, because there the disruptive effects of the industrial system on native values are intensified by the particular kind of industrial development that the pipeline represents — large-scale industrial development on the frontier. The values of white people working on the frontier are opposed to and inconsistent with the values that are embedded in native tradition in the villages and settlements of the North. The community life of native people emphasizes sharing and cooperation

between generations and among the member households of an extended family. The native community has a profound sense of its own permanence. The place is more important than economic incentive.

The frontier encourages, indeed depends upon, a footloose work force, mobile capital and all their ideological concomitants. It is not any particular location that matters but the profitability of an area; attachments are to reward, not to place, people or community. Individualism, uncertainty and instability are part and parcel of the frontier.

The native people are well aware of the difference between their own attitudes and values and those of a frontier work force. Agnes Edgi at Fort Good Hope told the Inquiry:

> We, the Dene people, were born on this land of ours. We are not like the white people who go wandering around looking for work. They are not like us ... who have a home in one place. They, the white people, move from one town to another, from one country to another, searching for jobs to make money. [C2003]

The frontier mentality exacerbates the processes whereby traditional social controls are broken down and pathological behaviour becomes a feature of everyday life.

Ethel Townsend, a native teacher from Fort Norman, told the Inquiry that construction of a pipeline will impose a great strain on the people of the Northwest Territories:

> The adaptability of our people will be stretched to its limits, and there is a breaking point. [C4388]

I have been describing here a complex process, one that may be difficult for people who have grown up within the industrial system to comprehend. Let us turn now to some of the easily understood and highly visible effects of industrial development on the northern people to date, and let me

suggest what the social impact of the pipeline would be.

Specific Impacts

The Costs of Welfare

Transfer payments in the North are made for a variety of purposes, which include payments to people who are in ill health, to single parents with dependent children, to persons caring for dependent relatives, to wives of men in prison, to the blind and to the aged. These payments also include "economic assistance" for people who would normally support themselves, but who cannot do so for lack of employment.

It is commonly believed that welfare payments are inversely related to the size of the employment base: the larger the employment base, the lower the welfare payments. This idea is widely accepted among northern policy-makers; it is one of the foundations of policies designed to expand northern industrial wage employment and, more generally, to industrialize the North. The reasoning is simple: people in the North require economic assistance because they lack employment. They believe that the traditional life based on the land has collapsed and that nothing has taken its place. The native people therefore require welfare — but only as a "transitional measure." When opportunities for wage employment have been sufficiently enlarged, they will no longer need economic assistance. Quite predictably, white northerners complain that native people are receiving too much welfare, and that industrial development is not proceeding fast enough to relieve the public of the substantial burden that native welfare represents.

What is the real relationship between elfare payments and the economic base of e North? Have welfare payments declined industrial activity has expanded? The idence strongly suggests that the convennal wisdom is wrong. So far, the expann of industrial activity in the North has en accompanied by a marked increase in onomic assistance and in other types of elfare payments. In a report prepared for rctic Gas entitled *Social and Economic* *pact of Proposed Arctic Gas Pipeline in* *orthern Canada,* Gemini North have own that welfare payments to residents of e Mackenzie Valley and the Mackenzie elta rose sharply during the period 1968-69 to 1972-1973. This period was one of pid industrial expansion; it witnessed the nstruction of both the Mackenzie and the empster Highways, and the oil and gas ploration in the Mackenzie Delta. In 1968-69, total welfare payments stood at 95,294. By 1972-1973, they had risen to ,002,504, an increase of well over 200 rcent. Throughout this five-year period, yments for economic assistance made up out half of the total, ranging from a low of .6 percent in 1968-1969 to a high of 55.6 rcent in 1970-1971. Gemini North ncluded:

It should be noted that job opportunities have also increased substantially for the Lower Mackenzie Delta, Central Mackenzie and Upper Mackenzie sub-regions, over the period under review. However, all [sub-regions] show an increase in the economic component of social assistance payments, in current dollar values. [Vol. 2, p. 629]

On a more local basis, Gemini North cited e case of Tuktoyaktuk:

Tuk represents the "Jesus factor" at work. Although oil exploration and development activity was at its maximum level in 1971/72 and 1972/73 social assistance payments have

increased phenomenally, 114 percent over the 1970/71 level. Furthermore, the economic component of total welfare rose drastically, from 32.7 percent in 1969/70 to 67.9 percent in 1972/73. [Vol. 2, p. 635]

The same substantial increase in welfare payments, largely for economic assistance, was evident at Coppermine following the introduction of Gulf Oil's recruitment program there. In 1972-1973, welfare payments in Coppermine were $27,000; by 1973-1974, they had risen to $51,000; and by 1974-1975, they amounted to $71,000.

There were no doubt many factors at work that could in part account for these dramatic increases. A more generous policy of welfare payments to meet inflation could account for some of the increase, and perhaps a greater tolerance by the staff who administer welfare payment programs may account for more. There may be other factors, quite incidental to the spread of industrial activity, that led to increased welfare payments. Nevertheless, the relation between the increase of industrial wage employment and the increase of welfare payments stands out as obvious and fundamental. No one has been able to show that industrial activity, which has so far directly affected Fort Simpson, Inuvik and Tuktoyaktuk, has played a major role in absorbing surplus labour and diminishing welfare dependence in those communities. Arctic Gas made that assertion, but advanced no evidence in its support.

Moreover, we must not fall into the trap of regarding total welfare payments as a measure of indigence. Moralistic judgments about "welfare bums" are wholly out of place in any discussion of the northern economy, for such judgments are little more than a denial of the serious issues under consideration.

Payment of economic assistance may be likened to reviving a boxer who is on the ropes to let him go another round — only perhaps to receive a knock-out blow. Welfare cannot solve the real problem. Welfare payments may be regarded as a recognition of social costs — by paying them we try to alleviate some of the hardships that the recipients have to endure. Nevertheless, these payments should, for the most part, be viewed as a short-term necessity; they should be paid until the fundamental issues are tackled. The problem of mounting welfare payments is a good reason for dealing with these issues now, but welfare is neither their cause nor their solution.

The recent increase in welfare payments and in related social problems that we have observed in the North has one basic cause: the force and suddenness with which industrial development has intruded into the region. During the past two centuries, the native people of the North have had to change a great deal and, by and large, they have shown a remarkable ability to adapt. But never before has there been such a sustained assault on their social institutions and relationships, on their language and culture, and on their attitudes and values. Never before have there been greater strains on the families. Should a husband and father stay in his community or work far away? Should the young people choose one way of life or another? Under the accumulated force of these pulls and pressures, communities are bound to disintegrate, families are bound to come apart, and individuals are bound to fail. The rising figures for welfare payments reflect to a considerable degree the impact of the industrial system on the native people of the North today.

Crime and Violence

Welfare and economic assistance payments may be regarded as the economic aspect of a much larger problem. We must also consider a range of social disorders, each of which, like dependence on welfare, can be seen in economic or in broader human terms. Crime and violence are already problems in northern native society; will the advent of large-scale industrial development ameliorate or compound these problems?

Native witnesses maintained that there is a correlation between social disorders and industrial development. Crime in the Northwest Territories increased between 1969 and 1975, a period of industrial expansion. The native people assert that the communities least involved in wage labour and least dominated by the frontier mentality are the communities with least crime and violence. Indeed, many native witnesses emphasized to me their fear that their particular settlements might become more like the "developed" communities.

It would be difficult to overstate the seriousness of social problems in the Northwest Territories. Death by violence — accident, homicide, suicide and poisoning — has been the main cause of death among native people in the Northwest Territories since 1967, and among the Yukon Indians for approximately 15 years. In the Northwest Territories, the figure for violent death rose from 14.1 percent of all deaths in 1966 to 23.4 percent in 1974. The most recent figures published by Statistics Canada for the whole of Canada are for 1973, when deaths caused by accident, homicide, suicide and poisoning comprised only 10.2 percent of the total number of deaths — less than half the percentage for the Northwest Territories.

All of the evidence indicates that an increase in industrial wage employment and disposable income among the native people in the North brings with it a dramatic increase in violent death and injuries. The experience at Fort Simpson, cited by Mr. Justice William Morrow of the Supreme Court of the Northwest Territories in *Observations on Resource Issues in Canada's North,* bears out this tendency:

> Until just recently, the present population [of Fort Simpson] of several hundred Indians and whites had led uneventful and relatively quiet lives. But the highway construction combined with pipeline speculation appears to have changed all of that. Last year [1975] the Magistrate's Court had more than seventy juvenile cases in one week, and my court was required to go there more times in that one year than in the previous eight-year total. To me this is a clear indication of what is to come. These small native communities are just not ready to take major developments. [p. 9]

I am persuaded that the incidence of these disorders is closely bound up with the rapid expansion of the industrial system and with its persistent intrusion into every part of the native people's lives. The process affects the complex links between native people and their past, their culturally preferred economic life, and their individual, familial and political self-respect. We should not be surprised to learn that the economic forces that have broken these vital links, and that are unresponsive to the distress of those who have been hurt, should lead to serious disorders. Crimes of violence can, to some extent, be seen as expressions of frustration, confusion and indignation, but we can go beyond that interpretation to the obvious connection between crimes of violence and the change the South has, in recent years, brought to the native people of the North. With that obvious connection, we can affirm

one simple proposition: the more the indu[strial] trial frontier displaces the homeland in t[he] North, the worse the incidence of crime ar[d] violence will be.

How, then, should we regard the soci[al] effects of a pipeline that would bring t[he] industrial frontier to virtually every part the Mackenzie Valley and Mackenzie Delt[a] The experience of the construction of pipeline in Alaska offers an indication what may happen. In the State of Alask[a] deaths by violence have risen from over [?] percent of all deaths in the 1950s, to mo[re] than 30 percent of the total between 19[69] and 1974. Significantly and ominously, th[e] increase was almost entirely accounted f[or] by a steep rise in violent deaths amor[g] native Alaskans — from less than 20 perce[nt] all through the 1950s to over 40 perce[nt] during the period of the oil boom, 1969-197[4].

In the North Slope Borough itself, whe[re] the majority of permanent residents a[re] Eskimo, the picture is worse. Suicides the[re] have gone up from two in 1968 to eight 1975; suicide attempts increased from sev[en] in 1973 to 23 in 1975. The figures for pu[r] posefully inflicted injury there are eve[n] more alarming. In 1973 there were 162 su[ch] injuries, 123 of which were alcohol-relate[d] in 1974, the figures dropped to 144 and 1[?] respectively; in 1975, however, they i[n] creased dramatically: there were 231 pu[r] posefully inflicted injuries, 180 of whi[ch] were alcohol-related. Preliminary figures midpoint 1976 show that the rate may ha[ve] nearly doubled in that year.

There is a small native village along t[he] Alaska pipeline corridor, which has a pop[u] lation of about 150 people. During 1973-197[?] the work force of this village was employ[ed] on the pipeline, and during that year t[he] local health aide treated nearly 200 purpos[e] fully inflicted injuries. The previous yea[r] there were only 15 such cases. In 1974-1975, after the villagers decided to give up working on the pipeline, the number of purposefully inflicted injuries treated declined to fewer than 30.

Dr. Otto Schaefer, Canada's foremost authority on northern health, and Director of the Northern Medical Research Unit, Charles Camsell Hospital in Edmonton, has concluded:

> Judging by the latest figures coming from Alaska as well as by disease patterns seen in our native population in the Northwest Territories, and considering the striking parallels in development ... one must fear that violent death in the Northwest Territories would climb to similar tragic heights (over 40 percent) or even worse, as the impact in the Northwest Territories would be concentrated on a smaller base, which therefore has less resilience to extra demands. [Exhibit F823, p. 2]

I see little reason to suppose, therefore, that the social and economic transformations associated with construction of the Mackenzie Valley pipeline will reduce crime and violence, both of which are already acute problems in the larger towns of the Northwest Territories. Rather, the evidence from both Alaska and the Mackenzie Valley and Western Arctic leads me to believe that construction of the pipeline would only aggravate a situation that is already alarming.

Health and Health Services

During the 1940s and 1950s, the health of the native people was one of the major problems confronting government in the North. By that time, the spread of infectious diseases, especially tuberculosis, had assumed appalling dimensions, and it was evident that medical services would have to be extended to even the remotest camps and villages. The

extension of these services was one of the reasons for the rapid growth of settlements in the 1950s and 1960s. However, improved medical services did not solve the native people's health problems. Certainly the devastation of pulmonary disease was eventually brought under control, and epidemics of influenza, measles and whooping-cough no longer caused so many deaths. But the former causes of sickness have, to some extent, been replaced by new ones — less deadly, but nonetheless debilitating.

The Inquiry heard evidence from doctors and dentists with wide experience of the health situation in northern communities. They told us that during the past decade venereal disease rates have risen rapidly in the Northwest Territories and are now many times higher than those for Canada as a whole. Dr. Herbert Schwarz, a physician from Tuktoyaktuk, told the Inquiry:

> Mr. Commissioner, if we apply these 1975 Inuvik percentages and figures for the seven-month period only [the first seven months of 1975], showing that one person in every six was infected with gonorrhea, and transpose these figures on a per capita basis to a city like Ottawa, then [it] would have from 80,000 to 100,000 people suffering with venereal disease. [The] city would be a disaster area and a state of medical emergency proclaimed.

> The incidence of venereal disease for the whole of the Northwest Territories was up 27 percent for the first seven months of 1975 over a similar period of a year ago. The Inuvik region contributed much more than its share to the territorial average. Cases reported and treated in the Inuvik zone were up 58 percent over a similar seven-month period last year, with 537 cases confirmed and treated to 339 confirmed cases treated last year. [C7532ff.]

In testimony, the medical authorities gave particular attention to changes in diet: native people are eating less meat, more sugar, and mothers have been encouraged to bottle-feed

rather than breast-feed their babies. Dr. Elizabeth Cass said the shift from country food to southern food has resulted in widespread myopia; Dr. Schaefer associated the change in diet with extremely high rates of child sickness in general and with middle-ear disease in particular. Dr. Mayhall described an epidemic of dental disease and the very high rates of tooth decay and gum disease in the North. We understand that a change in diet may cause such problems when we realize that local meat has a higher food value than meats imported to the North. Some changes in diet are plain to see, such as the consumption of great quantities of pop. (It has been estimated that in Barrow, Alaska, the average consumption of pop is seven cans a day for each man, woman and child.)

Construction of the pipeline would increase and intensify the impacts that recent changes have already had on the health of the native people. Accidents during construction, and incidents in the camps would require medical attention; these cases and the requirements of in-migrants who are not directly employed on the pipeline would impose a severe strain on existing health services. The pipeline companies may be required to supply additional medical services to attend to both their own workers and those working on pipeline-related activities. There may be some difficulty in recruiting medical staff to handle a sudden influx of several thousand people. But this is a problem associated with industrial expansion anywhere and, while it is acknowledged that it may be difficult to manage, it is regarded as a tolerable concomitant of industrial development.

These are not the problems that chiefly concern me. Change will come to the North,

---

as it does everywhere. There will be problems related to the delivery of health services in the North, pipeline or no pipeline. What we must understand is that the impact of a pipeline, with increased wage employment, rapid social change, and new ways and diet, will produce among the native people of the North particular and unfortunate effects that cannot be mitigated by any conventional means. There are real limitations to any preventive and curative measures that can be recommended.

I do not wish to leave the impression that I believe wage employment and an increased availability of cash to be the proximate cause of health problems. They are perhaps more generally attributable to rapid social change. But the situation is all of a piece: when the native people's own culture is overwhelmed by another culture, the loss of tradition, pride and self-confidence is evident in every aspect of personal, family and social life. The advance of industrial development has affected every part of native life, and there is every reason to believe that the construction of a pipeline and its aftermath would lead to further deterioration in the health of the native people.

Alcohol

The subjects of heavy drinking and drunkenness recur in every discussion of social pathology in the North. Both native and white people regard the abuse of alcohol as the most disruptive force, the most alarming symptom, and the most serious danger to the future of northern society. François Paulette of Fort Smith expressed the feelings of many native people in saying:

Today I feel sad when I see my people, the people who were so close together in the past ...fragmented with booze. [C4747]

Alcohol was introduced to northern natives by the fur traders in the Mackenzie Valley and by the whalers on the Arctic coast. Alcohol and other drugs were used in the Americas before the advent of Europeans, but only among agricultural peoples, not among hunters and gatherers. There is no evidence of the use of alcohol in any form by northern Indians and Eskimos before the coming of the white man.

Before the 1950s, alcohol was not an overriding problem in the North. Since then its use has increased and is still increasing. Northern natives were interdicted from drinking it before 1960. When the interdict was lifted, the consumption of alcohol began to increase, but it was only with the construction of the highways and with oil and gas exploration during the late 1960s, which brought high wages to native people, that the rate of consumption moved ahead of the Canadian average. Moreover, the higher rates of comsumption are in part the result of population increases in regional centres. However, now some of the smaller communities are also experiencing an alcohol problem.

The alcohol question points to an important distinction between the communities that the native people think of as having been influenced by the industrial system and those that have not. When the residents of Paulatuk or Colville Lake express their fears of increased white pressure, of a further weakening of the native economy, or of a pipeline, they point to the problems related to alcohol in other, more ''developed'' settlements. They fear an increase in wife beating, child neglect, violence, and other abuses they associate with drunkenness and drinking communities.

The reality of their fears, as well as of the kinds of change that can take place in a

small northern community, are illustrated by Hugh Brody's description of the experience of a settlement in the Eastern Arctic. In Pond Inlet in 1972, the per capita consumption of alcohol was 2.2 ounces per adult per month. In that year, Panarctic Oil began to recruit labour there, and in 1973-1974, the cash income of Panarctic employees from the village amounted to about $220,000. By 1974, the per capita consumption of alcohol was 30 ounces per adult per month. The Commissioner of the Northwest Territories tried to control the problem at Pond Inlet by forbidding mail-order deliveries of alcohol from the liquor store at Frobisher Bay. This action met with such hostility in Pond Inlet that he rescinded the order. By 1975, the Hamlet Council itself was preparing to regulate the importation of drink by mail order, and a jail had been built. In just three years, Pond Inlet had acquired a serious alcohol problem.

But although there was a 15-fold increase in per capita consumption of alcohol at Pond Inlet, that rate is still only 30 percent of the average consumption in the Northwest Territories. The disease there is still in its early stages, so to speak, but its impact can already be seen in the incidence of violence and child neglect: the number of cases related to drunken and disorderly behaviour went up from two in the year before Panarctic began to hire workers there, to 24 in the first year after hiring began. But, by comparison with settlements that have had a longer history of industrial impact and change, Pond Inlet has had only a glimpse of the alcohol-related disorders that may come.

At Fort McPherson, Neil and Elizabeth Colin, who helped found the Peel River Alcoholics Anonymous Centre, described for the Inquiry how the consumption of liquor increased when people from the village were

Alcohol education advertisements in northern newspapers. (GNWT)

Liquor store in Norman Wells. (GNWT)

Liquor misuse — a major northern problem. (Inuit Today)

Cocktail lounge in Yellowknife. (NFB—Grant)

employed on construction of the Dempster Highway:

> The beer sale here in Fort McPherson is $5.50 a dozen. In March 1975 they sold 1,413 cases, which cost $7,771.50. In April they sold 2,360 cases. It cost $12,980. In May they sold 2,489. It cost $13,690. Total sales is $34,441.50. That's in three months. This averages out to 7.3 dozen beer for every man and woman and child in this community. For this amount 10 men could purchase a freighter canoe and 20 [men a] kicker and skidoo every three months.

> The reason I put this up is because if the pipeline comes through it will be worse. [C1101]

The fact is, drinking has become an enormous problem throughout the Northwest Territories. When a traditional community becomes a drinking community, the whole atmosphere can change. Drunks can be seen staggering around the village, and people begin to lock their doors. People are apprehensive every time a plane lands: is it carrying liquor?

Let us look now at alcoholism in the Northwest Territories as a whole. In the year ending March 31, 1976, 877,000 gallons of alcohol were sold at a value of nearly $11 million. This volume represents 86,810 gallons of absolute (pure) alcohol: if that amount is divided by the population aged 15 and over, we see that the average consumption is roughly 3.4 gallons of absolute alcohol per person per year. With the exception of the Yukon, per capita consumption of alcohol in the Northwest Territories is higher than anywhere else in Canada. It is approximately one gallon of absolute alcohol over the national average.

Native leaders have questioned the wisdom of government policy on the price of alcohol and on the effect of its price on consumption. Frank T'Seleie at Fort Good Hope told the Inquiry:

> What else other than liquor is the territorial government willing to subsidize to make sure that prices are the same throughout the Northwest Territories? Does it subsidize fresh food or clothing or even pop in the same way? No, only liquor. [C1774]

Alcohol prices are the same throughout the Northwest Territories. The price of a given alcohol product is "set" f.o.b. Hay River, and markup and transportation costs are averaged throughout the distribution system. This practice is one of the factors contributing to the misuse of alcohol in the Northwest Territories. It is unfortunate that the Government of Canada, in granting this revenue source to the Government of the Northwest Territories, has placed the territorial government in a position where one of its principal sources of revenue comes from the sale of liquor. Tim McDermott, a white resident of Yellowknife, argued that there was a moral contradiction in encouraging "the people [to] work for the white man for reasonable money and then [to build] a liquor store for them to spend this money." [C8044]

Alcohol and the Pipeline

If we build the pipeline now, what will be its impact on native drinking? To understand what alcohol in its relation to accelerated industrial development will mean to Canadian native people, we have only to look at Alaska, where it is a problem of immense proportions. The rank of alcohol as a killer has risen from tenth place in 1960 to fourth in 1970, and it is still rising. Figures from the Office of Systems Development, Alaska Area Native Health Services, show that in 1960 the death rate attributed to heavy drinking and drunkenness (excluding deaths from cirrhosis of the liver) was 4.6 per 100,000 population; in 1970 that rate had risen to 41.1

per 100,000; and by 1973 the rate was 57.8 deaths per 100,000. In 1975, within the North Slope Borough, every single death was linked to heavy use of alcohol.

What might happen in Northern Canada? Dr. Ross Wheeler, a Yellowknife physician, outlined the problems he saw in the North. He mentioned suicide, mental illness, crimes of violence, and the exploitation of native women, and he concluded:

> The common theme running through all these social problems is alcohol. This single drug, more than any other factor, has been, is, and will be at the root of most of the social problems in the Territories. Facilities for dealing with alcoholism are in their infancy. More time and money are needed if the programs are to be built up. This need can only increase in the future.

> While treatment programs are necessary, they do not affect the basic problem causing alcoholism. Only the restoration of self-respect and a meaningful place in a society to which a person can relate, only basic dignity as a human being will reduce the problem of alcoholism. [C3401ff.]

Wheeler, like so many other witnesses, insisted upon the connection between the abuse of alcohol and industrial development. How, therefore, can we suppose that the construction of the pipeline will do anything but make the present situation worse?

The mindless violence and the social disarray that accompany drinking in the native communities are matters of grave concern to the native people themselves. They have spoken frankly to the Inquiry about the use of alcohol in the villages and of the measures they have taken to curb the problem.

Historically, measures to limit or prevent the misuse of alcohol have taken two forms: legislative sanction and remedial and educational activities. These efforts have not succeeded generally in North American society and they have largely failed in the North. But recently the native people have had some success with both methods: at Fort Rae and at Lac la Martre the people have adopted local prohibition, and in many native villages programs of self-help are underway. In my view, these programs will succeed only to the extent that the increasing self-awareness, self-confidence and self-respect among the native people provide a foundation upon which these programs can be built. I believe that the native organizations have created positive role models — exemplars, even heroes — for native people. These models may now be replacing the southern stereotype of the drunken Indian.

At the moment, it is impossible to say whether or not the native people's attempts to control the use of alcohol will succeed. But the construction of the Mackenzie Valley pipeline will certainly make the struggle more difficult, not easier. Elizabeth Colin, basing her remarks on her experience with the Peel River Alcoholics Anonymous Centre in Fort McPherson, told the Inquiry of her fears if the pipeline is built:

> Right now we are trying to get back on our feet. As natives. Trying to help ourselves. But what will happen if the pipeline comes through, and there is going to be a lot of money, and a lot of the Indians are going to be affected by alcohol? ... The people in the North are talking to the government for the first time now. If the government doesn't listen, how many more people will start drinking, just because they feel they have been fooled again? ... Maybe they will just drink more to try to forget what is happening to them. [C1102ff.]

The alcohol problem is bad now, but it could become far worse. There are communities in the Mackenzie Valley where alcohol-associated problems are severe, but there are other communities where these problems are relatively minor, still kept at bay by the enduring vigour of native society and its values. In the language of sociology, there continue to be well-integrated native families and communities. Rapid and massive change poses two threats: to communities of well-integrated families, whose satisfying lives may suddenly be disrupted, and to communities whose families have already been broken, and who will find attempts to improve their situation made more difficult or impossible.

I suggest that the problems of alcohol abuse are not insoluble, and that they have not proceeded so far in the North that all talk of native identity and self-respect is hollow rhetoric. The alcohol problem is secondary to other and more basic issues. Why should people not drink heavily when they have been separated from all the things they value? To the extent that the native people are obliged to participate in the type of frontier development that separates them from their traditional life, their chances of containing, and finally of ameliorating, the problems of alcohol grow worse and worse.

Some small groups of Dene and Inuit have, in various parts of the North, tried to move away from settlements that are afflicted with alcohol-related problems to create new communities of their own. These movements are a means that the native people themselves have found to solve the problem. In their view, the one way in which they can hope to ameliorate the alcohol problem is to ensure that they are *not* compelled to participate in industrial development, *not* compelled to leave their own lands, and *not* compelled to surrender their independence. Insofar as abuse of alcohol is a warning of the gravity of the native people's predicament, that warning is against unrestrained industrial development.

Social Impact and the Women of the North

Women from every town and village in which the Inquiry sat, described their hopes and fears for the future. The social impact of the pipeline will affect all members of the community, but it may have a particular effect upon women. Four women, Gina Blondin, Rosemary Cairns, Valerie Hearder and Mary Kerton, submitted a brief to the Inquiry at Yellowknife on this important subject:

> Looking at development from a woman's point of view is vital. Women are concerned with the human element of development, about what it will do to their children, their homes and their community. Women are the ones who end up coping with the results and effects of development decisions usually made by men. [Submission on the Merits 189, p. 1]

They suggested that the pipeline would aggravate the housing problem that now exists in communities such as Yellowknife, Fort Simpson and Inuvik. The pressures of overcrowding and the deterioration in the supply of public utilities such as electricity and water, and in communications, would fall mainly on women who, during the long northern winters, are often alone at home.

Of great concern to many women in the North is the likelihood of their being sexually exploited during the construction of a pipeline. Marie Anne Jeremicka at Lac la Martre pointed out this danger:

> There will be about six thousand men working on the pipeline and mostly these men will be from the South. What will it mean to us young people? It means, if these men come, they will take our young women away for a

A Yellowknife hotel. (NFB—Pearce)

Gina and Tina Blondin. (N. Cooper)

Government-run receiving home for children in Inuvik. (GNWT)

Three generations at Fort Providence. (GNWT)

year or two. Like the pipeline project will be going on for three years. They will take our young women away, probably shack up with them, make them pregnant, and leave them alone after the job is done. What will these young women do? They don't have education. Where will they get the money to support their children, and what will they do for a living? [C8224ff.]

Cassien Edgi of Fort Good Hope told the Inquiry:

I am 57 years old and have eight children and grandchildren. I am going against the pipeline which will give my children trouble and hardship. Every one of you sitting here love your children. Do you want them to suffer? What is going to happen if the pipeline goes through Fort Good Hope? Drugs, booze, family break-up and trouble. In the past we have a handful of white men. Still, how many girls have kids without fathers and live on welfare? If the pipeline goes through there will be thousands and thousands of white people. [C1884]

The women's brief also addressed this issue:

Teenagers are confused about sexual behaviour at the best of times and under the best of circumstances. But an imbalance in the number of males and females caused by a massive development intensifies this confusion for young girls and boys. In communities where the traditional pattern of life already has broken down, young girls have begun drinking and are being taken advantage of sexually. Recent reports point out that illegitimate pregnancies and venereal disease have skyrocketed in the Northwest Territories communities where development has taken place. But all these signs, which would be greatly intensified by development, are only the visible indicators of the real problem — a generation of confused young people and a disrupted community. [Submission on the Merits 189, p. 12]

Dr. Ross Wheeler of Yellowknife described to the Inquiry some of the implications of the pipeline for social contact between native women and a large number of transient white labourers, based upon the experience of Frobisher Bay:

This contact was characterized by a total lack of regard for native people as human beings. The male-female contact was invariably sexually exploitive in nature. The presence of a lot of money and easy access to alcohol were the catalysts. Young native women were drawn out by these features from their normal social patterns, and into patterns of drunkenness and overt sexuality. Little or no thought was given by the men involved to the consequences of their actions. These actions were totally irresponsible and devoid of emotional content. The effect on the native women was socially, physically and culturally destructive. They tended to be alienated from their people and were left alone to attend to their venereal disease, illegitimate children and incipient alcoholism.

In the past the social stigma of this type of contact happening occasionally could be absorbed. However, we have only to imagine this effect multiplied by a factor of a few thousand concentrated over three winters. It could be devastating. We could calculate the cost in terms of medical service. We could even "guesstimate" the cost of supportive social services, but it is impossible to assess the cost, the human price, for loss of dignity and social alienation.

Who is going to pay? The pipeline company? The oil company? The people of Canada? These people may pay the dollars; we already know who is going to pay the price in human misery. [C3400ff.]

Everywhere, the native people expressed the gravest concern about the potential dangers of having large construction camps near or with easy access to their villages. They insisted that these men must be prevented from disrupting community life. Jane Charlie of Fort McPherson said:

Now I worry about my own girls, how they will grow up. When I hear that there is going to be 800 people in every camp, I hope they make a law that the white people will have to stay away from the town of McPherson. Like I said before, the white people are good, but some are no good. [C1253B]

The pipeline companies, aware of this concern, have told the Inquiry that they will make every effort to minimize undesired communication between the construction camps and the villages and that, subject to union agreement, they will make the native villages "off limits" to men in the construction camps. They say that many of the proposed camps will be in remote locations, and that scheduling of construction during winter will prevent easy access to villages.

I do not doubt the good intentions of the companies in this regard. However, there is real doubt about the companies' legal right in Canada to restrict the access of their employees to native communities. In any event, as I have pointed out before, the companies will have no control over the influx of other workers who will come north to take advantage of the secondary employment generated by the pipeline.

It is, in my judgment, unrealistic to expect or hope that the villages can be immunized, as it were, against contact with the construction camps. Native people will be employed in those camps, and inevitably some of them will make friends with white construction workers and will wish to invite them home. We must also remember that many of the construction workers will be seeing the Canadian North for the first, and perhaps the only, time. Naturally, they will want to see something of the native villages, many of which are in locations of natural beauty. To expect anything else of them would be to deny the fascination that the North holds for Canadians as a whole. Unfortunately, that

NORTHERN FRONTIER, NORTHERN HOMELAND

fascination will inevitably lead to trouble when the leisure activities of large numbers of white male labourers begin to influence the social life of the small native villages. Other difficulties will be created by the attraction of young native people to the excitement and activity generated by the pipeline boom in the larger centres of settlement.

These attractions, together with the ready availability of alcohol, are the background to sexual exploitation and to family breakdown, two related and familiar aspects of social life in frontier settlements. Already there are towns in the Northwest Territories where Dene and Inuit women, many of them teenagers, are regarded as easy prey, an amusement for an evening or a week. Women, especially young women, will be vulnerable to the social impact of industrial development in the North.

If the young women, particularly those from traditional communities, are attracted by the company of white workers, they may reject — or be rejected by — their own families, a situation that has often occurred in the North in the past and that has led to much sorrow and disappointment. Less obvious, perhaps, but no less important is what happens to the young native men in such a situation. If the young men find that their company is rejected in favour of that of white workers, who are likely to be fully employed and to have a lot of money to spend, they will experience a whole range of frustration and despair. In such a situation, the temptation to turn to drink may be overwhelming. A drunken person who has these reasons for rage, anger and frustration inside him is a dangerous man, and he is likely to become violent. This situation, too, has often occurred in the North, but its

causes may not have been obvious to an outsider.

Social Inequalities

During the early 1950s, the swift growth of a strong governmental presence in the North was intended to bring to the native people the benefits of the modern liberal state and to give them equal opportunity with other Canadians. Paradoxically, it had the effect of producing yet deeper inequalities in the social structure of the North. The establishment and growth of Inuvik illustrate this point vividly.

Inuvik was intended to replace Aklavik as a centre for federal administration. All major commercial and government services were transferred to Inuvik, and new research and defence establishments were built there. Dr. Hobart described what the move from Aklavik to Inuvik entailed in terms of social impact:

> When whites first came to the Arctic, if they were to survive, much less live in comfort, they had in many ways to adopt the life-style of the native people. Thus, there was a basic similarity in the everyday living and survival patterns of everyone in the same community. As I heard people in this area say ten and more years ago, in Aklavik, the honey bucket was the great equalizer. At the risk of oversimplification, we could characterize the shift from Aklavik to Inuvik as the shift from egalitarianism to discrimination, from attitudes of acceptance to attitudes of prejudice against native people. ... If in Aklavik the honey bucket was the great equalizer, in Inuvik, particularly during the early years, the utilidor was the great discriminator. The planning of Inuvik provided that some would have to continue to carry the honey bucket and [others] would no longer have to. Thus, discrimination was built into the piling foundations of this community. You could see it from the air, before ever setting foot in town, in terms of where the utilidor did run, the

white serviced end of town — and where it did not — the native unserviced part of town. [F17160ff.]

Such inequalities have not gone unobserved by the native people, for they are to be seen in almost every community. Philip Blake, a Dene from Fort McPherson and a social worker there for five years, talked about the changes in that community:

> I am not an old man, and I have seen many changes in my life. Fifteen years ago, most of what you see as Fort McPherson did not exist. Take a look around the community now and you will start to get an idea of what has happened to the Indian people here over the past few years.
>
> Look at the housing where transient government staff live. And look at the housing where the Indian people live. Look at what houses are connected to the utilidor. Look at how the school and hostel, the RCMP and government staff houses are right in the centre of town, dividing the Indian people into two sides. Look at where the Bay store is, right on the top of the highest point of land. Do you think that this is the way that the Indian people chose to have this community? Do you think the people here had any voice in planning this community? Do you think they would have planned it so that it divided them and gave them a poorer standard than the transient whites who came in, supposedly to help them? [C1078]

We must ask ourselves, how will these inequalities be affected by the construction of the Mackenzie Valley pipeline? The likelihood is that the native people will be employed as unskilled workers on jobs that will not last beyond the period of construction. The social implications of this likelihood can be stated baldly: industrial expansion into the Western Arctic means the extension northward of southern wage-and status differentials. The native people will find themselves on the bottom rungs of the

Yellowknife. (DIAND)

Accommodation and recreation in Hay River:

House on Indian Reserve. (Native Press)

Highrise apartment. (DIAND)

Swimming pool. (GNWT)

---

ladder, and most of them are likely to remain there.

Any claim that equality of opportunity at the work place will prevent the coincidence of low pay and low status with brown skin is, to say the least, naive. Inequalities of income and of occupational level are intrinsic to the industrial system, and they will no doubt be features of its extension to any frontier. Nevertheless, it is not easy to accept the racial inequalities at the work place. Still less easy is it to accept the social tensions and disorders that such inequalities bequeath.

Only time and the establishment of options available to the native people will go any distance toward preventing such inequalities. Once again we must remember that industrial development of the frontier, without a parallel development of native self-determination and the native economy, will bring to bear on the native people immense pressure to give way to a style of life that they regard as alien and destructive. If we create a society in which the native people of the North are deprived of social and economic dignity by a process of development that they regard as an assault on their homeland and themselves, they will see this assault in racial terms and will protest and oppose it in the years to come.

Identity and Self-respect

By cataloguing the pathologies of society in the North today, I have tried to show the North as I see it. I have tried to predict what will happen in terms of social impact, if a pipeline is built now.

It should be plain enough that one of the most pervasive social problems in the North today is the loss of self-esteem that many native people have experienced. It may be no exaggeration to speak at times of a despair that has overwhelmed whole families, even whole villages. I want this point to be well understood because it is integral to many of the social pathologies of northern people, and the problem must be faced if we are to develop a rational social policy for the future of the North.

Many of us cannot easily imagine what it is like to be a member of a subject race. When you see your race, or a member of it, denigrated or insulted, then you too are diminished as an individual. The expression can be subtle and insidious, or it can be overt; it can be part of deliberate behaviour, or it can be unintentional. The disorders that such discrimination involves cannot be eliminated by psychiatric, health and counselling services. Although such services may palliate the disease, they will never cure it.

Pat Kehoe, a psychologist who practises in the Yukon, told the Inquiry:

> I have talked to numerous native people, many as clients, who described to me their personal frustration, despair and sense of worthlessness in the face of the growing white community, and as the numerical dilution continues, this feeling is likely to grow. [F28455]

He made this prediction of the likely consequences of the pipeline:

> From the model presented earlier and the abundant evidence of cultural breakdown, we should predict a high incidence of disordered behaviour or, if you prefer, mental illness, among the native people. I have described [a] population with limited access to highly valued, achieved roles, whether these be white or traditional; where people are given roles that are incompatible with their traditional values; where there is a discontinuity between the old ways and the new; where traditional roles, such as hunter, trapper [and] shaman, are devalued or discredited entirely;

and where the old standards by which self-esteem was regulated are increasingly identified as irrelevant. [F28457]

He summarized his conception of the problem by reference to the psychiatric disorder known as reactive depression:

> This disorder is recognized by a set of symptoms including passivity, lack of interest, decrease in energy, difficulty in concentration, lack of motivation and ambition, and a feeling of helplessness. These symptoms can vary in degree and from person to person and culture to culture. It has been suggested by many of my colleagues in psychology and psychiatry that this disorder is virtually endemic among the northern native people but at a sub-clinical level or [it is] perhaps simply unrecognized as depression. [F28458]

Dr. Pat Abbott, a psychiatrist with the Division of Northern Medicine, Department of Health and Welfare, made a point that is vital to understanding these problems. The establishment of new programs, the recruitment of personnel, the delivery of improved health services and social services by themselves are and will be an exercise in futility; it is the condition of the people that we must address. And here we have come full circle to return again to the question of cultural impact. Abbott elaborated upon the difference between disorders that are individual, and therefore amenable to treatment at the individual level, and those that are social, and therefore unamenable to individual treatment:

> In the same way that psychiatry throughout the world differs in its approach [in] different cultures, psychiatry in the North must also take into account the cultural and social conditions of the people. The vast majority of the problems that I have seen as a clinical psychiatrist cannot, in all honesty, be classified as psychiatric problems. Some problems such as the major psychoses occur in all people, and the treatment is largely medical in

the sense of medication. So at least in its initial stages, southern psychiatry is appropriate. However, many of the problems seen are so closely interwoven with the life-style of the native people in the North, which in turn is closely bound to such problems as economics, housing, self-esteem and cultural identity, that to label them as psychiatric disorders is frankly fraudulent and of no value whatsoever, as the treatment must eventually be the treatment of the whole community rather than [of] the individual. [F28437]

Social Impact and the Pipeline

Some advocates of the pipeline say that the wage employment it would provide, even though temporary, would ameliorate the social problems that underlie the psychological symptoms that Kehoe, Abbott and others have described. In the light of all of the evidence and our experience, this attitude must be regarded as wrong. We cannot ignore the truly frightening increases in crime, abuse of alcohol, diet-related illness, venereal disease rates and mental illness that have occurred during the past ten years in the North.

At the same time, we should acknowledge some encouraging trends: violent deaths of native people in the Northwest Territories fell from 28.4 percent of all deaths in 1974 to 22.5 percent in 1975. There was a reduction in the number of cases of venereal disease reported in 1976. I have described some local reactions against alcohol abuse that have led to measures of local prohibition. Why have these indicators of crime and social disease, which for years have gone from bad to worse, broken their upward trend? Perhaps it has been a result of heightened native consciousness, the determination of the native people to be true to themselves, that is responsible. But let us make no mistake: these improvements, although welcome, are

small, and they may prove to be merely an interruption of longer-term trends. In communities into which the industrial economy has only recently penetrated, the situation is deeply alarming.

The question we face is, will construction of the pipeline hamper social improvements? The answer must be yes. If pipeline construction goes ahead now, can we ensure that its effects will not halt these social improvements? The answer must be no. Although some ameliorative measures can be taken to lessen the social impact of pipeline construction and related activity on the northern people, no one should think that these measures will prevent the further and serious deterioration of social and personal well-being in the native communities.

The process of rebuilding a strong, self-confident society in the Mackenzie Valley has begun. Major industrial development now may well have a disastrous effect on that process. With the pipeline, I should expect the high rate of alcohol consumption to persist and worsen. I should expect further erosion of native culture, further demoralization of the native people, and degradation and violence beyond anything previously seen in the Mackenzie Valley and the Western Arctic.

The presence of a huge migrant labour force and the impact of construction over the years will mean that alcohol and drugs will become more serious problems. It is fanciful to think that greater opportunities for wage employment on a pipeline will stop or reverse the effects of past economic development.

Let me cite what Dr. Wheeler said of the Dene, because this statement applies to all the native peoples of the Mackenzie Valley

and the Western Arctic. His views exemplify those of every doctor and nurse who spoke to the Inquiry.

The Dene have great strength as a people. Part of this strength lies in their extended family ties which they have been able to maintain in close-knit communities. We white people know the value of these kinds of ties, as we are now feeling the loss of them in terms of the depersonalization and dehumanization of southern urban living. How long will the Dene family survive the loss of its young men and the degradation of its women?

We want to hear what plans the territorial and federal governments have or are developing for these kinds of social problems. But perhaps the answer lies not with increasing government bureaucracy, with all its controls. The solution to these problems, and with it the survival of the Dene, lies within the Dene. They must be allowed to develop these solutions within a time frame of their own choosing before we get stampeded into a social disaster from which the North may never recover. The people need time and freedom in order to survive. [C3402]

The Limits to Planning

I have been asked to predict the impact of the pipeline and energy corridor and to recommend terms and conditions that might mitigate their impact. Some impacts are easier to predict than others: there is a vast difference between the effects that are likely to occur in the first year and those that will be important in ten years. And there are difficulties in prediction that involve more than time or scale, for even short-term causal chains can be intricately connected. Moreover, some consequences of the pipeline will be controllable, but others will not. Just as there are limits to predicting, so also are there limits to planning.

Arctic Red River. (M. Jackson)

Café and bar in Fort Providence. (Native Press)

Elizabeth Mackenzie, activist against liquor abuse, being sworn in as a Justice of the Peace, Rae-Edzo. (Native Press)

People visiting outside the Bay, Fort Norman. (N. Cooper)

I can recommend terms and conditions that will to some extent mitigate the social impact of the pipeline and energy corridor, but some of the consequences I have predicted will occur no matter what controls we impose. Other consequences can be predicted only in a vague and general way: we can anticipate their scale, but cannot adequately plan for them. There is a gulf, therefore, between the nature of the predictions and the nature of the terms and conditions I am asked to propose. The one is imprecise and often speculative; the other, if the terms and conditions are to be effective, must be very precise. We must never forget their limitations; it is all too easy to be overconfident of our ability to act as social engineers and to suppose – quite wrongly – that all problems can be foreseen and resolved. The nature of human affairs often defies the planners. In the case of a vast undertaking like the Mackenzie Valley pipeline, overconfidence in our ability to anticipate and to manage social problems would be foolish and dangerous.

I am prepared to accept that the oil and gas industry, the pipeline company, and the contractors will be able to exercise a measure of control over the movement and behaviour of their personnel. I am prepared to accept that government will expand its services and infrastructure in major communities to serve the requirements of pipeline construction in the Mackenzie Valley and of gas plant development in the Delta. Where actual numbers of people can be predicted, planning is possible and orderly procedures and cost-sharing arrangements can be worked out. However, there are obvious limitations to planning of this sort. The cost of the project or the number of workers required may be so far in excess of the figures we have now that it will seem as though we had planned one project but had built another. There is the question of how many people will be involved in secondary employment: their number will be large, no matter what measures are taken to discourage them, and the costs associated with their presence in the North will be very high.

There are also political limits to planning. The impacts that lead to social costs vary in the degree to which they can be treated. There are matters over which government and industry can exercise some control; there are other matters over which control would not be in keeping with the principles of a democratic society. And there are social impacts over which no control could be exercised even under the most authoritarian regime.

Finally, I am not prepared to accept that, in the case of an enormous project like the pipeline, there can be any real control over how much people will drink and over what the abuse of alcohol will do to their lives. There can be no control over how many families will break up, how many children will become delinquent and have criminal records, how many communities will see their young people drifting towards the larger urban centres, and how many people may be driven from a way of life they know to one they do not understand and in which they have no real place. Such problems are beyond anyone's power to control, but they will generate enormous social costs. Because these costs are, by and large, neither measurable nor assignable, we tend to forget them or to pretend they do not exist. But with construction of a pipeline, they would occur, and the native people of the North would then have to pay the price.

Fort Simpson community hearing. (N. Cooper)

Native Claims

The paramount cry of the native people of the North is that their claims must be settled before a pipeline is built across their land. In this chapter, I shall outline the history of native claims in Canada. This history is important because the concept of native claims has evolved greatly in recent years: they have their origin in native use and occupancy of the land, but today they involve much more than land.

When treaties were signed during the 19th century, the settlement of the native people's claims was regarded primarily as surrender of their land so that settlement could proceed. The payment of money, the provision of goods and services, and the establishment of reserves — all of which accompanied such a surrender — were conceived in part as compensation and in part as the means of change. The government's expectation was that a backward people would, in the fullness of time, abandon their semi-nomadic ways and, with the benefit of the white man's religion, education and agriculture, take their place in the mainstream of the economic and political life of Canada.

The governments of the day did not regard the treaties as anything like a social contract in which different ways of life were accommodated within mutually acceptable limits; they gave little consideration to anything beyond the extinguishment of native claims to the land, once and for all. The native people, by and large, understood the spirit of the treaties differently; they regarded the treaties as the means by which they would be able to retain their own customs and to govern themselves in the future. But they lacked the power to enforce their view.

The native peoples of the North now insist that the settlement of native claims must be seen as a fundamental re-ordering of their relationship with the rest of us. Their claims must be seen as the means to the establishment of a social contract based on a clear understanding that they are distinct peoples in history. They insist upon the right to determine their own future, to ensure their place, but not assimilation, in Canadian life. And the Government of Canada has now accepted the principle of comprehensive claims; it recognizes that any settlement of claims today must embrace the whole range of questions that is outstanding between the Government of Canada and the native peoples.

The settlement of native claims is not a mere transaction. It would be wrong, therefore, to think that signing a piece of paper would put the whole question behind us. One of the mistakes of the past has been to see such settlements as final solutions. The definition and redefinition of the relationship with the native people and their place in Confederation will go on for a generation or more. This is because the relationship has never been properly worked out. Now, for the first time, the federal government is prepared to negotiate with the native people on a comprehensive basis, and the native people of the North are prepared to articulate their interests over a broad range of concerns. Their concerns begin with the land, but are not limited to it: they extend to renewable and non-renewable resources, education, health and social services, public order and, overarching all of these considerations, the future shape and composition of political institutions in the North.

Perhaps a redefinition of the relationship between the Government of Canada and the native people can be worked out in the North better than elsewhere: the native people are a larger proportion of the population there than anywhere else in Canada, and no provincial authority stands in the way of the Government of Canada's fulfilment of its constitutional obligations.

In considering the claims of the native people, I am guided primarily by the testimony that the Inquiry heard at the community hearings in the North. No doubt the native organizations will, in due course, elaborate these claims in their negotiations with the government but, for my own purposes, I have, in assessing these claims, relied upon the evidence of almost a thousand native persons who gave evidence in the Mackenzie Valley and the Western Arctic. Finally, I shall indicate what impact construction of the pipeline would have on the settlement of native claims and the goals that the native people seek through the settlement of these claims.

History of Native Claims

The Issue: No Pipeline Before Native Claims are Settled

All the native organizations that appeared at the hearings insisted that this Inquiry should recommend to the Minister of Indian Affairs and Northern Development that no right-of-way be granted to build a pipeline until native claims along the route, both in the Yukon and the Northwest Territories, have been settled. The spokesmen for the native organizations and the people themselves insisted upon this point with virtual unanimity.

The claims of the Dene and the Inuit of the North derive from their rights as aboriginal peoples and from their use and occupation of northern lands since time immemorial. They want to live on their land, govern themselves on their land and determine for themselves what use is to be made of it. They are asking us to settle their land claims in quite a different way from the way that government settled native land claims in the past; government's past practice, they say, is inconsistent with its newly declared intention to achieve a comprehensive settlement of native claims.

Arctic Gas suggested that the native people should not be permitted to advance such an argument before the Inquiry because it did not fall within my terms of reference. The Order-in-Council stated that I am "to inquire into and report upon the terms and conditions that should be imposed in respect of any right-of-way that might be granted across Crown lands for the purposes of the proposed Mackenzie Valley pipeline." Those words, they argued, limit the Inquiry to the consideration of only the terms and conditions that must be performed or carried out by whichever pipeline company is granted a right-of-way.

It is true that, according to the Pipeline Guidelines, any terms and conditions that the Minister decides to impose upon any right-of-way must be included in a signed agreement to be made between the Crown and the pipeline company. But the Order-in-Council does not confine this Inquiry to a review of the Pipeline Guidelines nor to the measures that the pipeline companies may be prepared to take to meet them. The Order-in-Council calls upon the Inquiry to consider the social, economic and environmental impact of the construction of a pipeline in the North. The effect of these impacts cannot be disentangled from the whole question of native claims. Indeed, the native organizations argue that no effective terms and conditions could be imposed on a pipeline right-of-way, with a view to ameliorating its social and economic impact, before native

claims have been settled. It was essential, therefore, if the Inquiry was to fulfil its mandate, to hear evidence on the native organizations' principal contention: that the settlement of native claims ought to precede any grant of a right-of-way.

Only the Government of Canada and the native people can negotiate a settlement of native claims in the North: only they can be parties to such negotiation, and nothing said in this report can bind either side. Evidence of native claims was heard at the Inquiry to permit me to consider fairly the native organizations' principal contention regarding the pipeline, and to consider the answer of the pipeline companies to that contention.

Native Lands and Treaties in North America

When the first European settlers arrived in North America, independent native societies, diverse in culture and language, already occupied the continent. The European nations asserted dominion over the New World by right of their "discovery." But what of the native peoples who inhabited North America? By what right did Europeans claim jurisdiction over them? Chief Justice John Marshall of the Supreme Court of the United States, in a series of judgments in the 1820s and 1830s, described the Europeans' claim in these words:

> America, separated from Europe by a wide ocean, was inhabited by a distinct people, divided into separate nations, independent of each other and of the rest of the world, having institutions of their own, and governing themselves by their own laws.

> It is difficult to comprehend the proposition that the inhabitants of either quarter of the globe could have rightful original claims of dominion over the inhabitants of the other, or over the lands they occupied; or that the

discovery of either by the other should give the discoverer rights in the country discovered which annulled the existing rights of its ancient possessors.

> Did these adventurers, by sailing along the coast and occasionally landing on it, acquire for the several governments to whom they belonged, or by whom they were commissioned, a rightful property in the soil from the Atlantic to the Pacific; or rightful dominion over the numerous people who occupied it? Or has nature, or the great Creator of all things, conferred these rights over hunters and fishermen, on agriculturists and manufacturers?

> To avoid bloody conflicts, which might terminate disastrously to all, it was necessary for the nations of Europe to establish some principle which all would acknowledge and which should decide their respective rights as between themselves. This principle, suggested by the actual state of things, was "that discovery gave title to the government by whose subjects or by whose authority it was made, against all other European governments, which title might be consummated by possession."

> This principle, acknowledged by all Europeans, because it was the interest of all to acknowledge it, gave to the nation making the discovery, as its inevitable consequence, the sole right of acquiring the soil and of making settlements upon it. [*Worcester v. Georgia* (1832) 31 U.S. 350 at 369]

The Europeans' assumption of power over the Indians was founded on a supposed moral and economic superiority of European culture and civilization over that of the native people. But it was, nevertheless, acknowledged that the native people retained certain rights. Chief Justice Marshall said:

> [the native people] were admitted to be the rightful occupants of the soil, with a legal as well as just claim to retain possession of it, and to use it according to their own discretion; but their rights to complete sovereignty, as

Hudson's Bay Company at Fort Resolution in the early days. (Alberta Archives)

Great Slave Lake Dene, 1903. (Alberta Archives)

Slavey Indians in the old days, Hay River. (Public Archives)

Hand-games and drums, Fort Good Hope, 1927. (Public Archives)

independent nations, were necessarily diminished and their power to dispose of the soil at their own will, to whomsoever they pleased, was denied by the original fundamental principle that discovery gave exclusive title to those who made it. [*Johnson v. McIntosh* (1823) 21 U.S. 543]

The concept of aboriginal rights has a firm basis in international law, and we subscribe to it in Canada. During the last century, the Supreme Court of Canada in the St. Catherines Milling case and this century in the Nishga case affirmed the proposition that the original peoples of our country had a legal right to the use and occupation of their ancestral lands. The courts have had to consider whether, in given cases, the native right has been taken away by competent authority, and sometimes the courts have decided it has been. But original use and occupation of the land is the legal foundation for the assertion of native claims in Northern Canada today.

From the beginning, Great Britain recognized the rights of native people to their traditional lands, and acquired by negotiation and purchase the lands the colonists required for settlement and cultivation. That recognition was based not only on international law, but also upon the realities of the times, for in those early days the native people greatly outnumbered the settlers.

The necessity to maintain good relations with the native people led the British to formulate a more clearly defined colonial policy towards Indian land rights in the mid-18th century. The westward expansion of settlers from New England during this period had given rise to discontent among the Indian tribes and during the Seven Years War (1756-1763), the British were at pains to ensure the continued friendship of the Iroquois Confederacy lest they defect to the French. When the war ended, the British

controlled the whole of the Atlantic seaboard, from Newfoundland to Florida, and the government promulgated the Royal Proclamation of 1763. This document reserved to the Indians, as their hunting grounds, all the land west of the Allegheny Mountains, excluding Rupert's Land, the territory granted in 1670 to the Hudson's Bay Company. The Proclamation stated that, when land was required for further settlement, it should be purchased for the Crown in a public meeting held for that purpose by the governor or commander-in-chief of the several colonies. This procedure for the purchase of Indian land was the basis for the treaties of the 19th and 20th centuries.

The Treaties

Following the Proclamation of 1763, the British made a series of treaties with the Indians living in what is now Southern Ontario. Many of these treaties were with small groups of Indians for limited areas of land, but, as settlement moved westward in the mid-19th century, there was a dramatic increase in geographical scale. The Robinson treaties, made in Ontario in 1850, and the "numbered treaties," made following Canada's acquisition from Great Britain in 1870 of Rupert's Land and the Northwestern Territory, covered much larger tracts of land.

The treaties concluded after 1870 on the prairies cleared the way for the settlement of Western Canada and the construction of the Canadian Pacific Railway. The government's instructions to the Lieutenant-Governor of the Northwest Territories in 1870, after the cession of Rupert's Land, were explicit:

> You will also turn your attention promptly to the condition of the country outside the Province of Manitoba, on the North and West; and while assuring the Indians of your desire

to establish friendly relations with them, you will ascertain and report to His Excellency the course you may think the most advisable to pursue, whether by Treaty or otherwise, for the removal of any obstructions that might be presented to the flow of population into the fertile lands that lie between Manitoba and the Rocky Mountains. [Canada, Sessional Papers, 1871, No. 20 p. 8]

Treaties 1 to 7, made between 1870 and 1877, covered the territory between the watershed west of Lake Superior and the Rocky Mountains. In 1899, Treaty 8 covered territory northward to Great Slave Lake. Then, in 1921, Treaty 11 dealt with the land from Great Slave Lake down the Mackenzie River to the Mackenzie Delta. Treaties 8 and 11 together cover the whole of Northern Alberta and the western part of the Northwest Territories, including the Mackenzie Valley.

The treaties conform to a distinct pattern: in exchange for the surrender of their aboriginal rights, the Indians received annual cash payments. The amount varied with the treaty: under Treaties 1 and 2, each man, woman and child received $3 a year; under Treaty 4, the chiefs received $25, headmen $15, and other members of the tribe $12. In addition, the government established reserves for the use of the Indian bands: the area in some cases was apportioned on the basis of 160 acres of land for a family of five; in other cases, it was one square mile of land for each family. The treaties also recognized the continued right of the native people to hunt and fish over all the unsettled parts of the territories they had surrendered. Beginning with Treaty 3, the government agreed to supply the Indian bands with farm and agricultural implements, as well as with ammunition and twine for use in hunting and fishing.

The spirit of these clauses, together with

the guarantee of hunting and fishing rights and the establishment of reserves was, according to the understanding of the Indians, to support their traditional hunting and fishing economy and to help them to develop a new agricultural economy to supplement the traditional one when it was no longer viable.

White settlers soon occupied the non-reserve land that the Indians had surrendered, and their traditional hunting and fishing economy was undermined. Legislation and game regulations limited traditional activities yet further. The land allocated for reserves was often quite unsuitable for agriculture, and the reserves were often whittled away to provide additional land for white settlement. The government never advanced the capital necessary to develop an agricultural base for the Indians, and when the native population began to expand, the whole concept of developing agriculture on reserve lands became impractical.

These prairie treaties were negotiated in periods of near desperation for the Indian tribes. The decimation of the buffalo herds had ruined their economy, and they suffered from epidemic diseases and periodic starvation. Often they had no alternative to accepting the treaty commissioner's offers.

The recent settlement of native claims in Alaska and the James Bay Agreement follow the tradition of the treaties. The object of the earlier surrenders was to permit agricultural settlement by another race. The objects of the Alaska Native Claims Settlement Act and of the James Bay Agreement are to facilitate resource development by another race. The negotiators for the Province of Quebec stated that, if the native people refused to approve the James Bay Agreement, the project would go ahead anyway, and they would simply lose the benefits offered by the Province. This attitude parallels the position of the treaty commissioners a century ago: they said that if the Indians did not sign the treaties offered them, their lands would be colonized anyway.

Treaties in the Northwest Territories

Throughout the British Empire, the Crown, not the local legislature, was always responsible for the welfare of the aboriginal people. In 1867, therefore, the British North America Act gave the Parliament of Canada jurisdiction over Indian affairs and Indian lands throughout the new country. This jurisdiction encompasses the Inuit, and the Metis as well, at least to the extent that they are pressing claims based on their Indian ancestry. With Canada's acquisition of Rupert's Land and the Northwestern Territory, and the entry of British Columbia into Confederation, that jurisdiction extended from the Atlantic to the Pacific, from the 49th Parallel to the Arctic Ocean.

The constitutional documents that effected the transfer to Canada of Rupert's Land and the Northwestern Territory all refer to "aboriginal rights." The Imperial Order-in-Council, signed by Queen Victoria, that assigned Rupert's Land to Canada provided that:

> Any claims of Indians to compensation for lands required for purposes of settlement shall be disposed of by the Canadian Government in communication with the Imperial Government; and the [Hudson's Bay] Company shall be relieved of all responsibility in respect of them. [Exhibit F569, p. 42]

It was upon these conditions that Canada achieved sovereignty over the lands that comprise the Northwest Territories and Yukon Territory, including the lands claimed today by the Dene, Inuit and Metis.

After the transfer of these territories, the federal government enacted the Dominion Lands Act of 1872, the first statute to deal with the sale and disposition of federal crown lands. It stated:

> 42. None of the provisions of this Act respecting the settlement of agricultural lands, or the lease of timber lands, or the purchase and sale of mineral lands, shall be held to apply to territory the Indian title to which shall not at the time have been extinguished. [Exhibit F569, p. 43]

All of these instruments acknowledge the rights of the native people. They illustrate that the recognition of aboriginal title was deeply embedded in both the policy and the law of the new nation.

Treaties 8 and 11, made with the Indians of Northern Alberta and the Northwest Territories, continue both the philosophy and the form of earlier treaties. These two treaties are the subject of a recent book by Father René Fumoleau, *As Long as this Land Shall Last.* I cite his text for many official and historical documents related to these treaties.

In 1888, government surveyors reported that there was oil in the Mackenzie Valley and that the oil-bearing formations were "almost co-extensive with the [Mackenzie] valley itself." The report of a Select Committee of the Senate on the resources of the Mackenzie Basin, in March 1888, has a familiar ring today:

> ... the petroleum area is so extensive as to justify the belief that eventually it will supply the larger part of this continent and be shipped from Churchill or some more northern Hudson's Bay port to England. ... The evidence ... points to the existence ... of the most extensive petroleum field in America, if not in the World. The uses of petroleum and consequently the demand for it by all Nations are increasing at such a rapid ratio, that it is probable this great petroleum field will assume an enormous value in the near future

Bishop Breynat testifying at First Dominion of Canada inquiry in the Far North, Fort Providence, 1928. (Public Archives)

Inspector Bruce of the RCMP, Indian Commissioner Conroy and Hugh Pearson, 1921 Treaty Party in Fort Providence. (Public Archives)

Dogrib Woman. (Public Archives)

René Fumoleau. (News of the North)

and will rank among the chief assets comprised in the Crown Domain of the Dominion. [cited in Fumoleau, op. cit., p. 40]

A Privy Council Report of 1891 set forth the government's intentions:

... the discovery [of] immense quantities of petroleum ... renders it advisable that a treaty or treaties should be made with the Indians who claim those regions as their hunting grounds, with a view to the extinguishment of the Indian title in such portions of the same, as it may be considered in the interest of the public to open up for settlement. [cited in Fumoleau, op. cit., p. 41]

No treaty was made, however, until the Klondike gold rush of 1898. It was the entry of large numbers of white prospectors into the Mackenzie Valley on their way to the Yukon gold fields and the desire of the government to ensure peaceful occupation of the land that led to the making of Treaty 8. The boundaries of Treaty 8 were drawn to include the area in which geologists thought oil or gold might be found; they did not include the area inhabited by the Indians north of Great Slave Lake because, in the words of the Indian Commissioner, Amédée Forget:

... their territory so far as it is at present known is of no particular value and they very rarely come into contact with Whites. [cited in Fumoleau, op. cit., p. 59]

Treaty 8 was signed at various points including Fort Smith in 1899 and Fort Resolution in 1900. While the treaty commissioners negotiated with the Indians, a Half-Breed Commission negotiated with the Metis. Following the procedure established in the prairies, the government gave the Metis the option of coming under the treaty with the Indians or of accepting scrip, which entitled the bearer either to $240 or to 240 acres of land. Many Metis chose to come under the treaty.

Treaty 8, like the prairie treaties, provided for an annual payment of $5 per head, the recognition of hunting and fishing rights, and the allocation of reserve lands. But these lands were not allocated then, and, with the sole exception of a small reserve at Hay River in 1974, none have been allocated to this day.

The Indian people did not see Treaty 8 as a surrender of their aboriginal rights: they considered it to be a treaty of peace and friendship. Native witnesses at the Inquiry recalled the prophetic words that Chief Drygeese spoke when Treaty 8 was signed at Fort Resolution:

If it is going to change, if you want to change our lives, then it is no use taking treaty, because without treaty we are making a living for ourselves and our families ... I would like a written promise from you to prove you are not taking our land away from us. ... There will be no closed season on our land. There will be nothing said about the land. ... My people will continue to live as they were before and no White man will change that. ... You will in the future want us to live like White man does and we do not want that. ... The people are happy as they are. If you try to change their ways of life by treaty, you will destroy their happiness. There will be bitter struggle between your people and my people. [cited in Fumoleau, op. cit., p. 91ff.]

In the years that followed, legislation was enacted restricting native hunting and trapping. In 1917, closed seasons were established on moose, caribou and certain other animals essential to the economy of the native people, and in 1918 the Migratory Birds Convention Act further restricted their hunting. The Indians regarded these regulations as breaches of the promise that they would be free to hunt, fish and trap, and because of them they boycotted the payment of treaty money in 1920 at Fort Resolution.

In 1907, and repeatedly thereafter, Henry Conroy, who accompanied the original treaty party in 1899 and who had charge of the annual payment of treaty money, recommended that Treaty 8 should be extended farther north. But, in 1910, the official position was still that:

... at present there is no necessity for taking that action. The influx of miners and prospectors into that country is very small, and at present there [are] no settlers. [cited in Fumoleau, op. cit., p. 136]

The official position remained unchanged until 1920, when the Imperial Oil Company struck oil on the Mackenzie River below Fort Norman. The government quickly moved to ensure that these oil-rich lands should be legally open for industrial development and free of any Indian interest. F.H. Kitto, Dominion Land Surveyor, wrote:

The recent discoveries of oil at Norman [Wells] have been made on lands virtually belonging to those tribes [of non-treaty Indians]. Until treaty has been made with them, the right of the Mining Lands and Yukon Branch [of the federal government] to dispose of these oil resources is open to debate. [cited in Fumoleau, op. cit., p. 159]

Treaty 11 was soon signed. During the summer of 1921, the Treaty Commission travelled down the Mackenzie River from Fort Providence to Fort McPherson, then returned to visit Fort Rae. In 1922, the treaty was made with the Dene at Fort Liard. As with Treaty 8, the Metis were given the option of taking treaty or accepting scrip. However, the parliamentary approval necessary to pay the scrip was delayed, and the Metis were not paid until 1924, when 172 Metis took scrip. The payments of $240 to each Metis represent the only settlement made with the Metis of the Northwest Territories who did not take treaty. Rick Hardy, President of the Metis Association,

TREATY INDIANS
AT
FORT McPHERSON
MacKENZIE RIVER
COPYRIGHT
E.B. 1824

told the Inquiry that the Metis do not consider that these payments extinguished their aboriginal rights.

The Dene do not regard Treaty 11, which followed the pattern of Treaty 8, as a surrender of their land, but consider it to be a treaty of peace and friendship. Father Fumoleau writes of Treaty 11:

A few basic facts emerge from the evidence of documents and testimonies. These are: treaty negotiations were brief, initial opposition was overcome, specific demands were made by the Indians, promises were given, and agreement was reached....

They saw the white man's treaty as his way of offering them his help and friendship. They were willing to share their land with him in the manner prescribed by their tradition and culture. The two races would live side by side in the North, embarking on a common future. [cited in Fumoleau, op. cit., p. 210ff.]

In 1921, as in 1899, the Dene wanted to retain their traditional way of life and to obtain guarantees against the encroachment of white settlers on their land. In fact Commissioner Conroy did guarantee the Dene full freedom to hunt, trap and fish, because many Dene negotiators were adamant that, unless the guarantee was given, they would not sign the treaty. To the Dene, this guarantee that the government would not interfere with their traditional life on the land was an affirmation, not an extinguishment, of their rights to their homeland.

It is important to understand the Dene's view of the treaty, because it explains the vehemence with which native witnesses told the Inquiry that the land is still theirs, that they have never sold it, and that it is not for sale.

Father Fumoleau has written an account of the Treaty negotiations at Fort Norman, based on the evidence of witnesses to the event:

Commissioner Conroy promised the people that this was their land. "You can do whatever you want," he said. "We are not going to stop you...." This was the promise he made to the people ... that we could go hunting and fishing....

Then the Treaty party, Commissioner Conroy ... said, "As long as the Mackenzie River flows, and as long as the sun always comes around the same direction every day, we will never break our promise." The people and the Bishop said the same thing, so the people thought that it was impossible that this would happen — the river would never reverse and go back up-river, and the sun would never go reverse. This was impossible, so they must be true. That is why we took the Treaty. [cited in Fumoleau, op. cit., p. 180ff]

Joe Naedzo told the Inquiry at Fort Franklin that, according to the native people's interpretation of the treaty, the government made "a law for themselves that as long as the Mackenzie River flows in one direction, the sun rises and sets, we will not bother you about your land or the animals." (C606)

When the treaty commissioners reached Fort Rae in 1921, the Dogrib people there were well aware that the promises the government had made to the Dogribs and Chipewyans, who had signed the treaty at Fort Resolution in 1900, had not been kept. The native people would not sign Treaty 11 unless the government guaranteed hunting and trapping rights over the whole of their traditional territory. This is Harry Black's account of the negotiations with the Dogribs:

Chief Monfwi stated that if his terms were met and agreed upon, then there will be a treaty, but if his terms were not met, then "there will be no treaty since you [Treaty Officials] are on my land." ... The Indian agent asked Chief Monfwi ... what size of land he wanted for the band. Monfwi stated

... "The size of land has to be large enough for all of my people." ... Chief Monfwi asked for a land boundary starting from Fort Providence, all along the Mackenzie River, right up to Great Bear Lake, then across to Contwoyto Lake ... Snowdrift, along the Great Slave Lake, back to Fort Providence.

The next day we crowded into the meeting tent again and began the big discussion about the land boundary again. Finally they came to an agreement and a land boundary was drawn up. Chief Monfwi said that within this land boundary there will be no closed season on game so long as the sun rises and the great river flows and only upon these terms I will accept the treaty money. [cited in Fumoleau, op. cit., p. 192ff]

The Government of the Northwest Territories had, by this time, begun to take shape. The first territorial government headquarters opened in Fort Smith in 1921, and its first session was the same year, with oil the main item on the agenda. The duties of the new administration included inspection of the oil well and of the country to see if it was suitable for a pipeline.

The Dene had signed Treaties 8 and 11 on the understanding that they would be free to hunt and fish over their traditional territory and that the government would protect them from the competition and intrusion of white trappers. Yet, contrary to treaty promises, an influx of white trappers and traders into the country was permitted to exploit the game resources almost at will, and soon strict game laws were necessary to save certain animal populations from extinction. The enforcement of these game laws caused hardship to the native people who depended on the animals for survival.

The encroachment of white trappers on lands that the native people regarded as their own led them to demand the establishment of game preserves in which only they would be permitted to hunt and trap. Fran

Treaty Indians at Fort McPherson.
(Alberta Archives)

Margaret Blackduck baking outdoors during Treaty Days in Rae, 1975. (Native Press)

Jim Sittichinli of Aklavik broadcasting in Loucheux language for Canadian Broadcasting Corporation. (Native Press)

Graveside service in the North. (R. Fumoleau)

Native Claims

T'Seleie told of such a request made by Father Antoine Binamé on behalf of the people of Fort Good Hope in 1928:

> At the present time the Indians are in fear of too many outside trappers getting into the districts outlined ... and should these preserves be granted ... the Indians would be more likely to endeavour to preserve the game in their own way. They at present are afraid of leaving the beaver colonies to breed up as the white man would in all likelihood come in and hunt them. [C1773]

The request was never granted, although some game preserves were established in other areas.

Wood Buffalo National Park was established in 1922 and enlarged in 1926. Shooting buffalo was strictly forbidden, although Treaty Indians were allowed to hunt other game and to trap furbearing animals in the park. These regulations were strictly enforced, and the protection of buffalo took precedence over the protection of Indian hunting rights.

In 1928, the government imposed a three-year closed season on beaver in the Mackenzie District. This regulation came at the worst possible time for the Dene, for that year they were decimated by an influenza epidemic. Other furbearing animals were scarce, and without beaver they were short of meat. The Dene at Fort Rae protested and refused to accept treaty payment until they had been assured that they could kill beaver. Bishop Breynat had appealed to the government on their behalf, and some modifications to the closed season were made. Despite continuing protests about the activities of white trappers, they received no protection from this threat. In 1937, the Indians of Fort Resolution again refused, as they had in 1920, to accept treaty payment in protest against their treatment by the government.

Finally, in 1938, legislation was passed to regulate the activity of white trappers and to restrict hunting and trapping licences only to those white persons who already held them. But, as Father Fumoleau told us, by this time most of the white trappers had turned from trapping to mining. At the same time that the native people had been restricted in their traditional activities, oil and mineral exploration and development had proceeded apace. In 1932, the richest uranium mine in the world began operation at Port Radium on Great Bear Lake. Gold was discovered in Yellowknife in 1933. In 1938, Norman Wells produced 22,000 barrels of oil, and in 1938-1939 the value of gold mined in the Northwest Territories exceeded for the first time the total value of raw furs produced.

The Dene insist the history of broken promises continues today. Jim Sittichinli, at the very first community hearing, held in Aklavik, related the recent experience of the native people:

> Now, at the time of the treaty ... 55 years ago ... they said, "As long as the river runs, as long as the sun goes up and down, and as long as you see that black mountain up there, well, you are entitled to your land."
>
> The river is still running. The sun still goes up and down and the black mountain is still up there, but today it seems that, the way our people understand, the government is giving up our land. It is giving [it up] to the seismic people and the other people coming up here, selling ... our land. The government is not keeping its word, at least as some of us see it.
>
> Now, there has been lots of damage done already to this part of the northland, and if we don't say anything, it will get worse....
>
> The other day I was taking a walk in Yellowknife ... and I passed a house there with a dog tied outside. I didn't notice it and all of a sudden this dog jumped up and gave me a big bark, and then, after I passed through there, I was saying to myself, "Well, that dog taught me a lesson." You know, so often you [don't] see the native people, they are tied down too much, I think, by the government. We never go and bark, therefore nobody takes notice of us, and it is about time that we the people of this northland should get up sometime and bark and then we would be noticed. [C87ff.]

So far I have been describing treaties made with the Indians and Metis. No treaties were ever made with the Inuit, although the boundaries of Treaty 11 include part of the Mackenzie Delta that was occupied and used by the Inuit. They were not asked to sign the treaty in 1921 and, when they were invited to do so in 1929, they refused.

The absence of a treaty has made little difference to the Inuit, although they have been spared the invidious legal distinctions introduced among the Dene by treaty and non-treaty status. The Inuit witnesses who spoke to the Inquiry made clear that they, no less than the Dene, regard their traditional lands as their homeland. They also demand recognition of their rights to the land and their right to self-determination as a people. At Tuktoyaktuk, Vince Steen summarized the historical experience of the Inuit:

> A lot of people seem to wonder why the Eskimos don't take the white man's word at face value any more.... Well, from my point of view, it goes way back, right back to when the Eskimos first saw the white man.
>
> Most of them were whalers, and the whaler wasn't very nice to the Eskimo. He just took all the whales he could get and never mind the results. Who is paying for it now? The Eskimo. There is a quota on how many whales he can kill now.
>
> Then next, following the whalers, the white traders and the white trappers. The white traders took them for every cent they could get. You know the stories in every history book where they had a pile of fur as high as your gun. Those things were not fair. The

natives lived with it — damn well had to — to get that gun, to make life easier for himself.

Then there was the white trapper. He came along and he showed the Eskimo how to use the traps, steel-jawed traps, leg-hold traps. They used them, well they're still using them today, but for the first 70 years when they were being used, there were no complaints down south about how cruel those traps are — as long as there was white trappers using them. Now for the last five years they are even thinking of cutting us off, but they haven't showed us a new way of how to catch those foxes for their wives though.

After them, after the white trappers and the fur traders, we have all the settlements, all the government people coming in and making settlements all over, and telling the people what to do, what is best for them. Live here. Live there. That place is no good for you. Right here is your school. So they did — they all moved into settlements, and for the 1950s and 1960s they damn near starved. Most of them were on rations because they were not going out into the country any more. Their kids had to go to school.

Then came the oil companies. First the seismographic outfits, and like the Eskimo did for the last 50 or 60 years, he sat back and watched them. Couldn't do anything about it anyway, and he watched them plough up their land in the summertime, plough up their traps in the wintertime. What are you going to do about it? A cat [caterpillar tractor] is bigger than your skidoo or your dog team.

Then the oil companies. Well, the oil companies, I must say, of all of them so far that I have mentioned, seem to ... have the most respect for the people and their ways; but it is too late. The people won't take a white man's word at face value any more because you fooled them too many times. You took everything they had and you gave them nothing. You took all the fur, took all the whales, killed all the polar bear with aircraft and everything, and put a quota on top of that, so we can't have polar bear when we feel like it any more. All that we pay for. Same thing with the seismic outfits....

Now they want to drill out there. Now they want to build a pipeline and they say they're not going to hurt the country while they do it. They're going to let the Eskimo live his way, but he can't because ... the white man has not only gotten so that he's taken over, taken everything out of the country ... but he's also taken the culture, half of it anyway....

For the Eskimo to believe now that the white man is not going to do any damage out there ... is just about impossible, because he hasn't proven himself. As far as I'm concerned he hasn't proven himself worthy of being believed any more....

The Eskimo is asking for a land settlement because he doesn't trust the white man any more to handle the land that he owns, and he figures he's owned for years and years. [C4199ff.]

Because the native people of the North believe the pipeline and the developments that will follow it will undermine their use of the land and indelibly shape the future of their lives in a way that is not of their choosing, they insist that, before any such development takes place, their right to their land and their right to self-determination as a people must be recognized. They have always held these beliefs, but their articulation of them has seldom been heard or understood.

Entrenchment, Not Extinguishment

Canadian policy has always contemplated the eventual extinguishment of native title to the land. The native people had to make way for the settlement of agricultural lands in the West, and now they are told they must make way for the industrial development of the North. But the native people of the North do not want to repeat the history of the native peoples of the West. They say that, in

the North, Canadian policy should take a new direction.

Throughout Canada, we have assumed that the advance of western civilization would lead the native people to join the mainstream of Canadian life. On this assumption, the treaties promised the Indians education and agricultural training. On this assumption, the federal government has introduced programs for education, housing, job training and welfare to both treaty and non-treaty Indians. Historical experience has clearly shown that this assumption is ill-founded, and that such programs do not work. The statistics for unemployment, school drop-outs, inadequate housing, prison inmates, infant mortality and violent death bespeak the failure of these programs. George Manuel, President of the National Indian Brotherhood, told the Inquiry that the programs failed because the native people were never given the political and constitutional authority to enforce the treaty commitments or to implement the programs. Every program has assumed, and eventually has produced, greater dependency on the government. Manuel told the Inquiry:

We, the aboriginal peoples of Southern Canada, have already experienced our Mackenzie Valley pipeline. Such projects have occurred time and time again in our history. They were, and are, the beginnings of the type of developments which destroy the way of life of aboriginal peoples and rob us of our economic, cultural and political independence....

Developments of this kind can only be supported on the condition that the [native] people must first be assured economic, political and cultural self-reliance. [F21761]

Manuel argued that the settlement of native claims in the North must recognize the native people's rights to land and to political authority over the land, as opposed to cash

People of Holman assemble for community hearing. (P. Scott)

Swearing in of witnesses Douglas Sanders, George Manuel and René Fumoleau. (D. Gamble)

Sign at Fort Good Hope airstrip. (N. Cooper)

Chief Billy Diamond, Premier Robert Bourassa, Hon. Judd Buchanan, Northern Quebec Inuit Association President, Charlie Watt and John Ciaccia at signing of James Bay Agreement, 1975. (DIAND)

compensation for the purchase of their land. The object of negotiations, he said, should be the enhancement of aboriginal rights, not their extinguishment. Only through transfer to them of real economic and political power can the native people of the North play a major role in determining the course of events in their homeland and avoid the demoralization that has overtaken so many Indian communities in the South. The determination to arrest this historical process, which is already underway in some northern communities, explains the native people's insistence on a settlement that entrenches their right to the land and offers them self-determination.

The demand for entrenchment of native rights is not unique to the native people of the North. Indians in Southern Canada, and aboriginal peoples in many other parts of the world, are urging upon the dominant society their own right to self-determination. As Manuel said:

> Aboriginal people everywhere share a common attachment to the land, a common experience and a common struggle. [F21760]

James Wah-Shee, voicing a sentiment shared by virtually all of the native people in the North, said:

> The general public has been misinformed on the question of land settlement in the North. What is at issue is land not money.
>
> A land settlement in the Northwest Territories requires a new approach, a break in a historical pattern. A "once-and-for-all" settlement in the tradition of the treaties and Alaska will not work in the Northwest Territories. What we are seriously considering is not the surrender of our rights "once and for all" but the formalization of our rights and ongoing negotiation and dialogue. We are investigating a solution which could be a source of pride to all Canadians and not an expensive tax burden, for ours is a truly

"developmental" model in the widest and most human sense of the word. It allows for the preservation of our people and our culture and secures our participation as equals in the economy and society of Canada. [*Delta Gas: Now or Later,* speech presented in Ottawa, May 24, 1974, p. 14]

The treaties already made with the Dene do not stand in the way of a new settlement. The Dene maintain that Treaties 8 and 11 did not extinguish their aboriginal rights, and the government, for its part, has agreed to negotiate settlement of native claims without insisting on whatever rights it may claim under the treaties. Since no reserves were ever set aside under the treaties (except one at Hay River), federal policy, therefore, is not impeded by the Indian Act, the provisions of which relate primarily to the administration of reserve lands.

In the case of the non-status Indians — treaty Indians who for one reason or another have lost their treaty status — the Indian Act has no application, and the federal government has agreed to negotiate with them on the footing that they are entitled to participate in a settlement in the same way as treaty Indians. The government has made the same undertaking to the Metis. The government is not, therefore, arguing that the payment of scrip by the Half-Breed Commissions in the past extinguished the aboriginal rights of the Metis. In the case of the Inuit, there are neither treaties nor reserves, and the provisions of the Indian Act have never been applied to them.

There is, therefore, no legal or constitutional impediment to the adoption of a new policy in the settlement of native claims. The federal government, in dealing with the claims of the northern people, has recognized both that there are new opportunities for the settlement of claims and that such claims must be treated as comprehensive claims.

The Honourable Judd Buchanan, in addressing the Territorial Council of the Northwest Territories on February 13, 1976, described the claims, as the government saw them:

> First, the claims involved are regarded as comprehensive in the sense that they relate to all native claimants residing in the area concerned, and the proposals for settlement ... could include the following elements: categories of land, hunting, trapping and fishing, resource management, cultural identity, and native involvement in governmental evolution. [p. 7ff.]

The native people of the North, for their part, also wish the settlement of their claims to be a comprehensive settlement. They, like the federal government, see their claims as the means of opening up new possibilities. Robert Andre, at Arctic Red River, articulated for the Inquiry the native people's view of the objectives of their claims:

> We are saying we have the right to determine our own lives. This right derives from the fact that we were here first. We are saying we are a distinct people, a nation of people, and we must have a special right within Canada. We are distinct in that it will not be an easy matter for us to be brought into your system because we are different. We have our own system, our own way of life, our own cultures and traditions. We have our own languages, our own laws, and a system of justice....
>
> Land claims ... [mean] our survival as a distinct people. We are a people with a long history and a whole culture, a culture which has survived. ... We want to survive as a people, [hence] our stand for maximum independence within your society. We want to develop our own economy. We want to acquire political independence for our people, within the Canadian constitution. We want to govern our own lives and our own lands and its resources. We want to have our own system of government, by which we can control and develop our land for our benefit. We want to have the exclusive right to hunt, to fish and to trap. [C4536ff.]

We are saying that on the basis of our [aboriginal] land rights, we have an ownership and the right to participate directly in resource development. [C4536]

We want, as the original owners of this land, to receive royalties from [past] developments and for future developments, which we are prepared to allow. These royalties will be used to fund local economic development, which we are sure will last long after the companies have exhausted the non-renewable resources of our land. The present system attempts to put us into a wage economy as employees of companies and governments over which we have no control. We want to strengthen the economy at the community level, under the collective control of our people. In this way many of our young people will be able to participate directly in the community and not have to move elsewhere to find employment.

We want to become involved in the education of our children in the communities where we are in the majority. We want to be able to control the local schools. We want to start our own schools in the larger centres in the North where we are in the minority....

Where the governments have a continuing role after the land settlement, we want to have a clear recognition as a distinct people, especially at the community level. Also at the community level, powers and control should lie with the chief and band council. To achieve all this is not easy. Much work lies ahead of us....

We must again become a people making our own history. To be able to make our own history is to be able to mould our own future, to build our society that preserves the best of our past and our traditions, while enabling us to grow and develop as a whole people.

We want a society where all are equal, where people do not exploit others. We are not against change, but it must be under our terms and under our control. ... We ask that our rights as a people for self-determination be respected. [C4539ff.]

Robert Andre was speaking only of the Dene land claims, but the evidence I have heard indicates that the claims of the Inuit coincide in principle with those of the Dene. The Metis Association of the Northwest Territories originally indicated its agreement with the Dene position, but they are now developing a claim of their own. I am satisfied that the position Andre articulated represents the concept of native claims held by the majority of the people of Indian ancestry in the Mackenzie Valley.

Self-Determination and Confederation

The Claim to Self-determination

Why do the native people in the North insist upon their right to self-determination? Why cannot they be governed by the same political institutions as other Canadians? Many white people in the North raised these questions at the Inquiry. Ross Laycock at Norman Wells put it this way:

> I don't see why ... we say Dene nation, why not a Canadian nation? The Americans in coping with racial prejudice have a melting pot where all races become Americans. We have a patchwork quilt, so let us sew it together and become Canadians, not white and Indians. [C2149]

But all of our experience has shown that the native people are not prepared to assimilate into our society. The fact is, they are distinct from the mass of the Canadian people racially, culturally and linguistically. The people living in the far-flung villages of the Canadian North may be remote from the metropolis, but they are not ignorant. They sense that their determination to be themselves is the only foundation on which they can rebuild their society. They are seeking — and discovering — insights of their own into the nature of the dominant white society and into the relationship between that society and their own. They believe they must formulate their claims for the future on that basis.

Native leadership can come only from the native people, and the reasons for this lie deep within man's soul. We all sense that people must do what they can for themselves. No one else, no matter how well-meaning, can do it for them. The native people are, therefore, seeking a fundamental reordering of the relations between themselves and the rest of Canada. They are seeking a new Confederation in the North.

The concept of native self-determination must be understood in the context of native claims. When the Dene people refer to themselves as a nation, as many of them have, they are not renouncing Canada or Confederation. Rather they are proclaiming that they are a distinct people, who share a common historical experience, a common set of values, and a common world view. They want their children and their children's children to be secure in that same knowledge of who they are and where they come from. They want their own experience, traditions and values to occupy an honourable place in the contemporary life of our country. Seen in this light, they say their claims will lead to the enhancement of Confederation — not to its renunciation.

It is a disservice to the Dene to suggest that they — or, for that matter, the Inuit or the Metis — are separatists. They see their future as lying with and within Canada, and they look to the Government of Canada, to the Parliament of Canada, and to the Crown itself to safeguard their rights and their future. Indeed it is this Inquiry, established

*Support for the Dene Declaration, Fort Simpson,
1975.* (Native Press)

*James Arvaluk, former President of Inuit Tapirisat,
and Ewan Cotterill, Assistant Deputy Minister of
Indian Affairs and Northern Development.*
(Inuit Today—T. Grant)

NWT Metis Association President, Rick Hardy.
(Native Press)

Fitz-Smith band office, Fort Smith. (Native Press)

by the Government of Canada under the
Territorial Lands Act, a statute enacted by
the Parliament of Canada, which they have
chosen to be a forum for the presentation of
their case before the people of Southern
Canada.

Self-determination and
the Canadian Constitution

Can a settlement that embraces the native
people's claim to self-determination be accommodated within our constitutional tradition and framework?

The roots of most Canadians lie in Europe,
but the cultures of the native peoples have a
different origin: they are indigenous to North
America. The Fathers of Confederation provided in the constitution that the Parliament
of Canada should protect the native people
of our country. There is no such provision in
the constitution for any other people.

Parliament has exclusive legislative jurisdiction in relation to the native peoples of
Canada, but the British North America Act
does not prescribe any particular legislative
arrangements for them. There is nothing in
the constitution that would preclude the
kind of settlement the native people of the
North are seeking.

Under the constitutional authority of
Parliament to legislate for the peace, order
and good government of Canada, there has
been a wide range of administrative arrangements in the Northwest Territories,
beginning with the Act of 1869 (S.C. 32-33
Victoria, Ch.3), which established a temporary system of administrative control for
Rupert's Land and the Northwestern Territory, right up to 1970 with the establishment
of the contemporary Territorial Council
under the Northwest Territories Act (R.S.C.

1970, Ch. N-22). It is certainly within Parliament's power to reorganize the territorial
government to permit a devolution of self-
government to Dene and Inuit institutions.
Parliament is competent, in the exercise of its
jurisdiction under Section 91(24) of the
British North America Act, to restrict participation in such institutions to persons of a
certain racial heritage.

Could the native people's claims to self-
determination, to the land, and to self-
governing institutions be accommodated
constitutionally within any future legislation that might establish a province in the
Territories? Under our constitution, specific
limitations and conditions could be attached
to the powers of a new province. Constitutionally, there is no bar to the native ownership of land nor to a guarantee of native
institutions of self-government in a new
province.

I think such special guarantees would be
in keeping with the Canadian tradition. Lord
Durham, in his report of 1839, looked toward
the assimilation of all Canadians into the
British culture. The Act of Union in 1840
established a framework of government
designed to promote this solution: one province and one legislature for both the French-
speaking people of Lower Canada and the
English-speaking people of Upper Canada.
But the people of Quebec would not be
assimilated. Thus, in 1867, as Dr. Peter
Russell wrote, "it was Cartier's ideal of a
pluralistic nation, not Durham's ideal of a
British nation in North America, that prevailed." The Dene, the Inuit and the Metis
call for the extension to Canada's native
people of the original spirit of Confederation.

Canada has not been an easy nation to
govern, but over the years we have tried to
remain true to the ideal that underlies
Confederation, an ideal that Canada and

Canadians have had to affirm again and
again in the face of continuing challenges to
their tolerance and sense of diversity. Why
should the native people of Canada be given
special consideration? No such consideration
has been offered to the Ukrainians, the
Swedes, the Italians, or any other race, ethnic
group or nationality since Confederation.
Why should the native people be allowed
political institutions of their own under the
Constitution of Canada, when other groups
are not?

The answer is simple enough: the native
people of the North did not immigrate to
Canada as individuals or families expecting
to assimilate. Immigrants chose to come and
to submit to the Canadian polity; their
choices were individual choices. The Dene
and the Inuit were already here, and were
forced to submit to the polity imposed upon
them. They were here and had their own
languages, cultures and histories before the
arrival of the French or English. They are the
original peoples of Northern Canada. The
North was — and is — their homeland.

Special Status

Experience has shown that our concept of
universal assimilation cannot be applied to
the native people. Dr. Lloyd Barber, Commissioner of Indian Claims in Canada, has said:

> ... native people are seriously talking about a
> distinctly different place within Canadian
> society, an opportunity for greater self-deter-
> mination and a fair share of resources, based
> on their original rights. No doubt this will
> require new and special forms of institutions
> which will need to be recognized as part of
> our political framework. [Speech to the Rotary
> Club in Yellowknife, 1974]

The idea of new political institutions that
give meaning to native self-determination
should not frighten us. Special status for the

native people is, and has been since Confederation, an integral part of our constitutional tradition. Their special status has, however, often led them into a state of enforced dependency. The self-determination that the native people of the North are now seeking is an extension of the special status they have always had under the constitution. In working out the nature and scope of that special status and of the political institutions that it will have, the native people of the North see an opportunity to break the cycle of dependency and to regain their sense of integrity and self-reliance. Barber had this to say about the importance of native self-determination:

> The old approaches are out. We've been allowed to delude ourselves about the situation for a long time because of a basic lack of political power in native communities. This is no longer the case, and it is out of the question that the newly emerging political and legal power of native people is likely to diminish. We must face the situation squarely as a political fact of life but more importantly, as a fundamental point of honour and fairness. We do, indeed, have a significant piece of unfinished business that lies at the foundations of this country. [ibid.]

I have used the expression "special status," and I do so advisedly. A special status for the native people is embodied in the constitution and reflected in the Indian Act and the treaties. In 1969, the Government of Canada proposed to end special status for the native peoples, and the native peoples throughout Canada opposed that idea so vigorously that the government abandoned it.

The Honourable Judd Buchanan, then Minister of Indian Affairs and Northern Development, in a statement of policy issued on July 26, 1976 — a statement of policy approved by the Cabinet and described as "the foundation for future policy" — reaffirmed the idea of special status. The statement of policy foresees "that there would continue to be recognition for Indian status, treaty rights and special privileges resulting from land claims settlements." This, of course, would apply to the treaty Indians in the Mackenzie Valley and the Western Arctic. But it must, in the Northwest Territories, entail also some form of special status for non-treaty Indians, Metis and Inuit because their aboriginal rights have been also recognized. The government cannot admit special status for treaty Indians, yet deny it to those living in the same village, even in the same houses. Special status for the native people has always been federal policy in Canada: the time has now come to make it work.

Local, regional, or territorial political entities may evolve that have a predominantly native electorate, an electorate in which a native majority might be entrenched by a suitable residency clause. Or political instruments may be developed by which the native people can, under an ethnic franchise and within a larger political entity, control matters that are, by tradition and right, theirs to determine. One approach would be geographical, the other functional. I am not attempting here to list all of the political possibilities. The native people and the Government of Canada must explore them together. I am saying that the Constitution of Canada does not necessarily require the imposition of existing political forms on the native people. The constitution offers an opportunity to deal comprehensively with native claims in the North, unfettered by real or imagined constitutional constraints. I express no opinion on the various options: I simply want it understood that all of them are open.

The claim by native people for institutions of their own is not going to be abandoned. In the North — indeed, all over Canada — it is gaining strength. It may seem odd — and out of keeping with liberal notions of integration and assimilation — but it is an ethnic strand in our constitutional fabric going back to 1867 and before. The European settlement of this country was an heroic achievement, but that history should not be celebrated in a way that fails to recognize the presence and history of the original inhabitants. We may take pride in the achievements of ancestors who settled the Atlantic coast, the St. Lawrence Valley, and then pushed on to the West and to the Pacific, but we should never forget that there were already people living in those lands. These peoples are now insisting that we recognize their right to develop political institutions in the North that will enable them to build on their own tradition and on their own past so they can share more fully in our country's future.

Evolution of Government in the Northwest Territories

The concept of native self-determination is antithetical to the vision of the future held by many white people in the Northwest Territories, who believe that, in due course, the Territories should become a province like the other provinces. They see no place for native self-determination in such a future. It is not surprising they should feel this way because their vision of the future is a reflection of what occurred during the settlement of the West. Agricultural settlers moved into Indian country, and when they were well enough established, they sought admittance to Confederation as a province. In 1870 Manitoba was carved out of the Northwestern Territory; in 1880 a large area

NWT Indian delegates meeting to choose a new leader, Fort Norman, 1976. (N. Cooper)

Fort Resolution Settlement Council. (GNWT)

Laing Building, Yellowknife, 1970, headquarters of the Government of the Northwest Territories. (NFB—McNeill)

John Steen, member from Tuktoyaktuk, addressing the Territorial Council. (GNWT)

of the Northwestern Territory was transferred to Ontario; in 1905 Alberta and Saskatchewan were created; and in 1912 a large area was added to the Province of Quebec. Many white northerners expected the Northwest Territories, following this process, to become a province like the others; a province in which white men govern a and that once belonged to others. Some witnesses have urged me to recommend to the federal government the granting of additional powers to the Territorial Council in order to bring the Northwest Territories closer to provincial status.

In fact, the evolution of political institutions in the Northwest Territories since 1905 has followed the pattern of the provinces. The Territorial Council is modelled after the provincial legislatures, although because it is the creation of Parliament, it has no standing under the constitution.

In 1966, the Carrothers Commission recommended that local municipal bodies should be the basis for the development of self-government in the Northwest Territories. As a result, institutions of local government were established following the model of municipal institutions as they exist in Southern Canada. In the larger centres, local government has a tax base founded on private property. The same system, whereby increased responsibility for local affairs is tied to the evolution of a tax base, was established in native communities. Even though there is virtually no private property in these communities, the assumption seems to have been that they would progress in time from settlements and hamlets — the most limited forms of local government — to the status of villages, towns and cities, like Fort Simpson, Inuvik and Yellowknife.

Settlements and hamlets, the highest levels of local government that the native

communities have so far achieved, have very limited authority. In practice, this authority relates only to the day-to-day operations of the community, such as roads, water, sewage and garbage. In the native communities, most members of the local council are natives, but the native people made it quite clear to me that these councils have no power to deal with their vital concerns, such as the protection of their land and the education of their children. These important decisions are still made in Yellowknife and Ottawa. The native people regard local government, as it exists at present, as an extension of the territorial government, not a political institution of the community itself. Paul Andrew, Chief of the Fort Norman Band, had formerly worked as settlement secretary at Fort Norman. He described local government in this way:

> It was quite obvious that this whole Settlement Council system has never worked and never will work because it is a form of tokenism to the territorial government.... [It is] an Advisory Board whose advice [is] not usually taken....
>
> The frustrations that I found for the position was that I was told that I was working for the people. But I was continuously getting orders from the regional office. They were the ones that finally decided what would happen and what would not happen. [C875ff.]

Though there is a majority of native people on the Territorial Council, it is not regarded as a native institution. The bureaucracy of the territorial government, concentrated in Yellowknife and the other large centres, plays a far more important part than the Territorial Council in shaping the lives of the native people and their communities. The native people see the Government of the Northwest Territories as a white institution; indeed, of the persons who hold the position of director in the

Government of the Northwest Territories, all are white. For the most part, native employees hold clerical and janitorial positions. Noel Kakfwi expressed to the Inquiry at Fort Good Hope the native people's sense of non-participation in the existing government:

> In Yellowknife last week I spent about eight days. Out of curiosity I went into the offices and I was exploring the building in different places. All I seen was those white people with the brown hair, white collar, neckties, sitting on the desk. I looked around if I could see one native fellow, one Dene. Nothing doing. [C1923ff.]

In developing institutions of government in the North, we have sought to impose our own system, to persuade the native people to conform to our political models. We have not tried to fashion a system of government based on the Dene and Inuit models of consensus, or to build on their traditional forms of local decision-making. So long as the native people are obliged to participate in political institutions that are not of their making or of their choosing, it seems to me their participation will be half-hearted. Indeed, two Dene members withdrew from the Territorial Council last year on the ground that such membership was inconsistent with the furtherance of the claims of the Dene.

To understand why Dene and Inuit models have not been used to develop local and regional government in the North, we have to look closely at our own assumptions about the native people. During the past few years, the native people have challenged the validity of these assumptions.

We have assumed that native culture is static and unchanging, and we have not seriously considered the possibility that the native people could adapt their traditional social, economic and political organization to deal with present realities. The native people are seen as a people locked into the past. Such an assumption becomes self-fulfilling. By not allowing them the means to deal with their present problems on their own terms, their culture does, in fact, tend to become degraded and static. Their challenges to our assumptions and their assertion of their rights have made many white people in the Northwest Territories uneasy. Native organizations are resented, and the federal government is criticized for providing funds to them. A world in which the native people could not assert their rights is changing into a world in which they can insist and are insisting upon them.

Many white people in the North are convinced that it is wrong to concede that differences based on racial identity, cultural values and economic opportunities even exist. But it is better to articulate and understand these differences than it is to ignore them. The differences are real. They have always existed, but they have been suppressed. Now the native people are proclaiming their right to shape their world in their own image and not in the shadow of ours. As a result, some white people now resent what they regard as an attempt to alter the political, economic and social order of the Northwest Territories. They are right to regard this as an attempt to change the existing order. But they should not resent it, because a growing native consciousness is a fact of life in the North. It was bound to come. It is not going to go away, even if we impose political institutions in which it has no place.

Both the white and the native people in the North realize that the government's decision on the pipeline and on the way in which native claims are settled, will determine whether the political evolution of the North will follow the pattern of the history of the West or whether it will find a place for native ideas of self-determination. The settlement of native claims must be the point of departure for any political reorganization in the Northwest Territories. That is why the decision on the pipeline is really a decision about the political future of the Northwest Territories. It is the highest obligation of the Government of Canada, now as it was a century ago in the West, to settle the native people's claims to their northern homeland.

The pipeline project represents a far greater advance of the industrial system into the North than anything that has gone before it. The native people throughout the Mackenzie Valley and the Western Arctic sense that the decision on the pipeline is the turning point in their history. For them the time of decision has arrived.

Native Claims: Their Nature and Extent

Two Views of a Settlement

Many white people see the settlement of native claims as a necessary preliminary to the pipeline, a clearing of the legal underbrush; such a settlement would follow the pattern established elsewhere in Canada and the United States, by which the goal of the settlement of native claims is to facilitate agricultural and industrial development. Upon these grounds, a settlement along the lines of the Alaskan settlement has been urged.

Under the Alaska Native Claims Settlement Act of 1971 the native people of the state, in consideration of the extinguishment of their aboriginal claims to some 375 million acres of land, were granted 40 million acres and close to $1 billion. The settlement includes more land than is held in trust for all other American Indians, and the compensation is nearly four times the amount that all other Indian tribes have won from the United States Indians Claims Commission during its 25 years of existence. Under the settlement, an elaborate system of regional and village corporations has been established to hold title to the lands and to receive the monetary benefits. But the settlement gives no special recognition to the native economy in the form of hunting, fishing or trapping rights; nor does it establish any native political structures. In fact, the Act specifically states that no permanent, racially defined institution, right or obligation can be established by it. Under the Act, the special status of native lands comes to an end in 20 years. Emil Notti, former President of the Alaska Federation of Natives, told the Inquiry that the settlement could be viewed as:

> ... a means of transforming native peoples from hunters and gatherers into entrepreneurs and capitalists in as short a time as possible. [F23344]

The ultimate goal of the settlement, therefore, is the assimilation of the native people. The Dene and the Inuit of Canada, however, oppose any settlement that offers to pay the native people for their land and then to assimilate them into the larger society without any special rights or guarantees for them or their land. Both the Government of Canada and the native people reject the policy of assimilation.

The differences between the two conceptions of what is involved in the settlement of native claims are fundamental. Many white northerners, who regard a settlement as the means of assimilating the native people, hold

The NWT Indian Brotherhood panel explains Dene use and occupancy of land. From left: Fred Greenland, Charlie Snowshoe, interpreter Louis Blondin, Wilson Pellissey, Betty Menicoche and Phoebe Nahanni. (D. Gamble)

Trapper David Nasagaloak with muskox Holman, 1976. (M. Jackson)

Harry Simpson and family in their tent, near Rae Lakes. (Native Press)

Winter hunting camp. (R. Fumoleau)

hat if the native people will not settle their claims on these terms and assimilate, then they must be prepared to return to the bush or the barrens, or to live on reserves, as Indians do in the South.

The native people say this choice is too limited. They believe they have the right to fashion a choice of their own. At the community hearings the native people were at pains to articulate the nature and extent of their claims, and the main lines of these claims are now reasonably clear.

The Land

The native people presented extensive evidence to the Inquiry to show that they have used and occupied vast tracts of the Mackenzie Valley and the Western Arctic since time immemorial, and they now seek recognition of their right as a people to their homeland. Only through their collective ownership can they ensure that their land will remain the birthright of future generations. Two members of the Andre family of Arctic Red River expressed the feelings of the Dene on this issue. Alice Andre:

> My grandfather, old Paul Niditchie, was elected first chief here in Arctic Red River in 1921. He was one of the chiefs that signed the treaty that year. . . . It's going on to 55 years since the treaty was signed . . . today no white man is going to make me give our land away. . . . I am saying this for myself and the people, especially the children and the future generations to come, so they can make use of this land. . . . There is no way I'm going to give this land away. I heard about Alaska and James Bay. I don't want it to happen around here. [C4579]

Agnes Andre:

> Should we be forced into a land settlement involving money, which we do not want, how long will the money last? Ten, fifteen, twenty years? . . . We don't want this kind of a land

settlement. We want a settlement where we can keep our land till the end of the earth and not have our future relatives to have to fight for it again and again, possibly till our land is ours no more. We want to keep our land, we don't want money. . . . We want a settlement where not only us and our children will be happy, but [also] our great-grandchildren. A million times our thoughts will be happy. [C4591ff.]

The Inuit, no less than the Dene, see the land as their birthright. Peter Thrasher of Aklavik expressed the views of the Inuit:

> In many ways I inherit what my grandfather and my father have given me; a place to live in, a place to own, something I have a right to. . . . I would like to give something for the future generations of my children, so they will have something . . . to live on, and they also should have the right to inherit this country. [C14]

The special character of native land use explains why they seek title to areas of land that are, by southern standards, immense. Within living memory, the Inuit of the Western Arctic have used nearly 100,000 square miles of land and water to support themselves. The Dene presented evidence to show that they have used and occupied 450,000 square miles of land in the Northwest Territories. The native people rely not only on the areas in which they actually hunt, fish and trap, but they also need the areas that are of critical importance to the animal populations. At Sachs Harbour, David Nasogaluak explained to the Inquiry how the Bankslanders rely upon the whole of Banks Island, an area of 25,000 square miles, even though they do not hunt or trap in the northern part of the island. Andy Carpenter added, "We are saving the north end of Banks Island for breeding areas. That's for foxes, caribou, muskoxen." [C4120]

Daniel Sonfrere, Chief of the Hay River

Indian Band, emphasized how his people saved some areas:

> . . . just like they are keeping it for the future because they don't want to clean everything out at once. So they are kind of saving that area out there. [C522]

The native people maintain that the use they make of the land requires them to control vast tracts of it. They reject a land settlement that would give them title only to discrete blocks of land around their villages. They reject any suggestion, therefore, of an extension of the reserve system to Northern Canada. For this reason, also, they reject the model of the James Bay Agreement as a means of settling their land claims.

Under the James Bay Agreement, the Cree and Inuit of Northern Quebec have agreed to surrender their aboriginal rights over their traditional territory in return for cash compensation and for a land regime that gives them specific interests in three categories of land. Category 1 lands, allocated for the native people's exclusive use, consist of land in and around the native villages. These lands will be administered by the native people themselves, and although there are some differences in law, they roughly correspond to reserve lands. Subject to some important exceptions, no economic development on these lands can take place without the consent of the native people. Category 1 lands cover about 3,250 square miles for the Inuit, and about 2,100 square miles for the Cree. The James Bay Agreement covers a total area of about 410,000 square miles (an area roughly equivalent to that covered by Treaties 8 and 11 in the Northwest Territories). Thus, in the words of John Ciaccia, who negotiated the settlement for the Government of Quebec, Category 1 lands comprise but "a tiny proportion of the whole territory." [*The James Bay and Northern Québec*

Agreement, p. xvii] The Agreement also gives the native people hunting, fishing and trapping rights in Category 2 and Category 3 lands, to which I shall return later.

The native people of the North also reject the model of land selection used in the Alaskan settlement because such a model would not support a land-based economy. Under the Alaskan settlement, the native people have the right to select some 40 million acres of land from a checkerboard grid. Although such a distribution enables village sites to be retained, it cannot accommodate trap lines nor the migratory movements of caribou or fish. It is not designed to protect, and is not capable of protecting, a land-based native economy.

Regulation of Land Use

The native people want to entrench their rights to the land, not only to preserve the native economy, but also to enable them to achieve a measure of control over alternative uses of land, particularly the development of non-renewable resources. With such control, they can influence the rate of advance of industrial development in the North. Alizette Potfighter of Detah, the Dene village across the bay from Yellowknife, explained why the native people regard such control as essential:

Yellowknife ... is in the process of becoming as large and as organized as the large towns down south. In the past, people here used to hunt moose and fish right by the Yellowknife Bay and used to hunt caribou. They used to go berry picking practically right in their back yards. Now the people have to travel miles and miles from home to hunt and trap, the fish are no longer good to eat, and [the people] have to go to the Big Lake if they want fish, which again means that we have to travel far.

The mines have polluted our waters and the fish. ... The arsenic has caused this; it also

affects the greenery around us. The people who live right in town are warned beforehand about planting gardens and how they may be affected by high arsenic levels....

The wildlife has been driven further into the bush. The coming of the white man and the development he brought with him has only served to take away our way of life. [C8426ff.]

In virtually every native community in the Mackenzie Valley and Mackenzie Delta, the people complained of the impact of seismic exploration on the habitat of furbearing animals. They have no means of controlling the activities of the oil and gas industry. The Land Use Regulations provide for consultation with the communities when a company applies to the federal government to carry out seismic work, but the communities can only advise. Even the right to advise proved, more often than not, to be illusory. In Aklavik, Billy Stoor offered an example of this.

We received the Land Use Application from Northwest Lands and Forests and they [said they] would like ... to take gravel out of the Willow River area, and they asked for Council's comments by April 2. That was yesterday and we only received the application today. The applications, when they are made, go to Fort Smith and [then] go to Inuvik and then they are forwarded to us for comment, if we have any, and it is supposed to be done in three weeks, but a lot of times they are late. And their application was received today, and they wanted our comments by yesterday, so they could start today. [C79ff.]

In light of their experience of the treaties, the native people insist that their hunting, fishing and trapping rights cannot be protected merely by just incorporating them in a settlement. They see ownership and control of the land itself as the only means of safeguarding their traditional economy.

The James Bay Agreement includes guarantees to protect hunting, fishing and trapping rights. Are they not adequate? In the Agreement, the native people have exclusive hunting, fishing and trapping rights in Category 2 lands, and the Cree may select 25,000 square miles, and the Inuit 35,000 square miles of such lands, but they have no special right of occupancy: the Government of Quebec may designate these lands for development purposes at any time, so long as the land used for development is replaced or compensation paid. Mining, seismic exploration and technical surveys are not, however, classified as development, so these activities may be carried out freely on Category 2 lands, without compensation or replacement of land, even though such activity may interfere with the native people's hunting, fishing and trapping. Category 3 lands are included in the public lands of the Province of Quebec: the native people have the right to hunt, fish and trap on them, and certain species of animals and birds may be reserved for their exclusive use. However, development of these lands may take place at any time without compensation in any form to native people.

The land regime of the Agreement is buttressed by provisions for sustained levels of harvesting, a guaranteed minimum annual income for hunters and trappers, and an elaborate scheme for the participation of native people in game management and environmental protection. However, in nearly every case, their participation in the scheme is advisory and consultative.

The native people of the North reject the James Bay Agreement model as inadequate to protect their traditional economy because it does not entrench hunting, fishing and trapping rights through ownership of the land. In that model, the native economy must

Assistant counsel for the Inquiry, Stephen Goudge, with Russell Anthony and Andrew Thompson, for the Canadian Arctic Resources Committee. (Native Press)

Contaminated water, a Yellowknife problem. (Native Press)

Glen Bell, counsel for the NWT Indian Brotherhood and the NWT Metis Association. (Native Press)

subservient and secondary to alternative uses of the land that will be incompatible with the native use.

There are other reasons why the native people of the North seek recognition of their right to ownership of the land. Not only will such ownership give them the legal basis from which they can negotiate with government and industry to ensure that any proposed developments are environmentally acceptable, it will also enable them to share in the benefits of economic development. Royalties from the development of non-renewable resources could be used to modernize the native economy and to promote development of renewable resources. There may be other benefits from joint-venture arrangements with outside developers, by which the native people who wish to participate in various forms of development may do so, not merely as employees at the lowest level — which has been the experience of the past — but also as managers and contractors.

The question of royalties on non-renewable resources brings us to the question of subsurface rights. Dr. Andrew Thompson, a professor of Law at the University of British Columbia, told the Inquiry that ownership of the surface of the land, without ownership of subsurface rights, is often of little value. Ownership of mineral rights usually carries with it a right-of-access: the surface owner has to give way when the owner of subsurface resources wants to exploit them. The James Bay Agreement, for example, requires, even in the case of Category 1 lands, the native people to permit subsurface owners to use the surface in the exercise of their rights. Indeed, they must permit surface use even to owners of subsurface rights adjacent to Category 1 lands.

The subservience of the surface owner is often economic as well as legal, particularly in the North, because the short-term value in dollars of oil, gas or minerals lying beneath a tract of land usually exceeds its short-term value for hunting, fishing and trapping. Thompson suggested that these legal and economic imperatives require that, if the integrity of surface rights granted by the settlement is to be ensured, the settlement of native claims should confer management rights over minerals, either by legislation or through ownership. There is significant support for this proposition from the Australian Aboriginal Land Rights Commission. The Commissioner, Mr. Justice A.E. Woodward, said in his report of April 1974 that oil, gas and minerals on aboriginal lands should remain the property of the Crown, but he recommended that the aborigines should have the right to refuse to allow exploration for such resources on their traditional lands:

I believe that to deny to aborigines the right to prevent mining on their land is to deny the reality of their land rights. [p. 108]

This recommendation brings us to what may be the most important question raised by native claims. Are the native people to own subsurface rights to the land, as well as the land itself? If they do, will they be in a position to stand in the way of exploitation of those subsurface resources?

Mr. Justice Woodward urged that, in ordinary cases the aborigines should be free to decide whether or not they were prepared to consent to industrial development. If they were, they should be free to negotiate for payment for exploration rights, royalty payments, joint-venture interests, protection of sacred sites, aboriginal employment, and establishment of appropriate liaison arrangements between the aborigines and the developing agency. He concluded that the aborigines' power to control the nature and extent of development should be subject to one qualification: their views might be overridden if the government of the day resolved that the national interest required it. This is how he stated that limitation:

In this context I use the word "required" deliberately, so that such an issue would not be determined on a mere balance of convenience or desirability, but only as a matter of necessity. [p. 108]

In reaching its decision the government will no doubt have regard not only for the particular mineral but also for the fact that the national interest requires respect for Aboriginal rights and Aboriginal wishes. [p. 119]

The Inuit Tapirisat of Canada, in a submission to the Government of Canada in February 1976, grappled with this issue. On behalf of the Inuit of the Northwest Territories, they claimed ownership in fee simple of some 250,000 square miles of land and water, including the surface down to 1,500 feet, and they laid down criteria for the selection of these lands. Of particular importance is this provision: the Inuit should have the right to select 50,000 square miles in respect of which they could seek the cancellation of existing rights, for example oil and gas leases, subject to compensation being paid by the federal government. Petroleum and mineral development could then take place on the lands selected only under "an agreement for consent" given by communities that hold title to these lands. Such an agreement would include wide-ranging provisions for economic participation in any development by joint management employment and fixed royalties, together with provisions designed to avoid or reduce adverse social and environmental impacts. Under the Inuit proposal, the lands selected could be expropriated only by a special Act of Parliament. The Inuit proposal has since been withdrawn, but I mention it here to demonstrate that

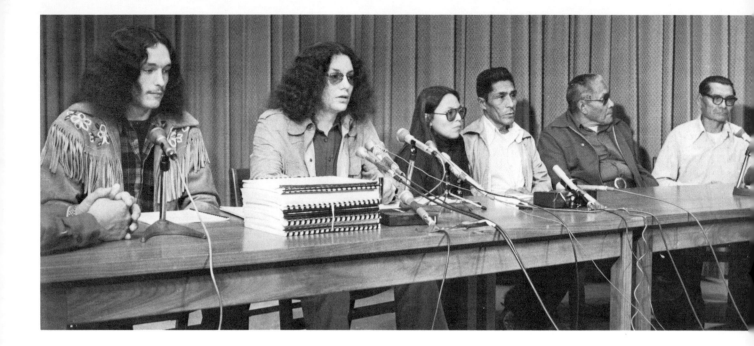

claims can be formulated that do justice both to the aspirations that the native people have for control of their homeland and to the national interest in vital non-renewable resources.

Self-Government

The native people have proposed a restructuring of political institutions in the Northwest Territories. This restructuring, which is the overarching feature of their claims, would reflect both in law and in fact the principle that the North is their homeland and that they have the right, under the constitution and within Confederation, to shape their future. The proposal of the Inuit Tapirisat of Canada called for the establishment of a new political entity comprising the land north of the tree line. Political control of that territory would lie with the Inuit, at least for the foreseeable future, by a 10-year residency requirement for voting.

The Dene, in their proposal to the federal government, stated:

> The Dene have the right to develop their own institutions and enjoy their rights as a people in the framework of their own institutions.

> There will therefore be *within* Confederation, a Dene government with jurisdiction over a geographical area and over subject matters now within the jurisdiction of the Government of Canada or the Government of the Northwest Territories. [para. 7 of the proposed Agreement in Principle]

The native people seek a measure of control over land use, and they see that the ownership of the land and political control of land use are intimately linked. They also seek control over the education of their children, and control over the delivery of community services, such as housing, health and social services. The native people acknowledge that these services have made important contributions to their material and physical well-being, but they reject the idea that they should continue to be passive recipients of these services.

These claims must be regarded together, for they are closely integrated. Many people in the native communities told the Inquiry that they want to continue living off the land. This would require changes in the present school curriculum and school year that would allow the children to accompany their parents into the bush without disrupting their education. Some families wish to move back into the bush more or less permanently. However, this option would require a change in not only educational policy, but also in housing policy to provide loans to build permanent log houses outside of the communities. Communications policy must be formulated to ensure an effective radio service between the bush and the communities. Transportation policy must be formulated to ensure the means of travel to and from bush camps. Land use and economic development policy must be formulated to ensure that the areas within which families are living the traditional life are not damaged by exploration for or development of non-renewable resources and to ensure that financial support is given to the native economy.

These claims leave unanswered many questions that will have to be clarified and resolved through negotiations between the Government of Canada and the native organizations. A vital question, one of great concern to white northerners, is how Yellowknife, Hay River and other communities with white majorities would fit into this scheme. Would they be part of the new territory? Or would they become enclaves within it? It is not my task to try to resolve these difficult questions. Whether native self-determination requires native hegemony over a geographical area, or whether can be achieved through the transfer political control over specific matters to the native people, remain questions to be resolved by negotiations.

Rick Hardy, President of the Metis Association of the Northwest Territories, told the Inquiry that his Association was considering yet other political possibilities. The Association is still formulating its claims, but Hardy intimated that it might propose that Metis guaranteed a minimum number of seats in the Territorial Council and positions with the territorial administration. The Territorial Council of the Yukon has made a similar proposal to secure the political rights of the Indian people of the Yukon. This approach originated in New Zealand, where the Maoris have a specified number of seats in the New Zealand legislature. This proposal proceeds on the assumption that native people are to be a minority in a larger political entity, without institutions of their own. That is the case in New Zealand. The Dene and Inuit proposals, on the other hand, seek to establish political institutions of their own fashioning.

Native Claims: A Closer Examination

I have outlined the native claims as they have been presented to the Inquiry. I intend now to deal with two specific areas of the claims at length because it is my judgment that the claims of the native people of the North deserve our most serious consideration. They are, I believe, basic to the native people's view of what the future should hold for them. Let us take a closer look at native

NWT Indian Brotherhood President, George Erasmus (second from left) presenting Dene land claim to federal government, 1976. (DIAND)

Education programs run by native people: Lunch at Koe-Go-Cho hostel in Fort Simpson. (Native Press)

Candy Beaulieu at Tree of Peace kindergarten, Yellowknife. (Native Press)

Florence Erasmus and kindergarten class, Yellowknife. (Native Press)

Native Claims
181

claims related to education and to renewable resource development, both of which are essential to the survival of the native culture and economy. Then we can understand better what a settlement of native claims would entail, both in terms of the kind of political control that the native people will require, and of the time that will be needed, not just to pass legislation, but to establish new institutions and to introduce new programs to make native self-determination a reality in the North. When we have done this, we shall be in a position to consider the impact of the pipeline on the achievement of the goals the native people seek through a settlement of native claims.

The Claim to Native Control of Education

The native people of the North claim the right to educate their children. This claim flows from their deeply felt need to transmit to their children their values, their languages and their history. It is also related to their experience with the present school system and its curriculum, which is based on Euro-Canadian ideals, values and standards. Bob Overvold, then Executive Director of the Metis Association, told the Inquiry:

... no imposed educational system, no matter how well-intentioned, will work for the Dene. Instead, only one that is initiated and developed by the Dene and that is rooted in Dene tradition, culture, and values will be successful. Such a system would be based upon a person's environment and then expanded to provide knowledge of the culture or society that surrounds him. [F23952]

Overvold explained that native children who enter the present system find that what they are taught in school is quite different from what they have learned in their homes. To Overvold,

The importance of the Dene developing [their own] educational system ... is quite self-evident. If one buys my evaluation of the present system in the Northwest Territories as being essentially no different than any other system in Southern Canada, then I see the essence of that system for the average white child being such that when a child enters this formal system at the age of five or six, the system takes up without any break, reinforces and builds upon all that the child has previously learned in his home and in the community. For the Dene entering the system, the case is the complete opposite. For the Dene, the same system means a severe break with his culture and starts him off at a disadvantage from which he most often never recovers. [F23953]

The Hawthorn Committee had earlier reached the same conclusion:

In sum, the atmosphere of the school, the routines, the rewards, and the expectations provide a critically different experience for the Indian child than for the non-Indian. Discontinuity of socialization, repeated failure, discrimination and lack of significance of the educational process in the life of the Indian child result in diminishing motivation, increasing negativism, poor self-images and low levels of aspiration. [*A Survey of the Contemporary Indians of Canada*, 1967, Vol. 2, p. 130]

The native people insist that they must control the education of their children, if it is to transmit their culture as opposed to ours. They say that the curriculum must include such subjects as native history, native skills, native lore and native rights; that they must determine the languages of instruction; and they insist that they must have the power to hire and fire teachers and to arrange the school year so that it accommodates the social and economic life of each community.

The native people's claim to control of education is not a rejection of all the knowledge that is basic to the society of Southern Canada. They made it quite clear that they seek a balance of the two cultures in the education of their children, but a balance of their own making. Nowhere did the native people contend that learning English was not worthwhile, but they insist that their own languages also be taught. Robert Sharpe, principal of the school at Old Crow, in outlining the mandate he felt he had from the local parents, said they had told him:

... we want our children to have the academic option open to them, so if they wanted, they could go on through university or whatever; but we don't want this at the cost of losing our life, our culture, our skills, our tradition, our language. [C1595]

Could not these aspirations be realized through a reform of the present system, a system under the control of the territorial government, rather than by transferring control to the native people? John Parker, Deputy Commissioner of the Northwest Territories, appeared before the Inquiry to argue that they could. He said that, since the early 1970s, the policy of the territorial government had been to transfer responsibility to the local communities, to make the curriculum culturally relevant, and to train native teachers. Other witnesses before the Inquiry, however, argued that, despite this new policy, little had changed in the schools in the native communities.

The new policy provides for instruction to native children in their mother tongue during the first three years of school. This has not come about: the language of instruction is still English, and the Alberta curriculum is still the basis of northern education. The new policy also provides a "cultural inclusion'' annual grant of $15 for each student to local school committees for their use in teaching native languages, arts and crafts, trapping or anything else that might be designated ''cultural.'' Paul Robinson, former Director of Curriculum for the Northwest Territories Department of Education, said that this $15 per student is insignificant when compared with the average cost of $1,700 for each student every year.

Bilingual and bicultural educational programs require bilingual teachers. In the Northwest Territories there has been an education program designed to prepare such teachers since 1968, but, according to Robinson, its effectiveness has been limited. In 1974, for example, six native students graduated from the program; these six represent approximately 1.5 percent of the total complement of northern teachers required and would fill only four percent of the teaching vacancies in an average year. The remaining 96 percent of the vacancies must be filled by teachers from the South.

Could these deficiencies in the bilingual education program be remedied if more money and better facilities were provided? With additional funds, could the territorial government expand the teacher education program and increase the amounts spent on ''cultural inclusion''? Robinson explained that these failures were not owing to lack of money:

> The question is not one of availability. In excess of $40 million is now spent on northern education.... How is the money expended?... The percentage increase in the cost of administration over the three-year period 1971-1974 indicates the priorities of the education system in this regard. The 45.5 percent increase in expenditures on administrative control of education can be contrasted with the 13.8 percent increase for improving education at the settlement level. [F27416]

The financial support available for higher education also indicates the priorities of the present education policy. In 1975-1976, some $311,500 was used to assist 183 students from the North. Of this number, only 10 were native. In the same year, native students were awarded two and one-half of the 18 bursaries available to university students. Robinson suggested that not only do these figures indicate the limited success that native students have in the schools, but they also reflect the motives underlying the system: higher education grants and bursaries are made available primarily as inducements to attract white public servants to the Northwest Territories. Robinson believes that, so long as control of education lies outside the hands of the native people, nothing in the system will really change:

> Native peoples continue to be regarded as essentially the wards of the state. The paternalistic, non-native administrators will determine the measure of local control to be permitted on the basis of the readiness of the Dene and Inuit ... but they are not ready. They are never ready. [F27418]

Bernard Gillie, former Director of Education for the Northwest Territories, told the Inquiry what he thought should be done to realize native aspirations:

> There must be an acceptance by all concerned ... that self-determination is the keystone of the new system. The decisions about what to do and how to do it must lie in the hands of the native people and reflect the values they believe in and respect. This is not to suggest that this should exclude the concepts and beliefs from other cultures, but the decisions as to what shall be incorporated in their own changing culture must be theirs to make. A mere patching up of the present system will not do what the Dene people want to accomplish. [F23924]

I think it should be understood that the Department of Education of the Government

of the Northwest Territories has sincerely tried to establish an education system that would reflect Dene and Inuit desires. Its administrators, supervisors and teachers are dedicated educators. But, with the best will in the world and with ample funds, the department has not succeeded, and there are no grounds for believing that it ever will succeed. The reason is simple: one people cannot run another people's schools.

Precedents for the Claim

The concept of native control of the education of their children is not revolutionary. In 1975, the Congress of the United States passed The Indian Self-Determination and Education Assistance Act, Section 2 of which states:

> The prolonged federal domination of Indian service programs has served to retard rather than enhance the progress of Indian people and their communities by depriving Indians of the full opportunity to develop leadership skills crucial to the realization of self-government, and has denied to the Indian people an effective voice in the planning and implementation of programs for the benefit of Indians which are responsive to the true needs of Indian communities. [p. 1]

Section 3 of the Act states:

> The Congress ... recognizes the obligation of the United States to respond ... by assuring maximum Indian participation in the direction of educational as well as other Federal services to Indian communities so as to render such services more responsive to the needs and desires of those communities.
>
> The Congress declares its commitment ... through the establishment of a meaningful Indian self-determination policy which will permit an orderly transition from Federal domination of programs for and services to Indians to effective and meaningful participation by the Indian people in the planning

Mary Rose Wright teaching bush life skills to Judy Wright, Drum Lake. (Native Press)

Bedtime at Whitehorse residential school. (J. Falls)

Loucheux child at Old Crow. (G. Calef)

White and native children in northern kindergarten class. (GNWT)

conduct, and administration of those programs and services. [p. 1]

Ethelou Yazzie, Director of the Rough Rock Demonstration School in Arizona, told the Inquiry that under this legislation the Navahos have established their own school system. She described how, under the control of the locally elected Navaho School Board, a bicultural, bilingual school has been developed at Rough Rock: "Navaho people, through their elected administrative officers, are running a sophisticated school, unabashedly oriented to Navaho children." Ex. F637, Appendix, p. 3] Navahos fill most of the administrative positions and more than 60 percent of the teaching positions at the school. All of the aides and support staff come from the native community.

The United States is not alone in accepting the principle of native self-determination in education. The principle has already been accepted in Canada. In 1972, the National Indian Brotherhood prepared a policy paper, *Indian Control of Indian Education,* which was accepted the following year by the Honourable Jean Chrétien, then Minister of Indian Affairs and Northern Development, as the basis for Indian education policy. The statement says:

> The past practice of using the school committee as an advisory body with limited influence, in restricted areas of the school program, must give way to an education authority with the control of funds and consequent authority which are necessary for an effective decision-making body. [p. 6]

From the Ts'zil Community School on the Mount Currie Reserve in British Columbia, to the Lesser Slave Lake Agreement in Northern Alberta, to the Tri-Partite Agreement involving the Micmac people in central Nova Scotia, the right to native control is being recognized and realized. The Ontario Task Force on Education has also recently supported this principle. In British Columbia, the Nishga Indian bands of the Nass Valley have recently established a fully native-controlled school board that will oversee bilingual and bicultural programs.

The James Bay Agreement provides for the establishment of Cree and Inuit school boards with all the powers of school boards under the Quebec Education Act. In addition, the native school boards may select and develop courses and teaching materials designed to preserve and transmit the languages and cultures of the native peoples; and they may, with the agreement of the Quebec Department of Education, hire native people as teachers, even though these candidates might not qualify as teachers under the normal provincial standards. The Agreement also provides that the languages of instruction shall be the native languages.

The Implications of the Claim

What is envisaged by the claim to control of education is the transfer from the territorial government to the native people of all authority over the education of native children. Whether or not there should be a native-controlled regional school board and native-controlled local school boards in each community, and other aspects of the institutional and legislative framework of native education would be resolved through negotiations. But it must be clearly understood that the transfer of control is not merely a decentralization of power under the general supervision of the territorial government — that would only perpetuate the existing state of affairs. The transfer of control must be real, and it must occur at all levels. Such a transfer can take place only over a period of time, but it must be agreed now that it will take place.

There are, at the present time, many white children in the schools of the North, and arrangements must be made for their education, also. It may be possible to incorporate a program for them into the native education system or a parallel school system for them may be necessary. Indeed, a combination of the two may be the best approach.

In the native villages, education would be under the direction of the native people. The children of white residents, the great majority of whom do not stay for very long, would attend local schools with native children. Because the native people think it is important for their children to learn English, as well as to preserve their own language, and to learn about white culture as well as to preserve their own, it is likely that white children who have spent a few years in such a school system would not suffer any disadvantage from it, and that in many ways they would benefit from the experience. It would also mean that only white families who have a genuine interest in the North and its people would choose to live in the native villages.

In the larger centres such as Yellowknife or Inuvik, where there are large numbers of white children, two parallel school systems may be the proper approach. Under such a system, the territorial Department of Education might continue to be responsible for the education of white children in the larger centres and to implement the kind of educational program that most of the white parents wish their children to have. However, there is no reason why the two school systems should have no relations with each other: some programs and facilities could be shared, and the special attributes of the two systems could be made available to students of both systems. With time, it may be possible to offer in the larger centres an educational experience that would be truly bicultural. But that prospect can never be realized unless the native people are given the right to build their own educational system.

Native Languages

In many of the communities of the Mackenzie Valley and the Western Arctic, the native languages are still strong. In those places, the native people spoke to the Inquiry through interpreters, and those who are bilingual often preferred to address the Inquiry in their mother tongue. In places like Fort Franklin, Rae Lakes, Fort Liard and Trout Lake, the first language of the children is still the native language. Indeed, until they go to school, it is their only language. In other communities, like those in the Delta, use of the native languages has been eroded so far that young children now commonly use English, rather than their native language. However, Dr. John Ritter, a linguist who has studied the use of Loucheux in the Mackenzie Delta, told the Inquiry that even in these communities, where outsiders often think that the native languages are dead, young people have what he called a passive competence in them. He concluded:

> ... the native languages continue to be a fact of life for the children and play a vitally deep role in their cognitive development. In no sense are the languages yet "dead." [F30000]

Many people think that native languages, like native cultures, are not capable of change and growth, and that the loss of the native languages is inevitable. Just as they assume that progress in the modern world requires a shift from native to white values,

so they assume that progress requires a shift from the native languages to English.

The evidence before this Inquiry showed this assumption to be mistaken. Dr. Michael Krauss, Alaska's leading expert on native languages, told the Inquiry:

> ... it is not the case that the native languages are intrinsically inferior to any other or incapable of development for meeting the needs of the twentieth century. ... The basic structures of the native languages are perfectly capable of handling modern ideas and concepts. [F29970ff.]

The native people want their languages to survive to become part of their future, not simply a reminder of their past. Krauss described in specific terms a program that would ensure the survival and development of the native languages. The first stage is the development of an orthography — a uniform system of spelling and writing the words of a language. Such an orthography, if properly designed, would enable native children to learn to read and write in their own languages faster than they can learn to read and write in English. The second stage is the development of general literacy, among both children and adults, in the native languages; and the third stage involves enlarging the vocabularies of the native languages. As an example of such a vocabulary development, Krauss cited the work done at the beginning of this century on the Hebrew language, which has meant that "men can successfully fly jet planes using the very language which in the past was the language of shepherds." [F29975] He pointed out, also, that the Inuit and Athabascan languages are renowned for their ability to form new words easily and quickly.

There are many elements and factors to be

considered in the implementation of a program to ensure the survival and development of the native languages, but it is quite clear that the school system is at the core of it. The time needed to develop a bicultural and bilingual school system is considerable for it will require not only trained teachers but also the preparation of new texts and educational aids that are either not available at present or are available in very small numbers.

The experience of other countries indicates that these goals can be achieved. New orthographies have been developed and standardized; native teachers have been trained; and adequate new teaching materials have been prepared for small native populations in, for example, Greenland and the Soviet Union.

The transfer of the control of the education of native children, with all that it implies in the way of institutions, finance, legislation, and language rights, must be part of the reordering of relationships between the native peoples and the federal government that is inherent in the settlement of native claims. It should be quite clear, however, that the objectives of these programs for cultural and linguistic survival cannot be achieved simply by signing a piece of paper. The settlement of native claims and consequent enabling legislation is not the culmination but the beginning of a new process.

*Learning in another language and in an alien way,
old residential school, Fort Resolution.*
(Public Archives)

Food from the land:
*Reindeer round-up at Atkinson Point. Left to right:
Jimmy Dillon, Mikkel Panaktalok and Don Pingo.*
(GNWT–D. Hanna)

Carving up caribou for a feast, Fort Good Hope.
(N. Cooper)

Holman hunters with winter harvest. (DIAND)

The Claim to Renewable Resources

The game, fish and fur, and the other renewable resources of the land are the foundation upon which the native people believe their economic future can and should be established. They seek to defend what is for many of them a way of life, and at the same time to modernize and expand the native economy.

A mixture of hunting and fishing and of trapping-for-trade is widely regarded by the Dene and Inuit as their traditional life. This economy is based on primary production at the individual or family level and, because it relies on traditional skills and a detailed knowledge of animal life and the land, this way of life is basic to native culture and gives meaning to the values that the native people still hold today.

If the economic future of the native people is to correspond with their declared preferences, the native economy of the bush and the barrens must be fortified. Small-scale harvesting of renewable resources must cease to be economically uncertain and insecure. The close links between primary production and the collective well-being of the native people should find a prominent place in planning for northern development.

The native people and the native organizations spoke to the Inquiry of the need for innovation in the use of renewable resources. Among their suggestions were the development of a fishery in the Mackenzie River, the systematic harvesting of caribou, the provision of incentives to fur trappers, and an orderly system for marketing fur.

Viability of the Renewable Resource Sector

The argument against too heavy reliance on traditional, small-scale primary production centres on the question: how many people can the land ultimately support even when the renewable resources of the North are fully utilized? There are now some 15,000 native people living in the Mackenzie Valley and the Western Arctic, and the population is increasing. It is argued, therefore, that the increase of the native people themselves will threaten the viability of their own resource base.

In the past, policies for the North have been influenced, if not determined, by the belief that the available renewable resources cannot support native populations. The conventional wisdom since the decline of the fur trade has insisted that economic development in the North ought to consist of mines, roads, oil and gas, and pipelines. This wisdom so overwhelmed any contrary suggestions that some of the native people themselves have been inclined to doubt the worth of their own economy. Such doubts tended to be confirmed by the consequences of the government policy of concentrating activity in the non-renewable resource sector, which of course increased the vulnerability of the traditional native economy. The prophecies of conventional wisdom thus tended toward self-fulfilment. The conviction that there was no hope for the old way made that way indeed hopeless.

Can the land support a larger native population? The native people testified that industrial development has driven the animals away from many places they used to inhabit. But despite this fact — which is very important from the hunter's and trapper's perspective because it makes his activities

more arduous — animal populations appear to be thriving throughout the Mackenzie Valley and the Western Arctic. It should also be remembered that in aboriginal times the land supported a larger native population than it does today. In fact, there is little evidence that native people are over-exploiting their resources at present, and there is much evidence that overall yields could be increased. I shall deal with this evidence when I turn to the proposals made to the Inquiry for the modernization of renewable resource harvesting.

Northerners point to many animal species that may have some potential for commercial or domestic use and that are not being harvested at the present time. Consider the Western Arctic, where you will find white whale, seal, char, herring, whitefish, trout, moose, caribou, bear, wolf, fox, numerous bird species, edible plants and berries. Consider the strong economy of the people of Banks Island, which is based on white fox trapping. Look at the Mackenzie Valley with its moose, caribou, beaver, muskrat, marten, mink, wolverine, lynx and coloured fox populations, river and lake fisheries, timber stands along the Liard River and the south shore of Great Slave Lake.

I do not want to be misunderstood here: the North is, in fact, a region of limited biological productivity. Its renewable resources will not support a large population. But through a long history the region has been productive enough for the native people, and they believe it could be made to be yet more productive in the years to come.

There has been a dearth of research into the means of improving productivity in the North. Assertions about the impossibility of strengthening the native economy have often been just that — assertions. We do not have adequate inventories of the various species available there — not even for the Mackenzie River. Nor for that matter do we know very much about the present intensity of renewable resource use. We do not know enough about food chains and ecological relationships in the North to be able to predict what effect an increased harvest of one species may have on other species. We have not considered whether or not new systems of marketing and price support might strengthen the native economy.

Some renewable resource development schemes have been tried in the North, including the fur-garment industry in Tuktoyaktuk and Aklavik, fisheries on Great Slave Lake and in the Mackenzie Delta, and sawmills at a few locations along the Mackenzie Valley, and some attention has been given to the support of trapping. These schemes have usually been undertaken without adequate funding and always without a clear acknowledgment that the native people should run these ventures themselves.

Proposals made to the Inquiry

The native organizations offered some ideas for strengthening the native economy by development of renewable game, fish and fur resources.

Dr. Robert Ruttan and John T'Seleie discussed the fishery potential of the Mackenzie Valley. They emphasized that the Mackenzie, Laird, Hay and Slave Rivers contain at least ten species of fish. Lake trout also occur in harvestable numbers in Great Slave Lake, and arctic char are found in certain tributaries of the Mackenzie River west of the Delta. They reminded the Inquiry that each community along the Mackenzie River makes extensive use of the river fishery during the summer months, and that the fish

of many large lakes along the Valley are a relatively untouched resource. The primary species available are lake trout, whitefish, grayling, pickerel, inconnu (coney), cisco (herring) and northern pike. Although many of these lakes have low temperatures and relatively low productivity, they have sustained for a long time fairly high levels of subsistence fishing. The people of Fort Good Hope and Colville Lake fish more than 50 lakes: in 1975, during a six-month period, the Fort Good Hope people harvested an estimated 127,000 to 186,000 pounds of fish.

The total value of the fishery resource of the Mackenzie River region has never been calculated. Ruttan and T'Seleie reckon the replacement value of the fish taken at Fort Good Hope over the six-month period in 1975 was between $143,000 and $209,000, and said that a potential annual production of 500,000 to 1,000,000 pounds of fish would not be unreasonable. They argued that, with a long-range fish management program, the economic value of the fishery could be maximized by the establishment of community and regional markets and by processing for domestic and commercial use or for resale. Certain lakes and streams could be used for sport-fishing camps. At present, several tourist lodges operate on Great Bear and Great Slave Lakes. However, the role of the native people in them is limited to that of guides; they have no control over the management of the lodges nor of the resource base.

Similarly, evidence was given on the possibilities for increased utilization of caribou. Three major herds range within or very near the Mackenzie drainage basin. The population of the Bathurst herd may be approaching 200,000 animals, and the potential annual harvest for this herd alone may well be 10,000 animals. The Bluenose herd,

which ranges in winter along the north shore of Great Bear Lake, is expanding at present and may now number as many as 50,000. In the chapter on the Northern Yukon, I have discussed the importance of the Porcupine caribou herd to the people of Old Crow. But the herd is utilized by native people in the Northwest Territories too. It is an important resource in spring and autumn for the native hunters from Fort McPherson and Aklavik.

These three herds now supply hundreds of thousands of pounds of meat to the native people of the Mackenzie Valley and the Western Arctic. With systematic management, they could constitute an even more important domestic resource and perhaps a commercial resource as well, but the potential harvest limits of this species cannot safely be determined without accurate estimates of their total populations, annual increments and long-term cycles.

From the beginning of the fur trade, furbearers have been a major source of income for native people. Although trapping has declined over the last 20 years, it still remains an important part of the native economy. Beaver, muskrat, marten, mink, fox, lynx and wolverine are the most important animals in the trapping economy. Even though, during the past few years, there has been some increase in trapping owing to higher fur prices, there is evidence to show that much higher levels of trapping could be sustained. A report entitled *Development Agencies for the Northwest Territories* prepared in 1973 by Edward Weick for a Special Staff Group of the Department of Indian Affairs and Northern Development under the chairmanship of Kalmen Kaplansky stated:

The number of pelts taken in 1970-71 as shown in Statistics Canada's data on fur

Herring fishing in Tuktoyaktuk harbour. (J. Inglis)

Fish drying, Trout Lake. (N. Cooper)

Tuktoyaktuk woman working in fur garment factory. (GNWT)

Government operated fish processing plant, Jacobshavn, Greenland. (E. Weick)

production is well below the optimum. Estimates suggest that muskrat production could be increased from 74,450 to 250,000 pelts; white fox, from 25,584 to 100,000 pelts; ermine, from 1,844 to 10,000 pelts; mink, from 4,021 to 10,000 pelts and beaver, from 6,888 to 12,000 pelts. Since Northwest Territories production is a small part of total international production, an increase in exploitation would not likely have a depressive effect on prices except, perhaps, in the case of distinctive species such as the white fox. [p. 20-21]

Ruttan and T'Seleie told the Inquiry that potential fur yields could readily be increased by more effective management. Values could also be increased by an improved marketing system, including public auctions and the development of trapper-owned trading stores to ensure the lines of credit so essential to trapping, sales to handicraft centres, and further development of a fur-garment industry within the North-west Territories. The Special Staff Group report indicated what would be required to modernize the trapping industry. It would have to include:

> ... better information on resource availability, restrictive licensing, improved equipment and access to remote, underexploited areas, adjustment of trapping, wage work and school term seasons, to avoid conflicts. It could also include more rational marketing mechanisms to minimize currently excessive control by middle-men, of both the primary production and the manufacturing-retailing markets. Standards of size and quality should be established and enforced. [ibid., p. 22-23]

At Fort Liard, Chief Harry Deneron explained that many trappers, who had no established lines of credit, were forced to sell their furs to local traders at prices much lower than the furs ultimately fetched at auctions in the South. He argued that a settlement of native claims that gave the native people control of the renewable

resources of their land and access to capital would enable trappers to maximize their returns.

Ruttan and T'Seleie also gave evidence on the forest resources of the Mackenzie River basin. The most extensive stands of commercially valuable timber occur along the Liard River and on the alluvial flood plains and islands along the Mackenzie River and its tributaries. The Special Staff Group report expressed some doubt on whether or not the forests of the Mackenzie Valley could support a pulp-and-paper industry, and it emphasized that the forest resource is better suited to supply the local and regional market and that forest products should be especially developed for use in the North. The report suggested:

> It should be possible to integrate the northern forest resource into the construction industry by planning in advance to use regional materials in housing programs and thus provide a basis for local development. It might be more expensive initially to supply northern lumber needs from territorial forest stands. Yet, when one considers the jobs that might be created in logging, sawmilling, perhaps transportation and prefabrication, probable reduction in welfare costs, the development of useful skills and competence, and the possible growth of a viable forest industry, these positive factors might offset the somewhat higher initial costs. [ibid., p. 40]

This view accords with what many native people in the villages told me. They maintained that housing constructed out of logs and designed locally would provide them with shelter that is better suited to their needs, and would permit them to use local materials and develop native skills.

Evidence From Other Countries

Substantial efforts have been made to develop native economies based on renewable resources in some other parts of the world. Some arctic countries have made serious attempts to maintain and strengthen native economies based on hunting, fishing and trapping. I think we may obtain a better idea of the opportunities that renewable resource development offers, if we look at the experience — and the mistakes — of some of these other countries.

EVIDENCE FROM GREENLAND

Qanak, an Inuit community, was established because the Greenlandic-Danish administration was alarmed by the possible consequences of the construction of a huge United States Air Force base at Thule. In particular, the hunters and trappers of the Polar Eskimo were thought to be culturally threatened.

To ensure their survival as harvesters of renewable resources, the Thule people moved during the late 1950s to Qanak and a number of nearby camps and small settlements. Qanak, a community of some 750 people, is an impressive example of how an economy and a society based on local renewable resources can be strengthened. Educational and medical services are delivered to all but the tiniest camps, and essential goods are sold in the stores at comparatively low prices.

Community rules limit the use of snow-mobiles and powerboats because these machines alarm and drive away the local populations of marine mammals. As a result, present-day hunting is an effective blend of traditional and appropriate modern technology: kayaks may be taken by powerboat to the bays and fiords, then paddled to the hunting locations. Hunters must harpoon a narwhal before shooting at it, thereby eliminating losses through sinking, for the harpoon lines are attached to floats; this rule also reduces the likelihood of a wounded animal escaping to die elsewhere.

In the Mackenzie Delta, the native hunters take approximately 300 white whales each year, but 150 of them are lost because of sinking and the escape of wounded animals. If rules such as those at Qanak were adopted, the whale harvest could be doubled without any increase in the kill.

The material well-being of the Qanak hunters is high by Greenlandic standards. Some furs have a guaranteed minimum price, and in 1971-1972 the earnings of many families from furs alone were above $5,000.

It is important to emphasize that this group of villages and camps, spread around the bays and fiords of the far northwest of Greenland, is at no great distance from the American base at Thule. The construction and maintenance of the base obviously could provide opportunities to move the Polar Eskimo into the wage-labour economy. However, the Greenlandic-Danish administration decided not to take that course; instead, they encouraged the development of the renewable resource economy. This decision did not create a zoo, in which an impoverished native people pursued their ancient practices for reasons based on southern sentimentality. Rather, with the assistance of the Danish Government, they modernized their traditional hunting, trapping and fishing economy. The Thule-Qanak people can choose between a life as a harvester of renewable resources or a life in town as a wage-earner. This example shows that it is possible to have an effective renewable resource sector that meets the aspirations and needs of the traditional culture, without creating small pockets of economically or culturally disadvantaged individuals. It must be added, however, that Thule-Qanak, along with the Scoresbysund settlement on the east coast, are exceptions to the general situation in Greenland today.

The present economy of Greenland came into being through a process of forced and rapid change during a relatively short period of time. In the late 1950s, the Danish government decided to develop the Greenland fishing industry, with large fish-processing plants and deep-water fishing fleets, to achieve economic self-sufficiency. Accordingly, shore plants and equipment, fishing boats and trained crews were built up; the people were concentrated into large communities both to achieve economies of administration and to facilitate the operations of large fish-processing plants and of offshore fishing fleets. The administration originally intended the fishing boats to be small and crewed by families, but in the 1960s a trend toward larger vessels, including factory boats, became predominant.

Unlike Thule-Qanak and Scoresbysund, the economic situation in most of the rest of Greenland gives rise to doubts about large-scale development of renewable resources. These doubts are reinforced by difficulties that the "developed" Greenlandic communities are now experiencing, where the incidence of alcohol abuse, violence and family break-down is causing alarm, and the Greenlanders' complaints over their loss of cultural identity and self-respect are becoming louder.

EVIDENCE FROM THE SOVIET UNION

It is not easy to obtain detailed information about economic developments in the Soviet Union, but I think we may learn something from what we know about the possibilities of harvesting renewable resources there. Northern minority peoples have, to some extent, been encouraged to maintain their own renewable resource base. In parts of the Soviet Union, particularly in the far northeast, an area that includes Chukchi and Eskimo communities, hunting has been professionalized.

In 1971 a Canadian party headed by the Honourable Jean Chrétien, Minister of Indian Affairs and Northern Development, visited the Soviet far North. Walter Slipchenko prepared a report of the party's trip, *Siberia 1971,* in which he notes that the native people work in government and industry and in such professions as medicine, teaching, and administration, but that most of them were still engaged in the traditional pursuits of hunting, fishing and reindeer herding.

Of the estimated 140,000 "small peoples" (a category that excludes the very numerous Komi and Yakut), a total of about 20,000 (the great majority of the work force) are engaged on a full-time basis in professionalized renewable resource activities, and of that number, about 12,000 are classified as hunters and fishermen. Slipchenko pointed out in his summary:

> A bonus is paid to trappers and hunters for whatever they catch in excess of the established norms. In order to ensure that a hunter works at his maximum effort the following steps are taken by each sovkhoz:
> — control and norms are established by fellow hunters;
> — each hunter is encouraged by a system of bonuses to catch as many animals as possible;
> — each hunter is regarded as a professional man and receives a guaranteed minimum monthly wage. [p. 89]

Let us see what these minimum earnings represent. A normal wage for someone employed full-time in the industrial sector

A Russian reindeer herder and family, Siberia, 1971. (DIAND)

Wood bison. (DIAND)

Cutting reindeer from the herd, Tuktoyaktuk, 1936. (DIAND)

Marten — an important northern fur resource. (NFB–Cesar)

of the Soviet North is 500 roubles per month. Full-time hunters or trappers earn between 200 and 1,000 roubles per month. Their guaranteed minimum is only about 50 percent of a low industrial wage, but the incentives scheme ensures that a successful full-time resource harvester is earning an income not much below that of the highest paid workers in the industrial sector. In other words, a hunter can earn as much as an engineer.

Resource harvesting remains the basis of many native peoples' lives in the Soviet Union. Despite collectivization, the links between hunters, trappers, and reindeer herders and their traditional resources have, to a considerable extent, been preserved. The fur trade in the skins of sea mammals tended in some places to result in overproduction of meat and in wastage. It was therefore decided to establish fur farms where fine-fur animals are fed on the excess meat of marine mammals that are killed for their skins or ivory.

Several Canadian missions have visited the Soviet Union, and the number is increasing as the result of a treaty made in 1970. The Soviets are eager to demonstrate their technological achievements, but they are less eager to let us see how the indigenous peoples of Siberia are making their living today. The Government of Canada should, nevertheless, continue its efforts to send a mission of hunters and trappers to see what they can learn from the Soviet experience.

EVIDENCE FROM THE UNITED STATES

Dr. Sam Stanley of the Smithsonian Institution presented to the Inquiry a summary of a study made in the early 1970s of economic development among seven Indian tribes in the United States. The study was designed to isolate the factors contributing to, or detracting from, the success of economic development programs on Indian reservations and in their communities. The study concluded that programs imposed from outside the native communities, which ignored the structure of native society and land use, failed in every case.

The experience of the aquaculture project among the Lummi Indians of Washington State is regarded as one of the most successful economic development programs in the experience of American Indian tribes. Vine Deloria, Jr. described this project in *The Lummi Indian Community: The Fishermen of the Pacific Northwest*. Although the Lummis had participated in the fur trade, and despite the government's efforts to convert them into farmers, their primary economic activity was fishing. The Lummis had participated in the rapid growth of commercial fishing in the 1940s and 1950s; they operated a small fleet of purse-seine boats, which provided employment for most of the men on the reservation. However, during the 1960s, the rationalization of the fishing industry increased the cost of operating a fishing boat far beyond the limited financial resources of the average Lummi. Lacking the capital to improve their fleet and to compete with white boat-owners, the Lummis were forced to give up their boats.

In search of a new economic base, the Lummi Tribal Council considered two very different proposals. One was a proposal by a large corporation to construct a magnesium-oxide production plant in Lummi Bay. The plant would have offered wage employment to members of the tribe, but it would have polluted tidal lands. The Lummis rejected it. The other proposal the tribe considered and adopted was aquaculture — the farming of

oysters, clams, sea trout, salmon and other seafood products.

Initially, the project required the construction of a research pond to test the growth of oyster and sea trout in salt water. The Lummis built this pond themselves, supplying manual labour, heavy equipment operators, and supervision of the work. The United States government, in funding construction of the main operating pond, designated the Lummi tribe as the prime contractor. Construction of the pond involved a dyke of a kind never before built in the United States: the tribe hired an outside firm to provide the necessary technical skills, but they performed the great majority of the work. They have also built a complete oyster-hatchery that is able to produce 100 million seed oysters a year, an exceptionally high rate of productivity.

The aquaculture project has other distinctive characteristics. The Lummis have matched every construction project with a training program that has prepared native people to assume leadership at the highest levels. The project has had a dramatic effect on the whole concept of education on the reservation. School drop-outs are now going back to school to study fisheries technology, marine biology and business management.

Aquaculture is a vital part of the Lummi economy, but it is not its sole component. The Lummis are searching out subsidiary occupations and training programs that will support total community development. To achieve this aim, profits generated by the aquaculture project are not distributed to members of the tribe, but are used to fund individual or community development to ensure that jobs are available for every Lummi who wishes to live and work on the reservation.

The success of the aquaculture project has

meant that the Lummis can maintain their close ties with the sea in a modern economic context. The project uses the tidal flats that the Lummis have traditionally used; it permits a blending of traditional knowledge of the sea and modern marine biology; it has permitted local control of development and has involved all members of the tribal community; and, perhaps most important, the project has realized the Lummis' desire to maintain their reservation as a source of community life. Deloria says the ultimate success of the project will depend upon the tribe's ability to defend its resource base (water) against inconsistent uses. He concludes:

> The programs that have been proposed by the federal government — designed to turn the Lummis into farmers, to make wage earners out of them, to relocate them in the cities, even to make craftsmen out of them — were all activities that did not speak to the Lummi community in terms of its deepest striving: to be itself. The aquaculture project related directly to Lummi traditions. It involved work at which the Lummi people were expert. [Ex. F681, p. 102]

The experience of the Lummis has already been followed in Canada. The Nimpkish Indian Band in Alert Bay, British Columbia, are now developing their own aquaculture project and have established an educational program designed to train native people in the technical skills necessary to manage such a project. They are also offering courses in navigation, net making and boat maintenance. In this way, they seek to ensure that native people maintain an important role in commercial fishing, a role that is consistent with their past and their preferences.

Some Implications for Canada

There are lessons to be learned from these experiences. On the one hand, development must be under the control of the people whose lives and economies are being changed: the strengthening of the renewable resource sector of the native economy must go forward under the direction of the native people themselves. If development proceeds in a manner and at a scale that is out of keeping with local needs and wishes, it will tend to be counterproductive at the local level — whether it is renewable or nonrewable resources that are being developed.

The contrast between Thule-Qanak and the new towns of Greenland is instructive. Greenlandic economic development was imposed from the outside, and we should likely learn as much about its economic and technical aspects in Copenhagen as in Godthaab. In essence, the problem of the Greenland fishery is that the Danes have done the thinking and planning and have provided the capital, whereas the Greenlanders have provided only the labour.

Thule-Qanak offers a much better example of the direction that small native communities may wish to take — development on a scale compatible with the traditions of the people whose economy is being developed. It corresponds with Dene and Inuit ideas of how their native economy should be developed. And, although we are uncertain about the details of the native economies in the Soviet Union, we have learned enough to urge that a closer examination be made of their scheme for professionalization of hunting. The contrast between the Lummi aquaculture project and other instances of economic development on Indian reservations in the United States also shows that the development of economic programs for native people must be firmly based upon the structures of native society and their pattern of land use.

If renewable resources are to be the basis of an economy, perhaps the native people will have to be subsidized. We already subsidize wheat farmers by price supports because we regard the production of wheat and the stability of farm families as an important goal. We subsidize fishermen on the Atlantic and Pacific coasts by the payment of extended unemployment insurance benefits in the off-season. But, until now, we have never regarded hunting and trapping in the same light. In the North, hunters and trappers have been subsidized — and stigmatized — by welfare. It should now be recognized that people who hunt and trap for a living are self-employed in the same way that commercial fishermen or farmers are.

There should be a reassessment of the goals of educational and social policy as they relate to the traditional sector and to wage employment. There are many young people today who want to participate in the renewable resource sector, not necessarily to the exclusion of other employment, and not necessarily as a lifetime career. They wish to choose and, perhaps, to alternate choices. The teaching of skills that are necessary to participate in a modernized renewable resource economy must therefore be integrated into the educational program, and the importance of these skills must be properly recognized in economic and social policies.

The native economy of the Western Arctic and the Mackenzie Valley is unfamiliar to urban southerners, and policy-makers are generally uncomfortable in thinking about it. They may regard the native economy as unspecialized, inefficient and unproductive. It is true that such economies have no

Sorting shrimp in government fish plant, Jacobshavn, Greenland. (E. Weick)

Abe Okpik examining fish nets at Trout Lake. (N. Cooper)

Hunter with white fox pelts in northern co-op. (GNWT)

Butchering white whale. (W. Hunt)

historically generated much surplus, nor have they produced a labour force that is easily adaptable to large-scale industrial enterprise. They can provide, however, for the needs of those who participate in them. The ways in which we measure economic performance in a modern industrial setting do not necessarily apply in other settings. Nevertheless, other economies can change and modernize in their own way, just as an industrial economy does.

It is increasingly recognized that the economic development of the Third World hinges on agrarian reform, on the modernization of existing agriculture to serve domestic needs; in the same way, and to a greater extent than we have been prepared to concede, the economic development of the North hinges on the modernization of the existing native economy, based as it is on the ability of the native people to use renewable resources to serve their own needs. Productivity must be improved and the native economy must be expanded so that more people can be gainfully employed in it. In my judgment, therefore, the renewable resource sector must have priority in the economic development of the North.

Native Management of Renewable Resources

The idea of modernizing the native economy is not new. It has been adumbrated in many reports bearing the imprimatur of the Department of Indian Affairs and Northern Development. But nothing has been done about it. Why? Because it was not important to us, whereas large-scale industrial development was. Indeed, such large-scale projects hold great attraction for policy-makers and planners in Ottawa and Yellowknife.

Small-scale projects, amenable to local control, do not.

The remarkable thing is that, despite two decades of almost missionary zeal by government and industry, the native people of the North still wish to see their economic future based on renewable resource development. They have argued that the renewable resource sector must take priority over the non-renewable resource sector. This was said in every native village, in every native settlement.

The native people claim the right to the renewable resources of the North. This claim implies that all hunting, trapping, and fishing rights throughout the Mackenzie Valley and the Western Arctic, along with the control of licensing and other functions of game management, should be given to the native communities, and that, for matters affecting all native communities, the control should be vested in larger native institutions at the regional or territorial level. The native people seek the means to manage, harvest, process and market the fur, fish and game of the Northwest Territories.

It is worth bearing in mind that modernization of the renewable resource sector can be achieved with a comparatively small capital outlay. A reasonable share of the royalties from existing industries based on non-renewable resources in the Mackenzie Valley and the Western Arctic would suffice. Huge subsidies of the magnitude provided to the non-renewable resource industries would not be necessary. And the possibilities for native management and control would be greater.

The question of scale, however, suggests that we may consider some resources that, although they are not renewable, are nonetheless amenable to the kind of development that is consistent with local interest

and local control. I have in mind here certain accessible surface resources, such as gravel. These and other resources will no doubt be of importance in the claims negotiations and in land selection. The native people will, in time, judge this matter for themselves, but they should not be constrained or limited by any narrow meaning of the word "renewable."

I do not mean to say that industrial development should not take place. It has taken place, and it is taking place. But unless we decide that, as a matter of priority, a firmly strengthened renewable resource sector must be established in the Mackenzie Valley and the Western Arctic, we shall not see a diversified economy in the North.

Native Claims and the Pipeline

We must now address the central question, can we build the pipeline and, at the same time, do justice to native claims?

The case made by the native people is that the pipeline will bring an influx of construction workers from the South, that it will bring large-scale in-migration, that it will entail a commitment by the Governments of Canada and of the Northwest Territories to a program of large-scale frontier development that, once begun, cannot be diverted in its course. They say it will mean enhanced oil and gas exploration and development throughout the Mackenzie Valley and the Western Arctic. They say that, to the extent that there is a substantial in-migration of white people to the North, there will be a still greater tendency to persist with southern patterns of political, social and industrial development, and it will become less and less likely that the native people will gain any measure of self-determination.

The native people say that the construction of a pipeline and the establishment of an energy corridor will lead to greater demand for industrial sites, roads and seismic lines, with ever greater loss or fragmentation of productive areas of land. Industrial users of land, urban centres, and a growing non-native population will make ever greater demands on water for hydro-electricity and for other industrial and domestic uses. The threats to the fishery will be increased. And last, but by no means least, the emphasis the Governments of Canada and the Northwest Territories have placed on non-renewable resources will become even greater than it is now, and the two governments will be less and less inclined to support the development of renewable resources.

Others argue that these developments are inevitable, and that there really is no choice. The industrialization of the North has already begun, and it will continue and will force further changes upon the native people. The power of technology to effect such changes cannot be diminished, nor can its impact be arrested. Rather than postponing the pipeline, we should help the native people to make as easy a transition as possible to the industrial system. This is the law of life, and it must prevail in the North, too.

The native people insist that a settlement of their claims must precede any large-scale industrial development. That, they say, is the essential condition of such development. They say that, notwithstanding any undertakings industry may give, and notwithstanding any recommendations this Inquiry may make, they will never have any control over what will happen to them, to their villages and to the land they claim, unless

they have some measure of control over the development of the North. The only way they will acquire that measure of control, they say, is through a settlement of their land claims.

The native people do not believe that any recommendations this Inquiry may make for the pipeline project will be carried out, even if the government finds them acceptable, and even if industry says they are acceptable, unless they are in a position to insist upon them. And they will be in that position only if their claims are settled, if their rights to their land are entrenched, and if institutions are established that enable them to enforce the recommendations. They say the experience of the treaties proves this.

Let us consider, then, whether construction of the pipeline and establishment of the energy corridor before native claims are settled, will retard achievement of the goals of the native people or indeed render them impossible of achievement?

Land and Control of Land Use

If the pipeline is built before a settlement of native claims is reached, then the land that is required for the pipeline right-of-way, the energy corridor, and their ancillary facilities will have been selected, and will thereby be excluded from any later selection of land for use by the native people. Under the Alaska Native Claims Settlement Act, the pipeline corridor from Prudhoe Bay to Valdez was excluded from the land selection process, and so was the proposed corridor for the Arctic Gas pipeline from Prudhoe Bay along the Interior Route to the International Boundary between Alaska and the Yukon.

I have recommended in this report that certain areas be withdrawn from industrial development to establish a wilderness park

in the Northern Yukon and a whale sanctuary in Mackenzie Bay. But all along the route of the proposed pipeline there are areas and places that are of special importance to the native people. If the pipeline is built now, prior to the native people's selection of land, these areas and places may well be lost.

In many villages along the Mackenzie River, the native people expressed great concern over the proximity of the proposed pipeline to their villages. These small villages are the hearth of native life, and the people in them can be expected to seek special protection for the lands near them. Inuit Tapirisat of Canada, in their submission to the federal government, asked for the native communities' right to select any land within a 25-miles radius, and the Dene may well seek similar protection for their villages. Acceptance by the government of the proposed route and the designation of an energy corridor along that route before native claims are settled would certainly prejudice those claims. The proposed pipeline route at present passes within 25 miles of Fort Good Hope, Fort Norman, Wrigley, Fort Simpson and Jean Marie River.

Of course, the Dene and Inuit claims are not limited to the vicinity of their villages. They seek ownership and control of the use of vast tracts of land to achieve a number of objectives. They seek to strengthen the renewable resource sector of the northern economy. This, they insist, must take place before a pipeline is built. Their reasoning is simple: once the pipeline is underway, the primary flow of capital will be to the non-renewable resource sector. Once the gas pipeline is built and the corridor is established, the gas pipeline will probably be looped, and after that, an oil pipeline may be constructed, and, of course, gas and oil exploration will be intensified all along the

Beaver pelts drying in Wrigley. (L. Smith)

John Bayly, counsel for COPE. ((T. Chretien)

Sam Raddi, President of COPE, with NWT Commissioner, Stuart Hodgson. (Inuit Today— T. Grant)

Ron Veale, counsel for Council of Yukon Indians. (T. Chretien)

corridor. Given the fact that over the past decade, in the pre-pipeline period, there has been a concentration on the non-renewable resource sector of the economy, the shift to that sector, and away from the renewable resource sector, once the construction of the pipeline is begun, will become complete.

A second objective of the claims to land and control of land use relates to non-renewable resources. The native people seek to exercise a measure of control over projects such as the pipeline to protect the renewable resource base and environment upon which they depend. If we build the pipeline now, the federal government will establish a regulatory authority to supervise its construction and enforce, among other matters, environmental protection measures. The authority will employ a large number of inspectors, monitors and other personnel. The public service population in the Northwest Territories, mainly white, will further increase. The necessity, acknowledged on all sides, for a regulatory authority will mean that its staff will have extensive power over land use all along the corridor. There is little likelihood of the native people having any control over land use, whether it be access roads to the pipeline, or seismic exploration, or extensions of the corridor. The machinery for regulating the pipeline will entrench and reinforce the existing federal and territorial bureaucracies.

The native people, through their claims, seek benefits from those industrial developments by which they are prepared to give their consent and which the government deems necessary in the national interest. Would they be in a position to take advantage of any benefits that might accrue from a pipeline, prior to a claims settlement? The native people, with some few exceptions, do not have the necessary capital or the experience to participate effectively in joint ventures on projects such as the pipeline. But a claims settlement would be the means of supplying capital to native development corporations so they could participate in such ventures. The Metis Association of the Northwest Territories told the Inquiry that they are eager to participate in such ventures.

Self-Government

The native people believe that, with a new wave of white in-migration in the wake of a pipeline, they will see repeated in the North the experience of native people throughout the rest of North America. An increase in the white population would not only reinforce the existing structure of government; it would reduce the native people to a minority position within that structure, thereby undermining their constitutional claim to self-determination.

We know there was virtually uncontrolled in-migration to Alaska of non-Alaskan residents as a result of the construction of the trans-Alaska pipeline. Arctic Gas say that measures can be taken to restrict such in-migration to the Northwest Territories. It is also said that stringent measures can be imposed to regulate housing, land use — indeed, the whole of northern life — in a way that was not possible in Alaska. But a proposal to use the power of the state in that way confirms the very fear that the native people have: a large-scale project such as the pipeline would lead to the further entrenchment of the existing, and largely white, bureaucracy in the North, and the chances of achieving a transfer of power to native institutions — one of the major objectives of native claims — would be made so difficult as to be impossible.

Since the Carrothers Commission in 1966, the development of municipal government has been the focus for the evolution of local self-government in the Northwest Territories. If this policy is to continue, then there is nothing further to be said. If it is to be changed — and the claims of the native people may require change in the existing institutions of local government — the change should be effected before construction of the pipeline is underway and before existing government structures become further entrenched. To the extent that the Dene and Inuit proposals call for the restriction of the franchise in local, regional and territorial political entities to long-term residents of the North, the effect of the construction of the pipeline, swelling the population of white southerners, would render the prospect of agreement on such a limitation that much more unlikely.

The native people seek control over social services so that they themselves can deal with the problems that already exist in the North. It would not be possible to achieve the same objective merely by pursuing a crash program making funds available to support existing local native rehabilitation programs and to establish new ones to deal with the problems associated with the pipeline. The sheer scale of the pipeline's impact on the social fabric of the small communities is likely to overwhelm the capabilities of such native programs as the Koe-Go-Cho Society at Fort Simpson and Peel River Alcoholics Anonymous at Fort McPherson.

At the same time, if the pipeline precedes a settlement of claims, the process of bureaucratic entrenchment will also take place in the social services. The services themselves will have to be expanded to deal with the anticipated increases in alcoholism, crime, family breakdowns, and other forms of social disorganization that experience in the North, and elsewhere, has shown to be associated with large-scale frontier development. This expansion will mean more social workers, more police, more alcohol rehabilitation workers and a corresponding increase in the size of the bureaucracy.

The idea that new programs, more planning and an increase in social service personnel will solve these problems misconstrues their real nature and cause. The high rates of social and personal breakdown in the North are, in good measure, the responses of individuals and families who have suffered the loss of meaning in their lives and control over their destiny. A pipeline before a settlement would confirm their belief that they have no control over their land or their lives. Whether that conviction is true or not, that will be their perception. These problems are beyond the competence of social workers, priests and psychiatrists. They cannot be counselled away.

Of course, a settlement of native claims will not be a panacea for all of the social ills of the North, but it would permit the native people to begin to solve these problems themselves. That would take time. But it is worth taking the time, because to build a pipeline before native claims are settled would compound existing problems and undermine the possibility of their solution.

I have said that control of education and the preservation of the native languages are central to the issue of cultural survival. The effects that prior construction of a pipeline would have on education and language could be regarded as a litmus test of prejudice to native claims.

The educational system in the North

already reflects the demands of white families, who, although they stay only a year or two in the North, insist upon a curriculum similar to that of Ottawa, Edmonton or Vancouver because they intend to return south. They do not want their children to lose a year or to have to adjust to a different school system in the North.

Pipeline construction would bring yet more white families north, and it would therefore entrench the present system and its curriculum. At the same time as the native people find themselves part of an industrial labour force, without having had a chance to build up and develop their own forms of economic development, they would find increasing difficulty in making their case that the curriculum does not meet the needs of their children.

If the native peoples' claim to run their own schools is to be recognized, it must be done now.

The Lessons of History

The native people of the North seek in their claims to fulfil their hope for the future. The settlement of their claims would therefore be an event of both real and symbolic importance in their relationship to the rest of Canada. The native people want to follow a path of their own. To them, a decision that their claims must be settled before the pipeline is built will be an affirmation of their right to choose that path. On the other hand, if the pipeline is built before native claims are settled, that will be a demonstration to the native people of the North that the Government of Canada is not prepared to give them the right to govern their own lives; for if they are not to be granted that right in relation to the decision which more than anything else will affect their lives and the

lives of their children, then what is left o that right thereafter?

What are the implications of not recogniz ing that right and proceeding with th pipeline before settlement? Feelings of frus tration and disappointment among the na tive people of the North would be trans formed into bitterness and rage. There is real possibility of civil disobedience and civi disorder.

These things are possibilities. But I ca predict with certainty that if the pipeline i built before a settlement is achieved, th communities that are already strugglin with the negative effects of industrial devel opment will be still further demoralized. T the extent that the process of margina ization — the sense of being made irrelevan in your own land — is a principal cause o social pathology, the native people wi suffer its effects in ever greater measure.

Can we learn anything from our ow history? I hope we can, if we examine th settlement of the West and the events tha led to the Red River Rebellion of 1869 an the Northwest Rebellion of 1885. Let m make it plain that, while I believe there is real possibility of civil disobedience and civ disorder in the North if we build the pipelin without a settlement of native claims, I d not believe that there is likely to be rebellion. Nevertheless the events of 1869 1870 and 1885 offer us an insight into th consequences of similar policies today. Thes events, and their aftermath, make it imposs ble to reconcile native claims with th demands of white advance to the frontier.

The establishment of a Provisional Go ernment by Louis Riel and his followers i 1869 in the Red River Valley was a cons quence of Canada's having acquired Ru pert's Land from the Hudson's Bay Com pany without recognition of the rights of th

Metis, Indians and whites living there. The list of Rights drawn up by the Provisional Government called for the settlement of the land claims of the Metis and the signing of treaties with the Indians. In the Manitoba Act of 1870, the claims of the Metis were recognized, and 1,400,000 acres were set aside for their benefit. But their claims were processed very slowly, and, with their lands in doubt and their hunting opportunities continually declining, many Metis migrated north and west to the Valley of the Saskatchewan. There they built a prosperous and stable society that was a product of both the old and new ways. In 1873 they established their own government in the unorganized territory of the Northwest with Gabriel Dumont as president. But the advance of white settlement soon reached them even there.

Manitoba entered Confederation in 1870, and the following year the Canadian Pacific Railway was incorporated. Between 1871 and 1877, the government signed seven treaties with the Indians to enable rail construction to proceed, and by the mid-1870s railway survey crews reached the Saskatchewan.

The CPR, built across the prairies in 1882 and 1883, with the labour of five thousand men, completed the displacement of Indian society that had begun with the treaty negotiations. The settlers who followed the laying of the track soon spread out across the hunting grounds of the Cree and the Blackfoot. The Indians, demoralized and racked by disease, watched from their newly established reserves as their lands were divided.

The construction of the railway was not without serious incident. In 1882, Chief Piapot's Cree pulled up some 40 miles of CPR survey stakes, and camped directly in the path of construction crews. Only the intervention of the Northwest Mounted Police averted violence then. When the railway crossed the Blackfoot reserve, the Indians again confronted the construction crews. Father Lacombe succeeded in persuading them to give up that land for a new reserve elsewhere.

The Northwest Rebellion of 1885 arose from the grievances and frustrations of the Metis and Indians. Dr. Robert Page, an historian from Trent University, told the Inquiry that, although the CPR acted as a catalyst to bring these tensions to a head, it was not the sole issue. In 1884, serious political agitation led the people in Saskatchewan to ask Riel to return. They sent a petition of rights and grievances to Ottawa which cited the government's failure to provide the Metis with patents to the land they already occupied, and the destitution of the Indians.

The government procrastinated in dealing with the claims despite official entreaties of Inspector Crozier of the Northwest Mounted Police urging that the claims should be settled immediately. In March 1885, the Metis rose in rebellion. The Cree, under Poundmaker and Big Bear, also took up arms. A military operation was organized, and the militia was sent to the west on the CPR. The Metis and Indians were defeated.

On November 7, 1885, the last spike was driven at Craigellachie. Nine days later, Louis Riel was hanged at the police barracks in Regina. Eight Indians were also hanged. The Metis were dispersed, and the Indians were confined to their reserves. Some Metis fled to the United States, some to Indian reserves and some to the Mackenzie Valley. In the years after the rebellion, some Metis were granted land or scrip, but the final settlement of their claims dragged on for years. Their scrip was often bought up by white speculators and, under the impact of advancing settlement, some of them retreated to the North.

The historical record shows that if the land claims of the Metis had been settled, there would have been no Northwest Rebellion. It is equally plain that the opening of the West to white settlers made it difficult, if not impossible, for the Government of Canada to recognize the land claims of the native people, who had lived on the plains before the coming of the railway.

There is a direct parallel between what happened on the prairies after 1869 and the situation in the Northwest Territories today. Then, as now, the native people were faced with a vast influx of whites on the frontier. Then, as now, the basic provisions for native land rights had not been agreed. Then, as now, a large-scale frontier development project was in its initial stages, and a major reordering of the constitutional status of the area was in the making.

The lesson to be learned from the events of that century is not simply that the failure to recognize native claims may lead to violence, but that the claims of the white settlers, and the railway, once acknowledged, soon made it impossible to carry out the promises made to the native peoples.

The Government of Canada was then and is now committed to settling the claims of the native people. White settlement of the West made it impossible for the government to settle native claims. Today, the Government of Canada is pledged to settle native claims in the North, and the pledge is for a comprehensive settlement. It is my conviction that, if the pipeline is built before a settlement of native claims is made and implemented, that pledge will not and, in the nature of things, cannot be fulfilled.

Hunting camp near Fort Resolution. (R. Fumoleau)

Postponement of the Pipeline

In my judgment, we must settle native claims before we build a Mackenzie Valley pipeline. Such a settlement will not be simply the signing of an agreement, after which pipeline construction can then immediately proceed. Intrinsic to the settlement of native land claims is the establishment of new institutions and programs that will form the basis for native self-determination.

The native people of the North reject the model of the James Bay Agreement. They seek new institutions of local, regional and indeed territorial government. John Ciaccia, speaking to the Parliamentary Committee convened to examine the James Bay Agreement, said that the Government of Quebec was "taking the opportunity to extend its administration, its laws, its services, its governmental structures through the entirety of Québec." [*The James Bay and Northern Québec Agreement,* p. xvi] The Dene and the Inuit seek a very different kind of settlement.

They also reject the Alaskan model. The Alaskan settlement was designed to provide the native people with land, capital and corporate structures to enable them to participate in what has become the dominant mode of economic development in Alaska, the non-renewable resource sector. This model is only relevant if we decide against the strengthening of the renewable resource sector in the Canadian North.

The Alaskan settlement also rejects the idea that there should be any special status for native people. That is a policy quite different from the policy formulated by the Government of Canada. In Alaska the settlement was designed to do away with special status by 1991 and to assimilate Alaskan natives. The Government of Canada faced that issue between 1969 and 1976 and decided against it.

The issue comes down to this: will native claims be rendered more difficult or even impossible of achievement if we build a pipeline without first settling those claims? Must we establish the political, social and economic institutions and programs embodied in the settlement before building a pipeline? Unless we do, will the progress of the native people toward realization of their goals be irremediably retarded? I think the answer clearly is yes. The progress of events, once a pipeline is under construction, will place the native people at a grave disadvantage, and will place the government itself in an increasingly difficult position.

In my opinion a period of ten years will be required in the Mackenzie Valley and Western Arctic to settle native claims, and to establish the new institutions and new programs that a settlement will entail. No pipeline should be built until these things have been achieved.

It might be possible to make a settlement within the year with the Metis, and perhaps to force a settlement upon the Inuit. It would, however, be impossible, I think, to coerce the Dene to agree to such a settlement. It would have to be an imposed settlement.

You can sign an agreement or you can impose one; you can proceed with land selection; you can promise the native people that no encroachments will be made upon their lands. Yet you will discover before long that such encroachments are necessary. You can, in an agreement, promise the native people the right to rebuild the native economy. The influx of whites, the divisions created among the native people, the preoccupations of the federal and territorial governments, faced with the problems o[f] pipeline construction and the developmen[t] of the corridor, would make fulfilment o[f] such a promise impossible. That is why th[e] pipeline should be postponed for 10 years.

A decision to build the pipeline no[w] would imply a decision to bring to produc[-] tion now the gas and oil resources of th[e] Mackenzie Delta and the Beaufort Sea. Th[e] industrial activity that would follow th[at] decision would be on a scale such as t[o] require the full attention of the governmen[t] and entrench its commitment to non-renew[-] able resource development in the North. Th[e] drive to bring the native people into th[e] industrial system would intensify, and ther[e] would be little likelihood of the nativ[e] people receiving any support in their desir[e] to expand the renewable resource sector.

If we believe that the industrial syste[m] must advance now into the Mackenzi[e] Valley and the Western Arctic, then w[e] must not delude ourselves or the nativ[e] people about what a settlement of the[ir] claims will mean in such circumstances.

It would be dishonest to impose a settle[-] ment that we know now — and that th[e] native people will know before the ink is dr[y] on it — will not achieve their goals. They wi[ll] soon realize — just as the native people on th[e] prairies realized a century ago as the settle[rs] poured in — that the actual course of even[ts] on the ground will deny the promises tha[t] appear on paper. The advance of the indus[-] trial system would determine the course [of] events, no matter what Parliament, th[e] courts, this Inquiry or anyone else may say.

If we think back to the days when th[e] treaties were signed on the prairies, we ca[n] predict what will happen in the North if [a] settlement is forced upon the native peopl[e.] We shall soon see that we cannot keep th[e] promises we have made.

12 Epilogue: Themes for the National Interest

Prime Minister Trudeau has said that Canada is a product of the providential encounter between the French and the English on this continent. Canada takes its identity from the evolution of that encounter. The contours of that meeting between the French and the English in North America define the political institutions of the nation, and constitute Canada's unique contribution to the search by man for a rational polity.

But there was an earlier encounter on this continent that made possible the very existence of the nation — between the Europeans and the indigenous peoples of the Americas. Here, in what is now Canada, it was an encounter first between the French and the native people, then between the English and the native people. It was an encounter which has ramified throughout our history, and the consequences of which are with us today. This encounter may be as important to us all, in the long sweep of history, as any other on this continent. And it is taking place in its most intense and contemporary form on our northern frontier.

It is for this reason that so many eyes are drawn to the North. As André Siegfried, the le Tocqueville of Canada, said:

Many countries — and they are to be envied — possess in one direction or another a window which opens out on to the infinite — on to the potential future.... The North is always there like a presence, it is the background of the picture, without which Canada would not be Canadian. [Canada p. 28-29]

It may be that, through this window, we shall discover something of the shape that our future relations with the native people of our country must assume.

The English and French are the inheritors of two great streams of western civilization. They hold far more in common than divides them: they have similar linguistic and literary traditions and rivalry and commonality of interests that have caused their histories repeatedly to overlap. What is more, the industrial system is the foundation for the material well-being they both enjoy.

Now the industrial system beckons to the native people. But it does not merely beckon: it has intruded into their culture, economy and society, now pulling, now pushing them towards another, and in many ways an alien, way of life. In the North today, the native people are being urged to give up their life on the land; they are being told that their days and their lives should become partitioned like our own. We have often urged that their commitment to the industrial system be entire and complete. Native people have even been told that they cannot compromise: they must become industrial workers, or go naked back to the bush.

Yet many of them refuse. They say they have a past of their own; they see that complete dependence on the industrial system entails a future that has no place for the values they cherish. Their refusal to make the commitment asked of them is one of the points of recurring tension in the North today. They acknowledge the benefits we have brought to them. They say that they are, in some respects, more comfortable now than they were in the old days. The industrial system has provided many things that they value, such as rifles, radios, outboard motors and snowmobiles. But they know that, in the old days, the land was their own. Even in the days of the fur trade, they and the land were essential to it. Now they recognize they are not essential. If it is in the national interest, a pipeline can and will be built across their land. They fear that they will become strangers in their own land. The native people know that somehow they must gain a measure of control over their lives and over the political institutions that shape their lives, and that they must do this before the industrial system overtakes and, it may be, overwhelms them. This is what their claims are about, and this is why they say their claims must be settled before a pipeline is built.

The native people know their land is important to us as a source of oil and gas and mineral wealth, but that its preservation is not essential to us. They know that above all else we have wanted to subdue the land and extract its resources. They recognize that we do not regard their hunting, trapping and fishing as essential, that it is something we often regard in a patronizing way. They say that we reject the things that are valuable to them in life: that we do so explicitly and implicitly.

We have sought to make over these people in our own image, but this pronounced, consistent and well-intentioned effort at assimilation has failed. The use of the bush and the barrens, and the values associated with them, have persisted. The native economy refuses to die. The Dene, Inuit and Metis survive, determined to be themselves. In the past their refusal to be assimilated has usually been passive, even covert. Today it is plain and unmistakable, a fact of northern life that must be understood.

The native people have had some hard things to say about the government, about the oil and gas industry and about the white man and his institutions. The allegation has been made that what the leaders of native organizations in Northern Canada are saying is not representative of the attitudes and thinking of northern native peoples. But this Inquiry not only has sought the views of the native organizations, but has obtained the views of the native people who live in every settlement and village of the Mackenzie Valley and the Western Arctic. There the native people, speaking in their own villages, in their own languages and in their own way, expressed their real views. About that I am in no doubt.

It would be a mistake to think that the native people are being manipulated by sinister forces, unseen by them, yet discernible to us. It is demeaning and degrading to tell someone that he does not mean or does not know what he is saying, that someone has told him to say it. It would be wrong to dismiss what they have said because we would rather believe that they are not capable of expressing their own opinions.

It may be uncomfortable to have to listen, when we have never listened in the past. But we must listen now. If we do not understand what is in the minds of the native people, what their attitudes really are toward industrial development, we shall have no way of knowing what impact a pipeline and an energy corridor will have on the people of the North.

We all have different ideas of progress and our own definitions of the national interest. It is commonplace for people in Southern Canada to dismiss the notion that a few thousand native people have a right to stand in the way of industrial imperatives. But many of the Dene intend to do just that. Philip Blake told the Inquiry at Fort McPherson:

> If your nation chooses ... to continue to try and destroy our nation, then I hope you will understand why we are willing to fight so that our nation can survive. It is our world.
>
> We do not wish to push our world onto you. But we are willing to defend it for ourselves, our children, and our grandchildren. If your nation becomes so violent that it would tear up our land, destroy our society and our future, and occupy our homeland, by trying to

impose this pipeline against our will, then of course we will have no choice but to react with violence.

> I hope we do not have to do that. For it is not the way we would choose. However, if we are forced to blow up the pipeline ... I hope you will not only look on the violence of Indian action, but also on the violence of your own nation which would force us to take such a course.
>
> We will never initiate violence. But if your nation threatens by its own violent action to destroy our nation, you will have given us no choice. Please do not force us into this position. For we would all lose too much. [C1085ff.]

Chief Fred Greenland said to the Inquiry at Aklavik:

> It's clear to me what the native people are saying today. They're discussing not their future but the future of their children and grandchildren, and if the government continues to refuse or neglect [us] ... I think the natives would just stop their effort and discussions and the opportunities for a peaceful settlement would be lost. We must choose wisely and carefully because there will be a future generation of Canadians who will live with the results. [C3863]

Frank T'Seleie, then Chief at Fort Good Hope, also spoke of the future generations, of the children yet unborn. He told the Inquiry:

> It is for this unborn child, Mr. Berger, that my nation will stop the pipeline. It is so that this unborn child can know the freedom of this land that I am willing to lay down my life. [C1778ff.]

Chief Jim Antoine of Fort Simpson:

> ... every time we try to do something, within the system ... it doesn't seem to work for us, as Indian people. We tried it, we tried to use it, it doesn't work for us. ... We're going to keep on trying to use the system until we get frustrated enough that we're going to try changing it. I think that's where it's directed, that's where it's going. I would stand with my brother from Good Hope that he would lay

down his life for what he believes in, and I feel the same way. There's a lot of us young people who feel the same way. [C2625]

Raymond Yakaleya, speaking at Norma Wells:

> Our backs are turned to the corners. This is our last stand.
>
> I ask each and every one of you in this room what would you do if you were in our shoes? How would you feel if you had these conditions on you? I ask you one more time, let us negotiate, there's still time, but don't force us, because this time we have nothing to lose. When I ask for the lives of my people, am I asking you for too much? [C2177]

I have given the most anxious consideration to whether or not I should make any reference in this report to these statements. I may be said that merely reciting them would be to invite a violent reaction to the pipeline if it were built without a just settlement of native claims. Yet these statements were no lightly made. No one who heard them could doubt that they were said in earnest. So have concluded that they cannot be ignored. They illustrate the depth of feeling among the native people.

I want to emphasize that my recommendation that the construction of a Mackenzie Valley pipeline should be postponed until native claims are settled is not dependent upon this evidence. That recommendation based upon the social and economic impact of a pipeline, and upon the impact it would have on native claims. I would be remiss in my duty, however, if I did not remind the Government of Canada that these things were said. I do not want anyone to think I am predicting an insurrection. But I am saying there is a real possibility of civil disobedience and civil disorder that — if they did occur — might well render orderly political evolution of the North impossible, and could poison relations between the Government of

Nahanni Butte Inquiry hearing. (N. Cooper)

Fort Simpson Chief Jim Antoine at Trout Lake with Judge Berger. (News of the North)

NWT Inuit leader Sam Raddi presenting land claims proposal to federal cabinet, Ottawa, 1976. (ITC–T. Grant)

Rick Hardy, **President** *of NWT Metis Association* (Native Press)

Canada and the native people for many years to come.

We ought not to be surprised that native people should express themselves so strongly. Julius Nyerere, President of Tanzania, said at a meeting commemorating the twenty-fifth anniversary of the United Nations on October 15, 1970:

> A man can change his religion if he wishes; he can accept a different political belief — or in both cases give the appearance of doing so — if this would relieve him of intolerable circumstances. But no man can change his colour or his race. And if he suffers because of it, he must either become less than a man, or he must fight. And for good or evil, mankind has been so created that many will refuse to acquiesce in their own degradation; they will destroy peace rather than suffer under it. [p. 4, no. 42]

It has been said that the native people have not articulated their claims, that they are taking too long over it. Yet, when you realize that we have tried to suppress systematically their own institutions, traditions and aspirations, why should we expect them to develop a blueprint for the future in haste?

It has also been suggested that the native people would not be able to manage their own affairs. In fact, they have brought before this Inquiry their own scheme for self-government and for the economic development of the North. And it would be wrong to dismiss this scheme out of hand. They have offered a first, not a final, draft. But it is founded on their own past and their own experience, on their own preferences and aspirations; they wish to see it realized in a future that is of their fashioning. The modernization of the native economy, the development of the renewable resource sector, constitutes as rational a program for the

development of the North as we have so far been able to devise.

All that has been said in this report should make it plain that the great agency of change in the North is the presence of industrial man. He and his technology, armed with immense political and administrative power and prepared to transform the social and natural landscape in the interests of a particular kind of society and economy, have a way of soon becoming pervasive. It is not just a question of a seismic trail being cleared across their hunting grounds, or of a drilling rig outside their village that troubles the native people. It is the knowledge that they could be overwhelmed by economic and political strength, and that the resources of their land — indeed the land itself — could be taken from them.

In each native village there is a network of social relationships established over many generations. If there were a pipeline, would all those threads linking family to family, and generation to generation, be snapped?

The native people are raising profound questions. They are challenging the economic religion of our time, the belief in an ever-expanding cycle of growth and consumption. It is a faith shared equally by capitalist and communist.

Dr. Ian McTaggart-Cowan has said:

> Is the only way to improve the lot of a country's citizens the way of industrialization, whether it be the western way or the forced march of the USSR?...

> Almost inevitably, diversity is sacrificed to a spurious efficiency. The loss of diversity is not merely a matter for sentimental regret. It is a direct reduction in the number of opportunities open to future generations.

> As we look toward the end of the twentieth century...we see...this diversity threatened by dominant societies pursuing goals that, though they have produced a rich material

culture, are already eroding the sources of their original stimulus. [In an address to the Pacific Science Congress, August 26, 1975]

The native people take an historical point of view. They argue that their own culture should not be discarded, that it has served them well for many years, and that the industrial system of the white man may not, here in the North, serve them as well for anything like so long a time. They do not wish to set themselves up as a living folk museum, nor do they wish to be the objects of mere sentimentality. Rather, with the guarantees that can be provided only by a settlement of their claims, and with the strengthening of their own economy, they wish to ensure that their cultures can continue to grow and change — in directions they choose for themselves.

Here on our last frontier we have a chance to protect the environment and to deal justly with some of the native people of Canada. If we postpone the pipeline, there will be an opportunity for the native people of the North to build a future for themselves. But if we build the pipeline now, there is every reason to believe that the history of the northern native people will proceed along the same lamentable course as that of native people in so many other places.

Now it has been said that, without the industry's drive to build a pipeline, there is unlikely to be a settlement of native claims. Why should this be so? The Government of Canada has an obligation to settle these claims, pipeline or no pipeline: a solemn assurance has been given. Postponement of pipeline construction will be no reason to turn away from the other issues that confront us in the North.

A settlement of native claims that does no more than extinguish the native interest in land will get us nowhere so far as the social

The Ramparts along the Mackenzie River. (R. Fumoleau)

and economic advancement of the native people are concerned. Those social and economic gains will follow from the achievement of a sense of collective pride and initiative by the Dene, Inuit and Metis, and not simply from a clearing away of legal complications to enable industrial development to proceed.

If the pipeline is not built now, an orderly program of exploration can still proceed in the Mackenzie Delta and the Beaufort Sea. And, even if the oil and gas industry withdraws from its exploration activities because of a decision to postpone the pipeline, the Government of Canada has the means to ensure the continuation of exploratory drilling if it were held to be in the national interest. Postponement of the pipeline would mean that, if continued drilling in the Mackenzie Delta and the Beaufort Sea reveals sufficient reserves, Canada can proceed to build a pipeline at a time of its own choosing, along a route of its own choice, by means it has decided upon, and with the cooperation of the native people of the North.

Let me make it clear that if we decide to postpone the pipeline, we shall not be renouncing our northern energy supplies. They will still be there. No one is going to take them away. In years to come, it will still be available as fuel or as industrial feedstocks.

We have never had to determine what is the most intelligent use to make of our resources. We have never had to consider restraint. Will we continue, driven by technology and egregious patterns of consumption, to deplete our energy resources wherever and whenever we find them? Upon this question depends the future of northern native people and their environment.

Maurice Strong, Chairman of Petro Canada, has written:

Man's very skills, the very technical success with which he overspreads the earth, makes him the most dangerous of all creatures.

One critical aspect of man's use of planetary resources is the way in which he is burning up more and more of the world's energy....

We can no longer afford to plan on the basis of past and current trends in consumption. If we assume that a decent standard of life for the world's peoples inevitably requires increasing per capita use of energy, we shall be planning for an energy starved world, or an ecological disaster, or both. Rather than searching endlessly for new energy sources, we must contribute to its wiser use....

At present, we are far from this ideal. We have recklessly assumed that no matter how wasteful our lifestyle, we shall somehow find the energy to support it....

In the last 15 years, world use of energy has doubled. North America now uses about five times as much energy as is consumed in the whole of Asia, and per capita consumption is about 24 times higher. The United States each year wastes more fossil fuel than is used by two-thirds of the world's population. [*Edmonton Journal,* September 22, 1976]

If we build the pipeline, it will seem strange, years from now, that we refused to do justice to the native people merely to continue to provide ourselves with a range of consumer goods and comforts without even asking Canadians to consider an alternative. Such a course is not necessary, nor is it acceptable.

I have said that, under the present conditions, the pipeline, if it were built now, would do enormous damage to the social fabric in the North, would bring only limited economic benefits, and would stand in the way of a just settlement of native claims. It would exacerbate tension. It would leave a legacy of bitterness throughout a region in which the native people have protested, with virtual unanimity, against the pipeline. For a time, some of them may be co-opted. But in the end, the Dene, Inuit and Metis will follow those of their leaders who refuse to turn their backs on their own history, who insist that they must be true to themselves and who articulate the values that lie at the heart of the native identity.

No pipeline should be built now. Time is needed to settle native claims, set up new institutions and establish a truly diversified economy in the North. This, I suggest, is the course northern development should take.

We have the opportunity to make a new departure, to open a new chapter in the history of the indigenous peoples of the Americas. We must not reject the opportunity that is now before us.

Appendices

The Inquiry
and Participants

The Hearings

The Mackenzie Valley Pipeline Inquiry was established on March 21, 1974 by Order-in-Council P.C. 1974-641 (as attached). The Expanded Guidelines for Northern Pipelines, which were tabled in the House of Commons on June 28, 1972, form part of the terms of reference of the Inquiry.

Preliminary hearings were held in April and May 1974 (at Yellowknife, Inuvik, Whitehorse and Ottawa) and in September 1974 (at Yellowknife) to hear submissions from all interested parties on the scope and procedures of the Inquiry. On the basis of these hearings, preliminary rulings were issued on July 12, 1974 and on October 29, 1974. On March 3, 1975 a week of overview hearings began in Yellowknife consisting of the opening statements of each participant and presentations by experts, without cross-examination, on general subjects of importance to the Inquiry.

The formal hearings began on March 11, 1975 with witnesses called by each participant presenting evidence that was subject to cross-examination. The evidence was divided into the following general areas: engineering and construction of the proposed pipeline, the impact of a pipeline and Mackenzie corridor development on the physical environment, the living environment and the human environment (social and economic).

In addition to the formal hearings, the Inquiry travelled to all of the 35 communities in the Mackenzie Valley region, the delta and Beaufort Sea region and the northern Yukon to hear evidence from the residents in their own languages, in their home communities. The first such hearing was held in Aklavik in early April 1975 and the last in Detah in August 1976.

Many written submissions and requests to be heard were received by the Inquiry from people and organizations in Southern Canada; consequently, in May and June 1976, hearings were held in ten cities from Vancouver to Halifax.

The hearings ended on November 19, 1976 in Yellowknife following a week of final argument during which the participants advanced their views on the terms and conditions for a pipeline and energy corridor across the Northern Yukon and along the Mackenzie Valley.

Documents and Records

A full record of the evidence presented verbally to the Inquiry is contained in the Inquiry transcripts. In addition, many reports, maps, pictures, and a few miscellaneous objects have been officially designated as Inquiry exhibits.

Perhaps the most important of all are the verbatim transcripts of the proceedings of both the formal and community hearings. The formal hearings have yielded over 906 exhibits and 32,353 pages of testimony bound in 204 volumes. The community hearings have been transcribed in 77 volumes with a total of 8,438 pages and 662 exhibits. The exhibits include such documents as the application and supporting materials submitted by Arctic Gas and Foothills (which run into many volumes), the Land Use and Occupancy maps prepared by the Indian Brotherhood of the Northwest Territories and by the Committee for Original Peoples Entitlement/Inuit Tapirisat of Canada, the 1974 report of the federal government's Pipeline Application Assessment Group, publications of the Environment Protection Board, and a number of the reports prepared for the Environmental-Social Program, Northern Pipelines and the Beaufort Sea Project.

Also included in the Inquiry documents are the final submissions of all the Inquiry participants, containing their recommendations supporting the terms and conditions that they propose should apply to the pipeline project. The Commission Counsel Submission is over 800 pages long, and has generated replies from several of the participants and from the Government of the Northwest Territories.

To assist in retrieval of information, the Inquiry has prepared a "key word" type index to the transcripts. This will be printed and distributed as a companion volume to the transcripts. Also, summaries of the proceedings cross-referenced to the transcripts were prepared by the Department of Indian Affairs and Northern Development, and published in six volumes.

Participants

Canadian Arctic Gas Pipeline Limited

Chairman: William Wilder

President: Vernon Horte

Counsel: Pierre Genest, Q.C., Michael Goldie, Q.C., Daryl Carter, Jack Marshall, John Steeves, G. Ziskrout.

Foothills Pipe Lines Ltd.

President: Robert Blair

Counsel: Reginald Gibbs, Q.C., Alan Hollingworth, John Lutes, Ian MacLaughlin.

Canadian Arctic Resources Committee (CARC)

Chairman: Andrew Thompson

Counsel: Russell Anthony, Alistair Lucas, Garth Evans.

The Canadian Nature Federation, the Federation of Ontario Naturalists, Pollution Probe and the Canadian Environmental Law Association were represented at the Inquiry through counsel for CARC.

Commission Counsel

Ian Scott, Q.C., Stephen Goudge, Ian Roland, Alick Ryder

Special Counsel

Michael Jackson, Ian Waddell.

Committee for Original Peoples Entitlement (COPE)

President: Sam Raddi

Counsel: John Bayly, Leslie Lane, Peter Cumming.

Inuit Tapirisat of Canada was represented at the Inquiry by COPE.

Council for Yukon Indians

President: Elijah Smith (until mid-1976) and Daniel Johnson (subsequently)

Counsel: Ron Veale.

Environment Protection Board

Chairman and Counsel: Carson Templeton.

Indian Brotherhood of the Northwest Territories/Metis Association of the Northwest Territories

President, Indian Brotherhood: James Wah Shee (until early 1976) and George Erasmus (subsequently)

President, Metis Association: Richard Hardy

Counsel: Glen Bell.

Northwest Territories Mental Health Association

Executive Director and Counsel: Jo MacQuarrie.

Northwest Territories Association of Municipalities

President: James Robertson

Executive Secretary: David Reesor

Counsel: Murray Sigler.

Northwest Territories Chamber of Commerce

President: Gordon Erion and Gerald Loomis (subsequently)

Counsel: David Searle, Q.C.

Imperial Oil Limited, Gulf Oil Limited and Shell Canada Limited

Counsel: John Ballem, Q.C.

CANADA

PRIVY COUNCIL · CONSEIL PRIVÉ

P.C. 1974-641

21 March, 1974

WHEREAS proposals have been made for the construction and operation of a natural gas pipeline, referred to as the Mackenzie Valley Pipeline, across Crown lands under the control, management and administration of the Minister of Indian Affairs and Northern Development within the Yukon Territory and the Northwest Territories in respect of which it is contemplated that authority might be sought, pursuant to paragraph 19(f) of the Territorial Lands Act, for the acquisition of a right-of-way;

AND WHEREAS it is desirable that any such right-of-way that might be granted be subject to such terms and conditions as are appropriate having regard to the regional social, environmental and economic impact of the construction, operation and abondonment of the proposed pipeline;

THEREFORE, HIS EXCELLENCY THE GOVERNOR GENERAL IN COUNCIL, on the recommendation of the Minister of Indian Affairs and Northern Development, is pleased hereby, pursuant to paragraph 19(h) of the Territorial Lands Act, to designate the Honourable Mr. Justice Thomas R. Berger (hereinafter referred to as Mr. Justice Berger), of the City of Vancouver in the Province of British Columbia, to inquire into and report upon the terms and conditions that should be imposed in respect of any right-of-way that might be granted across Crown lands for the purposes of the proposed Mackenzie Valley Pipeline having regard to

...2

(a)   the social, environmental and economic
       impact regionally, of the construction,
       operation and subsequent abandonment
       of the proposed pipeline in the Yukon
       and the Northwest Territories, and

(b)   any proposals to meet the specific
       environmental and social concerns
       set out in the Expanded Guidelines
       for Northern Pipelines as tabled in
       the House of Commons on June 28, 1972
       by the Minister.

HIS EXCELLENCY THE GOVERNOR GENERAL IN COUNCIL
is further pleased hereby

1.   to authorize Mr. Justice Berger

  (a)   to hold hearings pursuant to this Order in
              Territorial centers and in such other places
              and at such times as he may decide from time to
              time;

  (b)   for the purposes of the inquiry, to summon
              and bring before him any person whose
              attendance he considers necessary to the
              inquiry, examine such persons under oath,
              compel the production of documents and
              do all things necessary to provide a full
              and proper inquiry;

  (c)   to adopt such practices and procedures for
              all purposes of the inquiry as he from time
              to time deems expedient for the proper
              conduct thereof;

  (d)   subject to paragraph 2 hereunder, to engage
              the services of such accountants, engineers,
              technical advisers, or other experts, clerks,
              reporters and assistants as he deems necessary
              or advisable, and also the services of counsel
              to aid and assist him in the inquiry, at such
              rates of remuneration and reimbursement as
              may be approved by the Treasury Board; and

(e)   to rent such space for offices and hearing
        rooms as he deems necessary or advisable at
        such rental rates as may be approved by
        the Treasury Board; and

2.   to authorize the Minister of Indian Affairs and
        Northern Development to designate an officer of
        the Department of Indian Affairs and Northern
        Development to act as Secretary for the inquiry
        and to provide Mr. Justice Berger with such
        accountants, engineers, technical advisers, or
        other experts,clerks, reporters and assistants
        from the Public Service as may be requested by
        Mr. Justice Berger.

        HIS EXCELLENCY THE GOVERNOR GENERAL IN COUNCIL
is further pleased hereby to direct Mr. Justice Berger
to report to the Minister of Indian Affairs and Northern
Development with all reasonable despatch and file with
the Minister the papers and records of the inquiry as
soon as may be reasonable after the conclusion thereof.

        HIS EXCELLENCY THE GOVERNOR GENERAL IN COUNCIL,
with the concurrence of the Minister of Justice, is
further pleased hereby, pursuant to section 37 of the
Judges Act, to authorize Mr. Justice Berger to act on
the inquiry.

                              Certified to be a true copy

                              Assistant Clerk of the Privy Council

Bibliographic Note
and Terminology

Bibliographic Note

This volume contains sufficient bibliographic information to enable the reader to locate published material that is cited. The full bibliographic references will be listed in Volume Two. Where transcripts of the Inquiry hearings are cited, they are identified by the page number preceded by F (formal hearings) or C (community hearings). The Inquiry exhibits are similarly cited with the exhibit number preceded by F or C.

Note on Terminology

Throughout this report I have referred to the land claims of the native people as *native claims.*

Often I have referred to native people meaning all of the people of Eskimo and Indian ancestry, whether they regard themselves as Inuit, Dene or Metis. They are, of course, distinct peoples, yet they have an identity of interest with respect to many of the issues dealt with in this report and have often, in such instances, been referred to collectively as *native people.* Where only one of these peoples is meant, that is apparent from the text.

I have usually referred to present-day Eskimo peoples as Inuit: this is in keeping with their wishes today. Although many people of Eskimo ancestry of the Mackenzie Delta call themselves *Inuvialuit,* I have referred to them also as Inuit.

The term *Dene* refers to the status and non-status people of Indian ancestry who regard themselves as Dene. Native people who describe themselves as Metis and who see themselves as having a distinct history and culture, as well as aspirations and goals that differ from those of the Dene, I have referred to as Metis. I have dealt with the people of Old Crow separately because they live in the Northern Yukon, not in the Northwest Territories.

I have referred to the Mackenzie Valley and the Western Arctic. There is of course some overlap here, in that both geographical areas may be regarded as encompassing the Mackenzie Delta. The Mackenzie Valley includes the whole of the region from the Alberta border to the Mackenzie Delta, including the Great Slave Lake and Great Bear Lake areas. The Western Arctic encompasses the whole area on the rim of the Beaufort Sea, including the arctic coast of the Yukon.

I have referred to witnesses by their first name and surname when their names first appear, and thereafter by their surname only, except where the repetition of the first name is essential to avoid confusion. I have given the appellation "Mr." only to Ministers of the Crown. I have referred to witnesses holding doctorates as "Dr."

I have referred to government officials, the leaders of native organizations, band chiefs and others, by the offices they held when they gave evidence to the Inquiry.

I have often referred to *whites* and to the *white man.* It will be apparent that sometimes I mean western man and the representatives of the industrial system. Of course, in such a context the expression *white man* can, in fact, include people of many races. However, the native people throughout the Inquiry referred to the white man. They knew what they meant, and although they no doubt adopted the expression because the representatives of the larger Canadian society who come to the North are almost entirely Caucasian, they have not been inclined to make any finer differentiation. I think the phrase is not at all misleading under these circumstances. The alternative, which I have rejected, would be constantly to use such expressions as *non-native, southern* or *Euro-Canadian.* Instead, I have used these latter expressions where, in the context, no other would do.

Unless I have indicated otherwise, the term *the North* refers to the Northwest Territories and the Yukon Territory. *The South* generally refers to metropolitan Canada.

I have used the expressions *we* many times. I have meant by it the non-native population of Canada, north and south, and have sought merely to remind readers that I view the North as one who shares the culture, perceptions and ideas of Canadians as a whole.

Throughout the report, Canadian Arctic Gas Pipeline Limited is referred to as Arctic Gas and Foothills Pipe Lines Ltd. as Foothills. I have treated each of these informal terms as plural, recognizing that groups of companies are involved.

Photographs
and Diagrams

Colour Section Photographs

Front cover, clockwise from top right:
Drillers on arctic oil rig (GNWT);
Snowmobiles at Holman Island (E. Weick);
Muskrat skins on stretch boards
(R. Fumoleau); White whales (R. McClung);
Caribou on snow field (ISL—G. Calef);
Welding pipe (Arctic Gas); Johnny Crapeau
and grandson (R. Fumoleau); Teddy Tsetta
of Detah (R. Fumoleau).

Back cover: Drill rig on artificial island,
Beaufort Sea (J. Inglis); Hunter on arctic sea
ice (G. Bristow).

Title page, top left: Dogrib woman testifying
(M. Jackson); *top right:* Yellowknife formal
hearing (D. Gamble); *centre:* Hearing at Rae
(M. Jackson).

Page xxviii: Bowhead whale (W. Hoek);
White whales (R. McClung).

Page xxix, clockwise from top left: Polar
bear (H. Kiliaan); Grizzly bear (R. Russell);
Arctic fox (R. Russell); Cow moose
(R. Russell); Dall sheep (DIAND); Caribou
(N. Cooper); Black bear (A. Carmichael);
Muskrat (R. Russell).

Page xxx, clockwise from top: Arctic
landscape (TravelArctic—J. Swietlik); Ice-
floe (J. Burnford); Richardson Mountains
(ISL—G. Calef); Ice formation, Beaufort Sea
(Arctic Gas); Snow, ice and sun (GNWT); Ice
(ISL—G. Calef); Midnight sun on the
Mackenzie Delta (G. Calef).

Page xxxi, clockwise from top left: Well
head (GNWT); Grave, Fort Franklin
(D. Gamble); Mackenzie River at break-up
(ISL—G. Calef); Swimming Point stockpile
site (D. Gamble); Seismic line, Mackenzie
Delta (ISL—G. Calef); Evening at Rae
(M. Jackson); Inuit schooner (H. Lloyd).

Page xxxii, top: Lac la Martre children on
spring ice (M. Jackson); *clockwise from
right:* Blanket toss at Northern Games,
Coppermine (GNWT—R. Wilson); Charlie
Barnaby fishing near Fort Good Hope
(M. Jackson); Setting nets (DIAND); Helen
Tobie's beadwork (R. Fumoleau); Welder
(GWNT); Inuit seal catch (TravelArctic);
Judge Berger (A. Steen).

Acknowledgements

DIAGRAMS

Colour map: Surveys and Mapping Branch,
Department of Energy, Mines and Resources.

Photo mosaics: National Air Photo Library,
Surveys and Mapping Branch, Department
of Energy, Mines and Resources.

Maps and diagrams: Geological Survey of
Canada, Department of Energy, Mines and
Resources.

PHOTOGRAPHY

The photography appearing in this report
was made possible through the cooperation
of the following organizations and
photographers.

Alyeska Pipeline Service Company,
Anchorage, Alaska.

Canadian Arctic Gas Pipeline Limited,
Toronto.

Canadian Committee for the International
Biological Programme, Panels 9 and 10.

Canadian National, Montreal.

Canadian Press Pictures, Ottawa.

Department of Energy, Mines and Resources,
Geological Survey of Canada, Ottawa.

Department of the Environment, Canadian
Wildlife Service (CWS), Ottawa.

Department of Indian Affairs and Northern
Development (DIAND), Ottawa, Ontario;

Public Affairs, Yellowknife, Northwest
Territories; Fort Saskatchewan, Alberta.

Foothills Pipe Lines Ltd., Calgary.

Government of the Northwest Territories
(GNWT): Department of Information and
TravelArctic, Yellowknife.

Imperial Oil Company Ltd., Ottawa.

Inuit Tapirisat of Canada (ITC), Inuit Today,
Ottawa.

The Metis Association of the Northwest
Territories, Yellowknife.

National Film Board (NFB), Photothèque,
Ottawa.

National Museums of Canada (NMC):
National Museum of Man and National
Museum of Natural Science, Ottawa.

Native Communications Society of the
Northwest Territories, (Native Press)
Yellowknife. Photographers Tapwe
Chretien, Tony Buggins, and Tessa
Macintosh.

News of the North, Yellowknife.

Northern Environment Foundation,
Winnipeg.

Northern Transportation Company Ltd.
(NTCL), Edmonton.

Provincial Museums and Archives of
Alberta, Edmonton.

The Public Archives of Canada, Ottawa.

Templeton Engineering Company,
Winnipeg.

Ken Adam, Templeton Engineering
Company, Winnipeg.

Sam Barry, Edmonton.

Thomas Barry, Canadian Wildlife Service (CWS), Department of the Environment, Edmonton.

Larry Bliss, University of Alberta, Edmonton.

Gary Bristow, Holman, NWT.

Juliet Burnford, Yellowknife.

George Calef, Yellowknife (formerly with Interdisciplinary Systems Ltd. (ISL), Winnipeg).

David Campbell, National Museum of Natural Science, National Museums of Canada, Ottawa.

Wayne Campbell, Interdisciplinary Systems Ltd. (ISL), Winnipeg.

William Campbell, Dundas, Ontario.

A. H. Carmichael, Vancouver.

Tapwe Chretien, Yellowknife.

Michael Church, University of British Columbia, Vancouver.

Nancy Cooper, Yellowknife.

Diana Crosbie, Ottawa.

Charles Dauphiné Jr., Canadian Wildlife Service (CWS), Department of the Environment, Ottawa.

Elmer de Bock, Canadian Wildlife Service (CWS), Department of the Environment, Edmonton.

Jan Falls, Ottawa.

Whit Fraser, Yellowknife.

René Fumoleau, Yellowknife.

Richard Fyfe, Canadian Wildlife Service (CWS), Department of the Environment, Edmonton.

John Fyles, Ottawa.

Don Gamble, Ottawa.

R. O. Geddie, Hamilton.

Cy and Mary Hampson, Cymar Films, Edmonton.

Alan Heginbottom, Geological Survey of Canada (GSC), Department of Energy, Mines and Resources, Ottawa.

Wyb Hoek, Fisheries and Marine Service, Department of the Environment, Ste. Anne de Bellevue, Quebec.

J. C. Holroyd, Calgary.

W. J. Hunt, Fisheries and Marine Service, Department of the Environment, Inuvik, NWT.

Julian Inglis, Department of Indian Affairs and Northern Development, Ottawa.

Michael Jackson, Vancouver.

Hank Kiliaan, Canadian Wildlife Service (CWS), Department of the Environment, Edmonton.

Peter Lewis, Geological Survey of Canada (GSC), Department of Energy, Mines and Resources, Ottawa.

Hugh Lloyd, Ottawa.

Don MacKay, Inland Waters Directorate, Department of the Environment, Ottawa.

Ian MacNeil, Parks Canada, Department of Indian Affairs and Northern Development, Ottawa.

A. L. Maki, Thunder Bay.

R. McClung, Fisheries and Marine Service, Department of the Environment, Ste. Anne de Bellevue, Quebec.

Gilbert Milne, Toronto.

Guy Morrison, Canadian Wildlife Service (CWS), Department of the Environment, Ottawa.

Ted Owen, Geological Survey of Canada (GSC), Department of Energy, Mines and Resources, Ottawa.

A. M. Pearson, Canadian Wildlife Service (CWS), Department of the Environment, Edmonton.

Everett Peterson, Western Ecological Services Ltd., Edmonton.

Roy Read, Templeton Engineering Company, Winnipeg.

R. H. Russell, Canadian Wildlife Service (CWS), Department of the Environment, Edmonton.

Patrick Scott, Narnia Productions, Yellowknife.

Tomas Sennett, Northern Environment Foundation, Winnipeg.

Lorne Smith, Baffin Photo Services, Yellowknife.

M. W. Smith, Ottawa.

William Sol, Templeton Engineering Company, Winnipeg.

Andrew Steen, Yellowknife.

Ian Waddell, Vancouver.

E. R. Weick, Ottawa.

Robert Zrelec, Montreal.

Acknowledgements

want to extend my thanks to the people who gave their advice, assistance and cooperation to the Inquiry. It is not possible to refer to all of them by name. I am especially indebted to the witnesses who testified at the hearings — in the northern communities, the southern cities and at the formal hearings — upon whose evidence this report is based. Many of their names do not appear in these pages, but anyone who turns to the transcripts of the hearings will see there the wealth of knowledge, experience and understanding that they offered to the Inquiry.

The Inquiry has received full support and cooperation from the Department of Indian Affairs and Northern Development, and from the Ministers responsible for the Department: the Honourable Jean Chrétien, under whom the Inquiry was established, the Honourable Judd Buchanan, who succeeded Mr. Chrétien, and the Honourable Warren Allmand, to whom this report is submitted. Through their good offices the Inquiry was enabled to proceed with a full examination of the social, environmental and economic impact of the proposed pipeline and energy corridor. They saw to it that funds were provided to enable the native organizations, the environmental groups, northern municipalities and northern business to participate in the work of the Inquiry. They also used their good offices to ensure that all relevant government studies and reports were made available both to the Inquiry and to participants at the Inquiry. In addition, the Inquiry received the full cooperation of the Government of the Northwest Territories and the Government of the Yukon, as well as the Department of the Environment, the Department of Energy, Mines and Resources, the Secretary of State Department, and other departments of the Government of Canada.

The Inquiry was given full support by all participants at the Inquiry: the pipeline companies, the oil and gas industry, native organizations, the environmental groups, northern municipalities and northern business.

I wish to extend special thanks to the following persons who, at one time or another, have served on the Inquiry staff or contributed to its work.

Commission Counsel:

Ian Scott, Q.C.; Stephen Goudge, Ian Roland, Alick Ryder.

Special Counsel:

Michael Jackson (community hearings), Ian Waddell (administrative matters).

Secretary to the Inquiry:

Patricia Hutchinson.

Information Officer:

Diana Crosbie.

Yellowknife and Vancouver Offices:

Ruth Carriere, Valerie Chapman, Kay Trent.

Official Court Reporters:

Hugh Bemister, Ken Bemister, William Bemister; Dennis Baylis, Norma Bearcroft, Dawn Biden, Bim Bouchard, Rich Cartier, Alexandra Edlund, Lois Gillespie, Denise Graves, Ann Hardy, Sud Mann, George Mills, Beverley Parker, Alexis Passmore, Angela Ritter, Karen Smith, Ivadelle Trew.

Consultants:

Hugh Brody, Edward Chamberlin, P.K. Chatterji, Gordon Davies, Don Gamble, Valerius Geist, Christopher Hatfield, Ray Haynes, June Helm, Rolf Kellerhals, Ian McTaggart-Cowan, Steve Merrett, Graham Morgan, Larry Naylor, Thomas Pelton, Everett Peterson, Ron Pritchard, Michael Smith, John Sprague, Kenneth Torrance, Ian Whitaker, Peter Williams, Scott Wood.

Technical Staff and Public Service Advisors:

John Fyles (Head), Ed Weick (Socio-economic Advisor); Patricia Anderson, Kathy Arkay, Tom Barry, Kay Bowlby, Larry Burgess, Janice Falls, Sam Gelman, Daphne Greenwood, Vernon Hawley, Alan Heginbottom, Ellen Hughes, Owen Hughes, Herbert Inhaber, Hugh Lloyd, Fred McFarland, Sheila Meldrum, Richard Morlan, Robert Morrison, Mary Mussell, Christopher O'Brien, Phillip Reilly, Peter Rennie, Judy Rowell, Kay Shaw, Norman Simmons, Pamela White, Thomas Wood, Margot Young.

Ottawa Office:

Shirley Callard; Carolyn Bennett, Don Carter, Vicky Chase, Patricia Fournier, Leslie Gardiner, Betty Green, Barbara Jones, Sheila Kent, Anne-Marie Marion, Monika Plettenberg, Barbara Smith, Jean-Louis Vidal, Mireille Wensel, Annette Whyte.

Report Editing:

Rosemary Wallbank; Alan Cooke.

Report Translation:

Brian Peters; Richard Gratton, Pierre Guérin, Louise Morrison, Michèle Wilson.

Report Publication:

Bob Russell (Alphatext), Byrne Scott (Printing), Ken Slater (Design).

All the views expressed and all of the judgments made in this report are my own, and for them I bear complete responsibility.

NOTES ON BERGER REPORT

P. 72 WHAT WE DO KNOW SIMPLY REINFORCES THIS CONCLUSION! WE COULD NOT CLEAN UP A MAJOR OIL SPILL IN THE BEAUFORT SEA.

P. 72-73 IN THE FINAL ANALYSIS, WE MUST DETERMINE WEATHER OR NOT THE INDUSTRY OR THE GOVERNMENT FOR THAT MATTER ~ HAS THE CAPACITY TO CONTROL AND CLEAN UP A MAJOR, TODAY NEITHER OF THEM HAS.

88 AS NORTHERN SETTLEMENTS HAVE GROWN, WHITE COMPOUNDS HAVE BEEN ESTABLISHED WITHIN THEM, IN MANY PLACES IT IS NO EXAGGERATION TO SPEAK OF SOUTHERN ENCLAVES, OCCUPIED BY WHITES WHO HAVE NO LINKS WITH THE NATIVE POPULATION, BUT ARE THERE TO ADMINISTER THE PROGRAMS OF THE GOVERNMENT OF CANADA AND THE GOVERNMENT OF THE NORTH WEST TERRITORIES, MANY NATIVE WITNESSES EXPRESSED THE RESENTMENT THEY FEEL TOWARD THE WHITE PEOPLE WITHIN THEIR COMMUNITIES WHO HAVE LARGE HOUSES, CLEAN RUNNING WATER AND FLUSH TOILETS, WHILE THEY HAVE NONE OF THESE AMENITIES.

89 THE ATTITUDE OF MANY WHITE PEOPLE TOWARD THE NORTH AND THE NATIVE NORTHERNERS IS A THINLY VEILED EVOLUTINARY DETERMINISM! THERE WILL BE GREATER INDUSTRIAL DEVELOPMENT—:

90 THERE IS NO DOUBT ABOUT THE PURPOSE OF THE SCHOOLS! ----